THE WORLD SYSTEM

The historic long-term economic interconnections of the world are now universally accepted. The idea of the "world system" advanced by Immanuel Wallerstein has set the period of linkage in the early modern period. But some academics think this date is much too late and denies the much longer run of interconnection going back as much as 5,000 years.

Reframing the chronology of the world system exercises powerful influences on the writing of history. It integrates the areas of Asia and the East which were marginalized by Wallerstein into the heart of the debate and provides a much more convincing account of developments which cannot otherwise be explained. It undermines the primacy claimed for Europe as the major agent of economic change, an issue with implications far beyond the realm of history.

Andre Gunder Frank and Barry K. Gills have persuasively argued this case for several years. In this volume, they present the arguments of several academics including their own. The important foreword by William H. McNeill provides a context for the debate to which Immanuel Wallerstein and Samir Amin contribute.

Andre Gunder Frank is Professor of Development Economics and Social Science at the University of Amsterdam. His publications in 25 languages include 30 books, chapters in over 120 anthologies and articles in 500 periodical issues. His books include *World Accumulation 1492–1789* (1978), *Crisis in the World Economy* (1980), *Transforming the Revolution: Social Movements and the World System* (1990), and *Underdevelopment of Development: An Autobiographical Essay* (1991).

Barry K. Gills is Lecturer in Politics at the University of Newcastle-upon-Tyne. He is a Fellow of the Transnational Institute, Amsterdam. He is co-founder of the World Historical Systems Group of the International Studies Association. His recent works include *Low Intensity Democracy*, edited with Joel Rocamora and Richard Wilson, *Transcending the State-Global Divide: A Neo-structuralist Agenda in International Relations*, edited with Ronan Palan, and *The Crisis of Socialism in the Third World*, edited with Shahid Qadir.

THE WORLD SYSTEM

Five hundred years or five thousand?

Edited by

Andre Gunder Frank and Barry K. Gills

ROUTLEDGE

London and New York

First published 1993
by Routledge
11 New Fetter Lane, London EC4P 4EE

Simultaneously published in the USA and Canada
by Routledge
29 West 35th Street, New York, NY 10001

Typeset in 10 on 12 point Garamond by Intype
Printed in Great Britain by T.J. Press (Padstow) Ltd,
Padstow, Cornwall

British Library Cataloguing in Publication Data
A catalogue record for this book is available from the British Library

Library of Congress Cataloging in Publication Data
The world system : Five hundred years or five thousand? / edited by Andre Gunder Frank and Barry K. Gills.
p. cm.
Includes bibliographical references and index.
1. Economic history. 2. Historiography. I. Frank, Andre Gunder.
II. Gills, Barry K.
HC26.W67 1993
330.9–dc20 92–45844

ISBN 0–415–07678–1

CONTENTS

FOREWORD

There is no doubt that world-historians and would-be world-historians have proliferated in recent decades, and this book constitutes a notable contribution to the resulting discourse. This foreword ought therefore to suggest how the thought of the two editors and of the other authors represented here fits into that discourse. Their diversity makes the task more difficult than it would be were a single mind at work. Still, all the contributors have a good deal in common since they subscribe to the notion that a transcivilizational entity, inexactly dubbed "world system," existed in ancient and medieval as well as in modern times.

How to understand human history as a whole is problematic. Indeed some historians even deny that the subject is a proper object of attention since it is not possible to know the personalities, institutions, and other relevant facts about the history of every part of the inhabited earth. Such an observation about the unmanageable bulk of historical information is accurate, but irrelevant. If it were relevant, national and all other forms of history would also be impossible because personalities and other facts of local history of each part of a nation, not to mention the fleeting states of consciousness of individuals which constitute the ultimate ground of all history, are also too numerous for anyone to know.

Words, however, can extricate us from an excess of data by generalizing experience. Using words appropriately we habitually and as a matter of course understand whatever it is that confronts us by fixing attention on whatever matters most. In this fashion, words quite literally blind us to irrelevant dimensions of reality, and guide our action by turning the buzzing, blooming confusion that surrounds us into something intelligible. The whole trick is to exclude meaningless information from consciousness, even, or especially, when it is readily accessible.

This characteristic of human intelligence makes historical study and writing possible. Each scale of history has an appropriate set of terms and concepts for excluding irrelevancies. As a result, world history is as feasible as national or local history – no more, no less – as long as appropriate terms and concepts for each scale of history are employed.

But do appropriate terms for writing world history exist? And how can would-be world-historians cope with the diversity of tongues and concepts that different human groups have used to guide their conduct and understanding of the world? This is not a trivial question, nor is it likely to be resolved unambiguously and to universal satisfaction. As long as different peoples use different languages and subscribe to different outlooks on the world, terms of historical discourse that seem appropriate to some will repel others. Intensified communication across linguistic and cultural boundaries will not alter this situation, and is likely to reinforce conscious divergences.

Yet the rich diversity of human behavior guided by words of different languages operates within the same natural world. This means that words and actions that come closest to matching consequences with expectation have positive survival value for those using them; while words and actions that lead to disappointment and confusion have a contrary effect, hampering collective action by dividing a community between those who want to adjust the old, ineffective words and actions and those who wish to reaffirm the ancient verities more strenuously than ever just because they seem to be faltering.

Over time, natural selection for terms more nearly adequate to reality certainly does occur in technology and the physical sciences. In the social sciences, however, the pattern of selection is more complex because words that generate enthusiastic agreement and inspire energetic adhesion to collective courses of action often prevail in ambiguous situations, whether or not the words in question match any external or natural reality. Indeed, a sufficiently energetic faith can often create its object. Modern nations have been created from local, peasant diversity by bands of zealots; and many other groups – youth gangs, religious sects, secret societies, and the like – also affect behavior solely because their members agree among themselves. Indeed, all human society is founded very largely on agreements, expressed in words and ceremonies, that become ends in themselves and are almost independent of external reality.

Hence the stubborn diversity of human society persists. Ever since Herodotus, historians have noticed this fact. In modern times, a few historians, anthropologists, and other students of society have even attempted to pull away from naive attachment to the pieties and practices of their own local community – whatever it may be – seeking to understand what happened among the different peoples of the earth by using terms that try to take account of the diversity of local outlooks and behavior without subscribing wholeheartedly to any one of them. Whether the enterprise can be successful – and for whom – remains problematic.

For many but not for all of the contributors to this volume the conception of "world system" derived from a Marxist tradition, emphasizing the economic exploitation of marginal peoples by a capitalist core. But Marx's vision of the uniqueness of modern capitalism falls to the ground if one affirms, with the editors, that a capital-accumulating core has existed (though not always in the same location) for some five thousand years. This constitutes revisionism expected in liberal discourse but repugnant to dogmatic upholders of Marxist Truth. The volume will be judged accordingly. It may even signify for the history of ideas the confluence of Marxist with more inchoate liberal ideas about world history. Whether it will constitute such a landmark or not depends on the future of Marxism on the one hand and of the literary and intellectual enterprise of world history on the other.

That enterprise, in its inchoate, multiplex, and vaguely liberal form, seems fully capable of absorbing and profiting from a Marxist (or ex-Marxist) stream. It derives, like Marxism, from the west-European civilizational tradition, having absorbed data but no organizing concepts from encounters with the other cultural traditions of the earth, whether great or small. Within the west-European tradition, two incompatible models of universal or world history coexisted for many centuries. One was pagan and cyclical – a pattern of rise and fall that repeated itself in essentials among different communities at different times because human nature was everywhere the same. The other was Christian and linear, beginning with Adam and ending with the second coming of Christ as set forth in sacred scripture.

These models still lurk behind the scenes in the pages that follow. The world system as described by Frank and Gills is, after all, unique and linear, yet passes through a series of repetitive cycles. Other recent efforts at world history also combine linear and cyclical patterns, though where the emphasis is placed varies with every author.

The first notable departure from the Christian unitary and linear vision of the human past took form in the eighteenth century, when Vico, Herder, and others started to speak of separate civilizations or cultures, each with a language and life cycle of its own. Their vision of the rise and fall of separate peoples and cultures was focused almost entirely within the bounds of the ancient Mediterranean and medieval and modern Europe. Only in the twentieth century did the rest of the world enter seriously into the picture when Spengler first applied the notion of separate and equivalent civilizations to all of Eurasia and Toynbee then extended the scheme completely around the globe.

From the point of view of Spengler and Toynbee, differences among the peoples and languages of the classical Mediterranean lands and of medieval and modern Europe, which had loomed so large for Vico and Herder, became trivial. Instead, all the classical peoples belonged together in one civilization, and despite their differences medieval and modern Europeans shared another. Thus the civilizational building blocks for world history took on far larger proportions in their hands, and others, including myself, who came after, have continued to think and speak of multiple civilizations that embrace all of western Europe, all of China, and comparably massive groupings in India, the Middle East, and pre-Columbian America.

The idea that humankind had developed a number of comparable civilizations, whose rise and fall followed approximately parallel lines, constituted a notable departure from the naively ethnocentric vision of the past that treated any departure from local norms as deplorable error and corruption of right and truth. But by treating a plurality of civilizations as separate entities this vision of human reality minimized the importance of outside encounters and overlooked transcivilizational processes and relationships.

The historians represented in this book seek to correct this defect, affirming that interactions among the principal civilizations of Eurasia–Africa in the centuries before 1500 constituted a world system. This enlargement of scale resembles the shift Spengler and Toynbee achieved in the first half of the twentieth century, locating the most important entity of world history in a transcivilizational pattern of relationships that expanded geographically through time from an initial core in Mesopotamia.

It is undoubtedly true that some dimensions of human affairs transcended civilizational boundaries in ancient as well as in modern times. Traders, soldiers, and missionaries often operated among strangers of different linguistic and cultural traditions from themselves. Resulting contacts sometimes led one or both parties to alter their behavior by modifying old practices in the light of new information. Even in ancient and medieval times, a few really useful innovations spread very rapidly within the circuit of Old World mercantile, military, and missionary contact. Thus, the stirrup seems to appear simultaneously throughout Eurasia so that it is impossible to tell for sure where it was first invented. On the other hand, we know that the place value system of numerical notation originated in Indian mathematical treatises, where it remained safely encapsulated for many centuries before its sudden propagation throughout the Eurasian world for commercial calculations in the eleventh century.

Mere logical superiority could also provoke widespread alteration of belief and practice, though propagation of logically convincing ideas took longer. Nonetheless, the seven-day week, invented in ancient Sumer, proved contagious throughout Eurasia in very ancient times because it fitted obvious heavenly phenomena (the phases of the moon, and the seven movable lights of the firmament) so well. For similar reasons, Newtonian astronomy and the Gregorian calendar met with worldwide success in far more recent times.

All the same, commonalities that ran across the entire civilized world in ancient and medieval times remained exceptional. Differences of institutions, ideas, customs, and techniques were far more apparent, within as well as across civilizational lines. Is, then, the world system these authors explicate really significant? Equally, is the term "civilization," as used by

Spengler and Toynbee or by Vico and Herder, really meaningful in the light of all the local variability it overlooks? These are capital questions for world-historians, and deserve the most careful consideration by anyone who seeks to understand the human past as a whole, since these are the key terms currently available for the purpose.

To some degree the choice between the rival concepts of "world system" and "civilization" as building blocks for human history as a whole depends on whether one reckons that material life is more important than ideas and ideals. World-system thinkers are especially conscious of material exchanges and assert (or perhaps rather assume) that the accumulation of wealth in privileged centers through trade and the exercise of force conformed to a common norm regardless of local, cultural differences. Those who speak of "civilizations" tend to emphasize religious and other ideas, arguing that actual behavior in the pursuit of wealth and other human goals was subordinated to, or at least affected by, the ideals professed by the ruling elites of each civilization.

Even if one takes the view that pursuit of wealth was everywhere the same, regardless of religious and other professed ideals, the question remains whether long-distance trading and raiding were really massive enough to affect ancient societies in more than superficial ways. No one doubts that most people lived as cultivators and consumed little or nothing that was not produced within the local community itself. But luxury and strategic goods mattered for politics and war; and such goods often came from afar, delivered by merchants who systematically weighed local variations in price against local variations in security for their goods and person.

Such calculations established a market that extended as far as merchants traveled and exchanged information about the potential gains and risks of their profession. And this in turn, if we believe what the authors of this book have to tell us, established wealthy centers and dependent peripheries, even in ancient times when the physical volume of long-distance trade exchanges was comparatively small.

Incidentally, the phrase "world system" for such relationships is obviously a misnomer for ancient and medieval times inasmuch as large parts of the globe then remained outside the limits of the largest and most active transcivilizational market, which was based in Eurasia. Presumably, though the authors here assembled do not address the issue, smaller and less closely articulated "world systems" also existed in the Americas and elsewhere. A market that actually embraced the globe could only arise after 1500 when the opening of the world's oceans to regular shipping allowed the Eurasian world system to engulf all of humanity – a process that took some centuries but is virtually complete today.

But this awkwardness of terminology does not really matter if the reality of human interrelatedness which "world system" expresses really shaped the human past. This is the critical question for the architecture and arguments of this book, and it can only be answered individually and subjectively.

Across the past thirty years or so, my own view has been evolving away from "civilization" and toward "world system" as the best available framework for world history; but I have also concluded that both terms can best be understood as part of a far more inclusive spectrum of "communications nets," which are what really matter in defining human communities at every level of size, from biological family on up to the human race in its entirety.

Thus I agree with the authors of this book in thinking that the rise of specialized occupations producing goods for distant markets was a critical dimension of the deeper human past. Resulting alterations in everyday lives were among the most persistent and effective paths of innovation in ancient times as well as more recently. Yet markets and trade constituted only part of the communications network that crossed political, civilizational and linguistic boundaries. Soldiers and missionaries as well as refugees and wanderers also linked alien populations together, and carried information that sometimes altered local ways of life as profoundly as entry into market relationships did.

I conclude, therefore, that if the notion of a world system were tied more explicitly to a communications network and if more attention were paid to changes in that network as new means of transport and communication came into use, the notion of a "world system" would gain greater clarity and power. Moreover, the polarity between the terms "civilization" and "world system" would disappear and the language of world-historians might gain greater precision if communications networks were to become the focus of attention. For what we commonly mean by a "civilization" is a population whose ruling elite, together with at least some segments of the people they govern, shares norms of conduct, expressed through ceremonial and literary canons which are accepted in principle, however far actual conduct may fall short of the ideal prescriptions of the canon. Such agreement on norms of behavior is, of course, the result of communication across the generations as well as among contemporaries. It resembles the communication merchants and artisans engage in when learning the skills of their trade and the state of the market.

Indeed, norms of conduct shared with others – whether rulers, equals, or subordinates – constitute an essential ingredient of all social life, and are always established by communication. Communication is what makes us human; and if history were written with this simple notion in mind, networks of communication would become the center of attention, and a more satisfactory history of the world (and of all the innumerable subordinate groupings of humankind) might emerge.

World system history, exemplified here, is a step in that direction. At any rate, it seems so to me. But more explicit attention to communications networks, and a serious effort to understand how human activity altered the natural environments of the earth throughout the past must be added to the conceptions explored in this book before historians of the twenty-first century can be expected to produce a more nearly satisfactory world history.

William H. McNeill
25 May 1992

CONTRIBUTORS

Barry K. Gills is Lecturer in Politics at the University of Newcastle-upon-Tyne.

Andre Gunder Frank is Professor of Development Economics and Social Sciences at the University of Amsterdam.

K. Ekholm and **Jonathan Friedman** are at the Department of Social Anthropology, University of Lund.

David Wilkinson is at the Department of Political Science, University of California at Los Angeles (UCLA).

Samar Amin is at the Third World Forum, United Nations University, Dakar.

Janet Abu-Lughod is at the New School for Social Research, the Center for Studies of Social Change, New York.

Immanuel Wallerstein is at the Fernand Braudel Center for the Study of Economies, Historical Systems, and Civilizations, State University of New York (SUNY), Binghamton, New York.

PREFACE

> How did this book come into being? . . . I think authors ought to look back and give us some record of how their work developed, not because their works are important (they may turn out to be unimportant) but because we need to know more of the process of history-writing. Writers of history are not just observers. They are themselves part of the act and need to observe themselves in action. Their view of what "really" happened is filtered first through spotty and often hit-or-miss screens of available evidence, and second through the prisms of their own interest, selection, and interpretation of the evidence they see. . . . Once an author looks back at what he thought he was trying to do, many perspectives emerge. Foremost is that of ignorance. . . . Fortunately, no one has to regard it as the last word.
>
> (John King Fairbank [1969] *Trade and Diplomacy on the China Coast*, Stanford: Stanford University Press)

We emphatically agree with what the above-cited late dean of China historians at Harvard had to say. However, to relate the whole *Entstehungsgeschichte* of the present book might require still another one. It may be as long as the five thousand years of our topic itself! Our principal "prisms" of interpretation are center–periphery structures, hegemony/rivalry within them, the process of capital accumulation, cycles in all of these, and the world system in which they operate. They may be our modern prisms, but there is evidence that at least the first three also had their counterpart both in world reality and in the consciousness and expression of the same by the Akkadian King Sargon in 2450 BC.

Our guiding *non*-Eurocentrist idea of the unity and indivisibility of Afro-Eurasian history is at least as old as even the European "father of history" Herodotus, who already insisted on the same in and for his own time. The fact, but also the sociopolitical acceptance, of multicultural diversity within this unity is older than that. We suggest that racial, ethnic, cultural, religious, and other diversity has repeatedly been accepted and accommodated, at least in periods of (economic?) expansion. The affirmation and defense of separate identities, like today, has historically been the stuff of intermittent but recurrent political-economic crisis. Indeed, also like today, rallying around this or that alternative flag has historically been an attempt to defend shares of livelihood of a shrinking or more slowly growing economic pie during times of crisis. Historical *materialism*, both as a fact of life and as a "philosophical" reflection of and on it, has accompanied all history, and indeed also prehistory. Such materialism competes less than it complements idealism, both in history and among the historians who reflect (on) it. Complementary also are determinism or determination and (*not* or) free will in the age-old dilemma of "structure" and "agency" in new-fangled social-"scientific" terminology. In other words, regarding all three of these historical and contemporary dimensions, the varieties and alternatives of identity, the material limitations of idealism, and the challenge of wo/men making their own history but only in the historical conditions that they inherit, there is "unity in diversity." These more cultural and philosophical perspectives now emerge more clearly for the editors as we look back in this preface at what we thought we were trying to do with our (only?) apparently more structural analysis in the book itself.

It is not easy to follow Fairbank and say where and how this unity in diversity emerged and developed for each of the authors who contribute their diverse visions of it to this book. For, among the contributors, there is certainly much diversity both in their own histories and in their present-as-history rendition of history itself. Nonetheless, the contributors' unity about this historical unity is great enough at least to make this book possible, and indeed something of a common enterprise. As editors and principal contributors, it is both proper and easier to start with some record of how our own work developed and how it was and is related to that of other contributors to this book.

Frank has set on unity and structure for a long time, unity at least since high school and structure at least since studying social anthropology (extracurricularly to his economics studies) in graduate school at the University of Chicago in the mid-1950s. Then, also, Frank shared an apartment with Marshall Hodgson, who told him of an article he was then writing on eastern "Hemispheric interregional history as an approach to world history" for Unesco's *Journal of World History*, from which we quote in this book. Unfortunately, it would take Frank another three decades to understand what Hodgson was talking about. Nonetheless, Frank's writings in and on Latin America in the early 1960s not only featured dimensions of unity and structure, they also analyzed the history and present of Latin America and the "Third World" as part and parcel of a single "world system," to which he referred already in 1965 if not earlier. His reference then, however, was only to the capitalist world system during the past 500 years. Following *les événements* of May 1968 in Paris various common concerns put him in personal, political, and intellectual contact with Samir Amin, who had been writing his like-minded *Accumulation on a World Scale* and *Unequal Development*. Amin and Frank published three different books together in French, Italian, and Norwegian originals. Now Amin contributes chapter 8 in the present book, which both concurs with and dissents from the latest perspective of Frank.

In the early 1970s, Frank wrote a book on *World Accumulation*, which featured its long *cyclical* history since 1492. On then receiving the manuscript of Immanuel Wallerstein's *The Modern World-System*, Frank wrote a note that it would become an "instant classic." This note appeared as one of the three blurbs on the dust cover of the first edition (the other two were by Fernand Braudel and Eric Wolf). Since then, two joint books have appeared by Amin, Arrighi, Frank, and Wallerstein, in 1982 and 1990. Now Wallerstein also contributes a rejoinder to Frank and Gills in chapter 10 of this book. For Frank began tracing economic cycles backward through history and observing them also in the present "socialist system," which he increasingly regarded as part of the *same* world system. That far, Wallerstein agrees. However, both observations fed Frank's doubts about the uniqueness of the "modern capitalist world-system," on which Wallerstein continues to insist. An editor invited Frank among others to comment on an early version of our co-contributor Janet Abu-Lughod's "thirteenth-century world-system." That gave occasion to enquire if the long economic cycles *and* the world system in which they occur may not extend much farther back even than that. Frank was more and more persuaded that one should "*never* try to begin at the beginning. Historical research proceeds backward, not forward," as *per* another rule of Fairbank in the same preface already cited in our epigraph above. The result was a sort of critique of received theory under the title "A theoretical introduction to 5,000 years of world system history," which was graciously published in *Review* by Immanuel Wallerstein, who was one of the principal authors Frank subjected to critique. Successively less critique and more approval were "bestowed" on our present co-contributors Amin, Abu-Lughod, Ekholm and Friedman, McNeill, and Wilkinson. The article opened with an epigraph taken from Ranke: "no history can be written but universal history."

Gills read and during many hours in Frank's garden in spring 1989 critiqued a draft of that first article on the 5,000-year world system. Gills was earning his daily bread teaching contemporary international relations and Korean studies. Discussing the Frank manuscript offered him a welcome opportunity to return (alas on his own time) to his burning interest in, and to draw on, in many a desk drawer, aging manuscripts on his vision of synchronic timing, core–periphery relations, and hegemonic transitions in world history since ancient times. Gills's personal journey began in the ecology movement. In pursuit of a critical understanding of the nature of the modern ecological crisis, Gills turned to study of the origins of the state and civilization in order to understand the historical roots of the crisis. By 1982 in Hawaii, Gills was convinced that the patterns of the modern world system existed much earlier and in a real historical continuum. He even challenged Wallerstein, who was visiting Honolulu at the time, to extend his analysis backward in time; but Wallerstein answered that for the time being five hundred years was more than enough to work on. In 1984–5 at Oxford, Gills began systematic historical research into cycles of hegemony from a world-historical, comparative perspective. This work remained dormant and unfinished until spring 1989, when Gills produced his first paper on his general ideas on synchronization of cycles, which was publicly presented at a professional conference. There, Gills and Frank met and noted their general agreement of views that enabled their subsequent collaboration, which is now presented in this book.

Gills's and Frank's co-authored chapters, and indeed this book itself, are the fruit of collaboration that emerged from Frank's initial manuscript and Gills's critique thereof, which was in turn based in part on Gills's own old manuscripts. "The cumulation of accumulation," now chapter 3, was the "Theses and research agenda for 5000 years of world system history," which they proposed as their theoretical alternative to the received wisdom that Frank had critiqued. Gills also turned an earlier manuscript on "Hegemonic transitions" into chapter 4. Chapter 5 on "World system cycles, crises, and hegemonial shifts" represents their first joint attempt to apply their theoretical guidelines in chapter 4 to the reinterpretation of world (system) history. It presents the preliminary identification of system-wide, long economic cycles and their corresponding hegemonic shifts between 1700 BC and 1700 AD. Co-contributor David Wilkinson has begun to subject the identification of these cycles to empirical testing based on changes in city sizes (see the epilogue to chapter 5). Chapter 6 represents an application by Frank of the common theoretical categories to the long-standing question and particularly of co-contributor Immanuel Wallerstein's reading of "the transition from feudalism to capitalism." Frank has made individual attempts, not included here, to apply the same theory to the historical place of Central Asia and Latin America respectively in the history of the world system. Gills has done so for other Eurasian regions and especially East Asia. All of these, of course, are no more than initial steps, to be pursued by further study especially of the long cycles and also many shorter ones within them, which are set out in Gills's and Frank's chapter 5. In the meantime, as Fairbank suggested, the perspective that stands out foremost is that of our ignorance.

The historian William McNeill, who now graciously contributes a foreword here, is incomparably more erudite. He was writing his magisterial and now classic *The Rise of the West: A History of the Human Community* at the University of Chicago at the same time as the above-cited Marshall Hodgson worked there. The latter was writing his posthumously published, also magisterial three-volume *The Venture of Islam* and a manuscript on the ecumenical unity of world history (Hodgson 1993). Both stressed the word *oikumene*, and in their respective prefaces each acknowledged the influence of the other. McNeill went on to write many other books within the scope of his vision of one-world history. Then, returning to "*The Rise of the West* after twenty-five years," McNeill came to consider "the central methodological weakness" of his earlier emphasis on "interactions across civilizational boundaries and inadequate attention to the emergence of the ecumenical world system within which we live today." As he was so writing, McNeill and Frank met at 1989 meetings of the World History Association.

The political scientist David Wilkinson still speaks in terms of "civilization." However, he stresses the emergence and development of a single "Central civilization," which was formed out of the relations between Egypt and Mesopotamia around 1500 BC and then spread successively to incorporate all other "civilizations" within the "Central" one, which has been dominant long since. In so doing, Wilkinson debated with all other "civilizationists" and drew a line that was first *de facto* parallel and then asymptotic to that of Frank and Gills – until they were joined in the present book. Like them, he denies that the "civilization" or "system" is necessarily the same as their "mode[s] of production." So do Chase-Dunn and Hall, who also suggest that Frank and Gills should rename what they are talking about as "the Central world system." Wilkinson leans increasingly in their direction and tests some of their hypotheses (see the epilogue to chapter 5 below). Nonetheless, in chapter 7 below he still maintains his more political and civilizational outlook and of course his reservations *per contra* Frank and Gills. Wilkinson and Frank first met at the 1989 meetings of the International Society for Comparative Study of Civilizations, of which Wilkinson is a very active member and to which Chase-Dunn had invited Frank in part to present his world-system ideas and to meet Wilkinson. The same year, Gills and he met at the International Studies Association (ISA) and discussed the idea of forming a group there to study world-historical systems.

Kajsa Ekholm and Jonathan Friedman work in anthropology and archaeology, among other fields. In the postscript, republished here as chapter 2, of their 1982 article, they stress how they sought to counter the then dominant received wisdom of the Karl Polanyi school in anthropology and of Moses Finley and others in classical history. These writers deny any significant influences of *Trade and Markets in the Early Empires* (Polanyi *et al.* 1957). *Per contra*, Ekholm and Friedman trace the same, and indeed the capital accumulation and core–periphery relations that later reappear in Frank and Gills, back even much further than Wilkinson's Central civilization. Like these three, Ekholm and Friedman also deny the equiparity of "system" and "mode" of production. However, with most anthropologists, they stress greater multistructurality and multiculturality and, with some anthropologists, that ethnicity is circumstantial and relational rather than essentialist. There, however, they coincide with Frank and Gills, as they did in 1979, when they wrote that the so-called transition from feudalism to capitalism in Europe was essentially a shift in the center of capital accumulation from East to West. Friedman and Frank met at the former's university in Sweden and also with Gills at ISA.

The urban sociologist Janet Abu-Lughod returns to this theme in her *Before European Hegemony* in which she stresses that "the Decline of the East preceded the Rise of the West." As a long-time student of cities in contemporary times, she describes a chain of city-centered regions that were interlinked all the way across Eurasia in what she calls a "thirteenth-century world-system" from 1250 to 1350. However, she regards this world system as discrete and different from any previous ones and from the "modern world-system" described by Wallerstein. It was Frank's above-mentioned critique thereof that led to a meeting with Abu-Lughod. In her contribution here in chapter 9, she reconsiders the extent and timing of the development of the "world system" and explicates her agreements and disagreements with both Frank and Gills on the one hand and Wallerstein on the other.

The sociologist Immanuel Wallerstein comes from an Africanist background. His study of a region in the Third World was influenced by its dependence in and on the "world-system" and by the writings on the same by, among others, Frank and Amin. This influence and his subsequent book on *The Modern World-System* has led many commentators and critics, both friendly and unfriendly, to put "dependence" and "world-system" theory into the same bag. Brenner, Brewer, and many others speak of a single Frank–Wallerstein theoretical bag, into which some also throw Paul Sweezy and/or Samir Amin and others who publish in *Monthly Review*. However that may be with regard to dependence, *The Modern World-System* of Wallerstein and *World Accumulation 1492–1789* and *Dependent Accumulation and Underdevelopment* by Frank did refer to essentially the same historical unit, structure, and process during the past five hundred years. However, Wallerstein and Frank have since then come to a partial parting of the ways on earlier history. That has not prevented them from co-authoring in 1990 a book on social movements in the contemporary system, together with Amin. In his contribution to the present book in chapter 10, Wallerstein emphasizes the essential conceptual or theoretical difference between his 500-year modern and other earlier, and for a time also contemporaneous, "world-systems" (*with* a hyphen), on the one hand, and Frank and Gills's "world system," which extends at least 5,000 years back (*without* a hyphen). The former are characterized by a particular "mode of production," which is "capitalist" in the "modern" world-system. The latter exists prior to and independently of any particular mode of production or combination thereof, be they supposedly feudal or other tributary, capitalist, or socialist.

Samir Amin, *per contra*, considers these differences to have been and to continue to be of both paramount scientific and political importance. The Egyptian-born and French-educated political economist wrote a draft of his *Accumulation on a World Scale* as his doctoral dissertation in Paris in the mid-1950s. Literally countless books and articles later and also in his contribution to this book in chapter 8, Amin still emphasizes the important difference between "politics and ideology in command" that he sees in precapitalist tributary systems and the economic "law of value," which is in command in the "modern world-capitalist system." Wallerstein also affirms this difference, wording it slightly differently. He asserts that what distinguishes capitalism as a mode of production and therefore the modern world-system is the priority given to the "ceaseless accumulation of capital," whereas in the other historical systems, the accumulation of capital is subordinated to other politicocultural objectives. Frank and Gills, as well as Ekholm and Friedman and Wilkinson, dispute this difference and the related, supposedly fundamental break between the past and the "modern world capitalist system" around 1500. Abu-Lughod takes an intermediary position.

This book is devoted to elucidating this debate, and the introductory chapter 1 that follows details its far-reaching theoretical, political, and policy implications for some dozen-and-a-half social-scientific disciplines and philosophical positions ranging from archaeology and anthropology, via international and gender relations, to world systems theory. The introduction also supplies ample documentation of and detailed references to the above-mentioned discussions and publications, with which we did not wish to encumber this preface, seeking rather to focus on people and their ideas.

The publication of this book is meant to solicit and encourage the individual and collaborative work that we hope will diminish in the future the "foremost perspective, which is of ignorance." Our co-contributors, already named and introduced above, evidently have pride of place among the many people whose influence and help we would like to acknowledge in this enterprise. We are grateful also for their readiness once again to write or revise chapters of "discussion" for publication in this book.

A related step toward altering the perspective of ignorance was the recent founding of, and already very encouraging collaboration in, the World Historical Systems (WHS) Sub-Section of the International Political Economy Section of the International Studies Association, which emerged from the meeting between Gills and Wilkinson at ISA. Some of our co-contributors as well as we editors have been active members, and our agreements and dissensions are set out below. WHS has been organizing conference panels on which several of the chapters in this book have been presented and discussed. WHS has served as well as a forum of discussion of alternative and complementary perspectives of other friends and colleagues, with whose work ours and others' in this book also interact. Some of these friends in turn helped us along the way in the preparation and revision of one or another of the chapters below, and we wish to acknowledge their cooperation on both counts. These include especially the above-mentioned Christopher Chase-Dunn and Tom Hall, and Robert Denemark. Moreover, their own comparative work on world systems and on trade-generated linkages respectively is very much related to our own. George Modelski and William Thompson merit special mention here for their work on "political" long waves since 1494 and their current interest both in relating them more to economic ones and in extending them further back through history. They also served as panelists or discussants in WHS sessions. In addition to all these, Albert Bergesen, John Fitzpatrick, Mogens Larsen, K.P. Moseley, and Matthew Robertson have given complementary papers at WHS sessions. In turn, Michael Doyle, Joshua Goldstein, Frank Klink, and Mary Ann Tetreault have served as formal discussants on our WHS panels. We and some of our co-contributors have benefited from their insights and critiques. We would like to thank Sing Chew, Paulo Frank, Ronen Palan, and Peter Taylor who commented on one or more article manuscripts included as chapters here. We would also like to thank Sarah-Jane Woolley at Routledge for her constant assistance and Andrew Wheatcroft for his support. Of course, we have also benefited from the influence and help of many other people, known to us personally or not, too many to be able properly to acknowledge them here.

Andre Gunder Frank, Amsterdam
Barry K. Gills, Newcastle
16 May 1992

REFERENCE

Hodgson, Marshall (1993) in *Rethinking World History. Essays on Europe, Islam and World History*, ed. Edmund Burke III, Cambridge: Cambridge University Press.

Part I

INTRODUCTION

1

THE 5,000-YEAR WORLD SYSTEM

An interdisciplinary introduction

Andre Gunder Frank and Barry K. Gills

INTRODUCTION

Our thesis is that the contemporary world system has a history of at least 5,000 years. The rise to dominance of Europe and the West in this world system is only a recent – and perhaps a passing – event. Thus, our thesis poses a more humanocentric challenge to Eurocentrism.

Our main theoretical categories are:

1 The world system itself. *Per contra* Wallerstein (1974), we believe that the existence of the same world system in which we live stretches back at least 5,000 years (Frank 1990a, 1991a, chapter 6 below; Gills and Frank chapters 3 and 5 below). Wallerstein emphasizes the difference a hyphen makes. Unlike our nearly *world* (wide) system, world-*systems* are in a "world" of their own, which need not be even nearly worldwide. However, the "New World" in the "Americas" was of course home to some world-systems of its own before its incorporation into our (pre-existing) world system after 1492.

2 The process of capital accumulation as the motor force of (world system) history. Wallerstein and others regard continuous capital accumulation as the *differentiae specificae* of the "modern world-system." We have argued elsewhere that in this regard the "modern" world system is not so different and that this same process of capital accumulation has played a, if not the, central role in the world system for several millennia (Frank chapter 6 below; Gills and Frank chapter 3 below). Amin (chapter 8 below) and Wallerstein (chapter 10 below) disagree. They argue that previous world-systems were what Amin calls "tributary" or Wallerstein "world empires." In these, Amin claims, politics and ideology were in command, not the economic law of value in the accumulation of capital. Wallerstein seems to agree.

3 The center–periphery structure in and of the world (system). This structure is familiar to analysts of dependence in the "modern" world system and especially in Latin America since 1492. It includes but is not

limited to the transfer of surplus between zones of the world system. Frank (1967, 1969) wrote about this among others. However, we now find that this analytical category is also applicable to the world system before 1492.

4 The alternation between hegemony and rivalry. In this process, regional hegemonies and rivalries succeed the previous period of hegemony. World system and international-relations literature has recently produced many good analyses of alternation between hegemonic leadership and rivalry for hegemony in the world system since 1492, for instance by Wallerstein (1984), or since 1494 by Modelski (1987) and by Modelski and Thompson (1988). However, hegemony and rivalry also mark world (system) history long before that (Gills and Frank, chapters 3, 5 below).

5 Long (and short) economic cycles of alternating ascending (sometimes denominated "A") phases and descending (sometimes denominated "B") phases. In the real world-historical process and in its analysis by students of the "modern" world system, these long cycles are also associated with each of the previous categories. That is, an important characteristic of the "modern" world system is that the process of capital accumulation, changes in center–periphery position within it, and world system hegemony and rivalry are all cyclical and occur in tandem with each other. Frank analyzed the same for the "modern" world system under the titles *World Accumulation 1492–1789* and *Dependent Accumulation and Underdevelopment* (Frank 1978a, b). However, we now find that this (same) world system cycle and its features also extend back many centuries before 1492.

In this book, our thesis is introduced by the contribution of Kajsa Ekholm and Jonathan Friedman (chapter 2). It is extended by David Wilkinson (chapter 7) who argues that in 1500 BC relations between Egypt and Mesopotamia gave rise to what he calls "Central civilization," which has incessantly spread out through the world ever since. The "one world system" thesis is elaborated in our chapters.

Amin and Wallerstein critique this thesis and defend their own thesis that the "modern world-system" began 500 years ago. They argue in particular that its capitalist mode of production distinguishes it fundamentally from "world empires" and all previous world-systems, which Amin calls "tributary." In his critical reply to us, Wallerstein emphasizes the above-mentioned distinction between his plural "world-systems" with a hyphen and our singular "world system" without a hyphen. Janet Abu-Lughod, whose work we also review below, contributes a critical discussion of these issues and defends the existence of a "thirteenth-century world system," which she regards as distinguishable as it was distinguished (chapter 9).

Our thesis speaks to several disciplines or concerns and participates in long-standing controversies within and between them. Among these fields and concerns, beyond world-systems theory itself, we here note our challenge to Eurocentrism. Then we outline the connections of our thesis with historiography, civilizationism, archaeology, classicism in ancient history, medievalism, modern history, economic history, macrohistorical sociology, political geography, international relations, development studies, ecology, anthropology, race and ethnic relations and their study, gender relations and their study, etc. Our thesis, its similarities and differences with others, and the discussions of the same also have some important philosophical, social-scientific, and political implications, which we may briefly note in conclusion.

WORLD SYSTEM THEORY

We ask whether the principal systemic features of the "modern world system" can also be identified earlier than 1500 or not. Wallerstein (1974, 1984, 1989a, b, chapter 10 below), Modelski (1987), and Amin (chapter 8 below) argue that the *differentiae specificae* of our world system are new since 1500 and essentially different from previous times and places. However, Modelski (1991) includes leadership before 1500 in his analysis. Christopher Chase-Dunn (1986) and others find parallels in "other" and prior world systems. Wilkinson (1989) discovers at least some of these features in his "Central civilization" and elsewhere. However, he sees historical continuity, but no world system. Abu-Lughod (1989) sees a "thirteenth-century world system," but she regards it as different from the world system since 1500 or before 1250. Moreover, she is not so interested in comparing systemic features or characteristics. We combine all of the above into an analysis, or at least an identification, of the principal features of this world system over several thousand years of its history and development (Frank 1990a, 1991a, chapter 6 below; Gills and Frank chapters 3 and 5 below).

According to Wallerstein (1989b, c, 1988a, b and elsewhere) and many students of world capitalism, the *differentia specifica* of the modern world system is the ceaseless accumulation of capital: "It is this ceaseless accumulation of capital that may be said to be its most central activity and to constitute its *differentiae specificae*. No previous historical system seems to have had any comparable *mot d'ordre*" (1989b: 9).

Samir Amin (1991) also argues that this economic imperative is new and uniquely characterizes the modern capitalist world system. Of course, this is not the same as arguing that capital accumulation was absent, minor, or irrelevant elsewhere and earlier. On the contrary, capital accumulation did exist and even defined this (or another) world system before, indeed long before, 1500.

Yet, Wallerstein, Amin, and most others argue that there is something unique and uniquely powerful about modern capital, i.e. an imperative to accumulate "ceaselessly" in order to accumulate at all. We contend that this imperative, both in the familiar money form as well as other forms of capital, is not a unique systemic feature of modern "capitalism." Rather the imperative of ceaseless accumulation is a characteristic of competitive pressures throughout world system history. Moreover, in chapter 5 we note the existence of cycles in economic growth, both "pre-" and "post-" "capitalist," in the entire world system. Therefore, something more fundamental than "ceaseless" "capitalist" accumulation in its modern form seems to be at work in world (system) history throughout the millennia.

That is also the position of Ekholm and Friedman (chapter 2), who find "capital," as well as the now familiar logic of imperialism to accompany the expansion of capital, already existing from very ancient times in Mesopotamia. L. Orlin (1970), for instance, refers to "Assyrian colonies in Cappadocia" and Mitchell Allen (1984) to "Assyrian colonies in Anatolia." Ekholm and Friedman argue that ancient capital, particularly in its form of the accumulation of bullion (money capital), is essentially the same as capital in later, including modern times.

In this regard, and to anticipate our review of "archaeology" below, a generation and more ago the perhaps best-known polar-opposite positions were represented by Karl Polanyi *et al.* (1957) and Gordon Childe (1936, 1942). Polanyi is known for his deprecation of the role of markets and by extension of profit-driven accumulation. Yet even Polanyi concluded in a later essay, only posthumously published in 1975 and again in 1977, that

> throughout, the external origin of trade is conspicuous; internal trade is largely derivative of external trade, . . . [and] with trade the priority of the external line is evident . . . for what we term "luxuries" were no more than the necessities of the rich and powerful, whose import interest largely determined foreign policy. . . . Acquisition of goods from a distance may be practiced by a trader either from . . . (status motive) – or for the sake of gain . . . (profit motive). . . . [There are] many combinations of the two.
>
> (Polanyi 1975: 154, 135, 136–7)

Gordon Childe represented the historical-materialist and Marxist positions. Yet even so "Childe consistently underestimated the potential surplus that could have been generated by Neolithic economies," according to the archaeologist Philip Kohl (1987: 17). In a related vein, the well-known archaeological student of both Mesopotamia and Meso-America, Robert Adams (1974: 284), suggests "perhaps – to venture still a little further in this direction – we have wrongly deprecated the entrepreneurial element in the historical development of at least the more complex societies."

We also argue for this latter position, which is supported by more and more archaeological evidence and analysis, some of which is reviewed by Sherratt (n.d.) and Algaze (n.d.). However, we wish to expand the working definition of capital beyond the confines of current Marxism to encompass much wider manifestations of surplus transfer, both private and public. Therefore, we argue that for millennia already and throughout the world (system) there has been capital accumulation through infrastructural *investment* in agriculture (e.g. clearing and irrigating land) and livestock (cattle, sheep, horses, camels, and pasturage for them); industry (plant and equipment, as well as new technology for the same); transport (more and better ports, ships, roads, way stations, camels, carts); commerce (money capital, resident and itinerant foreign traders, and institutions for their promotion and protection); military (fortifications, weapons, warships, horses, and standing armies to man them); legitimacy (temples and luxuries); and of course the education, training, and cultural development of "human capital." Chapter 2 refers to capital accumulation already in prehistoric times, and it can also be inferred from the work of various archaeologists cited below. Even the drive to accumulate, or the obligation to do so in a competitive world, is not confined to modern capitalism.

Are other characteristics, in particular a core–periphery structure, of the modern world system unique to it since 1500? Or are they also identifiable elsewhere and earlier? In a short list of three main characteristics of his modern world-system, Wallerstein (1988b) identifies "this descriptive trinity (core–periphery, A/B [cycle phases], hegemony–rivalry) as a pattern maintained over centuries which is unique to the modern world-system. Its origin was precisely in the late fifteenth century" (108).

Wallerstein also makes lists of six (1989b) and twelve (1989a) characteristics of his modern world capitalist system since 1500. Frank (chapter 6) argues why all of them also apply earlier. The sections on archaeology, classicism, and medievalism below show how these categories, and particularly core–periphery, are also applicable to prehistory, the ancient world, and premodern history.

Another of the three world system characteristics mentioned by Wallerstein is hegemony–rivalry. But is this feature limited to the world since 1500? Or did it also exist elsewhere and earlier? Or, indeed, does it also characterize the same world system earlier? Wallerstein himself discusses the rise and fall of mostly economically based hegemony only since 1500.

Modelski (1987) and Modelski and Thompson (1988) as well as Thompson (1989) analyze largely politically based and exercised hegemony since 1494. Paul Kennedy's (1987) bestseller *The Rise and Fall of the Great Powers* went still farther back, but did not connect them in any systematic way.

Wallerstein employs a sequential model of hegemony which refers to productive competitiveness in other core markets, subsequent commercial competitiveness, and financial competitiveness. While this is a useful model of sequential attainment of different dimensions of hegemonic power, it leads to overemphasis on a temporary and fragile "moment" when a core power attains all three advantages simultaneously. It also confines our analysis of global hegemony too much to the single succession of a few such momentary hegemons, to the detriment of analysis of the total phenomena of global hegemony. Even when there is such a momentary hegemon, there are always other interlinked hegemonic powers. Wallerstein distinguishes modern "hegemony" from traditional "imperium." Yet all of his hegemonic powers themselves held colonial possessions and coexisted in a larger system of global hegemony in which other powers exercised imperium. Modelski (1987) and others emphasize political/military hegemony.

Our use of the term hegemony–rivalry refers to the political-economic predominance by a center of accumulation, which alternates with periods of rivalry among several such centers of accumulation. Therefore, we argue that hegemony–rivalry has also characterized the world system for thousands of years (chapters 3 and 5). As suggested above, hegemony is not only political. It is also based on center–periphery relations, which permit the hegemonic center to further its accumulation of capital at the expense of its periphery, hinterland, and its rivals. After a time, not least through the economic-military overextension signalled by Kennedy (1987), the hegemonic empire loses this power again. The decline in the hegemony of a great power gives way to an interregnum of economic, political, and military rivalry with others competing to take its place. After an interregnum of rivalry with other claimants, the previous hegemonic power is replaced by another one. Shifting systems of economic, political, and military alliances, reminiscent of those featured by George Orwell (1977) in his *1984*, are instrumental in first creating, then maintaining, and finally losing hegemonic imperial power.

We argue not only that there have been numerous and repeated instances of hegemony and rivalry at imperial regional levels. We also suggest that we may be able to recognize some instances of overarching "super-hegemony" and centralizing "super-accumulation" at the world system-wide level before 1500 (chapters 3 and 5). The Mongol empire certainly, and Song China perhaps, had a claim to super-hegemony. Thus, very significantly, the later rise to super-hegemony in and of western Europe, Great Britain, and the United States after 1500 did not constitute unique first instances in the creation of a hegemonic world system. Instead, as Abu-Lughod (1989: 338) persuasively argues, "'the fall of the East' preceded the 'Rise of the West'" and resulted in a hegemonic shift from East to West. This shift came at a time – and perhaps as a result – of overextension and political economic decline in various parts of the East, which suffered a period of cyclical economic decline so common to all as to have been world system-wide. Thus the "Rise of the West," including European hegemony and its expansion and later transfer of the "New World" across the Atlantic, did not just constitute a new, modern world-capitalist system. This development also – and even more so – represented a new but continued development and hegemonic shift within an old world system.

Janet Abu-Lughod (1989) makes a major contribution to the writing of world history in pushing the starting date for the world system back to 1250. In so doing, she has finally cut the Gordian knot of the supposed break in world history at 1500, as *per* Wallerstein (1974) and others. She denies that the present world system emerged in Europe through the transition from any previous mode of production. She argues instead that whatever mode of production existed in the sixteenth century also existed already in the thirteenth century in Europe – and in the "Middle East," India, and China.

Abu-Lughod shows that eight interlinking city-centered regions were united in a single thirteenth-century world system and division of labor. According to her reading, however, this world system economy experienced its apogee between 1250 and 1350 and declined to (virtual) extinction thereafter, before being reborn in southern and western Europe in the sixteenth century. In her words, "of crucial importance is the fact that the 'Fall of the East' preceded the 'Rise of the West.'" She argues that

> if we assume that restructuring, rather than substitution, is what happens when world systems succeed one another, albeit after periods of disorganization, then failure cannot refer to the parts themselves but only to the declining efficacy of the ways in which they were formerly connected. In saying the thirteenth-century world system failed, we mean that the system itself devolved. . . . From earliest times, the geographically central "core regions" . . . were Central Asia and the Indian Ocean, to which the Mediterranean was eventually appended. These cores persisted through the classical and thirteenth-century world systems. A decisive reorganization of this pattern did not occur until the sixteenth century.
>
> (Abu-Lughod 1989: 343–5)

It seems at least plausible, if not obvious, then to argue that between the fourteenth-century decline of the East and the fifteenth to sixteenth-century rise of the West there occurred a "declining efficacy" and "disorganization" of "the ways in which they were formerly connected." In that case, consequently there would have been a shift of the center of gravity in the system from East to West but not a complete failure of the system as a whole. On the contrary, this temporary disorganization and renewed reorganization could and should be read as the continuation and evolution of the system as a whole. Indeed, in our approach all history can and should be analyzed in terms of the shifts in centers of accumulation, as we emphasize in our titles "World system cycles, crises and hegemonial shifts 1700 BC to 1700 AD" (chapter 5) and "1492 and Latin America at the margin of world system history: East > West hegemonial shifts 992–1492–1992" (Frank 1993a).

Thus, Wallerstein (1989b) sees a single cycle in Europe (albeit "matched by a new market articulation in China . . . [in] this vast trading world-system"), and yet a variety of "unstable" systems around the world, each of which "seldom lasted more than 4–500 years" (1989b: 35). On the other hand, Abu-Lughod (1989) sees a single world system, certainly in the thirteenth-century cyclical conjuncture on which she concentrates, but also in earlier periods. Yet, successively each of her world systems cyclically rises (out of what?) and declines (into what?). However, neither Wallerstein nor Abu-Lughod is (yet?) willing to join their insights in the additional step to see both a single world system and its continuous cyclical development.

The third characteristic of Wallerstein's world system after 1500 is long economic cycles of capital accumulation. Their upward "A" and downward "B" phases generate changes of hegemony and of position in the center–periphery–hinterland structure. These cycles, and especially the Kondratieffs, play important roles in the real development of the world system and in its analysis by Wallerstein (1974), Frank (1978a), Modelski (1987), Goldstein (1988), and Thompson (1989). All emphasize the relations among cycles in the economy, hegemony, and war. However, are these cycles limited to modern times, or do they extend farther back? Wallerstein himself notes that

> It is the long swing that was crucial. . . . The feudal system in western Europe seems quite clearly to have operated by a pattern of cycles of expansion and contraction of two lengths: circa 50 years (which seem to resemble the Kondratieff cycles found in the capitalist world economy) and circa 200–300 years. . . . The patterns of the expansions and contractions are clearly laid out and widely accepted among those writing about the late Middle Ages and early modern times in Europe. . . . It is the long swing that was crucial. Thus 1050–1250+ was a time of the expansion of Europe (the Crusades, the colonizations). . . . The "crisis" or great contractions of 1250–1450+ included the Black Plague.
>
> (1989b: 33, 34)

Thus, even according to Wallerstein there was systematic cyclical continuity across his 1500 divide – in Europe. But Abu-Lughod (1989), McNeill (1983), and others offer and analyze substantial evidence that this same cycle was in fact world system wide. Wallerstein (1989b: 57, 58) also perceives some of the evidence. Moreover, all these developments were driven by the motor force of capital accumulation. The "crucial long swing" was a cycle of capital accumulation. Frank in chapter 6 tries to demonstrate that this same cyclical pattern definitely extends back through the eleventh century and that it could well be traced further back still. Gills and Frank in chapter 5 trace these long cycles much further back to at least 1700 BC in world (system) history.

So do these characteristic similarities with the modern world-capitalist system extend only to "other" earlier empires, state systems, or regional economies or to different "world systems"? We argue in chapters 3 and 6 that similar characteristics extend backwards through time in the same world system, which itself also extends much farther back in time. That is, we argue for the extension back in time through the same world system of the essential features of the modern-world-capitalist-system of Wallerstein (1974), Frank (1978b), Modelski (1987), Goldstein (1988), Thompson (1989), and others, and of the "other" world systems and civilizations of Chase-Dunn (1986, 1989), Wilkinson (1987, 1989), and others. This extension of the world system to at least 5,000 years has implications for many disciplines and concerns in history and social science, beginning with historiography and the Eurocentrism which underlies much of its other "scientific" and cultural endeavors.

EUROCENTRISM AND ITS ALTERNATIVES

Samir Amin (1989) in *Eurocentrism* and Martin Bernal (1987) in his *Black Athena: The Afroasiatic Roots of Classical Civilization* criticized Eurocentrism and offered alternative approaches, especially on an ideological level, which center on the eastern Mediterranean and north Africa respectively. Another alternative to Eurocentrism is the development of "Afrocentrism" by African-American historians and others in the United States, which as its name implies centers on Africa, specifically sub-Saharan Africa. We believe that these critiques of Eurocentrism are all to the good, but that they are too limited.

Our approach offers the basis for a wider world-historic humanocentric alternative to Eurocentrism. World history should be a reflection and representation of the full diversity of human experience and development, which far exceeds the limited and limiting recent bounds of the "West." Indeed, the "West" does not exist, except by reference to the "inscrutable" "East." Yet their historical existence is only a figment of "western" imagination. Eurocentrism and other centrisms prevent seeing or even asking how all the "parts" relate to the world [system] whole. Therefore, Eurocentrism is also an analytical fetter on world history.

A few generations ago, even some western historians, like Frederick

Teggart in 1918, criticized "Eurocentric" history and pleaded for a single "Eurasian" history in which

> The two parts of Eurasia are inextricably bound together. Mackinder has shown how much light may be thrown on European history by regarding it as subordinate to Asiatic. . . . The oldest of historians (Herodotus) held the idea that epochs of European history were marked by alternating movements across the imaginary line that separates East from West.
>
> (Teggart 1939: 248)

Yet since then, western domination in power and technology has further extended the domain of its culture and Eurocentric, western perspective through proselytizing religion, mass media, language, education, and, yes, "world" history writing and teaching, using the (in)famous Mercator projection maps, etc. Nonetheless, homogenization has proceeded less far and fast than some hoped and others feared; and many people around the world are seeking renewed and diverse self-affirmation and self-determination: "Think globally. Act locally." Some scholars also speak of this problematic in terms of "globalization-localization" (Featherstone 1991; King 1991; Lash and Urry 1987; Robertson 1990).

Western, Eurocentric world history and its distortions need not be replaced by "equal time" for the history of all cultures. Nor need we admit (a variety of competing) other centric histories, be they Islamo-, Nippo-, Sino-, or whatever other centric. No, we can and should all aspire to a nonexclusivist humanocentric history. This world history can be more than a historical "entitlement program," which gives all (contemporary) cultures or nationalities their due separate but equal shares of the past. Instead, a humanocentric history can and must also recognize our historical and contemporary unity in and through diversity beyond our ideological affirmations of cultural self.

WORLD HISTORIOGRAPHY

Although we should not aspire to "equal time" in the history of everybody in the world, world history also need not just concentrate on adding representative nonwestern civilizations and cultures to western ones. Nor should we limit our historical study of cultures and civilizations to the comparative examination of their distinctive and common features. This is the procedure of most so-called courses and textbooks on "world" history or "comparative civilizations."

Some examples of these approaches and their internal contradictions and limitations are examined in Frank (1990a). Two well-known examples to be examined below are the comparative studies of civilizations by Toynbee and Quigley. Another example is the approach to "Civilization as a unit of world history" by Edward Farmer (1985) and Farmer *et al.* (1977) in their *Comparative History of Civilizations in Asia*.

We argue that our world history can and should also make efforts to connect and relate the diversity of histories and times to each other. It may be empirically possible, and in that case it is historically important, to uncover all sorts of historical connections among peoples and places, not only over time but especially at the same time. These connections would lend additional meaning to our comparisons. Frederick Teggart (1939) made such connections, for instance, in his *Rome and China: A Study of Correlations in Historical Events*. Teggart correlated and connected diverse political and economic events (particularly wars, "barbarian" invasions, and interruption/resumption of trade) in these two areas and others in between. Teggart made these connections among contemporaneous events "for the purpose of gaining verifiable knowledge concerning 'the way things work' in the world of human relations . . . in the spirit of modern scientific work, on the study of World History" (Teggart 1939: v, xii).

A one-world history should also seek to systematize these connections and relations, as well as comparisons, into an analysis of a world system history. This is now the opinion of our contemporary dean of world history, William McNeill (1990). Recently, he reflected back over "*The Rise of the West* after twenty-five years" and concluded that:

> The central methodological weakness of my book is that while it emphasizes interactions across civilizational boundaries, it pays inadequate attention to the emergence of the ecumenical world system within which we live today. . . . Being too much preoccupied by the notion of "civilization," I bungled by not giving the initial emergence of a transcivilizational process the sustained emphasis it deserved. . . . In the ancient Middle East, the resulting interactions . . . led to the emergence of a cosmopolitan world system between 1700 and 500 BC. . . . There is a sense, indeed, in which the rise of civilizations in the Aegean (later Mediterranean) coast lands and in India after 1500 BC were and remained part of the emergent world system centered on the Middle East. . . . All three regions and their peoples remained in close and uninterrupted contact throughout the classical era. . . . [Moreover] one may, perhaps, assume that a similar [to the modern] primacy for economic exchanges existed also in earlier times all the way back [to] the earliest beginnings of civilization in ancient Mesopotamia.
>
> (McNeill 1990: 9–10, 12–14)

Thirty-five years earlier, Marshall Hodgson (1954) had already pleaded:

> During the last three thousand years there has been one zone,

> possessing to some degree a common history, which has been so inclusive that its study must take a preponderant place in any possible world-historical investigation. . . . The various lands of urbanized, literate civilization in the Eastern Hemisphere, in a continuous zone from the Atlantic to the Pacific, have been in commercial and commonly in intellectual contact with each other, mediately or immediately. Not only have the bulk of mankind lived in this zone, but its influence has emanated into much of the rest of the world.
>
> (Hodgson 1954: 716)

> [In] the following approach . . . events may be dealt with in their relation to the total constellation of historical forces of which they are a part. . . . This means that we are to consider how events reflect interdependent interregional developments.
>
> (Ibid.: 717)

Hodgson (1958: 879) thought that "few scholarly tasks are more urgent."

This same theme was taken up by L.S. Stavrianos (1970: 3–6) in *The World to 1500: A Global History*. In the "Introduction: nature of world history" he wrote:

> The distinctive feature of this book is that it is a *world* history. It deals with the entire globe rather than some one country or region. It is concerned not with Western man or non-Western man, but with all mankind. . . . The global approach to history represents a new departure in modern historiography. . . . The story of man from its very beginnings has a basic unity that must be recognized and respected. Neither Western nor non-Western history may be properly comprehended without a global overview encompassing both. Only then is it possible to perceive the interaction amongst all peoples at all times, and the primary role of that interaction in determining the course of human history. . . .
>
> World history is not the sum of histories of the civilizations of the world. . . . The structure of world history requires focusing on historical movements that have had major influence on man's development, so the geography of world history requires focusing on those regions that initiated those historical movements. When this is done, one land unit stands out uniquely and unchallengeable: Eurasia, the veritable heartland of world history since Neolithic times. . . . To an overwhelming degree, the history of man is the history of these Eurasian civilizations.
>
> (Stavrianos 1970: 3–6)

In volume 1, number 1 of the new *Journal of World History*, Allerdyce (1990: 62, 67, 69) quoted others to the effect that what world history "needs is a simple, all-encompassing, elegant idea, which offers an adequate conceptual base for a world history." We suggest that the basic elements of this idea may be found in the foregoing quotations from McNeill, Hodgson, and Stavrianos. The central concept of this all-encompassing idea advanced here is the process of capital accumulation in the world system.

This approach requires the rejection of still another historiographic tradition. We should not treat historical diversity and comparisons as Perry Anderson (1974) does. He goes beyond comparing the same or similar historical processes and formations like absolutism at *different* times. He also argues explicitly that "there is no such thing as a uniform temporal medium: for the times of the major Absolutism . . . were precisely, enormously diverse . . . no single temporality covers it." Instead, the systematization of interregional world history must realize, as Hodgson (1954: 719) argued, that "What is important is the recognition . . . that there has been some sort of developing pattern in which all these interregional developments can be studied, as they are affected by and in turn affect its elements as constituted at any one time."

Frank (1978a: 20) argued that

> Anderson's apparent attempt to make historiographic virtue out of empirical necessity when he argues that the historical times of events are different though their dates may be the same must be received with the greatest of care – and alarm. For however useful it may be [comparatively] to relate the same thing through different times, the essential (because it is the most necessary and the least accomplished) contribution of the historian to historical understanding is successively to relate different things and places at the same time in the historical process.

Much earlier, Teggart (1939)

> establish[ed] (for the first time) the existence of [temporal] correlations in historical events . . . which exhibits the relationship between contemporaneous disturbances in several areas . . . [and] awareness of the concurrence of events in different regions. . . . The study of the past can become effective only when it is fully realized that all peoples have histories, that these histories run concurrently and in the same world, and that the act of comparing is the beginning of knowledge. . . . It at once sets a new problem for investigation by raising the question of how the correspondences in events are to be accounted for.
>
> (Teggart 1939: 243, 245, 239)

Therefore, we should discard the usual western, Eurocentric rendition of history, which jumps discontinuously from ancient Mesopotamia to Egypt, to "classical" Greece and then Rome, to medieval western Europe, and then on to the Atlantic west, with scattered backflashes to China, India, etc. For meanwhile all other history drops out of the story. Or some people and places never even appear in history, unless they are useful as a supposedly direct descendant of development in the West.

Instead, any world history should try to trace and establish the historical continuity of developments between then and now in the world systemic whole and all its parts. Hodgson and McNeill already emphasized this continuity. David Wilkinson (1987) puts Hodgson's earlier suggestion into practice and demonstrates convincingly that "Central civilization" has a continuous and expanding (we would say world system) history since Mesopotamia and Egypt established relations in about 1500 BC. We return to his thesis below.

We argue that these relations extend even farther out and further back. During another millennium from 2500 BC or earlier, peoples established relations with each other around and through the Mediterranean to the Levant, Anatolia, Mesopotamia, and importantly on to the Persian Highlands and between them and the Indus Valley, as well as with many Central Asian "nomads." Gordon Childe (1942) already argued for the recognition and analysis of these and, even earlier and more widespread, of such relations in Neolithic times.

Moreover, world (system) history is not limited to that of sedentary "civilizations" and their relations. It also includes "barbarian" nomads and other peoples, and especially the multifarious relations among the former and the latter. Following Lattimore (1962) and others, we make a strong plea for much more study of Central and Inner Asian "nomadic" and other "peripheral" peoples. We recommend that special attention be given to the significance of their continuous trade and political relations with their "civilized" neighbors, and to the timing and causes of the recurrent waves of migratory and invasory incursions from Central/Inner Asia into east, south, and west Asia and Europe. Similarly, the nomadic tribes of the Arabian Peninsula long before the time of Mohammed merit more attention. Moreover, it is high time to drop and take exception to the now pejorative term "barbarian." The supposed differences between peoples who have been so called and those supposedly more "civilized" are doubtful at best. There is even reason to question many supposed distinctions between "nomad" and "sedentary" peoples. However that may be, there can be little doubt about "the Centrality of Central Asia" in world (system) history (Frank 1992b).

Africa has also received less attention than it merits in world (system) history. Curtin has done pioneering work on trade and migration in Africa, but in his *Cross-Cultural Trade in World History* (1984) he has not sought to pursue the African connection in Afro-Asia as far back in history as it may deserve. The south-east Asian peoples and their history were long since intimately related to and also influential on those of China and India, if only for the trade and migrations between them. Yet south-east Asia is often largely omitted from even those world histories that give their due to China and India.

CIVILIZATIONISM

Civilizationists and many historians as well as macrosociologists claim to write the history of the world, but without ever attempting to write world history. They distinguish various civilizations or other systems, and sometimes study one problem or another, like ideology, power, economy, or technology. Toynbee (1946), Quigley (1961), and more recently Mann (1986) are among them.

Arnold Toynbee (1946: 34–40) finds 19 or 21 separate civilizations, 5 still living and 16 dead, though "most of them [were/are] related as parent or offspring to one or more of the others." He rejects "the egocentric illusion [of] the misconception of the unity of history – involving the assumption that there is only one river of civilization, our own." We should indeed reject this Euro/western egocentric illusion, but it is Toynbee's misconception to assume that there cannot have been or be a single unifying river unless it was "our" western or another civilizational river. We suggest that there is a common river and unity of history in a single world system and that it is multicultural in origin and expression, which has been systematically distorted by Eurocentrism.

Toynbee also rightly rejects "the illusion of 'the unchanging East.'" "The East" has no historical existence. Indeed, it was a Euro/western-centric invention. Moreover, of course, the many peoples and regions of "the East" have been very different and ever changing. This fact and reading of history need and should not, however, exclude these peoples and regions from participation in a common stream of history or historical systemic unity.

Thirdly, Toynbee rightly rejects "the illusion of progress as something which proceeds in a straight line." Leaving aside for the moment the criterion of progress or not, we can nonetheless observe cyclical ups and downs in parts of the system and maybe in the whole system itself (chapter 5).

Finally, Toynbee rejects the "very different concept of the unity of history" as the diffusion of Egyptaic civilization over thousands of years. We accept the rejection of this diffusion, but not his unwarranted rejection of the unity of history or of a single historical world system.

Carroll Quigley (1961) devotes more attention than Toynbee to the interrelations and mutual influences among civilizations and their rise and decline through their seven stages of mixture, gestation, expansion, conflict, universal empire, decay, and invasion. Nonetheless, he still recognizes sixteen separate civilizations. Thus, Quigley also writes a history of the world without attempting to write world history. Instead, he emphasizes the separate internal logics of development in civilizations through a purportedly "universal" pattern of stages.

David Wilkinson (1987 and chapter 7), by contrast, writes a more unitary history about what he calls "Central civilization." It began in the west Asian part of the Eurasian landmass and spread eventually to encompass the entire globe.

> Central Civilization is the chief entity to which theories of class society, the social system, world-economy and world systems must apply if they are to apply at all. A suitable theoretical account of its economic process does not yet exist; one for its political process may.
>
> (Wilkinson 1987: 56–7)

Wilkinson's subtitles indicate his intent and recommended procedure:

> Recognizing Central Civilization as a Reality. . . . Recognizing a single entity in adjacent "civilizations". . . . Recognizing a single entity after civilizations collide. . . . Recognizing a single entity when "civilizations" succeed each other. . . . Did Central civilization ever fall?
>
> (Wilkinson 1987: 35–9)

Wilkinson's answer is no, since its birth when Mesopotamia and Egypt joined hands around 1500 BC. Therefore Chase-Dunn and Hall (1991) have suggested that we should "adapt Wilkinson's terminology and call their system the 'Central World System.'"

However, we are wary about the category of "civilization" itself. "Civilization" is ambiguous as a unit and terribly difficult to bound either in space or in time. When McNeill says he "bungled" by being too preoccupied with civilization as the unit of analysis, this was because it stands in the way of seeing and analyzing world [system] history as a whole.

ARCHAEOLOGY

As already observed in our discussion of capital accumulation and the role of markets and entrepreneurship in ancient history, the field was long dominated by the work of scholars such as Moses Finley (1985, original 1975) and Karl Polanyi *et al.* (1957). Both deny or downplay the role of market relations in the ancient economy, and by implication the scope for "capital" accumulation. Ekholm and Friedman (chapter 2) provocatively attempted to expand world system analysis to the ancient economy and to break with this predominant view. They put forward a bold thesis on the continuity of "capital" and imperialism in the ancient world. Archaeological critiques of Polanyi, in particular by Silver (1985), Kohl (1989), Woolf

(1990), and Sherratt and Sherratt (1991) re-examine the evidence. Archaeologists find ample empirical evidence of capital formation and for the operation of true price-setting markets in the ancient economy. Gills and Frank, chapters 3 and 5, rely on this evidence to systematize their reading of the role of capital accumulation and markets in the ancient world system.

Yet, all too often, historians and others have operated with the simplistic assumption that ancient states and empires were purely extractive, expropriating mechanisms. Anderson (1974) emphasizes the primacy of the political/coercive means of extraction of surplus in precapitalist social formations. Amin (1989 and chapter 8) similarly emphasizes the ideological and political-extractive character of surplus extraction in the "tributary" modes of production. We believe that the emphasis on these characterizations of ancient political economy are distorting. There is growing evidence of the vital and widespread role of private merchant capital and "free" imperial cities in generating the revenues on which the state lived in even the most militaristic and coercive of the ancient empires, Assyria, not to mention the more famous Phoenician commercial interests. What holds true for Assyria holds equally true for every other ancient empire and even China, though there perhaps to a somewhat lesser extent. Once this is recognized, the way is open to new studies of the transregional economic processes involving the transfer of goods and capital across ancient Eurasia and their effects "within" all the ancient empires.

Nonetheless, much of the work so far remains either civilizational or comparative civilizational in scope and conception. The leap to applying center–periphery and world system conceptual frameworks to the wider geographical, social and economic contexts we believe to exist has yet to be fully accomplished. There are a few glimmers of light on the horizon in this regard, for instance Sherratt's (1992) paper on the Bronze Age "world system" and McNeill's (1990) comments on the scope and significance of economic relations in the ancient world system quoted earlier. We believe that, given the state of the archaeological and historical evidence, there is good reason to encourage this nascent trend to analysis at the largest scale possible as the logical extension of the method and theses we advocate over the entire course of world history.

However, a new wave in archaeological studies has recently appeared. It applies center–periphery and/or world system analysis to the study of complex societies of the past. Thus, Rowlands, Larsen, and Kristiansen (1987) entitled a book *Centre and Periphery in the Ancient World*; Champion (1989) edited one on *Centre and Periphery: Comparative Studies in Archaeology* and Chase-Dunn and Hall (1991) on *Core/Periphery Relations in Precapitalist Worlds*; Greg Woolf (1990) discusses "World-systems analysis and the Roman Empire," Andrew Sherratt writes of "Core, periphery, and margin: perspectives on the Bronze Age" (n.d.) and asks "What would a Bronze Age world system look like?" (1992) and Frank (1993c) examines "Bronze Age world system cycles." Thus, much of this new literature and its titles about ancient and "precapitalist" societies or "worlds" imply that it is not only possible, but analytically fruitful to apply concepts developed for the analysis of the modern world also to the "premodern" and indeed the "prehistorical" world.

Progress in this direction has, however, been limited by the attempt to apply Wallersteinian categories too rigidly and/or by confining them to "world-systems" of excessively narrow scope. Guillermo Algaze (n.d.), for instance, comparatively examines "Prehistoric world systems, imperialism, and the[ir] expansion" in each of Egypt, southern Mesopotamia, and the Indus Valley, as well as central Mexico. Yet he does not consider the connections among the first three, as well as among them and northern Mesopotamia, Anatolia, the Levant, Persia, and Central Asia, which are examined in chapter 5. George Dales (1976) probed the "Shifting trade patterns between the Iranian Plateau and the Indus Valley in the third millennium BC." Hiebert and Lamberg-Karlovsky (1991) in turn examined the relations between "Central Asia and the Indo-Iranian borderlands." Shereen Ratnagar (1981) explored *Encounters: The Westerly Trade of the Harrapan Civilization* with Mesopotamia.

Philip Kohl (1991) also examines the connections between Persia and transcaucasian Central Asia, and between that and the Indus Valley. He sees parallels and shifts of center of gravity in the latter, but is reluctant to probe possible causal interrelations. Kohl (1987, 1989, 1991) has also written several times about center–periphery relations and "the use and abuse of world systems theory" regarding these areas. He concludes that "these Central Asian materials cannot easily be incorporated into an unmodified Wallersteinian world systems model. . . . Economic development and dependency were not linked phenomena during the Bronze Age. . . . Central Asia clearly interacted with South Asia and Iran in the late third millennium, but it was neither a core, a periphery, nor semi-periphery" (Kohl 1989: 235, 236, 237). Moreover, among others, Kohl also stresses the maritime connections with Oman.

From our perspective, all of these structures and processes, as well as the specific historical events, can and should be studied as part of a single world system process. It seems particularly opportune to do so when, as we write, a front-page headline in the *International Herald Tribune* (6 February 1992) reports the use of satellite observation to make the "major new find . . . of the Omanum Emporium" at or near "Ancient Arabia's Lost City" of (Omanian) Ubar, which was the center of the overland and maritime frankincense trade with most of the areas we have just discussed. Only extension and adaptation of world system analysis to earlier times can offer the analytical categories essential to examine all this in its then contemporary Bronze Age systemic interrelations. Moreover, we agree with the archaeologists like Kohl who suggest that the age-old inquiry into the origins of the ancient state also must be reoriented to take account of "international relations." However, these relations were competitive as states were rivals for economic suzerainty, and not only on a bilateral basis, but within an "interstate" world system. We return to this matter in our sections on international relations and anthropology below.

CLASSICISM IN ANCIENT HISTORY

In classicism, eurocentricity, as noted above, has been powerfully criticized by Martin Bernal (1987) and Samir Amin (1989). Both argue that ancient Greece was less the beginning of "western" than the continuation of "eastern" civilization and culture. However, we would caution against misuse of Bernal's work by some of his new "Afrocentrist" interpreters. Similarly, "poly-centrism" can be misused by multiculturalist counter-attacks on Eurocentric culture.

On a more material level, the archaeologists Andrew and Susan Sherratt insist similarly about Aegean civilization that "its growth can only be understood in the context of its interaction with these larger economic structures" in the Levant and "behind them stood the much larger urban economies of Mesopotamia and Egypt" where for "already 2000 years . . . the easterners had the gold, the skills, the bulk, the exotic materials, the sophisticated lifestyle, and the investment capacity" (Sherratt and Sherratt 1991: 355). Why else, we ask in chapter 5, would Alexander have turned East to seek his fortune?

Our world system perspective not only reinforces the Amin and Bernal ideological critique of Eurocentrism, but carries it much further still. We also offer an analytic framework, within which to perceive the "interaction with these larger structures" by Greek, Roman, and other "civilizations" in "classical" times. Thus, our perspective offers a powerful antidote to the Eurocentric classical historians, who imposed their bias upon studies of the ancient world by privileging the role of Graeco-Roman civilization in the story of world history. The contributions of nonwestern, and particularly "oriental," societies were systematically denigrated or dismissed as unimportant. Most importantly, Eurocentric classicism distorted the real political and economic position of the "West", i.e. the Graeco-Romans, in the ancient world as a whole. Yet we know that Hellas began its ascendance after a preparatory period of so-called "orientalizing," i.e. emulating and integrating with the more advanced and prosperous centers of civilization and commerce in the "East."

The Eurocentric distortions of classicism in ancient history can best be corrected by applying a world system approach in which all the major zones of ancient Eurasia are analyzed on the basis of their participation in a common economic process. Culturalism and the assumption of western superiority has distorted analyses of the true world historical position and relations of the west European and west Asian (Middle Eastern) regions. A world system framework clarifies that for most of world history, including ancient "classical" history, Europe was ever "marginal" and west Asia ever "central."

The ultimate center of economic gravity in the ancient world remained in the East even after the rise of Hellas, which is well attested in the history of the Hellenistic kingdoms. It can be argued that, even when Rome ascended to political predominance over these Hellenistic kingdoms, the real economic core of this pan-Mediterranean-oriental world system nevertheless decidedly remained in the East, whilst Rome itself played a largely parasitic role. The historical evidence corroborates the contention that the real position of the West relative to that of the East has been misunderstood.

Witness the ambition of Antony and Cleopatra to rule this world from the East; the secession of Queen Zenobia in the third century; the founding of Constantinople as the eastern capital, and its subsequent centuries-long tenure as the premier economic metropolis of the East. Indeed, the so-called "fall" of the Roman empire was mainly confined to the economically far weaker western provinces. It was primarily Eurocentric bias and privileging of Graeco-Roman civilization that produced the quite false dichotomy between the "fall" of Rome and the subsequent Byzantine empire. The latter, of course, was the same Roman empire; and it only retrenched and regrouped in its economic core in the East.

The true position and relations of the west European and west Asian (Middle Eastern) region have been analyzed even less within the context of the entire Eurasian economic world. Teggart (1939) established a model for how such a task might be accomplished. Such a project would need to incorporate the ancient history of every major region in Eurasia, especially those of China, India, Central Asia, and south-east Asia. Our world system history offers a framework to do so. In that framework as in world-historical reality, Europe was marginal and west Asia central. Gills and Frank in chapter 5 discuss a Eurasian-wide pattern of correlations in economic expansion and contraction and hegemonic rise and decline during the ancient period. They attempt to explore the synchronization and sequentialization of these patterns between all the major zones of ancient Eurasia, on the working assumption that they participated in a common world accumulation process.

MEDIEVALISM

Most study of medieval history is also extremely Eurocentric. The famous "Dark Ages" refer explicitly to Europe, indeed to western Europe. However, the implication is that either the rest of the world also experienced centuries of the same; or worse, that it did not exist at all, or if it did, there were no connections between (western) Europe and the remainder of the world. All these theses and their implications are directly challenged by our study of the Afro-Eurasian world system during "medieval" times in chapter 5.

In terms of twentieth-century European sociological historiography, the dispute could be summarized through the polar-opposite positions of the contemporaries Max Weber and Werner Sombart. The archaeologists Andrew and Susan Sherratt (1991) identify this contrast with regard to the ancient world. However, it also applies to medieval times; or rather, perhaps it was projected backward by Weber and Sombart from their study of medieval times and indeed from their concern with modern capitalism. Weber and Marx were antagonists in their interpretation of capitalism and in the theoretical apparatuses they bequeathed to twentieth-century social science and history. However, they were tactical allies with regard to their interpretation of medieval times, from which, however differently, both sought to distinguish modern capitalism. They saw medieval Europe as sunk in a Dark Age hole of immobility, which was closed in upon itself. For them and for their many and mutually antagonistic followers through most of the twentieth century, Europe was characterized by small-scale and agrarian feudal fiefdoms based on master–serf relations. The most important exponent of similar theses among historians was perhaps Marc Bloch. All of these followed in turn Edward Gibbon's renowned *Decline and Fall of the Roman Empire* from the eighteenth century and European Renaissance writers before that.

A contrary thesis was developed and defended by Sombart (1967, 1969), who laid much greater emphasis on commercial developments, by Alfons Dopsch (1918), and to some extent by Henri Pirenne (1936) and Henri See (1951). Dopsch emphasized the continued importance of trade after the decline of the Roman empire in the West and denied that Europe involuted completely. Pirenne recognized the integration at least of western Europe in the age of Charlemagne. Though See, like Marx and Weber, was concerned with "the origins of modern capitalism," he identified many medieval commercial precursors, also in the Church. Sture Bolin argued against Pirenne and suggested that without Mohammed – or indeed Rurik, the Swedish invader of Russia – there could have been no Charlemagne. That is, medieval western Europe was systemically related to eastern Europe and Islam. (For a discussion of these theses, see Adelson 1962.) The important place and role of Venice and Genoa in late medieval Europe were derived from their connections with the Byzantines and others in the "East." The Crusades went there because that was where the action was, while Europe still was in a backwater of world system history.

However, even if we start in Europe as we should not, these observations lead us much farther afield. The importance of the commercial and monetary ties between Europe and Islamic lands is emphasized by, among others, Maurice Lombard (1975). He rightly terms the medieval centuries as "the Golden Age of Islam." Marshall Hodgson (1974) sees medieval Islam as the veritable center and hub of a flourishing Eurasian oikumene, while (western) Europe – and by Eurocentric extension the world? – supposedly languished in the "Dark Ages." K.N. Chaudhuri (1990) goes on to analyze medieval splendor in *Asia Before Europe*. Countless historians of China have studied the rise and decline of the Sui, Tang, and Song dynasties; and the world-historian William McNeill (1983) ascribes world preeminence to the latter in the late Middle Ages. Christopher Beckwith (1987) insists on the systemic connection among all of these regions and other regions, in particular Central Asia including Tibet, and their polities throughout the medieval period. We rely heavily on all of these authors to construct our analysis of the world system during the medieval period (chapter 5, Frank 1991b).

From a world system perspective medieval Europe was socially, politically, and economically quite backward or less developed in comparison with the contemporary cores in the world system, all of which lay to the East. Perhaps no other region in Eurasia suffered so deep and prolonged a retrogression after the classical period. In this sense, medieval Europe was an exception rather than the rule, and Eurocentric preoccupation with feudal social forms distorts our appreciation of real social, political, and economic development in the world as a whole during those centuries. Thus, in this regard also, Eurocentrism distorts our understanding of human history.

FROM EARLY MODERN TO MODERN HISTORY

Early modern history is variously dated more or less from the thirteenth to the fifteenth centuries, depending on the specific historical topic under review. These include but are not confined to the following more or less contemporaneous or temporally overlapping events: the Wars of the Roses in England and/or the Hundred Years War, the Renaissance in Europe, Norman expansion southward through Europe, the end of the European Crusades, European expansion westward through the Mediterranean into and then across the Atlantic, Mamluk rule in Egypt, the decline of the Byzantine empire, the rise of the Ottoman empire and its expansion westward, Mongol expansion in all directions, the Black Death, the rise of the Safavid empire in Iran, India before and during the Muslim conquest, the Yuan dynasty in China and then its replacement by the Ming dynasty, and farther afield perhaps the Mali empire in west Africa, the rise of the Incas in Peru and of the Aztecs in Mexico. At best, some of these events or empires are treated comparatively, as in the "Early Modern Seminar" at the University of Minnesota led by Edward Farmer, whose approach was discussed above. Yet all of them are treated either independently of each other or at most in relation to their immediate neighbors.

Per contra, in our interpretation of the world system, all the Eurasian events would be supposed if not treated as having been interlinked and related to each other. We do not treat the Mongol expansion and the Black Death as arising, *deus ex machina*, out of nowhere and their impact on and reactions to them in China, India, Persia, and Europe as isolated instances. Instead, we treat all these events and others as integral parts of an integrated Eurasian-wide world system and historical process. Exceptionally, Janet Abu-Lughod's (1989) *Before European Hegemony* does the same. She treats eight of these areas as interlinked across Eurasia during the years 1250–1350. We already commented on her work in connection with "world system theory" above.

Palat and Wallerstein (1990) speak of an "evolving Indian Ocean world economy," which combined a set of intersecting trade and production linkages from Aden and Mocha on the Red Sea, and Basra, Gombroon, and Hormuz on the Persian Gulf, to Surat and Calicut on the western seaboard and Pulicat and Hughli on the Coromandel and Bengal coasts of India, Melaka on the Malay archipelago; and the imperial capitals such as Delhi and Teheran, connected by caravan trails. They "lived at the same pace as the outside world, keeping up with the trades and rhythms of the globe" (Palat and Wallerstein 1990: 30–1; also Braudel 1981–4: 18).

Nevertheless, Palat and Wallerstein insist that three autonomous historical systems existed: the Indian Ocean world economy, that centered on China, and the Mediterranean/European zones, which merely converged at intersections. Yet they note the "swift collapse of these cities once their fulcral positions were undermined." But they would have it that "their riches accumulated from their intermediary role in the trade between different world-systems" rather than acknowledging the existence of a single world economy. Furthermore, Palat and Wallerstein conclude that

> despite the temporal contemporaneity of post-1400 expansion of networks of exchange and intensification of relational dependencies in Europe and in the world of the Indian Ocean, the processes of large-scale socio-historical transformation in the two historical systems were fundamentally dissimilar. In one zone, it led to the emergence of the capitalist world-economy. In the other, to an expanded petty commodity production that did not lead to a real subsumption of labour.
>
> (Palat and Wallerstein 1990: 40)

We regard this as an excessively near-sighted view (see chapter 5 below for further discussion of this point).

Per contra other students of the world system therefore, if other parts of the world have been the most important players in the same world system earlier on, some of these players were important in the same world system after 1492 as well. Therefore, it is necessary to rephrase (or repose?) the question of "incorporation" into the system as perceived by

Hopkins and Wallerstein in their 1987 issue of *Review* dedicated to "Incorporation into the world-economy: How the world-system expands." Moreover, the hegemony first of Iberia in the sixteenth century and then of the Netherlands in the seventeenth, as well as the relative monopolies of trade on which they were based, came at the expense of still operative trading powers, e.g. the Ottomans and Indians.

However, beyond the retreat into greater isolation of China under the Ming at one end of Eurasia, another major reason that this historical development eventually became a more unipolar rather than a multipolar transition is explained by J.M. Blaut (1977, 1992) with reference to the other end: the western European maritime powers conquered the Americas and injected its bullion into their own processes of capital accumulation. The western powers then used the same to gain increasing control over the trade nexus of the still attractive and profitable Indian Ocean and Asia as a whole. Yet as late as 1680 the Director of the English East India Company Sir Josiah Child still observed that "we obstruct their [Mogul Indian] trade with all the Eastern nations which is ten times as much as ours and all European nations put together" (cited in Palat and Wallerstein 1990: 26). In that case, what was really in or out of the world system, what were its essential features, and when did these features and the world system itself begin?

In this regard, an argument similar to ours was already made by Jacques Gernet in his *History of China*:

> what we have acquired the habit of regarding – according to the history of the world that is in fact no more than the history of the West – as the beginning of modern times was only the repercussion of the upsurge of the urban, mercantile civilizations whose realm extended, before the Mongol invasion, from the Mediterranean to the Sea of China. The West gathered up part of this legacy and received from it the leaven which was to make possible its own development. The transmission was favored by the crusades of the twelfth and thirteenth centuries and the expansion of the Mongol empire in the thirteenth and fourteenth centuries. . . . There is nothing surprising about this Western backwardness: the Italian cities . . . were at the terminus of the great commercial routes of Asia. . . . The upsurge of the West, which was only to emerge from its relative isolation thanks to its maritime expansion, occurred at a time when the two great civilizations of Asia [China and Islam] were threatened.
>
> (Gernet 1985: 347–8)

ECONOMIC HISTORY

The same *problématique* marks much of economic history. In recent Eurocentric times, economic history has focused on Europe, its rise, and its expansion worldwide. Far too many books to mention have been written on the whys and wherefores of the "Rise of the West;" and almost all of them have sought the answer in this or that factor or combination of them *within* Europe. When the rest of the world *is* there, as for scholars such as Jones (1981), Hall (1985), or Baechler, Hall, and Mann (1988), it is there only to be found deficient or defective in some crucial historical, economic, social, political, ideological, or cultural respect in comparison to the West. Therefore, these authors also revert to an internal explanation of the presumed superiority of the West to explain its ascendance over the rest of the world. For all of them, the rise of Europe was a unique "miracle" and not a product of history and shifts within the world (system). The major exception in posing and answering this question is McNeill's *The Rise of the West*; and it is not an economic but a *world* history!

As for the others, we may choose *The Rise of the Western World: A New Economic History* by Douglass C. North and Robert Paul Thomas (1973) as an example. The reason is the explicitness of its title, its emphasis on "new," the renown of the authors, and their revision of received theory. Yet under their subtitles "Theory and overview: 1. The issue" and on the very first page, they clearly state "the development of an efficient economic organization *in Western Europe* accounts for the rise of the West" (North and Thomas 1973: 1, our emphasis). They then trace this institutional change, and especially the development of property rights, to increased economic scarcity, which was generated in turn by a demographic upturn in western Europe. The rest of the world was not there for them, but we shall return to its demographics in our discussion of macrohistorical sociology below. Here it is worthy of note, as North and Thomas (1973: vii) emphasize in their preface, that their economic history is "consistent with and complementary to standard neo-classical economic theory."

Marxist economic history, by contrast, has been dominated by concepts like "mode of production" and "class struggle." Yet, both these concepts have generally also been interpreted within a framework of a single "society" or social formation, or at least a single entity, whether that be a state or a civilization. That is, with regard to "the rise of the West" and "the development of capitalism," Marxist economic history has been equally or even more Eurocentric than its "bourgeois" opponents. Examples are the famous debate in the 1950s on "the transition from feudalism to capitalism" among Maurice Dobb, Paul Sweezy, Kohachiro Takahashi, Rodney Hilton, and others (reprinted in Hilton 1976) and the Brenner debate on "European feudalism" (Aston and Philpin 1985). De Ste Croix (1981) on the class struggles in the ancient "Graeco-Roman" civilization and Anderson (1974) on "Japanese feudalism" also considered these as a particular "society."

This limitation on the scope of analysis was not inevitable nor laid down by any law. Rather, it was the result of Eurocentrism and a preference for endogenous class-based, causal explanatory frameworks. In this preference for the limited and limiting units of analysis, like the national state or society or civilization, "transitions" occur mainly for "internal" "class" reasons. Central to these "transitions" have been the transitions between modes of production, which were usually analyzed as if they occurred wholly within each separate entity according to the development of its internal contradictions.

Thus Anderson (1974) analyzed the "fall" of late Rome in the West as the demise of the slave mode of production and its gradual replacement by the feudal mode of production. Brenner (in Aston and Philpin 1985) analyzes the transition from feudalism to capitalism in Europe as if it occurred primarily (if not solely) as a consequence of internal class contradictions that brought about a crisis of feudal relations in the European social formation – irrespective of external causes. This was also the central theme of Maurice Dobb (1963) which led to the debate between him and other "productionists" like Rodney Hilton versus the "circulationist" Paul Sweezy, who emphasized the contribution of world market relations to the transition from feudalism to capitalism in Europe, without however yet studying the dynamics of that world economy itself. Kohachiro Takahashi tried to take an intermediate position between the two sides in this debate in the early 1950s (reprinted in Hilton 1976). The same themes and theses resurfaced a generation later in the Brenner–Wallerstein exchange.

To re-examine the transition from feudalism to capitalism in western Europe and the simultaneous rise of the "second serfdom" in eastern Europe, Brenner takes a Dobbian productionist position; and Wallerstein focuses on the development of the capitalist modern world-system. Denemark and Thomas (1988) review this debate and contend that it is better to maintain a wider-system level of analysis and also to pay more attention to the concrete determinants of power within political systems. Denemark and Thomas point to the errors of overly state-centric analysis. Their refutation of Brenner's claims that Poland's relative status was primarily conditioned by its internal structure and not by trade is a useful empirical affirmation of the greater explanatory power of a world system framework of analysis. An illustration of the importance of these long-term and large-scale structural factors is that from his vantage point as a Hungarian Jeno Szücs could observe that in drawing the line between east and west Europe at their meetings in Moscow and Yalta,

> It is as if Stalin, Churchill and Roosevelt had studied carefully the *status quo* of the age of Charlemagne on the 1130th anniversary of his death. . . . [Also] the old Roman limes would show up on Europe's morphological map, thus presaging right from the start the birth of a "Central Europe" within the notion of the "West". . . . The whole history of the Hapsburg state was an attempt to balance the unbal-

> anceable while being squeezed somewhere between the two extremes of East–Central Europe. The only consequent structural element in that formula . . . [was] the setting up by the Hapsburgs of a diminished East-Central European-copy on an "imperial scale" of the division of labour drawn up by the nascent "world economy" on a larger scale . . . between West (industrial) and East (agricultural). . . . In the "Hapsburg division of labour," Hungary was cast in the East's role [with its East European hinterland and Austria governing Bohemia in the West's].
>
> (Szücs 1983: 133, 172, 173)

The issue of how to combine the respective strengths and insights of the global and state levels of analysis is taken up in a collection on "neostructuralism" (Palan and Gills 1993).

At the center of these still very relevant discussions is a vital methodological issue. Should we take as the primary unit of analysis a single society (if such a thing can be said to exist!), or a single state, or even a single mode of production (if there ever was one in isolation)? Doing so leads us to privilege production and endogenous factors in formulating our causal explanations of social change. Or should we take on the largest unit of analysis suggested by the material and political-military interactions in which any particular geographical area is involved? That leads us to privilege (or at least to emphasize) accumulation, exchange, and hegemonic influences or rivalries. That is our methodological choice. Of course, we differ from Wallerstein in that we do not see the world system as arising from 1500, but much earlier. Therefore, we do not regard the "transition," if any, as an intra-European process, but more as the consequence of a shift in the economic center of gravity from East to West. That is our argument explicitly in chapters 5 and 6 and in Frank (1992a, 1993a). Thus, we then find "systemic" and conjunctural causal explanations of "transitional" change that appear "external" to Europe and its "internal" relations of production. Since these appear primary to the "productionists," they therefore accuse us of "circulationism." Frank in chapter 6 in turn inveighs against "Transitional ideological modes: feudalism, capitalism, socialism."

In this regard, we may perhaps be permitted a personal but revealing aside. In 1965, one of us debated with Rodolfo Puiggros in the Sunday supplement of a Mexican newspaper about the transition between feudalism and capitalism in Latin American agriculture (Frank 1965). The title was "With what mode of production does the hen convert maize into golden eggs?" The answer was that the hen's mode of production in agriculture and *a fortiori* Latin America itself was capitalist since its conquest and incorporation into the capitalist system by the newly hegemonic Europe. Fifteen years later, Frank's then 17-year-old son Paulo suddenly said like a bolt out of the sky that "obviously Latin America *could not have been feudal*, since it was colonized by Europe."

The 1965 article began by inviting readers to solve a puzzle: connect nine points, which visually *seem* to form (and enclose) a square, with a single line of four continuous and straight segments. The point was – and still is – that it is impossible to find the solution as long as we stay within the limited frame that the nine points appear to impose on us: "The solution is that we must emerge from the limited and self imposed frame" by going *outside* it. The argument in 1965 was that "if we are to understand the Latin American *problématique* we must begin with the *world system* that creates it and go outside the self-imposed optical and mental illusion of the Ibero-American or national frame" (reprinted in Frank 1969: 231).

That is still the point, and it applies equally to understanding "the transition from feudalism to capitalism" in Europe and to "the rise of the western world: a new economic history." In the last generation, all sides of the Dobb–Sweezy debates, the Brenner debates, the Brenner–Wallerstein debates among Marxists and neo-Marxists, as well as the debates between neoclassicists and other Eurocentric scholars before them have posed all their questions and sought all their answers only or primarily *within* Europe, be it in its "mode of production," "institutions of property," or otherwise. Yet if we are to understand this apparently European *problématique* we must begin with the world system that creates it and go outside the self-imposed optical and mental illusion of the European or national frame.

We recommend the world system as the locus, and the process of accumulation within it as its motor force of development, as the primary determinants of the historical process. In this regard we are very much in agreement with Wallerstein, Amin, Abu-Lughod, and others – as far as they go. However, as noted in our discussion of world system theory above, we want also to apply the same methodology much further in space and time. We believe that Marxist and neo-Marxist historiography also should not be confined in its self-imposed "isolationist" orthodoxy. Rather, historical–materialist analysis, Marxist or otherwise, should move in ever more holistic and inclusive directions, which were proposed by earlier materialist economic historians, like Gordon Childe (1936, 1942), and later by Fernand Braudel's (1953, 1981–4) "total history." Only then can we hope to comprehend the full causal frameworks for transitions – be they in modes, centers of accumulation, or hegemonic power – on the scale of the "world-as-a-whole."

(MACRO) HISTORICAL SOCIOLOGY

Both the Marxist heritage and its self-limitations impinge on macrohistorical (political) sociology, and so do our critiques thereof from a world system perspective. For example, Michael Mann (1986) sums up his approach in two statements. Both could offer justification and basis for a world system historical approach. However, in Mann's hands they do rather the opposite:

> Societies are not unitary. They are not social systems (closed or open); they are not totalities. We can never find a single bounded society in geographical or social space. Because there is no system, no totality, there cannot be "sub-systems," "dimensions," or "levels" of such a totality. Because there is no whole, social relations cannot be reduced "ultimately," "in the last instance," to some systemic property of it – like the "mode of material production," or the "cultural" or "normative system," or the "form of military organization." Because there is no bounded totality, it is not helpful to divide social change or conflict into "endogenous" and "exogenous" varieties. Because there is no social system, there is no "evolutionary" process within it. . . . There is no one master concept or basic unit of "society." . . . I would abolish the concept of "society" altogether.
>
> The second statement flows from the first. Conceiving of societies as multiple overlapping and intersecting power networks gives us the best available entry into the issue of what is ultimately "primary" or "determining" in societies. . . . [There are] four sources of social power: ideological, economic, military, and political (IEMP) relationships.
>
> (Mann 1986: 1–2)

We can only agree to Mann's proposal to abolish the concept of society and to his rejection of the search for some single ultimately determinant property thereof. For most of Mann's rejection of the premises of orthodox history and social science, Right and Left, also eliminates many underbrush obstacles on the way to the world system history we propose. However, we have some reservations about his *prima facie* rejection of all totality and systemic property as well as about his singular preoccupation with power alone. In particular, we cannot be satisfied by his enquiry only into "the sources of social power" at different times and places, without a systematic attempt to investigate possible connections between here and there, and to trace possible continuities between then and now. Moreover, we suggest that Mann's focus on power itself devotes insufficient attention to the use, if not the motive, of power for ulterior economic ends.

This more materialist perspective is much more pervasive in Jack A. Goldstone's (1991) *Revolutions and Rebellions in the Early Modern World*. This book is not so much, and certainly not just, another study of revolutions and rebellions. In addition, indeed instead, it offers a demographic/structural and cyclical analysis of economic, political, social, cultural, and ideological factors responsible for state breakdown. The revolutions are only the straw that break the camel's back; and the rebellions are those that fail to do so, because the structural conditions are not ripe. "Any claim that such trends were produced solely by unique local conditions is thoroughly undermined by the evidence" (Goldstone 1991: 462). To explain, we may best let Goldstone speak for himself:

EARLY MODERN HISTORY: A WORLD HISTORY

> My primary conclusion is quite beautiful in its parsimony. It is that *the periodic state breakdowns in Europe, China and the Middle East from 1500 to 1800 were the result of a single basic process*. . . . The main trend was that population growth, in the context of relatively inflexible economic and social structures, led to changes in prices, shifts in resources, and increasing social demands with which the agrarian-bureaucratic states could not successfully cope. The four related critical trends were as follows: (1) Pressures increased on state finances and inflation eroded state income and population growth raised real expenses. . . . (2) Intra-elite conflicts became more prevalent as larger families and inflation made it more difficult for some families to maintain their status . . . while creating new aspirants to elite positions. . . . (3) Popular unrest grew, as competition for land, urban migration flooding labor markets, declining real wages, and increased youthfulness raised the mass mobilization potential of the populace. . . . (4) The ideologies of rectification and transformation became increasingly salient . . . and turned both elites and middling groups to heterodox religious movements in the search for reform, order, and discipline. The conjunctures of these four critical trends . . . combined to undermine stability on multiple levels of social organization. This basic process was triggered all across Eurasia by periods of sustained population increases that occurred in the sixteenth and early seventeenth centuries and again in the late eighteenth and early nineteenth centuries, thus producing worldwide waves of state breakdown. In contrast, in the late seventeenth and early eighteenth centuries populations did not grow, and the basic process and its four subthemes were absent. Political and social stability resulted.
>
> (Goldstone 1991: 459–60, his emphasis)

What lies behind the long cycles of expansion and contraction at least of "economic" growth rates and their political consequences, which are identified by us in chapter 5? Perhaps demographic changes, due in turn to Eurasian-wide ups and downs in mortality rates, as Goldstone persuasively argues. They could well combine with the long cycles of typically 200 years expansion and contraction, which we identify. Alas, we have not even investigated this possibility – if it is possible to do so with available demographic evidence. However, ecological cycles, as Goldstone also calls them, perhaps based on climatic changes, have also been suggested and investigated by others; and they are discussed in Frank (1990a and 1991a, 1992b). Goldstone's kind of analysis could and should be extended beyond the cases he studied.

Goldstone's demographically based economic, political, and social cycles challenge of course both the view that history is only linearly progressive and the view that, at least since early modern times, it is determined by the development of capitalism. We agree (chapter 5, Frank 1991a). Of course Goldstone's point is even better taken if the demographic and political economic cycles extend farther back than the supposed origin of capitalism around 1800, 1500, or whenever. Indeed, and although Goldstone himself does not go so far as to say so, his materialist analysis undermines the very idea of capitalism as a separate and useful category, not to mention system. That is what Frank in chapter 6 argues, also on materialist grounds.

A related major case in point is the insistence, against all the evidence, that class struggle is the motor force of history. Goldstone denies that, and adduces contrary evidence again and again. Alvin Gouldner (1980) already emphasized the contradiction between "the two Marxisms." One holds that material economic conditions shape social relations and form consciousness, and the other claims that the class struggle and consciousness thereof drive history. Yet, at about the same time, the Polish Marxist Leszek Nowak (1983 translation) pointed out that the transition from slavery to feudalism was not generated by interclass slave revolts against their masters, and the transition from feudalism to capitalism was not due to interclass uprisings by serfs against their lords. In both "transitions", if any, the conflicts and "struggles" were intraclass within the old and emerging new ruling classes, which responded to underlying economic changes. Slave and serf revolts were at best secondary and supplementary. Now Goldstone demonstrates that in each of the cases he analyzes, the important conflicts and struggles were among the existing and emerging elites, and not between the "people" and those elites. "Factional conflict within the elites, over access to office, patronage, and state policy, rather than conflict across classes, led to state paralysis and state breakdown" (Goldstone 1991: 461), as we also observed (chapter 3). Grassroots social movements from below were supplementary in that they helped further destabilize an already unstable state, if only by obliging it to spend already scarce resources to defend itself; and in that the popular movements favored the interests of some elite factions against others. "I know of no popular rebellion that succeeded by itself without associated elite revolts or elite leadership in creating institutional change" (Goldstone 1991: 11). All this would be obvious, if it were not so frequently denied by those whose ideology leads them to claim to know better.

Gills (1989) also refers to the intra-elite struggles underlying periodic crisis. He sees this pattern virtually everywhere prior to 1500. The pattern is driven not only demographically, but more fundamentally as a cyclical struggle among elites for control over shares of the surplus and state power. The typical pattern, as evident in the history of east Asia, is for privatization of accumulation to grow to a point at which it threatens the stability of the state, whose revenue declines as the rate of exploitation increases. This immiserates the peasantry and impoverishes the economy, and precipitates rebellion. In east Asian history, the timing of major rebellions is closely correlated to the entropic nadir in this cycle of accumulation and hegemony.

These and other revolts and revolutions have been the object of long study by Charles Tilly and his associates. They help fill an important void in the analysis of world system history, in which people's participation often does not receive the attention it rightfully deserves. Under the suggestive title *Big Structures, Large Processes, Huge Comparisons* Tilly (1984) asks "how can we improve our understanding of the large-scale structures and processes that were transforming the world?" Tilly answers and argues that "the most pressing theoretical problems are to connect local events to international structures of power and to improve existing models of these international structures."

He considers doing so at the world-historical, the world-systemic, the macrohistorical, and the microhistorical levels. "If the world forms but a single coherent network, the first two levels collapse into one. . . . How many levels exist and what units define them are partly empirical questions." But "if any connection counts, we will most likely discover that with trivial exceptions the world has always formed a single system." Tilly rightly rejects counting any connection; but he jumps to the unfounded conclusion that therefore "only in the last few hundred years, by the criterion of rapid, visible, and significant influences, could someone plausibly argue for all the world as a single system. . . . [This] implies that human history has seen many world systems, often simultaneously dominating different parts of the globe." Therefore, Tilly argues, we must study many "big structures, large processes, huge comparisons." Yet Tilly's own objectives and alternative criteria to pernicious postulates also permit alternative plausible arguments. To begin with, there could have been a multicentered and yet a single system. Nonetheless, Tilly himself still does not accept these arguments. On the contrary, in private correspondence (30 July 1989) he suggests that we would have to adopt precise numerical criteria of degrees of influence to measure significance, which in turn we reject as deleterious. Thus, we could say that Tilly's study of social movements breathes welcome life into the baby; but he throws out much of the wider social bath water, all of the systemic bath tub, and leaves the baby perilously suspended in midair.

POLITICAL GEOGRAPHY

Political geography as a world-encompassing subject is concerned primarily with analysis of the spatial dimensions of global political economy. Formerly, the dominant form of international political geography was geopolitics, which was preoccupied with strategic studies and power politics. Global rivalry among the great powers called into being a social-science discipline to inform strategists and statesmen. As such, geopolitics was the handmaiden of international relations, a similarly policy-oriented academic discipline. Mahan and Mackinder epitomized the infancy of geopolitics and its strategic obsession, e.g. in Mackinder's famous "heartland" theory.

Fortunately, in recent years political geography has been taken in new directions by critical scholarship addressing the spatial dimensions of the modern capitalist world economy. Particularly instrumental therein have been geographers like Peter Taylor (1989) who also edits the journal *Political Geography*, R.J. Johnson and P.J. Taylor (1986), Richard Peet (1991), and A.D. King (1991). Wallerstein (1991) has also contributed in this direction.

The spatial analysis of capitalism on a world scale has become more "fluid." It is moving away from notions of fixed territoriality, particularly when addressing questions of nation and nationalism, identity and locality, and the organization of production. The burgeoning literature on globalization/localization, postmodernism and critical human geography, and global culture indicates the still increasing intellectual interest in new ways of incorporating the spatial dimension into analyses of global processes (Soja 1988; Lash and Urry 1987; Jameson 1984; Anderson 1983; Featherstone 1991; A.D. King 1991).

The debates about world system theory and history intersect with these spatial explorations in political geography and critical social theory. Taken to its logical conclusion, our approach to cycles of accumulation and hegemony at the scale of the world system as a whole implies a new conceptualization of the spatial dimension of world accumulation/hegemonic processes (chapter 5). The fluidity of the spatial organization of the world system becomes all the more sharply apparent in a perpetual process of restructuring, which has been continuous for not only the past 500, but throughout 5,000 years of world system history.

The "geography of imperialism" should be understood not merely territorially, but temporally and sequentially, via the shifts in centers of accumulation that occur over time, and which themselves reflect the underlying processes of competitive accumulation that forever restructure the spatial organization of the world economy. In reality, no political geographical/spatial unit or entity, be it nation or state, is fixed. Instead, all have historically been and still are being kaleidoscopically transformed on the wheel of the processes of accumulation in the world system.

INTERNATIONAL RELATIONS AND INTERNATIONAL POLITICAL ECONOMY

Of all the academic disciplines our world system history should speak to, international relations (IR) and international political economy (IPE) are the most obvious candidates. World system analysis established its value by challenging both disciplines by its very multidisciplinary and holistic approach. By insisting on studying 500 years of world system history, world system analysis broke with the short-term post-1945 self-definition of both IR and IPE. It also broke with the then predominant state-centric approach in IR, which was mirrored in the modernization approach in development studies. World system theory made a case for the superiority of taking the world system as a whole as the unit of analysis. Since its first onslaught on the state-centric approach, conventional IR has been influenced by growing dissatisfaction with traditional realist state centrism. A number of prominent IR theorists have turned their attention instead to IPE (Gilpin 1981; Keohane 1984; Krasner 1983).

Our approach to hegemonic transitions also complements rather than competes with or contradicts the new Gramscian school in IPE of, for instance, Stephen Gill (1990) and Robert Cox (1981, 1983, 1987). They use larger frameworks of global hegemony, but also incorporate class and social forces, as well as their relationship to world order. This work complements our insistence on analyzing "interlinking hegemonies" in world historical processes. Gills (1993) attempts new synthesis of the Gramscian and world system approach in an analysis of hegemonic transitions in east Asia. However, most adherents of the new Gramscian approach to IR/IPE do not (yet) extend their analysis back in time beyond the relatively recent modern period.

However, the main point of continuing contact and dialogue between IR theorists and world system theorists has been long-cycle theory. Both were concerned with understanding the relationship between economic cycles of expansion and contraction and leadership/hegemonic cycles. These relationships were explored especially in Modelski (1987) and Modelski and Thompson (1988) coming from the "political" IR side; Wallerstein (1974) and Frank (1978a) on the "economic" world system side; the reader on both edited by Thompson (1983); the reworking of all of the above and much more in the magisterial study on long cycles and war by Goldstein (1988); and are reflected in recent discussion of world leadership and hegemony (Rapkin 1990). In addition to establishing historically grounded empirical studies of long-term cyclical change in the international/world system, they also made a contribution to cumulative social science knowledge, as reviewed by Chase-Dunn (1989).

This dialogue and growing interest in historically grounded IR and IPE theory also led to the establishment of the World Historical Systems

(WHS) sub-section of the IPE section in the International Studies Association (ISA). However, the 1991 and 1992 meetings of the WHS showed that a growing number of its members and others are now applying the study of a combination of both "political" and "economic" long cycles, and also of center–periphery structures, to world-systems – or, as we are, to the world system – before 1500. Our theses on world accumulation attempt to push the historical agenda of research even further back in sociohistorical time. Thereby, the established virtues of the world system and long-cycle approaches are extended to contribute to the study of world history. Premodern history and archaeology in turn can contribute to and perhaps "redefine" the study of IR and IPE.

The key question we pose to both existing world system theory and to IR and IPE theorists in whether there are fundamental historical cyclical patterns that shape not only the present and the past 500 years, but also much more of human history. Do the patterns of historical cyclical development of the present originate only 500 years ago with the emergence of the "capitalist mode of production" and the "modern interstate system," or do they emerge much earlier, as we suggest in chapter 5? If these patterns transcend transitions between modes of production and hegemonic power, as we think the evidence indicates, then the implications for social science are far-reaching indeed. We do not want to fall into some trap of "transhistoricism" by claiming that all world history is the same. We do not deny the reality of constant change and restructuring in the world economy. Far from it; what we seek to establish is that a process of accumulation existed in a world economic system long before the emergence of the "capitalist modern world-system" and that rhythms of expansion and contraction in this world system/economy have a continuity, which long predate – and indeed contribute to and help account for – the emergence of this "capitalist modern world-system." These patterns are interlinked with the historical rise and decline of hegemonic powers and shifts in the centers of power, whose fundamental characteristics, as we maintain, also long predate modern states systems.

Our hypotheses not only counter the short-term and state-centric views of much of IR and some of IPE, they also challenge these disciplines and their concerns to encompass more of the human experience and to analyze it more holistically. Ultimately, our position makes a case for both a macro- and a microhistorical sociology as the basis of any IR and/or IPE theory to understand and formulate policy for the modern world. The call for a world-historical approach to IR and IPE does not mean that current changes and conditions in the world system are irrelevant or a distraction. The real purpose of world-historical approaches is to inform and enrich our understanding of and policy for these on-going sociopolitical processes in the world today – and tomorrow. We explore some of these social-scientific, political and practical implications below in our conclusions.

DEVELOPMENT STUDIES

Development studies as such was born only after the Second World War and is, not unlike its second cousin "socialist development," already over the hill if not downright dead (Seers 1979; Hirschman 1981). The present world economic crisis has replaced concern for "development" by that for crisis management in the South and East. Moreover "development" has been replaced by the new buzzword "democracy," although managing the crisis allows for hardly any democratic control of public policy (Frank 1993b). On the other hand, as we contend, the world system has been around for over 5,000 years already; and its systematic study along these lines has only just begun. However, both the existence and the study of this world system have far-reaching implications for both development studies and "development" itself.

A world system perspective on "development" helps clarify how much – that is how little if at all – the "development" we have known has been good for people. "Development is bad for women," feminists say (Frank 1991b). If that is true, development is already bad for over half the world's population. However, "development" has also been bad for most men, as Wallerstein explicitly and Amin implicitly point out: over the five centuries existence of the modern world-system, as they see it, the growing polarization of income and wealth in the world has not benefitted most men (and still less women). Today, roughly speaking, 20 per cent of the population get 80 per cent of the world's goods, and 80 per cent have to share the poverty of the remaining 20 per cent of the goods. Wallerstein argues that as a result, the majority of the people in the world are absolutely worse off than 500 or even 200 years ago. If now we extend the idea of the world system still much farther back in history, the perspective on polarization and "development" becomes dimmer still, even if Amin argues that world-scale polarization only began with the birth of the modern world (capitalist) system.

However that may be, if there is only one world system, then "national" (state) development within it can only bring about a (temporary) improvement of a region's or a people's position within that system. In that case indeed, the very term "development" makes little sense unless it refers to the development of the whole world system itself, and not just of some part if it (Frank 1991b). That is, the entire (national state/society) foundation of "modernization" theory and policy, whether "capitalist" or "socialist," is challenged by the world system (theory) as well as by the bitter experience of those who put their faith in it and/or were obliged to suffer its costs.

The verity of this discovery is spectacularly illustrated by the experience with "socialist development." To begin with, the "development of socialism" was always little more than misnamed "socialist" development, as distinct from some "other" development, but nonetheless (national/state) development above and before all else. That has now been unmasked as a snare and a delusion. Unfortunately, perhaps even more on the ideological Right than on the Left, the blame for the failure is falsely attributed to the "socialist" part of this [non]development. In fact, "socialist development" was tried and failed exclusively in underdeveloped regions, which has been underdeveloped for ages and remain so – for that reason, that is because of their inherited and still continuing position in the world system, and not because of their supposed socialism. To the possible retort that some "capitalist" countries did develop, however, the answer is that most capitalist countries, regions, etc., in the world also did not "develop" and that they failed to do so for the same reason: not their "capitalist" or "socialist" "system," but their position in the world system! So the existence of, participation in, and awareness of the world system puts the *problématique* of development in a completely different light from that which was mistakenly and ideologically thrown upon it during the four postwar decades.

Development "policy" – and "theory" – has largely been a sham. Very few actors in this drama (farce? tragedy?) have sought anything other than their own profit and enrichment – at the expense of others. That has been true not only of "capitalists" for whom it comes naturally, but also of "socialists" for whom it may come unnaturally, but it comes nonetheless. The development theory either had policy-makers as its referent who turned out not to exist, or it had none at all to begin with. How could it have been otherwise, if all are part and parcel of the same dog-eat-dog competitive world system? In that system only a few can win the "development" race at any one time; and apparently they cannot even maintain their lead for long.

If world system theory is an outgrowth of dependence theory, as is often claimed especially by observers who subscribe to neither, then it should not be surprising if "world system" also has implications for "dependence." Briefly, they are that dependence exists – indeed has existed for millennia – within the world system; and that eliminating dependence or being/becoming independent of the world system is impossible. Thus, *dependentistas*, including Frank (1967, 1969), were right in giving structural dependence a central place in their analysis. Indeed, they did not know how right they were; for that dependence cannot be eliminated simply by replacing one "system" by another, because there is only one world system. On the other hand, therefore, the *dependentistas* were wrong in proposing easy solutions for dependence, as Frank (1991b) acknowledges under the title "The underdevelopment of development." It has been an essential part in the center–periphery structure of the world system for thousands of years; and it is not likely to be overcome easily or to disappear soon. Although they are not unrelated, concern about "dependent [under]development" has been shifting to concern for ecologically "sustainable development" (Redclift 1987).

ECOLOGY

Our thesis also touches on the contemporary and growing globe-embracing ecological threat and worldwide consciousness about the same. We argue that it was ecological considerations that led to the formation of the world system in the first place (chapter 5). The initial connections between Mesopotamia and Anatolia, Egypt and the Levant, etc., were forged to overcome ecologically determined regional deficiencies: Mesopotamia had to import metals from Anatolia, and Egypt wood from the Levant. Ecological considerations and changes also underlay many of the migrations and invasions from Central Asia into their neighboring regions to the east, south, and west. The resulting human activity, in turn, however, also had far-reaching ecological effects. Some may have been regionally beneficial for, or at least supportable by, the environment. Others, however, caused far-reaching environmental damage and, perhaps in combination with climatic and other environmental changes, led to regional environmental disasters. As a result, entire civilizations disappeared, like the Harappan in the Indus Valley.

Once formed, the "central" world system as a whole survived, however. Indeed, it expanded to incorporate ever more of the globe. Eventually, technological development, population growth, and of course the exploitation both of others and of the environment in the world system led to the growing globe-embracing environmental damage and threats, of which consciousness is only just emerging. However, vast regional environmental damage and awareness thereof – for instance in the Americas – occurred before in the world system and as a result of its expansion in what Alfred Crosby (1986) called *Ecological Imperialism: The Biological Expansion of Europe, 900–1900*. Analogous, if perhaps less dramatic, human-caused ecological scourges also occurred earlier in various Eurasian parts of the world system. Now, however, ecological disaster in the world system has itself become altogether global. Yet, the existence of the world system means that the causes of this disaster are generated primarily among the rich, who most benefit from the system, and that the damage and costs are visited selectively upon the poor, who can least defend themselves and their meager livelihood against the ecological threat and the structure and operation of the world system. Some of these people(s) have traditionally been the object of study by anthropologists.

ANTHROPOLOGY

Pursuing the world system back over thousands of years also touches some concerns of anthropologists. We have already considered the concern of archaeologists among them and some of the issues they debate. Evolutionism or neo-evolutionism *à la* White and Steward fell on hard times among anthropologists. However, there is certainly an overlap of interest with the longer historical view of a world system theory for 5,000 or more years, even if that is perhaps an exceedingly short view. The Lenskis (1982) referred to a 10,000-year world system, and physical anthropologists are of course concerned with more and more millions of years of humankind and its migration. Another issue is that of independent invention vs. diffusion. Emphasis on ties over long distances, not to mention participation in the same system, lends additional credence to diffusion and/or to simultaneous or repeated invention in response to common problems and stimuli.

A related recurrent issue among anthropologists is the question whether the societies they study are or were pristinely independent or related to others and participants in a wider system of societies. Currently, the long-held thesis that the !Kung Kung (Bushmen) led an independent existence in the Kalahari Desert has been the subject of increasing disconfirmation. Like most peoples, they have long participated in broader relations. It may nonetheless not be legitimate to say that these have long included the world system. Nor should it be excluded. However, the long-standing "substantivist" vs. "formalist" debate among economic anthropologists may find its Gordian knot cut when the "societies" they discuss are found to be part of the world system. The formalists argued that the same economic "laws" (e.g. of supply and demand) operate in all societies and times. The substantivists disagreed and countered that most societies were organized around "redistribution" and "reciprocity" instead. Reference in this regard has already been made above to the major substantivist writer Polanyi, who has been challenged by new archaeological finds. These finds and authors support a 5,000-year world system without, however, becoming formalists.

The transition from roaming if not nomadic hunters and gatherers to settled agriculturalists has not been as unidirectional as was once claimed. Instead, adaptive "transitions" have gone back and forth in response to ecological but also socioeconomic changes in the areas that particular peoples inhabited, which often formed part of and were subject to the influences of the world system (cf. Lattimore 1962). Thus, the anthropological concern with kinship-based social organization also appears in a different context, if kinship-based "societies" are viewed as part of the world system.

In particular, political organization that is supposedly derived only or primarily from kinship organization is subject to reinterpretation. Political organization and especially state formation has responded not only or even primarily to "internal" needs within this or that "society" but has been a function of contacts and rivalries with neighbors and/or invaders from afar within the world system. They in turn often responded to world system wide circumstances and changes. A survey of the related anthropological literature on state formation based on "internal" factors or on "interpolity relations" may be found in Cohen (1978). For Central Asia and its relations with its neighbors in east, south, and west Asia, this *problématique* is analyzed by among others the anthropologists Khazanov (1979) and Barfield (1989) and in Frank (1992b). Barfield (1989: 6–7) summarizes, following Irons (1979): "Among pastoral nomadic societies hierarchical political institutions are generated only by external relations with state societies and never develop purely as a result of internal dynamics of such societies." The anthropologists Talal Asad (1973) in *Anthropology and the Colonial Encounter* and Eric Wolf (1982) in *Europe and the People without History* deal with the relations between colonial powers and indigenous peoples. Although their concern is with relatively recent times, analogous problems also existed during encounters within the world system before modern times. Of particular interest in this regard are the related issues of ethnicity and race, their relations and study.

ETHNIC AND RACE RELATIONS/STUDIES

Another vital concern for anthropologists is ethnogenesis and ethnicity, which is of special relevance to ethnic identity, not to mention racial identification, today. The recurrent major and incessant more minor *Völkerwanderungen* in, through, and out of Eurasia have certainly mixed and mixed up ethnicity and race. So how can they be identified today?

Whatever the gaps in our knowledge, or the disputes, about past enthnogenesis and present ethnicity, their fundamentals are clear: ethnogenesis is less traditional than situational, and ethnicity is less an identity among "us" than a relation with "them." Both the situation and the relation are substantially defined by state and other political power; and the presence, absence, and especially the change in economic welfare occasion changes in the perception of ethnic identity and in the urgency of its expression. The anthropologist Frederick Barth (1969) persuasively argued for the recognition of situational and relational ethnic identity in his *Ethnic Groups and Boundaries*. The same was reiterated in more general terms in Nathan Glazer and Daniel Moynihan's *Ethnicity: Theory and Experience*. Summarizing in the words of Roger Ballard's (1976) review of the latter, "ethnicity is then, a political phenomenon, in which material interest unites with moral and emotional bonds." We argue in chapter 5 that all of these in turn are part and parcel of participation and changing circumstances in the world system, to which ethnic identity and racial identification are the responses. Therefore, our study of the millennial world system also bears on these vital concerns, which are convulsing the former Soviet Union and Yugoslavia as we write. In this regard, we may also recall again the previously cited literature on globalization and localism by among others Featherstone (1991), Friedman (1991), S. Hall (1991), King (1991). To summarize in the words pronounced by Mikhail Gorbachev before the United Nations, and we believe by Hegel before him: "unity in diversity."

GENDER RELATIONS

Feminist archaeologists and historians (thank Goddess for them!) have begun to dig up or reinterpret a Palaeolithic and Neolithic past supposedly governed by nonpatriarchal "partnership" relations. However, these relations were found to be "indigenous" particularly in Catal Huyuk and Hacilar in Anatolia, the site of Jericho in the Levant, later in Minoan Crete, and in the Balkans (Eisler 1987, following especially Marija Gimbutas 1980, 1981 and James Mellaart 1975). Figurines that suggest nonpatriarchal goddess-worship have also been found farther eastward into India. These scholars argue that these societies, and by extension western Judaeo-Christian society, only switched to patriarchy later, after armed invaders from Inner and Central Asia brought them warfare, military technology, oppression, and therewith the "diffusion" of patriarchy. Thus, these feminists suggest that western patriarchy is the result of its (unwelcome) diffusion from farther east in Inner Asia. This thesis is supported by the work of James DeMeo (1987, 1990, 1991). He claims that "matrist" (but not matriarchal) relations were "original" in much of the wetter and greener world before Arabia and Central Asia dried up about 4,000–3,500 BC. Then desertification expanded through what he calls the 1,000-mile-wide Saharasian belt stretching 8,000 miles from Africa through Inner Asia to China. As a result, many of its inhabitants suffered famines and were obliged to become pastoralist nomads, whose harsh and competitive realities then fostered "patrism" including patriarchy.

(Re)writing history from a more gender-balanced or feminist perspective is very welcome as all to the good. We particularly need more "feminist historical-materialist" analysis of different and changing gender and family relations, accumulation, politics, and culture/ideology. For much of history has been dominated by men in their own interest and written by them from their own perspective. However, the above-cited feminist version of history seems less than satisfactory and has at least the following four weaknesses and limitations: 1) it focuses rather selectively on some circum-Mediterranean societies with supposedly indigenous partnership societies and sees patriarchy as having been only belatedly diffused there from Inner Asia; 2) patriarchy was well established very early even in several societies to the east of the Mediterranean; 3) patriarchy was *not* comparatively more evident in Central Asian nomad societies, but rather the contrary. Frank (1992b) reports

> I asked every professional Central Asianist I have met whether the evidence available to them supports the Eisler and DeMeo theses. Unanimously, they have all said that it does not. According to their evidence on the contrary, Central Asian nomad societies accorded women higher status and had more egalitarian gender relations than their sedentary neighbors in Eurasia. I hesitate to cite the people who could only offer their evidence to me orally. However, I can quote some who have written something about this matter (of which we here reproduce short selections from a sample of two): "Women had more authority and autonomy than their sisters in neighboring sedentary societies. . . . Although the details cannot be confirmed for the entire history of Inner Asia, most visitors made comments [to this effect]" (Barfield 1989: 25). "Information dating from Mongol times suggests that women in the steppe empires had more rights and independence than their counterparts in sedentary states. These indications are confirmed for the Uighur empire" (Kwanten 1979: 58).
>
> (Frank 1992b: 20)

Finally, 4) to go to the roots of a *worldwide* problem like patriarchy, these primarily Euro-Mediterranean-centered feminist historians would do well to expand their scope to that of the world, if not also to the world system, as a whole. Beyond DeMeo's multicultural data, drawn from all around the world, a world *systemic* analysis could perhaps throw some additional light on this worldwide gender problem. For instance, just as emphasis on the competitive process of capital accumulation in the world system puts class and state formation in a different light, so may the same also offer a better perspective on the formation of the gender structure of society.

SOME PHILOSOPHICAL, SOCIAL SCIENTIFIC, AND POLITICAL IMPLICATIONS

This thesis and approach also speaks to the age-old philosophical dilemma about determinism and free will. The formation of and incorporation within the world system may or may not have been necessary and "determined." However, the world system both limited or "determined" and expanded the options or "free will" once the world system came into existence and/or incorporated a region or people within it. Surely, the formation and expansion of the world system and its "division of labor" increased material possibilities and cultural options for at least those who benefit from the system and probably for those who propagate it. However, the division of labor also assigned roles and strengthened social structures and historical processes, which limited the options and perhaps determined some of the choices of all participants in the system. Of course, those who are directly exploited and/or oppressed in, not to mention those who are eliminated by, the system have their options limited and perhaps largely determined. However, even those who derive most of the benefits from their positions "on top" of the system probably have some of their behavior "determined" by the exigencies of maintaining and/or furthering their positions within and their benefits from the system. Thus the unequal structure and the cyclical process, as well as the "progressive development" of the system simultaneously expand the "free will" possibilities and "determine" the limited options within the system. However, the "determinism" is not predetermined. The options are determined in and by the structure and process of the system at each point in time. They were not predetermined beforehand by some "invisible hand" and for all time. Like a glacier, the historical process within the system and indeed the world system itself make their own way, both adapting to and changing the ecology.

The recognition and analysis of the system, as distinct from its existence independently of its recognition, further holism in social science. Many social scientists and historians reject holism in theory, and/or they are not very holistic in (their) practice. We seek to make our analysis as holistic as possible. So do "world-systems" theorists. Yet, we do so in different ways, guided by our respective visions of the "whole." For Amin (chapter 8) and Wallerstein (chapter 10 and 1989b), the important whole system is the modern capitalist world-system. Perhaps it is for Abu-Lughod (chapter 9 and 1989) as well, although she also devotes her attention to the "thirteenth-century world system." All three also recognize other historical world-systems, as do Ekholm and Friedman (chapter 2), who devote more attention to studying ancient ones. We extend the same kind of holism to the study of a single world system and its development over 5,000 years. We suggest that this approach is an appropriate application both of the world system idea or approach and the holist mandate in social science and history. Ekholm and Friedman are receptive thereto; Abu-Lughod is skeptical; and Amin and Wallerstein reject this extension of the world-system and use of holism. The latter altogether, and the former partly, argue that before 1500 there were other world-systems, which can and should also be studied holistically, but on their own terms. Of course, if our present world system really has had a millennial existence and history as we claim, then our holistic long-view approach is all the more appropriate.

Like our "world-systems" colleagues, we also subscribe to and practice what we call the "three-legged stool" approach: like that stool, our study of the social world system is supported equally by three ecological/economic, political, and cultural/ideological/ethical legs. At one time or another, some of us may concentrate excessively or inadequately on one or two of these legs to the apparent exclusion of the other(s). However, in principle, if not always in practice, we recognize the role of all three legs. The most neglected one, perhaps, is the ecological material of the economic leg. That, unfortunately, is a shortcoming we still share with all too many other students of society.

Our thesis, as well as the related debates reviewed above, also have far-reaching political implications. Amin and Wallerstein identify the world system with its mode of production. Our study of the millennial world system and how it operates leads us to demur. Gills insists that the world system must not be confused with its "modes of production." Instead, he sees a complex mixture or articulation of modes at all times in the development of the world accumulation process and the world system and cannot accept the identification of the world system with a single dominant mode. Frank (chapter 6) goes further and argues that feudalism, and socialism, but also capitalism, are only "ideological modes," which should be excluded from our social-scientific analysis altogether.

This issue is perhaps the central political point in the social-scientific debate, which Amin and Wallerstein also join. They argue that the modern world-system is uniquely characterized by the capitalist mode of production. That is why they will not accept the proposal that the analysis of this world system can and should be pushed back before 1500. Before that, they argue and are joined by Abu-Lughod, there were other world-systems. Amin and Wallerstein insist, like probably all Marxists and most others, whether or not they see other prior world-systems, that in earlier times other modes of production were dominant. Amin sums them all up as "tributary" modes of production, in which "politics [and ideology] is/was in command," to recall Mao Zedong. In the modern capitalist world-system, by contrast, the economic law of value is in command, and that on a world-system scale.

We insist that this is nothing new. Therefore, Frank also suggests that it would be senseless to call all that previous history throughout most of the world "capitalist." If "capitalism" does not distinguish one "thing" from another, then there is no point in maintaining that label. Amin, Wallerstein, and most others insist that "capitalism" is distinguishable. Of course, today especially the political/ideological Right finds "capitalism" particularly distinguished and distinguishable from "socialism." Frank denies that any of these categories have any social-scientific and/or empirical content and suggests that they serve only ideological "false-consciousness" purposes to confuse and confound instead.

The (mis)use and replacement of these categories bears importantly on the analysis and understanding of some major world events today, particularly the end of "socialism" and of American "hegemony," albeit not of the "end of history." We believe that ideological blinkers – or worse, mindsets – have too long prevented us from seeing that the world political-economic system long predated the rise of capitalism in Europe and its hegemony in the world. The rise of Europe represented a hegemonic shift from East to West within a pre-existing system. If there was any transition then, it was this hegemonic shift within the system rather than the formation of a new system. We are again in one of the alternating periods of hegemony and rivalry in the world system now, which portends a renewed westward shift of hegemony across the Pacific. To identify the system with its dominant mode of production is a mistake. There was no transition from feudalism to capitalism as such. Nor was there (to be) an analogous transition from capitalism to socialism. If these analytical categories of "modes of production" prevent us from seeing the real world political-economic system, it would be better to abandon them altogether.

We should ask: what was the ideological reason for Wallerstein's and Frank's "scientific" construction of a sixteenth-century transition (from feudalism in Europe) to a modern world capitalist economy and system? It was the belief in a subsequent transition from capitalism to socialism, if not immediately in the world as a whole, at least through "socialism in one country" after another. Traditional Marxists, and many others who debated with us, even more so, were intent on preserving faith in the prior but for them more recent transition from one (feudal) mode of production to another (capitalist) one. Their political/ideological reason was that they were intent on the subsequent transition to still another and supposedly different socialist mode of production. That was (and is?) the position of Marxists, traditional and otherwise, like the above-cited Brenner (in Aston and Philpin 1985) and Anderson (1974). That is still the position of Samir Amin (1989), who, like Wallerstein, now wants to take refuge in "protocapitalism" – and by extension "protosocialism." (Before he was ousted after the Tiananmen massacre, Chinese Premier Zhao Ziyang came up with the idea that China is now only in the stage of "primary" socialism.)

If people would dare to undertake a "transition" from their "scientific" categories, they could spare themselves and their readers some of the political (dis)illusions regarding recent events in the "Second" and "Third" Worlds. These categories of "transition" and "modes" are not essential or even useful tools, but rather obstacles to the scientific study of the underlying continuity and essential properties of the world system in the past. They also shackle our political struggle and ability to confront and manage the development of this same system in the present and future.

We would all do better to see the reality of the globe-embracing structure and the long historical development of the whole world system itself, full stop. Better recognize this system's "unity in diversity." That would really be a "transition" in thinking. This "transition" would help us much better to choose among the diversities which are really available in that world system – *Vives cettes differences!* Moreover, this transition in thinking could also help us to understand the real transitions that there are and to guide us in the struggle for the good and against the socially bad difference.

In particular, we suggest that these labels confuse and confound the real world system issues about which people have to and do dispute and fight. The belief in these labels supports disputes about political "systems" and self-determination, which have little or no real possibilities to be put into practice in the single really existing world system. The same labels serve to misguide or defuse the real social movements. About these, Amin, Frank, and Wallerstein agree enough, despite their disagreements about world system history, to have written a book jointly with Giovanni Arrighi and Marta Fuentes under the title *Transforming the Revolution: Social Movements and the World-System* (Amin *et al.* 1990). Our joint conclusion was – *A luta continua!*

NOTE

This chapter first appeared in 1992 as "The Five Thousand Year World System: An interdisciplinary introduction," in the *Humboldt Journal of Social Relations* 18 (1): 1–79. (Special issue: World Systems Analysis.)

REFERENCES

Abu-Lughod, J. (1989) *Before European Hegemony. The World System* AD *1250–1350*, New York: Oxford University Press.

Adams, R.M. (1974) "Anthropological perspectives on ancient trade," *Current Anthropology* 15 (3) (September).

Adelson, H.L. (1962) *Medieval Commerce*, Princeton: Van Nostrand.

Algaze, G. (n.d.) "Prehistoric world systems, imperialism, and the expansion of some early pristine states" (manuscript).

Allen, M. (1984) "Assyrian colonies in Anatolia," published as "The mechanisms of underdevelopment: an ancient Mesopotamian example," *Review* 15 (3) (summer).

Allerdyce, G. (1990) "Toward world history: American historians and the coming of the world history course," *Journal of World History* 1 (1) (spring): 23–76.

Amin, S. (1989) *Eurocentrism*, London: Zed.

Amin, S., Arrighi, G., Frank, A.G., and Wallerstein, I. (1990) *Transforming the Revolution: Social Movements and the World-System*, New York: Monthly Review Press.

Anderson, B. (1983) *Imagined Communities: Reflections on the Origin and Spread of Nationalism*, London: Verso.

Anderson, P. (1974) *Lineages of the Absolutist State*, London: New Left Books.

Asad, T. (ed.) (1973) *Anthropology and the Colonial Encounter*, London: Ithaca Press.

Aston, T. and Philpin, C. (eds) (1985) *The Brenner Debate. Agrarian Class Structure and Economic Development in Pre-Industrial Europe*, Cambridge, MA: Cambridge University Press.

Baechler, J., Hall, J.A., and Mann, M. (eds) (1988) *Europe and the Rise of Capitalism*, Oxford: Basil Blackwell.

Ballard, R. (1976) "Ethnicity: theory and experience (a Review Article)," *Journal of the Community Relations Commission* 5 (3) (autumn).

Barfield, T. (1989) *The Perilous Frontier. Nomadic Empires and China*, Oxford: Basil Blackwell.

Barth, F. (ed.) (1969) *Ethnic Groups and Boundaries*, Boston: Little, Brown.

Beckwith, C. (1987) *The Tibetan Empire in Central Asia*, Princeton: Princeton University Press.

—— (1990) "The concept of the 'barbarian' in Chinese historiography and western Sinology: rhetoric and the creation of Fourth World nations in Inner Asia" (manuscript).

Bernal, M. (1987) *Black Athena. The Afroasiatic Roots of Classical Civilization*, New Brunswick: Rutgers University Press.

Blaut, J. (1977) "Where was capitalism born?" in *Radical Geography*, ed. R. Peet, Chicago: Maasoufa Press, 95–110.

Braudel, F. (1953) *El Mediterraneo y el Mundo Mediterraneo en la Epoca de Felipe II*, Mexico: Fondo de Cultura, vol. 1 of two.

—— (1981–4) *Civilization and Capitalism*, 3 vols, New York: Harper & Row.

Cameron, R. (1973) "The logistics of European economic growth: a note on historical periodization," *Journal of European Economic History* 2 (1): 145–8.

Champion, T.C. (ed.) (1989) *Centre and Periphery: Comparative Studies in Archaeology*, Boston: Unwin Hyman.

Chase-Dunn, C. (1986) "Rise and demise: world-systems and modes of production" (manuscript).

—— (1989) "Core/periphery hierarchies in the development of intersocietal networks" (manuscript).

Chase-Dunn, C. and Hall, T.D. (eds) (1991) *Core/Periphery Relations in Precapitalist Worlds*, Boulder, CO: Westview Press.

Chaudhuri, K.N. (1985) *Trade and Civilization in the Indian Ocean. An Economic History from the Rise of Islam to 1750*, Cambridge, MA: Cambridge University Press.

—— (1990) *Asia Before Europe. Economy and Civilization of the Indian Ocean from the Rise of Islam to 1750*, Cambridge, MA: Cambridge University Press.

Childe, G. (1936) *Man Makes Himself*, New York: Mentor.

—— (1942) *What Happened in History*, Harmondsworth: Pelican.

Cohen, R. (1978) "State origins: a reappraisal," in *The Early State*, ed. H.J.M. Claessen and P. Skalnik, The Hague: Mouton.

Cox, R.W. (1981) "Social forces, states and world orders: beyond international relations theory," *Millennium: Journal of International Studies* 10 (2): 126–55.

—— (1983) "Gramsci, hegemony and international relations: an essay in method," *Millennium: Journal of International Studies* 12 (2): 162–75.

—— (1987) *Production, Power, and World Order*, New York: Columbia University Press.

Crosby, A.W. (1986) *Ecological Imperialism: The Biological Expansion of Europe, 900–1900*, Cambridge, MA: Cambridge University Press.

Curtin, P.D. (1984) *Cross–Cultural Trade in World History*, Cambridge, MA: Cambridge University Press.

Dales, G.F. (1976) "Shifting trade patterns between the Iranian Plateau and the Indus Valley in the third millennium BC," *Colloques Internationaux*, dur CRNS No. 567.

DeMeo, J. (1987) "Desertification and the origins of armoring: the Saharasian connection," *Journal of Orgonomy* 21 (2), 22 (1 & 2), 23 (2).

—— (1990) "Origins and diffusion of patrism in Saharasia: evidence for a worldwise, climate-linked geographical pattern in human behavior," *Kyoto Review* 23 (spring).

—— (1991) "Origins and diffusion of patrism in Saharasia c. 4000 BC: evidence for a worldwide, climate-linked geographical pattern in human behavior," *World Futures* 30 (4).

Denemark, R. and Thomas, K. (1988) "The Brenner–Wallerstein debate," *International Studies Quarterly* 33 (March).

de Ste Croix, G.E.M. (1981) *The Class Struggle in the Ancient Greek World*, London: Duckworth.

Dobb, M. (1963) [original 1946] *Studies in the Development of Capitalism*, London: Routledge & Kegan Paul.

Dodgshon, R.A. (1987) *The European Past: Social Evolution and Spatial Order*, London: Macmillan.

Dopsch, A. (1918 & 1923/4) *Wirtschaftsliche und soziale Grundlagender Europäischen Kulturentwicklung aus der Zeit Caesar bis Karl den Grossen*, Vienna: L.W. Seidel & Sohn.

Eisler, R. (1987) *The Chalice and the Blade. Our History, Our Future*, San Francisco: Harper & Row.

Fairbank. J.K. (1969) *Trade and Diplomacy on the China Coast*, Stanford: Stanford University Press.

Farmer, E.L. (1985) "Civilization as a unit of world history: Eurasia and Europe's place in it," *The History Teacher* 18 (3) (May): 347–63.

—— *et al.* (1977) *Comparative History of Civilizations in Asia*, Reading, MA: Addison-Wesley.

Featherstone, M. (ed.) (1991) *Global Culture: Nationalism, Globalization and Modernity*, London: Sage.

Finley, M.I. (1985) *The Ancient Economy*, London: Hogarth Press, 2nd edn.

Frank, A.G. (1965) "Con que modo de produccion convierte la gallina maiz en huevos de oro?" *El Gallo Ilustrado Suplemento de El Dia, Mexico*, 31 October and 25 November.

—— (1967) *Capitalism and Underdevelopment in Latin America*, New York: Monthly Review Press.

—— (1969) *Latin America: Underdevelopment or Revolution*, New York: Monthly Review Press.

—— (1978a) *World Accumulation 1492–1789*, New York: Monthly Review Press; London: Macmillan.

—— (1978b) *Dependent Accumulation and Underdevelopment*, New York: Monthly Review Press; London: Macmillan.

—— (1990a) "A theoretical introduction to five thousand years of world system history," *Review* 13 (2) (spring): 155–248.

—— (1990b) "The thirteenth century world system: a Review Essay, *Journal of World History* 1 (2) (autumn): 249–56.

—— (1991a) "A plea for world system history," *Journal of World History* 2 (1) (winter): 1–28.

—— (1991b) "The underdevelopment of development," *Scandinavian Journal of Development Alternatives*, special number, 10 (3): 5–72. Published in Spanish as *El Subdesarrollo del Desarrollo: Un Ensayo Autobiografico*, Caracas: Editorial Nueva Sociedad, 1991.

—— (1992a) "Fourteen Ninety-Two Once Again," *Political Geography* 11 (4) (July): 386–93.

—— (1992b) *The Centrality of Central Asia*, University Press, Center for Asian Studies Amsterdam (CASA), Comparative Asian Studies (CAS), 8.

—— (1993a) "1492 and Latin America at the margin of world history: East >

West hegemonial shifts 992–1492–1992," *Comparative Civilizations Review* 28 (spring): 1–40.
—— (1993b) "Marketing democracy in an undemocratic market," in *Low Intensity Democracy: Political Power in the New World Order*, ed. Barry Gills, Joel Rocamora, and Richard Wilson, London: Pluto Press and Transnational Institute.
—— (1993c) "Bronze Age world system cycles," *Current Anthropology* 34 (4), (August to October).
Friedman, J. (1991) "Being in the world: globalization and localization," in *Global Culture: Nationalism, Globalization and Modernity*, ed. M. Featherstone, London: Sage.
Gernet, J. (1985) *A History of China*, Cambridge, MA: Cambridge University Press.
Gill, S. (1990) *American Hegemony and the Trilateral Commission*, Cambridge, MA: Cambridge University Press.
Gills, B.K. (1989) "Synchronization, conjuncture and centre-shift in east Asian international history," paper presented at the International Studies Association meetings, London (April).
—— (1993) "The hegemonic transition in east Asia: a historical perspective," in *Gramsci and International Relations*, ed. Stephen Gill, Cambridge: Cambridge University Press, 186–212.
Gilpin, R. (1981) *War and Change in World Politics*, Cambridge, MA: Cambridge University Press.
—— (1987) *The Political Economy of International Relations*, Princeton, NJ: Princeton University Press.
Gimbutas, M. (1980) *The Early Civilization of Europe*, Los Angeles: UCLA Indo-European Studies Center.
—— (1981) *The Goddesses and Gods of Old Europe*, 7000–3500 BC, Los Angeles: University of California Press.
Glazer, Nathan and Moynihan, Daniel P. (1975) *Ethnicity: Theory and Experience*, Cambridge, MA: Harvard University Press.
Goldstein, J.S. (1988) *Long Cycles. Prosperity and War in the Modern Age*, New Haven: Yale University Press.
Goldstone, J.A. (1991) *Revolutions and Rebellions in the Early Modern World*, Berkeley: University of California Press.
Gouldner, A. (1980) *The Two Marxisms*, London: Macmillan.
Hall, J.A. (1985) *Powers and Liberties: The Causes and Consequences of the Rise of the West*, London/Oxford: Penguin, with Basil Blackwell.
Hall, S. (1991) "The local and the global: globalization and ethnicity," in *Culture, Globalization and the World-System*, ed. A.D. King, London: Macmillan.
Hiebert, F.T. and Lamberg-Karlovsky, C.C. (1992) "Central Asia and the Indo-Iranian borderlands", in *Iran* 30: 1–15.
Hilton, R.H. (ed.) (1976) *The Transition from Feudalism to Capitalism*, London: New Left Books.
Hirschman, A.O. (1981) *Essays in Trespassing: Economics to Politics and Beyond*, Cambridge, MA: Cambridge University Press.
Hodgson, M.G.S. (1954) "Hemispheric interregional history as an approach to world history," *Unesco Journal of World History/Cahiers d'Histoire Mondiale* 1 (3): 715–23.
—— (1958) "The unity of later Islamic history," Unesco *Journal of World History* 5 (4): 879–914.
—— (1974) *The Venture of Islam*, Chicago: University of Chicago Press, 3 vols.

Hopkins, T. and Wallerstein, I. (1987) "Capitalism and the incorporation of new zones into the world-economy," *Review* 10 (5/6) (summer/Fall): 763–79.

Huntington, E. (1907) *The Pulse of Asia: A Journey in Central Asia illustrating the Geographic Basis of History*, New York: Houghton Mifflin.

Irons, W. (1979) "Political stratification among pastoral nomads," in *Pastoral Production and Society* ed. L'Equipe Ecologie et Anthropologie des Sociétés Pastorales, Cambridge, MA: Cambridge University Press.

Jameson, F. (1984) "Postmodernism, or the cultural logic of late capitalism," *New Left Review* 146 (July–August): 53–92.

Johnson R.J. and Taylor, P.J. (eds) (1986) *A World in Crisis? Geographical Perspectives*, Oxford: Blackwell.

Jones, E.L. (1981) *The European Miracle: Environments, Economies and Geopolitics in the History of Europe and Asia*, Cambridge, MA: Cambridge University Press.

Kennedy, P. (1987) *The Rise and Fall of the Great Powers*, New York: Random House.

Keohane, R.O. (1984) *After Hegemony: Cooperation and Discord in the World Political Economy*, Princeton: Princeton University Press.

Khazanov, A.M. (1979) *Nomads and the Outside World*, Cambridge, MA: Cambridge University Press.

King, A.D. (1990) *Urbanism, Colonialism and the World-Economy*, London: Routledge.

—— (ed.) (1991) *Culture, Globalization and the World-System*, London: Macmillan.

Kohl, P.L. (1978) "The balance of trade in southwestern Asia in the mid-third millennium," *Current Anthropology* 19 (3) (September): 463–92, including comments pp. 476–85.

—— (1987) "The ancient economy, transferable technologies and the Bronze Age world-system: a view from the northeastern frontier of the ancient Near East," in *Centre and Periphery in the Ancient World*, ed. M. Rowlands, M. Larsen, and K. Krisitansen, Cambridge, MA: Cambridge University Press, 13–24.

—— (1989) "The use and abuse of world systems theory: the case of the 'Pristine' west Asian state," in *Archaeological Thought in America*, ed. C.C. Lamberg-Karlovsky, Cambridge, MA: Cambridge University Press, 218–40.

—— (1991) "The Transcaucasian 'periphery' in the Bronze Age: a preliminary formulation," in *Resource, Power and Interregional Interaction*, ed. E.M. Shortman and P.A. Urban, New York: Plenum.

Krasner, S. (ed.) (1983) *International Regimes*, Ithaca and London: Cornell University Press.

Kwanten, Luc (1979) *Imperial Nomads*, Leicester: Leicester University Press.

Lash, S. and Urry, J. (1987) *The End of Organized Capitalism*, Oxford: Polity Press.

Lattimore, O. (1962) *Inner Asian Frontiers of China*, Boston: Beacon Press.

Lenski, G. and Lenski, J. (1982) *Human Societies*, New York: McGraw-Hill, 4th edn.

Lombard, M. (1975) *The Golden Age of Islam*, Amsterdam: North Holland.

Mann, M. (1986) *The Sources of Social Power*, vol. 1: *A History of Power from the Beginning to AD 1760*, Cambridge, MA: Cambridge University Press.

McNeill, W.H. (1963) *The Rise of the West: A History of the Human Community*, Chicago: University of Chicago Press.

—— (1964) *Europe's Steppe Frontier, 1500–1800*, Chicago: University of Chicago Press.

—— (1983) *The Pursuit of Power: Technology, Armed Force and Society since* AD *1000*, Oxford: Basil Blackwell.

—— (1990) "*The Rise of the West* after twenty-five years," *Journal of World History* 1 (1).

Mellaart, J. (1975) *The Neolithic of the Near East*, London: Thames & Hudson.

Modelski, G. (1987) *Long Cycles in World Politics*, London: Macmillan.

—— (1991) "World system evolution: a learning model," paper presented at the 32nd annual meeting of the International Studies Association, Vancouver, 20–23 March.

Modelski, G. and Thompson, W. (1988) *Sea Power in Global Politics 1494–1993*, London: Macmillan.

North, D.C. and Thomas, R.P. (1973) *The Rise of the Western World. A New Economic History*, Cambridge, MA: Cambridge University Press.

Nowak, L. (1983) *Property and Power. Towards a Non-Marxian Historical Materialism*, Dordrecht/Boston/Lancaster: D. Reidel.

Orlin, L.L. (1970) *Assyrian Colonies in Cappadocia*, The Hague: Mouton.

Orwell, G. (1977) *1984*, San Diego, CA: Harcourt Brace Jovanovich.

Palan, R. and Gills, B.K. (eds) (1993) *Transcending the State/Global Divide: The Neo-Structuralist Agenda in International Relations*, Boulder, CO: Lynne Rienner.

Palat, R.A. and Wallerstein, I. (1990) "Of what world system was pre-1500 'India' a part?" paper presented at the International Colloquium on "Merchants, companies and trade," Maison des Sciences de l'Homme, Paris, 30 May–2 June. Revision to be published in *Merchants, Companies and Trade*, ed. S. Chaudhuri and M. Morineau (forthcoming).

Peet, R. (1991) *Global Capitalism: Theories of Societal Development*, London: Routledge.

Pirenne, H. (1936) *Economic and Social History of Medieval Europe*, London: Routledge & Kegan Paul.

Polanyi, K. (1975) "Traders and trade," in *Ancient Civilization and Trade*, ed. J.A. Sabloff and C.C. Lamberg-Karlovsky, Albuquerque: University of New Mexico Press.

—— (1977) *The Livelihood of Man*, ed. H.W. Pearson, New York: Academic Press.

Polanyi, K., Arensberg, C., and Pearson, H.W. (1957) *Trade and Markets in the Early Empires*, Glencoe: The Free Press.

Quigley, C. (1961) *The Evolution of Civilizations. An Introduction to Historical Analysis*, New York: Macmillan.

Rapkin, D.P. (1990) *World Leadership and Hegemony*, Boulder: Lynne Rienner.

Ratnagar, S. (1981) *Encounters: The Westerly Trade of the Harappan Civilization*, Delhi: Oxford University Press.

Redclift, M. (1987) *Sustainable Development: Exploring the Contradictions*, London and New York: Methuen.

Robertson, R. (1990) "Globality, global culture and images of world order," in *Social Change and Modernity*, ed. H. Haferkamp and N. Smelser, Berkeley: University of California Press.

Rowlands, M., Larsen, M. and Kristiansen, K. (eds) (1987) *Centre and Periphery in the Ancient World*, Cambridge, MA: Cambridge University Press.

See, H. (1951) [original 1926] *Les Origines du Capitalisme Moderne*, Paris: Armand Colin.

Seers, D. (ed.) (1979) *Dependency Theory: A Critical Reassessment*, London: Frances Pinter.

Sherratt, A. (n.d.) "Core, periphery and margin: perspectives on the Bronze Age" (manuscript).
—— (1992) "What would a Bronze Age world system look like?" paper presented at the Prehistoric Society meeting, Bristol, 10–12 April.
Sherratt, A. and Sherratt, S. (1991) "From luxuries to commodities: the nature of the Bronze Age trading system," in *Bronze Age Trade in the Mediterranean*, ed. N.H. Cole, Jonsered: Paul Aströms Förlag, 351–84.
Silver, M. (1985) *Economic Structures of the Ancient Near East*, London: Croom Helm.
Soja, E.W. (1988) *Postmodern Geographies: The Reassertion of Space in Critical Social Theory*, London: Verso.
Sombart, W. (1967) *Luxury and Capitalism*, Ann Arbor: University of Michigan Press.
—— (1969) *The Jews and Modern Capitalism*, New York: B. Franklin.
Stavrianos, L.S. (1970) *The World to 1500: A Global History*, Englewood Cliffs: Prentice Hall.
Szücs, J. (1983) "The three historical regions of Europe," *Acta Historica Academiae Scientiarum Hungaricae* 29 (2–4): 131–84.
Taylor, P.J. (1989) *Political Geography: World-Economy, Nation-State and Locality*, London: Longman.
Teggart, F.J. (1939) *Rome and China: A Study of Correlations in Historical Events*, Berkeley: University of California Press.
Thompson, W.R. (ed.) (1983) *Contending Approaches to World System Analysis*, Beverly Hills: Sage.
—— (1989) *On Global War: Historical-Structural Approaches to World Politics*, Columbia: University of South Carolina Press.
Thrift, N. (1986) "The geography of international economic disorder," in *A World in Crisis? Geographical Perspectives*, ed. R.J. Johnson and P.J. Taylor, Oxford: Blackwell, 12–67.
Tilly, C. (1984) *Big Structures, Large Processes, Huge Comparisons*, New York: Russell Sage Foundation.
Toynbee, A. (1946) *A Study of History* (Somervell abridgement), Oxford: Oxford University Press.
Wallerstein, I. (1974) *The Modern World-System*, vol. 1, New York: Academic Books.
—— (1980) *The Modern World System*, vol. 2, New York: Academic Books,
—— (1984) *The Politics of the World-Economy*, Cambridge: Cambridge University Press.
—— (1988a) *The Modern World System*, vol. 3, New York: Academic Books.
—— (1988b) "The 'Discoveries' and Human Progress", *Estudos e Ensaios*.
—— (1989a) "World system analysis: the second phase," paper presented at the annual meetings of the PEWS Section of the American Sociological Association in San Francisco, 13 August.
—— (1989b) "The West, capitalism, and the modern world-system," prepared as a chapter in J. Needham, *Science and Civilization in China*, vol. 7: *The Social Background*, part 2. sect. 48: "Social and economic considerations" (forthcoming), published in *Review* XV, 4, Fall, 1992.
—— (1989c) "Culture as the ideological battleground of the modern world-system," *Hitotsubashi Journal of Social Studies* 21 (1) (August).
—— (1991) *Geopolitics and Geoculture: Essays on the Changing World System*, Cambridge, MA: Cambridge University Press.

Wilkinson, D. (1987) "Central civilization," *Comparative Civilizations Review* 17 (Fall): 31–59.

—— (1989) "The future of the world state: from civilization theory to world politics," paper presented at the annual meeting of the International Studies Association, London, 28 March–1 April.

Wolf, E. (1982) *Europe and the People without History*, Berkeley: University of California Press.

Woolf, G. (1990) "World-systems analysis and the Roman empire," *Journal of Roman Archaeology* 3.

Part II

BUILDING BLOCKS OF THEORY AND ANALYSIS

2

"CAPITAL" IMPERIALISM AND EXPLOITATION IN ANCIENT WORLD SYSTEMS

K. Ekholm and J. Friedman

INTRODUCTION

The above title may appear provocative to those who would maintain that capital is, by definition, wage-labor capital, that imperialism is the highest stage of capitalism, and that before the industrial revolution there were only "embedded" economies whose goals were related to the gaining of prestige, conspicuous consumption, and the maintenance of alliances for "social reasons" (Polanyi 1947; Finley 1973: 130, 158). This is because our argument is aimed at a tendency in anthropology and anthropologically influenced history and archaeology to divide the world's history into distinctive market/nonmarket or capitalist/precapitalist systems. We feel that such "substantivist" and "historical-materialist" categorizations are based on false abstractions from reality that obscure some of the essential continuities of social evolution from the rise of the first civilizations. Our own point of view is that there exists a form of "capitalism" in the ancient world, that there are "world economies," and that many properties of the dynamics of such systems are common to our own world economy. This is not to take a stand for the "formalist" approach in economic anthropology. The entire substantivist/formalist debate, which centers on the question of market rationality versus socially prescribed nonoptimizing behavior in precapitalist society, is very much a distortion of the original primitivist/modernist debate. The latter was not concerned with general models of individual behavior but with the macrostructure of ancient (not primitive) economies (Bücher 1893; Meyer 1910; Rostovtzeff 1957; for a discussion see Humphreys 1970). The opponents of the primitivists did not stress the praxeology of individual maximizing agents, but rather the substantive existence of a kind of capital accumulation in the ancient world. Their argument was, in Polanyi's own definition, a substantivist one insofar as they attempted to characterize a specific social system and not to assert a basic propensity of the human species.

We do not deny that there are important differences between industrial capitalism and the ancient systems. It is clear that the modern system in which industrial capitals compete for survival by direct investment in the productive forces implies a kind of dynamic unknown in the past. The accumulation of capital as a form of abstract wealth, however, is a truly ancient phenomenon. To say that this ancient "capital" played a fundamental economic role is not to say that it functioned directly in the production process, but that its accumulation and control were dominant features of those economies. The system to which we refer is characterized not only by an accumulation of capital, but by the emergence of an imperialist pattern: center/periphery structures are unstable over time; centers expand, contract, and collapse as a regular manifestation of the shift of points of accumulation. These phenomena are, we think, more general than modern capitalism. Similarly, the world economic crisis that we are experiencing today can be understood in terms of processes more general than a capitalist mode of production, processes that constitute a disastrous dynamic that has been the driving force of "civilized" history.

Our point of departure is that the forerunner of the present kind of world-system first emerged in the period following 3000 BC in southern Mesopotamia. Here we can describe the first example of the rise of a center of accumulation within a larger economic system and the development of an imperialist structure.

GENERALITIES

We refer repeatedly to "larger economic systems," to center/periphery relations, etc. Our object of analysis here is not the institutional structures of society, but the processes of reproduction within which such local structures are formed and maintained. To the extent that a society is not a self-contained unit of production and consumption, it becomes necessary to take up the larger system within which that society, in conjunction with others, reproduces itself. It is at this level that we can grasp the total economic flow, the dynamic, and the conditions of existence of the society in question.

1 Supralocal exchange systems existed long before the rise of the first civilizations, and, when considered as systems in evolution, they are crucial to an understanding of the emergence of civilization. A great many examples from late Palaeolithic and early Neolithic Europe and the Middle East demonstrate the existence of trade over rather wide areas. The obsidian trade of the Near East predates the formation of urban settlements by several thousand years, and the total process of exchange which accompanied it is clearly linked to economic growth in the area (Wright 1969; Lamberg-Karlovsky 1975). Early "tribal" systems

may have differed from later systems insofar as the exchange was not absolutely necessary to the maintenance of local productive forces, but socially necessary to the maintenance of internal group relations in the local population – i.e. as when prestige goods necessary for local transactions (brideprice and other services) and defining social position were imported objects. Ethnographic examples of such systems can be found throughout Africa, Melanesia, and Indonesia (Ekholm 1972, 1977a; Friedman 1975; Friedberg 1977).

2 With the rise of civilization we have a new situation in which we may speak of a technologically integrated system. The emergence of a developed center of "high culture" depends on the accumulation of resources from a wide area so that the very economic base of the locally developed society is likely to be the result of its center position within a larger system. Civilization is here coterminous with the existence of a center/periphery relation (Ekholm 1976, 1977b).

Generally speaking, the center is the center of most advanced industrial production based on raw materials and semifinished products imported from the periphery, which in exchange obtains some of the manufactures of the center.[1] The very maintenance of the center depends on its ability to dominate a supralocal resource base. Mesopotamia is the clearest example of the extent to which a center's industrial base can be imported. To insist, as is usually done, that the evolution of high cultures is based on the agricultural surplus of intensive irrigation is systematically to avoid the problem that surplus grain cannot be locally transformed into bronze, cloth, palaces (of imported stone), fine jewelry, and weapons – hallmarks of the great civilization. Even stone and wood were imports in the case of Mesopotamia.

Center/periphery relations are not necessarily defined in terms of their import–export pattern. Thus, it is unnecessary that a center be the sole locus of industrial manufacturing in the system, or that the periphery be the sole supplier of raw materials. A relation based on a technical division of labor does not correspond to either the mechanisms of development or the functioning of global systems. Center/periphery relations refer, rather, to different structural positions with respect to total accumulation. The possession of extremely "valuable" commodities such as silver (Athens) makes it possible to accumulate a disproportionate part of the production of the larger system. If Athens only imported and exported goods, it would never have become a great center. Its accumulation of wealth was, in the first instance, a result of large-scale military tribute-taking and plunder, mercantile profit, and the export of silver. This primary accumulation laid the foundation for a formidable expansion of industrial production. Generally speaking, industrial production is not the means by which centers accumulate initially, and accumulation of wealth from the larger system proceeds well in advance of home production. This initial and often continual "primitive accumulation" has always taken the form of tribute, booty, and enormous mercantile profits.

It is usually argued that capitalism can be reduced to the production of industrial capital to the exclusion of all other accumulative activities. Imperialism in such a system is a logically secondary phenomenon related to the needs of *self-expanding* industrial capital. This construct is opposed to the ancient economy where the struggle for prestige and political power predominated, thus where industrial growth, imperialism, and profit were marginal phenomena. It is assumed that capitalism is a self-igniting and self-accumulative process while the ancient economy was a more "embedded" system in which production for specific social uses determined the degree and form of growth. This distinction builds upon the subjectivity of the industrial capitalist in one case and on that of the classical Greek and Roman aristocrat in the other. In neither case is the structure of the total reproductive cycle taken into account in the definition. In the modern capitalist mode of production, for example, the accumulation of money capital is not a dependent function of production but rather operates parallel and in contradiction to production. The purpose of production here is the accumulation of money and it is certainly not the only means although it establishes the limit conditions of that accumulation. Large portions of the total liquid wealth of capitalist society are invested in "nonproductive" and even noncommercial activities. Similarly, while it is clearly the case that the landed aristocracy and, later, the imperial bureaucracy may have been the dominant class faction in ancient society, their power depended upon the enormous wealth and profit gained in commercial agriculture, and their direct involvement in urban and international commerce, as well as their access to imperialist tribute. This situation is not different in kind from the medieval Arab economy or early modern Europe. It is often overlooked that mercantile Europe operated very much like Rome in its expansion, that it accumulated and "squandered" great amounts of wealth, not primarily by producing, but by pillaging large parts of the globe, and that capitalist production only began *within* this larger imperialistic process upon which it was, materially speaking, entirely dependent. That a capitalist mode of production became dominant in Europe is, of course, related to specific local structures. The emergence of wage labor in one place and slavery in another is dependent on a difference in initial conditions, but the resultant social forms may be worlds apart.

Our argument is that the general properties of imperialist mercantilist expansion are common to ancient and modern worlds irrespective of specific local forms of accumulation. The growth of industry and commercial agriculture by whatever form of exploitation occurs within an already constituted imperialist structure and is not a local and closed process.

3 Center/periphery systems are, by definition, imperialistic insofar as the center of a system accumulates wealth based on the production of a wider area. While the existence of larger exchange systems is linked to and reinforced by the emergence of local hierarchy and class domination, the center/periphery relation further integrates such local class structures into a differentiated pattern where the central class becomes increasingly elaborated into factions: landed aristocrats, bureaucrats, merchants, etc. – exploiting by direct taxation, slavery, and even contract and wage labor, while the peripheral class structure is more or less restricted to a chiefly or feudal elite (that may become more elaborate in the development process) which mediates the export of raw materials and controls all imports.

The kinds of structure that develop internally depend, as we shall suggest later, upon the regional structure of the larger system. The center need not be a single political unit which would, in fact, require an extraordinary degree of direct control over the accumulation process. More often it tends to consist of a number of competing/exchanging political units, one of which may exercise hegemony within the center. Galtung (1971) represents a generalized imperialist structure (see Figure 2.1).

4 Center/periphery structures are drastically unstable because of the vulnerability of centers in the external (supply/market) realm which is so difficult to control. The existence of a production/resource area wider than that of the political unit which must be maintained by it is the fundamental weakness of such systems. Evolution is, as a result, a necessarily discontinuous process in space. Centers collapse and are replaced by other areas of high civilization. The development of total systems is not equivalent to the development of individual societies. On the contrary, the evolution tends to imply the shift of centers of accumulation over time. The "rise and fall" phenomenon is thus a manifestation of a more continuous process as a higher level of organization.

5 Imperialism is the characteristic of a center/periphery process that tends to reproduce simultaneous development and underdevelopment within a single system. "Empire" is a political mechanism, the control over a larger multisociety region by a single state. Empire, in functional terms, is a political machine for the maintenance and/or direct organization of imperialistic economic processes. In other words, it consists in the direct control over an *already existing* larger economic network.

THE EVOLUTION OF INTERLOCAL STRUCTURES

1 The Early Dynastic period in Mesopotamia represents the earliest emergence of a center/periphery structure which is at all well documented.

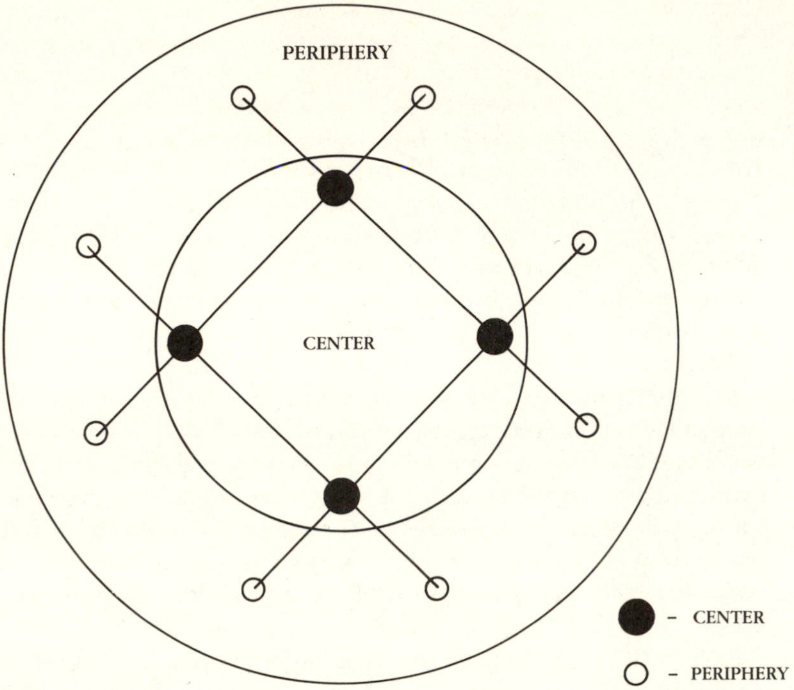

Figure 2.1

The import of wood, copper, stone, and later tin as well as increasing quantities of precious metals and stones (silver, gold, lapis lazuli) is an indication of the degree to which Mesopotamian civilization must be defined in terms of a larger system.

2 The Early Dynastic period is also the period of the formation of large walled cities in the center,[2] emerging from a period in which population is more evenly distributed in smaller settlements of varying sizes probably organized in larger regional political hierarchies (Wright 1972). The urban implosion leads to the formation of many compact, warring city states.[3] If we compare Mesopotamian development generally with that, for example, at Susiana in the fourth millennium BC there is a striking contrast between the settlement hierarchy in Susiana, where a single center apparently controlled the external trade for a whole local region, and the final situation in the plain where a number of neighboring centers all competed autonomously in the same larger network.[4]

3 The decentralized or city-state organization of a center results from the impossibility of monopolizing the relations between the center as a whole and the rest of the system, so that instead of a local control hierarchy there is competition among equals. Mesopotamia emerges as

a dense trade network linked to Anatolia and the Mediterranean in the West and to Iran and India in the East.[5] There are no local resources within Mesopotamia that can be monopolized and no single trade route out of the area. From the start, the main export is food, then textiles and manufactures produced from imported raw materials; this is possible for all cities.[6]

4 Egypt, as opposed to Mesopotamia, is an isolated area with respect to external trade networks. Trade can move up and down the Nile, and there are several points where raw materials, especially gold, might conceivably be controlled, although, as these areas are parallel to the Nile, local access is not clearly determined. There are, however, two areas that are crucial in terms of the larger system. In the north control over the delta area means control over the only real access to the Mesopotamian–Mediterranean trade area. In the south, control over the raw material and labor resources of Nubia is crucial as a means of economic power – as a supply zone for the larger area. What is crucial here is the absence of a multitude of points of access either to important raw materials, or especially to external trade.[7] Egypt is not, like Mesopotamia, located in the midst of a vast trade network. Rather it opens out at only a very few points, thus permitting the maintenance of a monopoly over the area's relation to the larger economy. As a result, internal competition and decentralization do not occur – no city states emerge. Theocratic and bureaucratic structures are increasingly elaborated. The redistributive structure based on various forms of direct taxation is extended. No private economic sector develops outside the state sphere and the upper class continues to be identified with the state itself.[8]

5 The different evolutions of Egypt and Mesopotamia, perhaps from similar original structures, are of great significance. The former is based on central monopoly and territorial annexation; the second on political fragmentation, competition, warfare, and empire. The second is apparently the more dynamic: the early and explosive developments of bronze, advanced weaponry, commercial techniques, abstract-formal writing all emerge in Mesopotamia long before they are introduced in Egypt.

6 Without here describing the precise nature and social categories of functioning of the Early Dynastic economic system we can link together some fundamental external characteristics.

The economy is clearly expansionist in nature. The form of expansion implies continuous increase in the work force by the mechanisms of slavery (captive or in other ways imported). Agricultural production is intensified, both to supply export needs and to support an increasing division of labor linked to the elaboration of textile, metal, and stone production, much of which is clearly for export. Such economic growth and differentiation lead to territorial expansion and a resultant conflict between political units of similar type.[9] Warfare leads to the intensification of weapon production and to its technological development, instrumental, perhaps, in the very evolution of bronze technology (bronze is harder and clearly superior to copper as material for weapons).[10] The growth of weapon production implies a further division of labor entailing a double demand to increase subsistence goods to support specialized labor power, and to increase exports in order to obtain copper and tin. This, in turn, leads to a further effort to increase the area of land in agriculture, to territorial expansion, and interstate conflict. As a result, the very survival of the city state in this system becomes totally dependent upon the secure control over the external resource base necessary for the maintenance of the production apparatus, especially the growing military sector, which is the foundation for the defense of all other economic and political activities.[11]

7 Externally, i.e. without considering the social form of the system, it can be said that the center as a whole comes increasingly to be the major exporter of manufactured goods, final consumption goods, and arms in exchange for the necessary materials for the very production of those goods. The principal effect of this development is the increased need for *control over the external conditions of local reproduction*.

The expansion of the center as a whole is based on widening rather than deepening of the production/consumption area. As the system is directed by an upper class that remains the principal consumer, there is no room for "market" expansion except in the realm of long-distance trade. This is partially offset by the expansion of wage sectors in the military and the bureaucracy and by the increase in monetary circulation in urban areas. The principal tendency is expressed in the fact that the expansion of the Early Dynastic system eventually incorporates the entire region from the Indus to the Mediterranean in a regular trade network.

CAPITAL AND EXPLOITATION: THE INTERNAL STRUCTURE

As it is difficult, on the basis of our familiarity with existing data, to analyze the specific categories of the operation of the economies of Mesopotamia, we can only attempt to offer some tentative characterizations of the way they may have developed.

1 To contrast Egypt and Mesopotamia again, we venture to say that from the start they are both temple-dominated, conical clan-type structures. This implies that the upper class is a theocratically defined, hierarchically organized group of aristocratic lineages that dominate a population distributed into a scalogram of larger and smaller centers.

a) The upper class is identical with the state.

b) The accumulation of wealth is centralized at the top of the hierarchy.[12]
c) The top of the hierarchy is thus in a position of control over external trade, export production, and the local distribution of imports (Johnson 1973).
d) The forms of exploitation in this predynastic structure consist of direct taxation of "commoners" and the use of varying forms of slavery – internal debt-slaves and imported – in expanding sectors of production, i.e. in temple agriculture and some craft sectors.

2 The stragegy in the early system was one based on a temple economy fulfilling ritual functions, where, within the larger region, control depended upon the accumulations of "means of circulation," prestige goods – obsidian, metals, etc. – necessary for the social transactions of all local kinship or corporate units. The centralized control over the flow of such goods implies control over aristocrats inhabiting the hinterland and secondary centers, as well as over real wealth and labor power.[13] The control over such circulation by a central group depends upon a monopoly over external relations. Wealth measured in prestige goods is equivalent to control over labor whose surplus product reproduces the ability of the ruler to maintain his nodal position between local production and the production of other areas.

3 This kind of structure breaks down throughout the Early Dynastic period, but not in Egypt where continued control over interregional trade enables the conical structure to become increasingly elaborate. The same kind of phenomenon that occurs within the region occurs within the evolving city state. With the whole aristocracy now in the same enclosed area and with increasing economic competition, possibilities for a more decentralized accumulation of wealth emerge within the ruling class. The increasing acquisition of formerly monopolized means of circulation by other members of the upper class is part of a crucial differentiation in the economic system. While previously, religious, political, and economic power were one, they now begin to be differentiated.

a) A class of wealthy aristocrats (great families) develops alongside the temple. Their access to liquid wealth enables them to buy land and set up estates, apparently as early as 2700 BC (Diakanoff 1959: 9).
b) A secular palace sector emerges out of the temple, specializing in political-administrative, trade, and warfare functions. This corresponds to a sector of the upper class with access to a share of the total wealth and, in this case, direct control over industrial production, as with the temple.
c) A merchant class increasingly monopolizes the interregional circulation process and is able to accumulate substantial portions of the total wealth through mercantile profit.

d) The differentiation of wealth accumulation in the upper class is reflected in the division of production into private and public sectors. The forms of exploitation, about which there is much debate, include labor which is directly dependent on the state ("helots" in Diakanoff 1977), private and state slaves, and a "free" population exploited by taxation. There is also evidence, perhaps in the free labor sector, of contract or wage labor connected with skilled or more specialized tasks. The unfree classes are only different from one another with respect to the degree to which their members exist as property.[14]

4 The significant internal phenomenon here is the development of a process of wealth accumulation as a private or, at least, as an extrastate process. While it is, in fact, the members of the state class who first engage in such accumulation, the end product of internal differentiation is the development of several potentially opposed upper-class factions.[15]

5 We use the word "capital" to refer to the form of abstract wealth represented in the concrete form of metal or even money that can be accumulated in itself and converted into other forms of wealth; land, labor, and products. It is this abstract form that increasingly becomes the economic organizational basis of control in the system, competing with the older direct forms of state control, taxation, and slavery. "Capital" is not tied to a specific form of exploitation. It is, rather, the forerunner of, or perhaps identical to, merchant capital in its functioning. What is important here is that it is an independent form of economic wealth and power and not merely a means of circulation or a measuring device.

6 Private capital is probably not a major driving force in itself. It is not directly invested in production nor linked in a necessary cycle of production and realization. The state is in fact the major investor as well as the major producer and consumer, and, while the accumulation of abstract metallic wealth by the state is necessary to pay for the maintenance of the system, the accumulation includes direct taxation in kind as well as the proceeds of import–export activity. We may, however, speak of a kind of state capital in this system to the extent that the accumulation by the state of abstract wealth becomes increasingly necessary to maintain import flows and the internal system of payments. This fund of wealth reveals its importance when there is a decline in other forms of production for export (e.g. in the Roman empire).[16]

7 In decentralized center/periphery systems where competition and warfare are necessary components of the functioning of the system, arms production tends to become the leading sector in the economy. The state–palace sector in such a phase of development tends to dominate the rest of the local economy, and it may be in severe conflict with the temple and private sectors.

8 A significant dialectical mechanism in this economy consists in the complementarity/contradiction among the economic goals of the different sectors.

a) Private accumulation removes necessary wealth from the state sector, striving to reproduce this privilege. But the conditions of private accumulation depend on the successful functioning of the state sector which is the source of manufactures and military power.
b) The merchant class is necessary to the realization of state-produced goods in the larger system, but its increased accumulation removes wealth from the state sector which, in turn, is necessary for the political and economic maintenance of mercantile activity.

9 With the development of the city-state economy, various forms of exploitation accrue to the former tax/state–slavery combination: private slavery on private estates, forms of contract and wage labour in craft and military sectors, and some form of corporate guild structure in the mercantile sector are common developments.

INTERNAL STRUCTURES AND THE LARGER SYSTEM

1 Dense trade networks correspond to competitive centers. Sparse networks correspond to hierarchical territorial structures. In Mesopotamia, the Aegean, and eastern Mediterranean, territorial hierarchies break down due to the impossibility of monopolizing trade in the larger region. The increasing density of trade may also have led to the transition from Western Zhou hegemony to the Warring States period in China.[17] Similar kinds of phenomena have been observed at various levels of economic organization. Thus, recent analyses of the evolution of Melanesian social systems in terms of trade structures would seem to indicate a fragmentation of larger political structures with the increasing density of trade (Allen 1977; Ambrose, n.d.).

2 Compact city states correlate with the loss of monopoly over the local economy by a state class and the development of a structure of class factions. In Phoenicia and Greece, there is an apparent transition from a palace-based (or royally controlled) economy to an oligarchic class structure. While there are conflicts between state and private sectors in Athens, the private sector is clearly in command in the classical period (this is also true for Phoenicia).[18] In Mesopotamia, the state sector and its bureaucratic membership remain a powerful force, maintaining a monopoly over industrial if not agricultural production.

3 There is a clear differentiation between agricultural-based production states and trade states within the larger system. The latter are, by definition, later developments that necessarily have to import subsistence

goods to support their specialized labor. Mesopotamia (southern) represents an agricultural-based production center surrounded by trade states such as Assur, in the north, and Phoenicia, in the west. Trade states specialize in specific forms of industrial production, the carrying trade, and middleman activity between other production areas. They must necessarily control the larger market network to which they belong. Dense local network conditions generate competitive expansion in the form of colonization. Empires in such systems as Athens, are, again, political-military devices for maintaining control over the larger network. It would appear, however, that the absence of a previous state-bureaucratic sector in such systems implies the continued dominance of the private, oligarchic, class and the continued furthering of their interests. The establishment of empire can take on a more or less bureaucratic form. In southern Mesopotamia the empire is the work of the state bureaucracy, and their interests, in terms of their own level of consumption and military needs, take precedence over the interests of private accumulators. The result is a great bureaucratic machine and a strictly controlled economy, centralized at the expense of private interests.

DYNAMICS IN EMPIRES

1 Empires that develop in the core/periphery systems that we have described are political mechanisms that feed on already established forms of wealth production and accumulation. Where they do not overtax and where they, simultaneously, maintain communication networks, they tend to increase the possibilities of production and trade in the system, i.e. the possibilities for all existing forms of wealth accumulation.

2 Empires maintain and reinforce core/periphery relations politically, by the extraction of tribute from conquered areas and peripheries. But insofar as empires do not replace other economic mechanisms of production and circulation, but only exploit them, they may create the conditions for their own demise.

3 This occurs where the revenue absorbed from the existing accumulation cycles increases more slowly than total accumulation itself. In such a case an economic decentralization sets in, resulting in a general weakening of the center relative to other areas. The classic example that is well documented is the decentralization that occurs in the Roman empire, resulting in the virtual bankruptcy of the center itself, which becomes a net importer, and where its costs of imperial maintenance far outstrip its intake of tribute. In the case of Rome, where the class of private capitalists and landowners is dominant, the decentralization process is probably much more rapid and uncontrolled than in Mesopotamia, where the state sector can maintain stricter surveillance of the private sector and

where a large portion of production is state monopoly. It is the Roman upper class itself, after all, that is largely responsible for the decentralization of the economy.[19]

4 Grossly stated, the balance of empire is determined by:

(booty + tribute [tax] + export revenue) - (cost of empire + cost of imports)

The maintenance of the center position in an empire depends on the mechanisms that determine the net economic flows in the larger system. When the empire does not organize those flows directly, there will be a tendency in the "capitalist" structure, referred to above, for the center eventually to decline.

CONCLUSION

Our aim has been to present the sketch of an argument and not a definitive analysis of any kind. Our point has been to stress the fundamental continuity between ancient and modern world-systems. We have repeatedly stressed the larger-system aspect in opposition to models that take society as the sufficient unit of analysis, thereby, as we see it, implicitly removing the question of dynamics, evolution, and devolution. In such a short space we have not attempted to take up more specific aspects of the available data, choosing instead to state a number of points that we feel are important areas of further discussion.

The general properties that we have discussed apply, at a sufficiently high level of abstraction, to all systems of "civilization." We are, perhaps, talking about the same system. The forms of accumulation have not changed so significantly. The forms of exploitation and oppression have all been around from the earliest civilizations although, of course, they have existed in different proportions and in varying combinations. Even in our own recent past, a major form of the accumulation of capital was by means of slavery, and it might be argued that today's eastern-bloc economies are but another (ancient) form of exploitation linked to the same process of accumulation (Frank 1977). There are, to be sure, a great many differences, but the similarities are, perhaps, a more serious and practical problem.

NOTES

1 The center need not, of course, be the originator of new technology. It need only concentrate that technology within its boundaries. While a good deal of military technology has been invented by peripheral nomadic groups, it is only in the centers that it has been mass-produced on a large scale.

2 Before the Jemdet Nasr period there are virtually no walled settlements. By the Early Dynastic (ED) period all cities are walled (Adams 1971: 581).

3 Young (1972: 832), for example, states that the "concentration of population into the larger urban centers appears to take place at the expense of the countryside."

4 Extensive discussions of the predynastic situation in southern Mesopotamia can be found in Johnson (1973, 1976) and Johnson and Wright (1975), where a case is made for the existence of hierarchical control over trade. We feel that the evidence they present can be interpreted in this way in spite of the perhaps unwarranted use of central-place theory.

5 The import of raw material is already evident in the Ubaid (Stigler 1974: 114).

6 Crawford (1973) points out that there is little clear evidence of large-scale production for export in the ED period in spite of the massive import of raw materials. In her argument for the existence of invisible exports from Mesopotamia which do not leave clear material traces, she stresses the importance of grain and dried fish in the initial periods. Spindle whorls are found at least as early as the Ubaid period (Kramer 1970), but it is difficult to determine exactly when textiles become an exported item. Later in the ED period, at Lagash there is mention of 200 slave women engaged in the various moments of textile production (Deimel, cited in Adams 1971: 5114). Adams (1971: 583) also mentions the export of tools and weapons.

7 It is, in fact, only in the delta area, where there are several possible outlets to the Mediterranean, that there was any serious competition between centers.

8 A long line of scholarship has stressed this specific property of Egyptian civilization. Weber (1976), for example, emphasizes the long-term maintenance and development of a bureaucratic state-class as opposed to the more mercantile and decentralized structure of Mesopotamia. Notable in Egypt is the lack of an urban civilization and its expression in walled towns, the very restricted use of a monetary medium up until a relatively late date (Janssen 1975a), the state monopoly over external trade, also until very late, and the lack of an independent class of "great families" or a merchant class. For further discussion see Janssen (1975a, 1975b), Morenz (1969), Kemp (1972), O'Connor (1972), Smith (1972) and Uphill (1972).

9 It might be hypothesized that territorial expansion was the direct outcome of competitive export of food (possibly the first major export) before ED in exchange for raw materials, and that this export agriculture was a key factor in the territorial conflicts that led to the formation of walled city states.

10 Metal was relatively rare in ED I, but there is a clear development of metallurgy in ED II and "lost wax process reached a climax in ED III when armourers made heavy and efficient weapons of war, axes, spears, and adzes" (Mallowan 1971: 239 f.).

11 The importance of warfare is stressed in Childe (1952), who refers to the first example of "organized homicide" (30) in c. 3000 BC.

12 In the Jemdet Nasr period and earlier in Susa, there are large storerooms attached to the central temple (Frankfort 1971: 1; 2: 84). "It has been said that the larger Ubaidian settlements were probably market towns as well as religious centers, both for the local satellite communities and for wider trade" (Stigler 1974: 114). See also Adams and Nissen (1972).

13 Long before bronze technology, copper makes its appearance in the form of copper beads in Iran at Ali-Kosh from 6750–6000 (Hole *et al.* 1971: 278) and in Egypt c. 4000 (Stigler 1974: 135).

14 Diakanoff claims, *contra* Gelb, that state sector "slaves" or helots are the equivalent of patriarchal slaves at the state level and not of serfs. They are, in any case, quite unlike the classical slaves of Greece and Rome. It is not clear

that his attempt at differentiating ancient Mesopotamia from the Mediterranean classical period is theoretically valid, especially in light of the massive expansion of the slave sector following 2000 BC.

15 The existence of a sphere of private capital accumulation is well documented for areas that are traditionally thought to be characterized by theocratic centralized economies. Thus, Larsen (1967, 1976) has shown that Assur, for example, in the Old Assyrian period, is very much a private commercial economy. His analysis of caravan-procedure texts, of costs and methods of trade, demonstrates the existence of a considerable profit-oriented private sector. Similar evidence exists for Ur (Oppenheim 1954) and for Lagash (Lambert 1953). Adams (1974) has discussed how the *dam.gar*, merchant, who begins as a state official, becomes an increasingly private operator (1974: 248). Farber's material (1978) demonstrates the very high degree of commercialization of the Babylonian economy (the existence of parallel movements of prices of different goods and services and wages, a general price level, and economic cycles).

16 Hopkins' (1978) work represents a sophisticated attempt at developing a model of the dynamic of the Roman economy that shows the fundamental importance of the imperialist drive of the state in the fueling of the other forms of accumulation in the system. The classical discussion of the relation between the decentralization of capital accumulation in the Roman empire as linked to the crisis of the state can be found in Rostovtzeff (1957).

17 A general discussion of the breakdown of trade monopolies and the development of city and territorial states can be found in Friedman and Rowlands (1977). Hsu (1965) discusses the internal transformations in China in the Zhou period, especially the emergence of private accumulation and the breakdown of the earlier aristocratic bureaucracy.

18 There is, however, a large-scale regional oscillation between private and state-controlled economies in the long run. Thus, the development of the Hellenistic states marks the emergence of state control after a period of more "democratic" oligarchic rule in the Mediterranean.

19 A pattern in the Roman imperialist system which may be common to all such systems is one that we can clearly see in modern imperialism. The first period would consist in military or military backed expansion where large areas are taxed at exorbitant rates. Such areas, e.g. Greece in the Roman period, being short of means of payment, borrow from Roman capitalists, a phenomenon reminiscent of the nineteenth and early twentieth centuries. The result is a double flow of tribute and debt service payments back to the center and a deindustrialization of the periphery. The enormous accumulation of capital in the center leads to a great deal of unproductive as well as productive investment. But the generally high rate of accumulation compared to the increase in production leads to increasing costs at home, increasing taxation, and conditions generally unfavorable for home producers on the world market. At this point the pattern shifts from a center/periphery structure toward a decentralization of production as well as accumulation. Rome's relative monopoly over certain mass-production items for the empire is lost in the imperial period, and its ability to maintain its increasingly expensive social complex at Rome becomes a serious problem leading to a more or less continual crisis of the state. It has been observed by some (Ekholm 1977b; Friedman 1978; Froebel *et al.* 1977) that a similar deindustrialization of capital accumulation is occurring today and that it, too, is directly linked to the present general economic crisis and to the crisis of the state in the West.

POSTSCRIPT

This article was published for the first time in 1979 in part as the result of work carried out in the framework of an interdisciplinary seminar on exchange systems in a historical perspective. It was also a product of the application of a global systemic anthropology that was emerging in our cooperative work in that period.

Just as there was heated debate concerning our general approach, there was quite some debate about this particular presentation. Moses Finley was one of those with whom we, quite understandably, had several heated discussions in the late 1970s. All this was a reflex of the dominant society-centered focus of the social sciences at the time.

Since that time we have had little chance to return to the issues of ancient civilizations although many of our colleagues have continued to develop the global approach in ancient history and prehistory (Spriggs 1988; Rowlands *et al.* 1987; Thomas 1989). Since the publication of that article other research has applied the global approach to the prehistory of Oceania (Friedman 1981, 1982, 1985) and to the relation between global processes and the emergence in the nineteenth century of social and cultural forms in central Africa that are today regarded as traditional (Ekholm 1991). Given the initial skeptical reception of the 1979 article as well as a number of similar endeavors (Ekholm 1975; Ekholm and Friedman 1980), it is indeed gratifying to discover that it has now been incorporated into a growing field within anthropology and "archaeology and related subjects." After quite a few years of global anthropology in the field (Ekholm 1991; Friedman 1992a, b) we have been prompted to begin looking again into the data of ancient societies and of prehistory in general. At present we can do no more than confine ourselves to several brief remarks concerning the status of the article today. A more systematic summary of our work is forthcoming in *Review* (Friedman 1992c).

The general argument of this article consisted in the assertion that the dualist division of world history that was so prevalent in anthropologically inspired economic history following Polanyi and disciples, in Marxist economic history, and even in the then emergent world-systems theory of Wallerstein (also partially informed by Polanyi), one that envisioned world history as divided into pre- and post-European Renaissance eras, was an ethnocentric misunderstanding. Frank and Gills have recently developed a similar theme, perhaps more extreme, that the past 5,000 years of world history can be understood as the continuity of the same system. In another article published at about the same time (1980) we emphasized the degree to which global systems are multistructural, i.e. that they contain numerous articulations among local and global processes and that system refers to the systemic properties of globally open processes rather than to an operationally definable empirical entity. This has been further elaborated in a series of articles dealing with the relation between global processes and cultural processes (Friedman 1988, 1989, 1990, 1991). In another article from the early phase of our work it was suggested (Friedman 1979) that the so-called transition from feudalism to capitalism was essentially a shift of capital accumulation from East to West in a declining Middle-East-dominated world system in the Middle Ages. This argument was taken from the pioneering work of Maurice Lombard, and since then Abu-Lughod has brilliantly made this kind of argument definitive, thus effectively forcing other researchers to rethink if not eliminate previous discussions of the internal transition in Europe.

While clearly sympathetic to the gist of the argument advanced by Frank, we think it should be reframed in more hypothetically interesting terms lest the notion of system become so diluted as to be nearly useless as a theoretical tool. Frank has claimed that we have sometimes shied away from the assumption of a single world-historical system. In the article reprinted here we do not make it a central issue since the empirical foundations are quite lacking. We suggest it as an avenue of research and concentrate instead on the issue of continuity. We have attempted to understand the degree to which such continuity exists. This is a more complex problem than the enduring appearance of empires, world markets, the accumulation of capital, and cycles of hegemony. It is related to the nature of the local structures as well, and the degree to which they are products of the same larger system. It is necessary to understand how different kinds of local organization arise, why caste here and ethnic pluralism there, why class in one situation and region and ranked estates in another. Now we have gone so far as to suggest that different kinds of social-identity formation are related to differences in the degree of capitalization of social relations, differences in the degree of resultant social individualization; that western ethnicity is, as a result, a product of what might be called the culture of "modernity" understood as a general phenomenon, as opposed to the kinds of cultural identity that we find today in India and south-east Asia (Friedman 1991). That so-called modern ethnicity may have appeared in earlier periods, i.e. the Hellenistic, to a greater or lesser extent might have significant implications for the continuity hypothesis. If Protestant ethics are more general than Christianity, as they would appear to be, this is also an important argument for continuity. There is more to the configuration of global systems than simply the general economics of wealth accumulation. One might, for example, take up the issue of the emergence of feudal structures as opposed to what we have described elsewhere as kin-based prestige-good systems on the peripheries of commercial civilizations. One might ask whether different proportions of different dominant forms of accumulation of wealth, mercantile (abstract wealth) vs. control over products and/or labor, affect the dynamic properties of the overall "system." We are not saying all this in order to play a Tilley-like role of devil's advocate, but because these are absolutely fundamental issues for the understanding of how global systems or the system function(s) and change(s).

The question of system vs. systems is not as simple as Frank defines it, although we are sympathetic to his point, since we have ourselves argued that the similarities are "a more serious and practical problem" (Ekholm and Friedman 1980) in political terms. It is necessary to come to grips with the questions of transformation even while assuming a continuity. Now we have suggested on several occasions that the similarities between empirically delimited systems are great enough to warrant a continuist hypothesis. But this does not eliminate the need to understand the conditions for the emergence of modern industrial capitalism and with those aspects of modernity that diverge from earlier social orders. If the family resemblances we discover enable us to talk of variations within the same system instead of the emergence of new systems this remains a complex empirical and theoretical problem of boundaries (not geographical). That China need not have been dynamically connected to the India–Mesopotamia–Mediterranean nexus in the third millennium BC for us to say that their regional histories can be seen as dependent on one another ought not to dismay us. The New World was not, in all probability, systemically connected to the Old in any strong sense until quite late. But it clearly displays global systemic processes of a similar order. In our argument the continuity of global systems concerns the continuity of global processes and not of a physically delimited portion of the globe. Contractions in such systems have not infrequently created "isolates," "untouched primitives," and Shangri-las. These are, of course, global products, but they are not globally connected in the sense demanded by Frank's model. Conditions and structures of reproduction must be examined in order to ascertain the way in which empirical global systems are constituted, the way in which regions and populations are linked, the degree to which the local is produced rather than simply connected to the larger whole and the degree to which its historical trajectory is tied to that whole. We are still operating with a working hypothesis and there is no obviously established 5,000-year-old system even if there might be much to suggest the existence of a system variable in extent and connectivity over time.

On the other hand there is also much to suggest that world history is like a Kafkaesque nightmare of repetition compulsions, more a scenario of imprisonment in larger systems than one of self-control led and empowering evolution.

NOTE

This chapter first appeared in 1982 as " 'Capital' imperialism and exploitation in ancient world-systems," in *Review* 4 (1) (summer): 87–109.

REFERENCES

Abu-Lughod, J. (1989) *Before European Hegemony: The World System A.D. 1250–1350*, New York: Oxford University Press.

Adams, Robert (1971) "Developmental stages in ancient Mesopotamia," in *Prehistoric Agriculture*, ed. S. Streuver, New York: Natural History Press, 572–90.

—— (1972) "Patterns of urbanization in early southern Mesopotamia," in *Man, Settlement and Urbanism*, ed. P. Ucko, G. Dimbleby, and R. Tringham, London: Duckworth, 735–50.

—— (1974) "Anthropological perspectives on ancient trade," *Current Anthropology* 15 (3) (September): 229–58.

Adams, Robert and Nissen, H. (1972) *The Uruk Countryside*, Chicago: University of Chicago Press.

Allen, Jim (1977) "Sea traffic trade and expanding horizons," in *Sunda and Sahul*, ed. J. Allen, J. Golson, and R. Jones, London: Academic Press, 187–417.

Ambrose, W.R. (n.d.) "Obsidian and its prehistoric distribution in Melanesia," (manuscript).

Bücher, K. (1893) *Die Enststehung Volk der Volkwirtschaft*, Tübingen: Laupp.

Childe, Gordon (1952) *New Light on the Most Ancient East*, New York: Praeger.

Crawford, H.E.W. (1973) "Mesopotamia's invisible exports in the third millennium BC", *World Archaeology* 5: 232–41.

Diakanoff, I.M. (1959) "The structure of society and state in early Sumer," translated from *Sumer: Society and State in Ancient Mesopotamia*, Moscow: Nauka.

—— (1977) "Slaves, helots and serfs in early antiquity," *Soviet Anthropology* 15 (2–3) (autumn/winter): 50–102.

Duncan-Jones, Richard (1974) *The Economy of the Roman Empire*, Cambridge: Cambridge University Press.

Ekholm, K. (1972) *Power and Prestige: The Rise and Fall of the Kongo Kingdom*, Uppsala: Skrivservice.

—— (1975) "On the limits of civilization: the dynamics of global systems," *Dialectical Anthropology* 5 (2): 155–66.

—— (1976) "Om studiet av det globala systemets dynamic," *Antropologiska Studier* 20: 5–32.

—— (1977a) "External exchange and the transformation of central African social systems," in *The Evolution of Social Systems*, ed. J. Friedman and M. Rowlands, London: Duckworth, 115–36.

—— (1977b) *Om studier av riskgenerering och av hur risker kan avvärjas*, Göteborg: Samrbets Kommittén för långsiktsmotiverad forskning, rapport 11.

—— (1991) *Catastrophe and Creation: The Formation of an African Culture*, London: Harwood.

Ekholm, K. and Friedman, J. (1980) "Towards a global anthropology," in *History and Underdevelopment*, ed. L. Blussé, H. Wesseling, and C.D. Winius, Leiden and Paris: Center for the History of European Expansion.

—— (1985) New introduction to "Towards a global anthropology," *Critique of Anthropology* 5 (1): 97–119.

Farber, Howard (1978) "A price and wage study of northern Babylonia during the

Old Babylonian period," *Journal of the Economic and Social History of the Orient* 21 (1): 1–51.

Finley, Moses (1973) *The Ancient Economy*, Berkeley: University of California Press.

Frank, Andre Gunder (1977) "Long live trans-ideological enterprise! Socialist economics in the capitalist international division of labour," *Review* 1 (1) (summer): 91–140.

Frankfort, Henry (1971) "The last Pre-Dynastic period in Babylonia," in *The Cambridge Ancient History*, 1 (2), London: Cambridge University Press, 71–92.

Friedberg, C. (1977) "The development of traditional agricultural practices in western Timor: from the ritual control of consumer goods to the political control of prestige goods," in *The Evolution of Social Systems*, ed. J. Friedman and M. Rowlands, London: Duckworth, 137–71.

Friedman, Jonathan (1975) "Religion as economy and economy as religion," *Ethnos* 40 (1–4): 4–63.

—— (1978) "Crises in theory and transformations of the world economy," *Review* 2 (2) (Fall): 132–46.

—— (1981) "Notes on structure and history in Oceania," in *Folk* 23: 275–95.

—— (1982) "Catastrophe and continuity in social evolution," in Renfrew *et al.* (eds) *Theory and Explanation in Archaeology*, London.

—— (1985) "Captain Cook, culture and the world system," *Journal of Pacific History* 20.

—— (1988) "Cultural logics of the global system," *Theory, Culture and Society* 5: 447–60.

—— (1989) "Culture, identity and world process," in *Review* 12 (1): 51–69.

—— (1990) "Being in the world: localization and globalization," in *Global Cultures*, ed. M. Featherstone, London: Sage.

—— (1991) "Notes on culture and identity in imperial worlds," in *Religion and Religious Practice in the Seleucid Kingdom*, ed. P. Bilde, Engberg-Pedersen, L. Hannestad, J. Zahle, Aarhus: Aarhus University Press.

—— (1992a) "Narcissism and the roots of postmodernity," in *Modernity and Identity*, ed. Lash and Friedman, Oxford: Blackwell.

—— (1992b) *Paradise Lost Paradise Regained: The Global Anthropology of Hawaiian Identity*, London: Harwood.

—— (1992c) "General historical and culturally specific properties of global systems," in *Review*, 15 (3): 3 5–72.

Friedman, Jonathan and Rowlands, M. (1977) "Notes towards an epigenetic model of the evolution of 'Civilization,'" in *The Evolution of Social Systems*, ed. J. Friedman and J. Rowlands, London: Duckworth, 201–76.

Fröbel, Folker, Heinrichs, Jurgen, and Krey, Otto (1977) *Die neue internationale Arbeitsteilung*, Hamburg: Towahlt Taschenbuch.

Galtung, Johan (1971) "A structural theory of imperialism," *Journal of Peace Research* 8 (2): 81–117.

Gelb, I. J. (1971) "From freedom to slavery", BAW, ph-Hist. K1. Abh. nf 75.

Hole, Frank, Flannery, Kent, and Beely, James (1971) "Prehistory and human ecology of the Del Luran Plain (excerpts)," *Prehistoric Agriculture*, Garden City: Natural History Press, 258–312.

Hopkins, Keith (1978) "Economic growth in towns in classical antiquity," in *Towns in Societies*, ed. P. Abrams and E.A. Wrigley, London: Cambridge University Press, 35–77.

Hsu, Cho-Yun (1965) *Ancient China in Transition*, Stanford: Stanford University Press.

Humphreys, S.C. (1970) "Economy and society in classical Athens," *Annali Scuola Normale Superiore de Pisa*, series II, 39: 11–26.

Janssen, Jac (1975a) *Commodity Prices from the Ramessid Period*, Leiden: Brill.

—— (1975b) "Prolegomena to the study of Egypt's economic history during the New Kingdom," *Studier zur altagyptischen kultur* 3: 127–85.

Johnson, Gregory (1973) *Local Exchange and Early State Development in Southwestern Iran*, Anthropological Papers 51, Ann Arbor: Museum of Anthropology, University of Michigan.

—— (1976) "Locational analysis and the investigation of Uruk social exchange systems," in *Ancient Civilization and Trade*, ed. J. Sabloff and C. Lamberg-Karlovsky, Albuquerque: University of New Mexico Press, 285–340.

Johnson, Gregory and Wright, Henry (1975) "Population, exchange and early state formation," *American Anthropologist* 127 (2 June): 267–89.

Jones, Arnold H.M. (1974) *The Roman Economy*, Oxford: Oxford University Press.

Kemp, Barry (1972) "Temple and town in ancient Egypt," in *Man, Settlement and Urbanism*, ed. P. Ucko, G. Dimbleby, and R. Tringham, London: Duckworth, 657–80.

Kramer, S.N. (1970) *The Sumerians*, Chicago: University of Chicago Press.

Lamberg-Karlovsky, C. (1972) "Trade mechanisms in Indus-Mesopotamian Interrelations," *Journal of the American Oriental Society* 92: 222–9.

—— (1975) "Third millennium modes of exchange and modes of production," in *Ancient Civilization and Trade*, ed. J. Sabloff and C. Lamberg-Karlovsky, Albuquerque: University of New Mexico Press.

Lambert, M. (1953) "Textes commerciaux de Lagache (epoque pre-Sargonique)," *Revue d'Assyriologie* 47: 105–21.

Larsen, Mogens-Trolle (1967) "Old Assyrian caravan procedures," Nederlands Historisch-Arekaeologish Institut te Instanbul, 22.

—— (1976) *The Old Assyrian City State and its Colonies*, Copenhagen: Akademisk Forlag.

Mallowan, M. (1971) "The Early Dynastic period in Mesopotamia," in *The Cambridge Ancient History*, 1 (2), London: Cambridge University Press, 238–314.

Meyer, Edward (1910) *Kleine Schriften*, Niemeyer: Halle.

Morenz, Siegfried (1969) *Prestige Wirtschaft im Alten Agypten*, München: Verlag der Bayerischen Akademie der Wissenschaften.

O'Connor, David (1972) "The geography of settlement in ancient Egypt," in *Man, Settlement and Urbanism*, ed. P. Ucko, G. Dimbleby, and R. Tringham, London: Duckworth, 8–20.

Oppenheim, A.L. (1954) "The seafaring merchants of Ur," *Journal of the American Oriental Society* 64: 6–17.

Polanyi, Karl (1947) "Our obsolete market mentality," in *Commentary* 13 (2) (February): 109–17.

Rostovtzeff, Mikhail (1957) *The Social and Economic History of the Roman Empire*, Oxford: Clarendon Press.

Rowlands, M.J., Larsen, M.T., and Kristiansen, K. (eds) (1987) *Center and Periphery in the Ancient World*, Cambridge: Cambridge University Press.

Smith, H.S. (1972) "Society and settlement in ancient Egypt," in *Man, Settlement and Urbanism*, ed. P. Ucko, G. Dimbleby, and R. Tringham, London: Duckworth.

Starr, Chester (1977) *The Economic and Social Growth of Early Greece*, Oxford: Oxford University Press.

Spriggs, M. (1988) "The Hawaiian transformation of ancestral Polynesian society," in *State and Society: The Emergence and Development of Social Hierarchy and Political Centralization*, ed. J. Gledhill, B. Bender, and M.T. Larsen, London: Unwin Hyman 57–73.

Stigler, Robert (ed.) (1974) "The concept of the Egyptian palace as a 'Ruling Machine,' " in *Man, Settlement and Urbanism*, ed. P. Ucko, G. Dimbleby, and R. Tringham, London: Duckworth, 721–34.

Thomas, N. (1989) *Out of Time: History and Evolution in Anthropological Discourse*, Cambridge: Cambridge University Press.

Uphill, E. (1972) "The concept of the Egyptian palace as a ruling machine," in *Man, Settlement and Urbanism*, ed. P. Ucko, G. Dimbleby and R. Tringham, London: Duckworth, 721–34.

Weber, Max (1976) *The Agrarian Sociology of Ancient Civilizations*, London: New Left Books.

Wright, Gary (1969) *Obsidian Analysis in Pre-Historic Near Eastern Trade: 7500–3500*, Anthropological Papers 37, Ann Arbor: Museum of Anthropology, University of Michigan.

Wright, Henry (1972) "A consideration of interregional exchange in Greater Mesopotamia, 4000–3000 BC," in *Social Exchange and Interaction*, ed. E.N. Wilmsen, Anthropological Papers 46, Ann Arbor: Museum of Anthropology, University of Michigan.

Young, T.C. (1972) "Population densities and early Mesopotamian urbanism," in *Man, Settlement and Urbanism*, ed. P. Ucko, G. Dimbleby, and R. Tringham, London: Duckworth, 827–42.

3

THE CUMULATION OF ACCUMULATION

Barry K. Gills and Andre Gunder Frank

WORLD SYSTEM ORIGINS

The historical origins

The designation in time of the origin of the world system depends very much on what concept of system is employed. We may illustrate this problem by analogy with the origins of a major river system. For instance, look at the Missouri–Mississippi river system. In one sense, each major branch has its own origin. Yet the Mississippi river can be said to have a later derivative origin where the two major branches join together, near St Louis, Missouri. By convention, the river is called "the Mississippi" and it is said to originate in Minnesota. Yet the larger and longer branch is called "the Missouri," which originates in the Rocky Mountains in Montana. Of course, all these also have other larger and smaller inflows, each with their own point(s) of origin. The problem in how to set a fixed point of origin when in fact no such single point of origin exists for the river system as a whole. In the case of the world system it would be possible to place its origins far up stream in the Neolithic period. However, it may be more appropriate to discuss the origins further down stream, where major branches converge.

By the river-system analogy, we may identify the separate origins of Sumer, Egypt, and the Indus as at some time in the fourth to the third millennia BC. The world system begins with their later confluence. David Wilkinson (1989) dates the birth of "Central civilization," through the political-conflictual confluence of Mesopotamia and Egypt into one overarching states system, at around 1500 BC. Wilkinson's work is of very great value to the analysis of world system history. Essentially, the confluence of "Mesopotamia" and "Egypt" gave birth to the world system. However, by the criteria of defining systemic relations, spelled out below, the confluence occurs considerably earlier than 1500 BC. By economic criteria of "interpenetrating accumulation," the confluence included the Indus valley and the area of Syria and the Levant. Thus, the confluence occurred some time in the early or mid-third millennium BC, that is by about 2700–2400 BC.

The ecological basis

Historical-materialist political economy begins with the recognition that "getting a living" is the ultimate basis of human social organization. The ultimate basis of "getting a living" is ecological, however. The invention of agriculture made possible the production of a substantial surplus. Gordon Childe (1951) made famous the term "Neolithic Revolution" to describe the profound effects on human social organization brought about by the production of an agricultural surplus. The subsequent "Urban Revolution" and the states that developed on this basis contributed to the formation of our world system.

From the outset, this social organization had an economic imperative based on a new type of relationship with the environment. The alluvial plains of Egypt, Mesopotamia, and Indus are similar in that their rich water supply and fertile soil make possible the production of a large agricultural surplus when the factors of production are properly organized. However, all three areas were deficient in many natural resources, such as timber, stone, and certain metals. Therefore, they had an ecologically founded economic imperative to acquire certain natural resources from outside their own ecological niches in order to "complete" their own production cycles. Urban civilization and the state required the maintenance of a complex division of labor, a political apparatus, and a much larger trade or economic nexus than that under the direct control of the state. Thus, the ecological origins of the world system point to the inherent instability of the urban civilizations and the states from which it emerged. This instability was both ecological-economic and strategic. Moreover, the two were intertwined from the beginning.

Economic and strategic instability and insecurity led to efforts to provide for the perpetual acquisition of all necessary natural resources, even if the required long-distance trade routes were outside the direct political control of the state. This was only possible through manipulated trade and through the assertion of direct political controls over the areas of supply. The internal demographic stability, and/or demographic expansion, of the first urban centers depended upon such secure acquisition of natural resources.

However, in a field of action in which many centers are expanding simultaneously, there must come a point when their spheres of influence become contiguous, and then overlap. As the economic nexus of the first urban civilizations and states expanded and deepened, competition and conflict over control of strategic sources of materials and over the routes by which they were acquired tended to intensify. For example, control over certain metals was crucial to attaining technological and military superiority vis-à-vis contemporary rivals. Failure to emulate the most advanced technology constituted, then as now, a strategic default.

The ultimate rationale for the origins of the world system were thus embedded in the economic imperative of the urban-based states. A larger and larger economic nexus was built up. Specialization within the complex division of labor deepened, while the entire nexus expanded territorially "outward." In the process, more and more ecological niches were assimilated into one interdependent economic system. Thereby, the world system destroyed and assimilated self-reliant cultures in its wake.

By the third millennium BC, the Afro-Eurasian economic nexus, upon which the world system was based, was already well established. Thereafter, the constant shifts in position among metropoles in the world system cannot be properly understood without analysis of the ecological and technological factors "compelling" certain lines of action. The rise and decline of urban centers and states can be made more understandable by placing them within the world systemic context. This also involves paying attention to their role in the economic nexus, particularly with regard to the sources and supply of key commodities and natural resources. The logic of the political structure of the world system is one in which the security of the member states, and their ability to accumulate surplus, is perpetually vulnerable to disruption. This situation created a dynamic of perpetual rivalry. Thus, attempts are made to extend political control over strategic areas of supply in the overall economic nexus.

Economic connections

New historical evidence suggests that economic connections through trade and migration, as well as through pillage and conquest, have been much more prevalent and much wider in scope, than was previously recognized. They have also gone much farther back through world history than is generally admitted. By the same token, manufacturing, transport, commercial, and other service activities are also older and more widespread than often suggested. The long history and systemic nature of these economic connections have not received nearly as much attention as they merit (Adams 1943). Even more neglected have been these trade connections' far-reaching importance in the social, political, and cultural life of "societies" and their relations with each other in the world system as a whole. Even those who do study trade connections, as for instance Philip Curtin's (1984) work on cross-cultural trade diasporas, often neglect systematic study of the world systemic complex of these trade connections.

Historical evidence to date indicates that economic contacts in the Middle East ranged over a very large area even several thousand years before the first urban states appeared. The Anatolian settlement Catal Huyuk is often cited as an example of a community with long-distance trade connections some 7,000–8,000 years ago. Jericho is another often cited example. Trade or economic connections between Egypt and Mesopotamia were apparently somewhat intermittent before 3000 BC, and therefore possibly not systemic. However, both Egypt and Mesopotamia very early on developed economic connections with Syria and the Levant, which formed a connecting corridor between the two major zones. The putative first pharaoh of unified Egypt, Narmer, may have had economic connections to the Levant. Certainly by 2700 BC, Egypt had formal political and economic relations with the city of Byblos on the Levantine coast. Byblos is probably the earliest port of economic contact mentioned in both Egyptian and Mesopotamian historical sources.

For both Egypt and Mesopotamia, war and trade with Syria and the Levant involved the search for access to strategic and other materials, such as timber, metals, oils, and certain luxury consumption goods. The apparent goal of Akkadian imperial expansion was to benefit from putting all the most strategic routes in one vast corridor from the Mediterranean to the Persian Gulf under its sole control. There is evidence that Akkad maintained maritime economic connections with the Indus, known as "Meluhha," via ports in the Persian Gulf. Thus, Akkad consolidated a privileged position in the overall economic nexus. The city states of Syria and the Levant became the objects of intense rivalry between Egypt and Mesopotamia. Oscillation occurred in the control of these areas: from the first and second dynasties of Egypt, over to Akkad, then to the third dynasty of Ur. By the nineteenth century BC, Egypt again exercised influence over most of the Levant as vassal states. It is clear that throughout a considerable historical period, even to the time of the Assyrian and then the Persian empires, Syria and the Levant played a crucial role as logistical interlinkage zones and entrepôts within the world system. They linked the Mesopotamian, Egyptian, and Indus zones in one world system.

World system extension

Accumulation is a major incentive for, and the ultimate cause of, economic, political, and military expansion by and interlinkage within the world system. Therefore, the process of accumulation and its expansion is also importantly related to the extension of the boundaries of the world system. Two additional analogies of expansion may be useful in understanding the process: the glacier analogy and the ink-blot analogy. By analogy to a glacier, the world system expanded along a course of its own making, in part adapting to pre-existing topology and in part itself restructuring this topology. By analogy to an ink blot, the world system also spread outward, beyond its area of early confluence. Probably the most spectacular single instance of this expansion was the "discovery" of the New World and later Oceania. David Wilkinson (1987) also sees Central civilization as expanding into other areas and societies and incorporating them into itself. In one sense, the process is one of simple incorporation of previously unincorporated areas, by analogy with the expansion of an ink blot.

However, the incorporation of some regions into the world system also involved processes more like merger than mere assimilation, as when two expanding ink blots merge. For instance, the incorporation of India, and especially of China, appear to be more merger than assimilation. Mesopotamian trade with the Indus was apparently well established at the time of the Akkadian empire. Repeated evidence of economic contact with India exists, though with significant periods of intermittent disruption. These disruptions make it difficult to set a firm date for the merger of India with the world system. Chinese urban centers and states appear to have developed essentially autonomously in the archaic Shang period. However, the overland routes to the central world system to the west were already opened by the end of the second millennium BC, particularly as migratory routes for peoples of Central and Inner Asia. The actual historical merger of Chinese complexes into the world system comes only after state formation in China reached a more advanced stage, in the late Zhou period. A series of loose hegemons began with Duke Huan of Qi (685–43 BC) and a process of unification of smaller feudatories into larger territorial states occurred. According to Wolfram Eberhard (1977), the eventual victory of the state of Qin and the creation of the first centralized empire in China was influenced by Qin's strong trade relations with Central Asia. These economic connections allowed Qin to accumulate considerable profit from trade. The Wei and Tao valleys of the Qin state were "the only means of transit from east to west. All traffic from and to Central Asia had to take this route" (Eberhard 1977: 60).

The maintenance of maritime and overland trade routes, and the peoples located in the areas between major zones, play key logistical interlinkage roles in the process of merger. In the formation of the world system, the interaction of high civilization with tribal peoples, especially in Inner and Central Asia, but also in Arabia and Africa, played a crucial but largely neglected role, to which we shall return below.

WORLD SYSTEM ROUTES AND NEXUSES

Maritime routes

The advertising blurb of *The Seacraft of Prehistory* by Paul Johnstone (1989) reads:

> the nautical dimension of prehistory has not received the attention it deserves. . . . Recent research has shown that man travelled and tracked over greater distances and at a much earlier date than has previously been thought possible. Some of these facts can be explained by man's mastery of water transport from earliest times.

Generally the sea routes were cheaper and favored over the overland ones. Some particularly important maritime routes are discussed below.

The silk roads

The silk roads formed a sort of spinal column and rib cage – or, more precisely perhaps, the circulatory system – of the body of this world system for some 2,000 years before 1500 AD. These "roads" extended overland between China, through Inner and Central Asia, to the "Middle East" (west Asia). From there, they extended through the Mediterranean into Africa and Europe. However, this overland complex was also connected by numerous maritime silk-"road" stretches through the Mediterranean, Black Sea, Red Sea, and Persian Gulf, and along many rivers. Moreover, the predominantly overland silk-road complex was complemented by a vast maritime silk-road network centered on the Indian Ocean through the Arabian Sea and Bay of Bengal, and on the South China Sea. These maritime silk roads in turn were connected by overland portage across the Kra isthmus on the Malay Peninsula, as well as by ship through the Malaccan Straits between it and Sumatra, etc.

The silk roads of course derive their name from China's principal export product to the West. However, the trade of items and peoples extended far beyond silk alone. Indeed, the silk had to be paid for and complemented by a large variety of other staple and luxury goods, money, services, and enslaved and other people who performed those services. Thus, the silk roads also served as the trade routes, urban and administrative centers, and military, political, and cultural sinews of a vast and complex division of labor and cultural diffusion.

Central Asia

If one looks at a map of Eurasia, it becomes clear that Central Asia (in present Afghanistan and former Soviet Central Asia) was well positioned to act as the ultimate nodal center. Central Asia was the crossroads of a world system in which China, India, Persia, Mesopotamia, the Levant, and the Mediterranean basin all participated. For instance, Central Asia played a key role in the joint participation in the world system of Han China, Gupta India, Parthian Persia, and the Roman empire.

However, Central and Inner Asia were also more than the meeting points of others. Inner and Central Asia also originated their own cycles of outward invasory/migratory movements in all directions. These cycles lasted an average of approximately two centuries and occurred at roughly half-millennium intervals. For instance, there were waves of invasions in 1700–1500 BC, in 1200–1000 BC, around 500 BC, around 0, in 400–600 AD and 1000–1200/1300 AD. Each inner wave pushed out outer waves, except the last one of Genghis Khan and his successors to Tamerlane, who overran all themselves.

Whether or not all these invasions responded to climatic changes, presumably they were both cause and effect of changes in rates of demographic growth and decline, which may in turn have climatic causes. However, they were also caused by – and in turn had effects on – the ecological, socioeconomic, and political relations with their civilized neighbors. Thus, Inner and Central Asia and its pulse require special attention in world system history. How central was Central Asia to world system history? To what extent was Central Asia, and not primarily the other civilized areas, something of a motor force of change in the whole system? How was the rise and decline of various cities (Samarkand!) and states in this area related to system-wide developments in trade?

The place and role of Central Asia are as important as they are neglected. The entire development of the world system has been profoundly affected by the successive waves of invasion from the Eurasian steppes on the perimeter of the agroindustrial zones. This "system implosion" is such a major phenomenon that it cries out for systemic study and explanation. These system implosions were not *deus ex machina*, but integral to the overall developmental logic of the world system's expansionary trajectory. In particular, the invasions and migrations from Inner and Central Asia were always instrumental in transforming the economic, social, political, and cultural life of their neighboring civilizations – and in forming their racial and ethnic complexions. Nor has the enormously important role of Central Asia as an intermediary zone in the world system received the systematic analysis which its functions merit. Other nomadic and tribal peoples, for instance on the Arabian Peninsula before Mohammed and in much of Africa, also participated in world system history and world accumulation in ways which have not been acknowledged except by a very few specialists.

The three corridors and logistic nexuses

Three magnets of attraction for political-economic expansion stand out. One is sources of human (labor) and/or material (land, water, raw materials, precious metal, etc.) and technological inputs into the process of accumulation. The second is markets to dispose of one zone's surplus production in exchange for more inputs, and to capture stored value. The third, and perhaps most significant, are the most privileged nexuses or logistical corridors of interzonal trade. Bottleneck control over the supply routes of raw materials, especially of metals and other strategic materials, plays a key role in attracting powers to such areas. This may also provide a basis upon which to make a bid for expansion of imperial power. Especially here, economic, political, and military conflict and/or cultural, "civilizational," religious, and ideological influence all offer special advantages for tapping into the accumulation and the system of exploitation of other zones to benefit one's own accumulation. Therefore, it is not mere historical coincidence that these three nexus areas have recurrently been the fulcra of rivalry, commerce, and of religious and other cultural forms of diffusion.

Certain strategically placed regions and corridors have played such especially important roles in world system development. They have been magnets which attracted the attention of expansionist powers and also of migrants and invaders. Major currents of thought also migrated through them. This attention is based on their role in the transfer of surplus within the world system, without which the world system does not exist. Certain metropoles have become attractive in and of themselves due to their positions along trade corridors, the growth of a market within the metropolitan city, and the accumulated wealth of the metropole itself. The rise and fall of great regional metropolitan centers and their "succession" reflects extra regional changes in which they participate. For example, the succession of metropoles in Egypt from Memphis to Alexandria to Cairo reflects fundamental underlying shifts in world system structure. So does the succession in Mesopotamia from Babylon to Seleucia to Baghdad.

Three nexus corridors have played a particularly pivotal and central logistical interlinkage role in the development of the world system.

1 The Nile–Red Sea corridor (with canal or overland connections between them and to the Mediterranean Sea, and open access to the Indian Ocean and beyond).
2 The Syria–Mesopotamia–Persian Gulf corridor (with overland routes linking the Mediterranean coast through Syria, on via the Orontes, Euphrates, and Tigris rivers, to the Persian Gulf, which gives open access to the Indian Ocean and beyond). This nexus also offered connections to overland routes to Central Asia.
3 The Aegean–Black Sea–Central Asia corridor (connecting the Mediterranean via the Dardanelles and Bosporus to the overland silk roads to and from Central Asia, from where connecting routes extended overland to India and China).

The choice between the two primarily sea-route corridors mostly fell to the Persian Gulf route. It was both topographically and climatically preferred to the Red Sea route. Moreover, the Persian Gulf corridor had connecting routes overland to Central Asia, which came to serve as a central node in the transfer of surplus among the major zones of the world system.

These three nexus corridors represented not only mere routes of trade. Repeatedly, they were integrated zones of economic and political development and recurrently the locus of attempts to build imperial systems. As the world system expanded and deepened, attempts were made by certain powers to place either two or all three corridors under a single imperial structure. Thus, such a power would control the key logistical interlinkages which have been central to the world system. For instance, the Assyrian empire attempted to control both the Syria–Mesopotamia corridor and the Nile–Red Sea corridor, but succeeded only briefly and sporadically. The Persian empire likewise controlled both these corridors for a time, and it also had partial control over the Aegean–Black Sea–Central Asia corridor. Thus the Persian empire is the first historical instance of a "three-corridor hegemony." Alexander the Great's grand strategic design for a world empire, or "world system hegemony," included plans to control all three corridors, plus the Indus complexes and the west Mediterranean basin. His successors split the Macedonian conquests almost precisely into realms parallel to the three corridors. They allowed the Indus to fall from Seleucid influence to the Mauryan empire and the west Mediterranean basin to control by Carthage and Rome. During the Hellenistic period, the recurrent rivalries between the Ptolemaic and Seleucid dynasties are indicative of continued struggles between the corridors for a privileged position in the world system's accumulation processes. Even the Roman imperium did not entirely unify the three corridors, however, since Mesopotamia was denied to Rome first by the Parthians, and later by the Sassanian Persians. They used their control of this area to extract considerable profit from the trade among Rome, India, and China.

Of course, each of these three main corridors had competing/complementary alternative variants and feeder routes of its own. For instance, there were several silk roads between East and West and different feeder routes in east and Central Asia and to/from south Asia. There were also routes connecting northern and western Europe through the Baltic Sea via the Dnieper, Don, Volga, and other Ukrainian and Russian routes. There were routes connecting the Adriatic to continental Europe, and the east Mediterranean to the west Mediterranean. Similarly, topological and other factors also favored some locations and routes as magnets of attraction and logistic nexuses in and around Asia. They deserve much more attention than they have received in world history. As the Afro-Eurasian nexus expanded and deepened, the number and role of these routes and chokepoints increased. At the same time, their relative importance changed vis-à-vis each other as a result of world system development. Locations such as the Straits of Malacca and of Ceylon had significant logistical roles for very long periods of world system development.

The three overland and sea-route corridors and their extensions were the most important nexuses between Europe and Asia for two millennia before the shift to transoceanic routes in the fifteenth and sixteenth centuries. This historic shift from the centrality of the three corridors to that of transoceanic logistical interlinkages was probably the single most important logistical shift in world history and world system development. However, rather than creating it as Wallerstein (1974) argues, the shift occurred within the already existing world system.

INFRASTRUCTURAL INVESTMENT, TECHNOLOGY, AND ECOLOGY

Infrastructural investment and accumulation

Accumulation implies infrastructural investment and technological development. Infrastructural investment takes many forms in many sectors, such as agriculture, transportation, communications, the military, industrial and manufacturing infrastructure, and bureaucratic administration. There is investment even in ideological (symbolic) infrastructure, both of the cult of the state and of religion. In the state form of accumulation, the state seeks to create social wealth in order to extract it. By laying the basis for increases in production and facilitating accumulation, the state increases its own access to surplus and therefore its potential capabilities vis-à-vis rival states. This in turn helps it to protect "what we've got" and to get more. In the private form, the propertied elites likewise create wealth in order to extract it and invest in infrastructure to facilitate production and thereby accumulation. The ultimate rationale of such investment would in all cases be to preserve, enhance, and expand the basis of accumulation itself. The development of infrastructure and the technology it embodies feed back into the generation of surplus and accumulation. This growth of surplus in turn feeds back into further growth and development of infrastructure and technology in a cumulative fashion. The pattern is spiral, whereby the world system itself grows and becomes more firmly "established" via infrastructural investment and accumulation.

Technological innovation

Technological progress in techniques of production, organization, and trade, both military and civilian, has long played an important, and often neglected, role in the history of the world system and in the changing relations among its parts. Technological advance and advantage have been crucial throughout history in armaments, shipping, and other transportation as well as in construction, agriculture, metalworking, and other manufacturing methods and facilities. Progress, leads, and lags in all of these have had significant contributory if not causative effects on (and also some derivative effects from) the regional and other relations of inequality within the world system. Some examples were examined by William McNeill (1982) in *The Pursuit of Power*.

Infrastructural investment is linked to technological change and to organizational innovation. Technological change in archaic and ancient periods, and even in medieval periods, was mostly slower than in modern industrial times. However, the essence of patterned relationships among technological innovation, infrastructural investment cycles, and the cycles of accumulation and hegemony (discussed below) probably have existed throughout history. When and what were the most significant technological innovations in world system history? Which innovations brought about restructuring of accumulation and of hegemony in the world system and which altered the logistical interlinkages? The diffusion of technology across the world system is another major area for systematic and systemic analysis.

In the general period of the contemporaneous Roman/Byzantine, Parthian/Persian Sassanian, Indian Mauryan/Gupta, and Chinese Han empires, cumulative infrastructural investments integrated each of these empires into a single world system. This high level of systemic integration was achieved via the well-developed logistic nexuses and the simultaneity of imperial expansion. At the end of that period, the entire world system experienced a general crisis. Hinterland peoples from Inner and Central Asia invaded Rome, Persia, India, and China. They caused (or followed?) a decline in infrastructural investment and (temporary) serious disruption of the world system's logistical interlinkages compared to the previous era.

How is infrastructural investment linked to productivity, and increases in productivity to the processes of accumulation in the world system? Technological innovation and technological change have been pervasive in world system development. Gordon Childe (1942) pioneered a materialist analysis of the effects of technology on the ancient economy. Logistic capabilities, for instance those of maritime trade, depend on technological capability. So does the dynamic of military rivalry. Indeed, the expansion of the world system depended from the outset on technological capabilities. Invasions from the "barbarian" perimeter to the civilized centers depended upon the technological and military superiorities of the barbarians. Such invasions did not cease until "civilized" technological developments made the attainment of military superiority by the barbarians virtually impossible. By asserting a new military-technological superiority, the Russian and Manchu empires finally put an end to the strategic threat of Inner Asia in the seventeenth and eighteenth centuries AD.

The industrial revolution gave European powers the military capability to destroy or subordinate contemporary empires in the world system such as the Mughal in India, the Qing in China, and the Ottoman in the three-corridors region.

Ecology

Technology has always been intimately associated with the ecological interface of the world system and its natural resource base. For instance, the technologies of farming created a secular trend to place more and more areas under agricultural production, thus to increase the sources of agricultural surplus. Particular technological innovations have dramatically affected the ecological interface, particularly those of industrialized production. Since the introduction of these technologies, the trend has been their extension across more and more of the world system, often with devastating ecological consequences.

There have been instances when environmental conditions brought about major changes in world system development. For instance, the salination of soils and silting up of irrigation works affected the relative economic strength of certain zones. For example, already before and even more after the sacking of Baghdad by the Mongols in 1258, Mesopotamia experienced relative decline. This was partly due to such environmental factors, and partly to shifts in logistical interlinkages in the world system.

Certain areas have been extremely difficult to incorporate into the world system for primarily ecological and/or topographical reasons. These difficulties (still) characterize, for instance, the Tibetan plateau, the Amazonian basin, the Great Northern Arctic of Canada and the former Soviet Union, and Antarctica. The social ecology of the peoples of Inner Asia, which Owen Lattimore (1940) contrasted to that of sedentary agricultural peoples, was a major factor in the world system's development for most of world history. The present ecological crises of industrial civilization remind us that ultimately ecology and the natural environment set limits on the expansion of the world system and on sustaining production and accumulation. If there have been any ecological cycles, rhythms, or trends, we should investigate what they are and how they have affected world system development.

SURPLUS TRANSFER AND ACCUMULATION RELATIONS

Surplus transfer and interpenetrating accumulation

The capture, say, by elite A here (with or without its redistribution here) of part of the economic surplus extracted by elite B there means that there is "interpenetrating accumulation" between A and B. This transfer or exchange of surplus connects not only the two elites, but also the economic, social, political, and ideological organization of their "societies". That is, the transfer, exchange, or "sharing" of surplus connects the elite A here not only to the elite B there. Surplus transfer also links the "societies' " respective processes of surplus management, their structures of exploitation and oppression by class and gender, and their institutions of the state and the economy. Thus, the transfer or exchange of surplus is not a socially "neutral" relationship, but rather a profoundly systemic one. Through sharing sources of surplus, the elite A here and the classes it exploits are systemically interlinked to the "mode of production," and even more important, to the *mode of accumulation* in B there. By extension, if part of the surplus of elite B here is also traded, whether through equal or more usually unequal exchange, for part of the surplus accumulated by elite C there, then not only B and C but also A and C are systemically linked through the intermediary B. Then A, B, and C are systemically connected in the same overarching system of accumulation.

This means that surplus extraction and accumulation are "shared" or "interpenetrating" across otherwise discrete political boundaries. Thus, their elites participate in each others' system of exploitation vis-à-vis the producing classes. This participation may be through economic exchange relations via the market or through political relations (e.g. tribute), or through combinations of both. All these relations characterize the millenarian relationship, for instance, between the peoples of China and Inner Asia. This interpenetrating accumulation thus creates a causal interdependence between structures of accumulation and between political entities. The structure of each component entity of the world system is saliently affected by this interpenetration, and empirical evidence of such interpenetrating accumulation through the transfer or exchange of surplus is the minimum indicator of a systemic relationship. Concomitantly, we should seek evidence that this interlinkage causes at least some element of economic and/or political restructuring in the respective zones. For instance, historical evidence of a fiscal crisis in one state or a zone of the world system (e.g. in third-century Rome) as a consequence of an exchange of surplus with another zone would be a clear indicator of a relationship at a high level of systemic integration. Evidence of change in the mode of accumulation and the system of exploitation in one zone as a function of the transfer of surplus to another zone would also constitute evidence of systemic relations. Evidence of political alliances and/or conflict related to participation in a system of transfer of surplus would also be considered evidence of a systemic relationship. According to these criteria, if different "societies," empires, and civilizations, as well as other "peoples," regularly exchanged surplus, then they also participated in the same world system. That is "society" A here could and would not be the same as it was in the absence of its contact with B there, and vice versa.

Trade in high-value luxury items, not to mention precious metals in particular, may, *contra* Wallerstein (1974, 1989), be even more important than lower-value staple trade in defining systemic relations. This is because the high-value "luxury" trade is essentially an interelite exchange. These commodities, besides serving elite consumption, or accumulation, are typically also stores of value. They embody aspects of social relations of production, which reproduce the division of labor, the class structure, and the mode of accumulation. Precious metals are only the most obvious example, but many "luxury" commodities have played a similar role (Schneider 1977). Thus, trade in *both* high-value "luxury" items and staple commodities are indicators of interpenetrating accumulation.

Center–periphery–hinterland complexes

Center–periphery–hinterland (CPH) complexes and hierarchies among different peoples, regions, and classes have always been an important part of world system structure. However, the occupancy of musical-chair places within this structure has frequently changed and contributed to the dynamics of world system historical development. To what extent (and why) have the world system and its parts been characterized by center–periphery and other structural inequalities? Wallerstein (1974 and other works) and Frank (1978a, b, 1981), among others, have posed questions and offered answers about the center–periphery structure of the world system since 1500. Ekholm and Friedman in chapter 2 above, Chase-Dunn (1986, 1989), and others are trying to apply similar analyses to world systems before 1500. The "necessity" of a division between center and periphery and the "function" of semiperipheries in between are increasingly familiar, not the least thanks to the widespread critiques of these ideas. Chase-Dunn (1986, 1989) surveys the propositions and debates. Wilkinson (1989) examines center–periphery structures all over the world for 5,000 years. Rowlands, Larsen, and Kristiansen (1987) analyze center and periphery in the ancient world. Chase-Dunn and Hall (1991) examine precapitalist center–periphery relations.

Chase-Dunn (1989) and Wilkinson (1989) have already made the argument that center–periphery hierarchies characterize systemic development much further back in world-historical development than 1500 AD. In fact, center–periphery relations characterize development since the origins of the state and systems of states. However, we need a more comprehensive CPH concept than most other scholars have used. The hinterland is not directly penetrated by the extracting classes of the center, but nevertheless it has systemic links with the center–periphery zone and its processes of accumulation. Wallerstein's use of the term hinterland to mean external to the world system is insufficient because it neglects the structural and systemic significance of zones which are "outside," but nonetheless related to, the center–periphery complex. These CPH relationships have been insufficiently analyzed.

The CPH complex does not refer to mere geographical position, nor only to unequal levels of development. CPH also refers to the relations among the classes, peoples, and "societies" that constitute the mode of accumulation. The CPH complex is the basic social complex upon which hegemony, as discussed below, is constructed in a larger systemic context. More research is necessary on how "geographical" position in a hegemonic structure affects class position in the CPH complex. We could expect to find that the class structure of a hegemonic state may be significantly altered by the surplus that this state accumulates from its subordinates in the CPH complex. For example, the subsidy to the plebeian class of Rome may be taken as an example of such systemic effects. Conversely, we might expect a CPH complex to give rise to increased exploitation of producers in subordinate positions.

The "hinterland" contains natural resources, including human labor, which are tapped by the center–periphery. However, what distinguishes the hinterland from the periphery is that the peoples of the hinterland are not fully, institutionally, subordinate to the center in terms of surplus extraction. That is, they retain some degree of social autonomy. If a hinterland people come under political means of extraction by the center, then the process of "peripheralization" begins. Nevertheless, despite a degree of social autonomy from the center, the hinterland is in systemic relations with the center. The frequency of center–hinterland conflict is one indicator of such systemic relations. The hinterland may also have functional roles in logistical interlinkage. In this sense, the hinterland may facilitate the transfer of surplus between zones of the world system. These roles of hinterlands merit as much theoretical attention in determining positional shifts and system change as those of semiperipheries.

The center– (or core–)periphery–hinterland concept is not intended to replace, but to extend, Wallerstein's (1974 and elsewhere; Arrighi and Drangel 1986) core–semiperiphery–periphery formulation. However, the semiperiphery has always been a weak and confusing link in the argument. The hinterland "extension" may confuse it still further and may counsel reformulation of the whole complex. For instance at a recent conference (with Wallerstein, Arrighi, and Frank among others), Samir Amin suggested that the semiperiphery has functionally become the real periphery, because it is exploited by the center; while the "periphery" has been marginalized out of the system, because it no longer has anything (or anybody) for the center to exploit for its own accumulation. As argued above, however, historically the hinterland has also contributed to core accumulation in the CPH complex.

Thus, CPH complexes are integral to the structure of the world system in *all* periods. They must be studied, not only comparatively, but also in their combination and interaction in the world system. It is important to examine how center–periphery zones expanded into the hinterland in order to understand the way in which accumulation processes were involved. The rationales of expansion and assimilation in the hinterland appear to be related to the "profitability" of such expansion, in terms of tapping new sources of surplus. They also help resolve internal contradictions in the center–periphery complex brought about as a result of exploitation and demographic pressure. Class conflict in the center–periphery complex is affected by the expansion of accumulation into the hinterland. Demographic trends are an important factor; the hinterland provides new resources to sustain the growing population of the center–periphery zone. The physical geographical limits of hinterland peripheralization by the center seem to be set by both logistical capabilities and by a cost–benefit calculus. Areas are occupied primarily if they can be made to pay for the cost of their own occupation or are deemed to be strategically necessary to protect another profitable area. Conversely, such areas are again abandoned if, or when, their occupation proves too costly. Fortification at such systemic boundaries has a dual function of keeping the barbarians out and keeping the producers in. That is, such fortification impedes military disruption of the zone of extraction and also impedes the escape of dependent/subordinate producers into the "free" zone.

"Barbarian" nomad–sedentary "civilization" relations

It is important to examine how systemic links between center and hinterland are formed. How does the hinterland interact over time with the center–periphery complex and thereby affect changes in the structure of that complex itself, and vice versa? A particularly important aspect of this question is the nature of the historical relations between the so-called tribal "barbarians" and the so-called "civilized" "societies." How are the barbarians "assimilated" into civilization and yet also able to transform civilization? Throughout most of world history, this barbarian–civilization relationship has been crucial to the territorial expansion of the state, imperialism, and "civilization."

The work of Arnold Toynbee (1973), Tom Hall (1986), Eric Wolf (1982), William McNeill (1964), and Owen Lattimore (1940, 1962) illuminates many aspects of how these center–periphery–hinterland hierarchies are created, deepened, and systemically transformed. Toynbee's "system implosion" is of particular interest. Robert Gilpin (1981) follows Toynbee to show how an older center is eventually encircled and engulfed by new states on the periphery, which implode into the center. Thus, a "center shift" takes place by way of an implosion from the former periphery to the center of the system. For instance, this occurred with the creation of the Qin empire at the end of the Warring States period in China. It also happened with the creation of the Macedonian empire at the end of the classical period in Greece. In even earlier examples of such hinterland impact, the "tribal" Guti, the Amorites, the Kassites, and the Akkadians were intimately involved in the political cycles of archaic Mesopotamia. Each of these peoples made a transition from hinterland roles to that of ruling class in the center. Moreover, these invasions of the center by the hinterland took place for systemic reasons, not just gratuitously. Eberhard (1977) and Gernet (1985) analyze how Inner Asian nomads repeatedly invaded China to appropriate its productive structure and economic surplus. Frederick Teggart's (1939) study of correlations of historical events in Rome and China analyzes the systemic causal connections across the whole Afro-Eurasian economic nexus, which caused hinterland–center conflict in one zone to affect relations in another zone. The sequencing of conflicts follows a logic that corresponds to both logistical elements in the nexus, struggles over shares of accumulation, and social tensions due to the expansionary pressure of the center–periphery complex into the hinterland.

POLITICAL-ECONOMIC MODES OF ACCUMULATION

Modes of accumulation

If we are to study any "modes" at all, we might better study the modes of accumulation, instead of the "mode of production." In the world system, production is the means to an end. That end is consumption and accumulation. It may be useful to study the differences, and also the mutual relations and combinations, of the "articulation" of "public" (state) and "private," "redistributive" and "market" modes of accumulation. It is doubtful that any of these modes, or other modes, have ever existed alone in any pure form anywhere. However, we should study not only how modes of accumulation differ and combine with each other "locally," but also how they interconnect with each other throughout the world system as a whole. Thus, world system history should both differentiate and combine modes of accumulation: horizontally through space as well as vertically through time. The "articulation" of modes is a way of analyzing how the mode(s) of accumulation in one zone of the world system is (are) affected by systemic links with other zones' mode(s) of accumulation. Can the overall world system be characterized by a single mode of accumulation? If not, why not?

Shifting the focus of analysis from production to accumulation need not mean abandoning analysis of the class structure. In fact, a focus on the relations of accumulation should sharpen the analysis of class relations. Geoffrey de Ste Croix (1981) argues that the key to every social formation is how the "propertied classes" extract the surplus from the working classes and ensure themselves a leisured existence. He defines a mode of production based on the means by which the propertied classes obtain most of their surplus. This approach is an alternative to trying to determine what form of relations of production characterize the entire social formation. That is, he focuses on the dominant mode of accumulation. Ste Croix delineates several means of extracting surplus: wages, coerced labor (in many variants), rent, and through the state (via taxes and corvée labor, and through "imperialism"). Interestingly, Ste Croix explains the fall of the late Roman empire as due primarily to gross overextraction of surplus, overconcentration of wealth in the hands of the upper classes, and the overexpansion of the bureaucratic and military apparatus (1981: 502–3). The latter is similar to Paul Kennedy's (1987) argument about military-economic overextension in *The Rise and Fall of the Great Powers*. This analysis implies a link between cycles of accumulation and cycles of hegemony, to which we will return below.

Equal, or perhaps even greater, analytical emphasis must be placed on horizontal interelite conflicts over apportioning "shares" of the available social surplus. This struggle has its focus in the ultimate political determination of the mode of accumulation. To say that the elites of different zones of the world system share in each others' system of exploitation and surplus extraction through interpenetrating accumulation is not to deny possible differences between these zones in terms of the mode of accumulation. The exchange or transfer of social surplus both affects and is affected by class structure. However, interpenetrating accumulation affects both the producing strata and the extracting/accumulating strata, though in different ways.

Transitions in modes of accumulation

Perhaps the single greatest weakness in historical materialism to date has been the failure to theorize transitions between modes in a world systemic context. Traditional Marxist interpretations of world historical development relied heavily on a schema of transitions between modes of production in a predetermined unilinear progression. This oversimplistic framework of analysis has long since been abandoned and revised by most historical-materialists. We propose instead to study transitions between modes of accumulation. However, they did not occur merely within each "separate" zone of the world system. Rather they were the key determinants of transition in both the "parts" and especially the whole of the world system. Therefore, the research task is not to search solely or even primarily for indigenously generated determinants of transition between modes, but rather to analyze the overall interactions of each zone of the world system with the dynamic of the entire world system. This is true of both the economic and the political aspects of modes of accumulation.

It would also be a mistake to attempt too strict an analytical separation between "agrarian" and "industrial" modes of accumulation in the world system. Even in very archaic phases of the world system, the economic nexus included nonagricultural sources of production and accumulation. The roles of industry and commerce before the onset of "industrialization" in the modern world system require much more study than they have received. The associated social and political relations of accumulation have changed very significantly across world-historical time, but not in any predetermined or unilinear progression of modes of accumulation. The precise nature and timing of such transitions is still an open empirical question.

Public/private accumulation

In principle, there are four possible permutations of private and public accumulation:

1 Dominant private accumulation (the state "facilitates" private accumulation).
2 Dominant state accumulation (private accumulation "facilitates" state accumulation).
3 All private accumulation.
4 All state accumulation.

Type 1, dominant private accumulation, may correspond to mercantile states and to modern democratic states. Type 2, dominant state accumulation, may characterize a number of bureaucratic states and empires as well as certain modern authoritarian regimes. Type 4, all state accumulation, might be characterized by states such as ancient Sparta, the Inca empire, and some modern (state) "socialist" states. Type 3, all private accumulation, raises the theoretical question of whether private accumulation is in fact possible at all without the state, or at least without the presence of the state somewhere in the overall economic nexus. There may be niches in the world system's economic nexus where all private accumulation may occur, but it has been difficult to identify instances of this.

State accumulation is typically characterized by a much larger scale and much greater potential capabilities to extract surplus than any sole private accumulator is capable of organizing. That is why "imperialism" is such an attractive means of accumulation. State accumulation centralizes accumulation more than private accumulation. For this reason, these two modes of accumulation and their respective elites are locked into a perpetual conflict over apportioning the shares of the surplus. Both private accumulating classes and the state elite, as a "state class," struggle to form a coalition of class fractions. Such a "hegemonic bloc" of class fractions allows them to cooperate to utilize the political apparatus to establish the dominant mode of accumulation. The oscillation between predominance by the private accumulators and the state class in a social formation is a key dimension of the cycles of accumulation, discussed below.

Economy/polity contradictions

There is a contradiction between a relatively unbounded economic nexus and a relatively bounded political organization of this economic nexus in world system development. The total economy of the major states and centers of the world system is not under their sole political control. This tension is universally recognized today as affecting the structure of modern capital accumulation. However, this phenomenon is not new. This economy/polity contradiction is characteristic not only of the so-called contemporary age of "interdependence," but has in fact *always* been a factor in world system development.

Even though the world system has since its origin developed logistical interlinkages that create a single overarching economic system, the political organization of the world system has not developed a parallel unity. Why is that? For the modern world system, Wallerstein (1974 and other works) argues that the capitalist mode of production structurally inhibits the creation of a single "world empire." That is, in this view the resolution of the economy/polity contradiction in the modern world system by a single overarching political entity is inhibited by its *capitalist* mode of production. However, it appears that even in other modes of accumulation it has not been possible to create a single political structure for the entire world system. Attempts to do so have been failures. The Mongol attempt in the thirteenth century perhaps came closest to success. The question of why the world system has never successfully been converted into one political entity should be seriously posed. The answer may be structural, or simply a matter of logistical and organizational limitations. Whatever the answer to this question about politics in the world system, it need not deny and may even strengthen the thesis of its essential economic unity.

HEGEMONY AND SUPER-HEGEMONY

Hegemony

Hegemony is a hierarchical structure of the accumulation of surplus among political entities, and their constituent classes, mediated by force. A hierarchy of centers of accumulation and polities is established that apportions a privileged share of surplus, and the political economic power to this end, to the hegemonic center/state and its ruling/propertied classes. Such a hegemonic structure thus consists schematically of a hierarchy of center–periphery–hinterland complexes in which the primary hegemonic center of accumulation and political power subordinates secondary centers and their respective zones of production and accumulation.

The rise and decline of hegemonic powers and cycles of hegemony and war have lately received increasing attention, e.g. by Modelski (1987),

Thompson (1989), Wallerstein (1974, 1988), Wight (1978), and Goldstein (1988), and even bestseller status (Kennedy 1987). Most of these studies confine themselves to the world system since 1500. However, we argue that the world system began earlier and was previously centered outside Europe. Therefore, the same, and more questions, about hegemonic rise, decline, cycles, and shifts apply – even more interestingly – to the larger and older world system, prior to Europe's rise to super-hegemonial economic and political power within it. Where and when were there hegemonic centers in the world system before 1500, and in what sense or how did they exercise their hegemony? David Wilkinson (1989) has made a systematic study of world states and hegemonies that could serve as the starting point for an answer.

The following are some other important questions. As one hegemonic center declined, was it replaced by another, and which and why? Were there periods with various hegemonic centers? Did they "coexist" side by side, or with how much systemic interconnection? In that case, did they complement each other, or did they compete with each other, economically, militarily, or otherwise until one (new?) center achieved hegemony over the others? Rather than continuing to look merely comparatively at contemporary hegemonic structures in different zones of the world system or to investigate the dynamic of each region separately, we must look at systemic links among all the constituent political organizations of the world system. Of course, these especially include contemporaneous hegemonic structures.

Hegemony takes a variety of historical forms. They vary from highly centralized integrated bureaucratic empires, to very loosely structured commercial or maritime hegemonies. In the latter, much of the surplus is captured not via direct political coercion, but via commodity exchange, albeit via unequal exchange. How and why do these various forms of hegemony occur at particular times and places? How do they reflect the interests of the actors which choose them and the prevailing conditions in the world system at the time?

Given the absence in the historical record of any single "world system hegemony," we must look to the rise and decline of hegemonies in each of the major zones of the world system in order to construct an overall picture of the hegemonial cycles, rhythms, and trends in the various regions and their possible relations. For instance, the oscillation between unitary hegemonies and multi-actor states systems has already been recognized as a key pattern of world-historical development (Mann 1986; Wilkinson 1989). These oscillations and the succession of hegemonies in each part of the world system should not be analyzed only on a comparative basis, but from a world systemic perspective. Only in this way can the dynamics of the world system's economy/polity contradiction be more fully understood.

All this suggests that the primary object and principal economic incentive of a bid for hegemony is to restructure the overarching system of accumulation in a way that privileges the hegemon in capital/surplus accumulation. Simply put, hegemony is a means to wealth, not merely to "power" or "order." That is, "power" in the world system is both economic and political at all times. In fact, economic power is political power, and vice versa. Turning Mann (1986) on his head, the ends of power are above all control over accumulation processes and the determination of the dominant mode of accumulation. The processes of accumulation are more fundamental to world system history than Mann's forms of social power *per se*. The political and economic processes in the world system are so integral as to constitute a single process rather than two separate ones. Success in accumulation plays a critical role in success in a bid for hegemony. This is true not only of modern states, but even of archaic ones. For instance, the victory of the state of Qin in the Warring States period in Chinese history depended greatly on its innovations in tax structure, infrastructural investments, bureaucratic administration, and trade links to the world system. All of these gave the Qin very real advantages in accumulation and in military capabilities over its more traditional, "feudal" rivals.

Cycles of accumulation and hegemony

The perpetual "symbiotic conflict" between private accumulating classes and state accumulating classes is indicative of cycles of accumulation. The oscillation between unitary hegemonies and multi-actor states systems is indicative of cycles of hegemony in the world system. Cycles of accumulation and cycles of hegemony are probably causally interrelated. This causal interrelationship appears to date from very early in world system history in various parts of the world system.

These cycles and their interrelationship are the central phenomena of the world system's longest cumulative patterns. These cycles have partly been analyzed by Gills's (1989) analysis of synchronization, conjuncture, and center shift in the cycles of east Asian history. Briefly, prior to the industrialization of production, the phase of accumulation in which private accumulating classes become dominant seems to be closely associated with the decline of hegemonies and their political fragmentation. That is, decentralization of accumulation affects the decentralization of political organization. These processes may be called "entropic." Phases of accumulation in which the bureaucratic state elite is dominant seem to be associated with the consolidation of hegemonies. That is, the centralization of accumulation affects the centralization of political organization, and vice versa. However, rising and declining hegemonies also call forth opposing (and also temporarily supporting) alliances to thwart existing and threatening hegemonial powers. Shifting alliances seem to promote some kind of "balance of power." All this may seem obvious, but the cyclical dynamic of hegemony (also through political conflict and shifting alliances) in relation to the process of accumulation has not previously been given the attention it deserves.

Implosion from the hinterland upon the center appears to be most likely to occur in entropic phases of the system. The hinterland, and perhaps the periphery, take advantage of weakness or entropy in the center to restructure the structure of accumulation. This may occur by usurping political power at the center, or by "secession" from the center altogether.

Too much attention has been given to the political and strategic aspects of long cycles of war and leadership with the exclusion of the underlying dynamics of accumulation. General war, as Modelski (1987) argues, does indeed produce new sets of victors who go on to establish a new order. However, one should not merely examine the political and military aspects of these cycles. The new victors, without exception, also proceed to restructure world accumulation. This and not mere political realignments or "order" alone is the ultimate end of such general conflict. The intense military rivalry that preceeds hegemony may stimulate production, but much of the economic benefit is consumed in the process of rivalry and war. Typically, a new hegemony is followed by a period of infrastructural investment and economic expansion, which is "the hegemonic prosperity phase" of accumulation. A unified hegemony usually reduces or even eliminates previous political obstructions to the greater integration of the economic nexus. This has a tremendous impact on the process of accumulation.

We must contemplate the existence, and study the development, of a wider world system farther back in world history to find answers to a host of questions about the dynamics of states systems and cycles of accumulation and hegemony. Particularly important are questions about the existence of world system wide accumulation processes and shifts in the centralization of accumulation from one zone of the world system to another. How do such shifts affect cycles of hegemony? What are the real patterns and "laws" of the world system's overall expansion, transformation, and decay?

Super-hegemony

The historical process of economic surplus management and capital accumulation is so interregional and inter-"societal" as to lead to the conclusion that it constituted a process of world accumulation in the world system over the millennia. A privileged position therein, in which one zone of the world system and its constituent ruling and propertied classes are able to accumulate surplus more effectively and concentrate accumulation at the expense of other zones, could be called "super-hegemony."

Thus, super-hegemony is also a class position in the overarching world-accumulation processes of the world system. A research agenda would be to examine the causes of possible super-hegemony, positional shifts from one zone to another, and the degree to which super-hegemony is transformed into further economic and political power within the world system. While hegemony is built up of center–periphery–hinterland complexes, super-hegemony occurs in the largest field possible, that of the entire world system and all its constituent hegemonic structures.

Super-hegemony links all the constituent hegemonies into one overarching systemic whole. Of course, the degree of institutional integration among distinct hegemonies is not as great as the degree of integration within each hegemony. Nevertheless, contemporary and/or contiguous hegemonies are not autonomous if interpenetrating accumulation exists. In the entire class structure of the world system, in whatever mode of accumulation, the super-hegemonic class position is the most privileged and the ultimate "center of centers" in the world-accumulation process.

To what extent did this overarching super-hegemony rest or operate on more than the mere outward exercise of political power and the radiation of cultural diffusion? In particular, to what extent and through what mechanisms did such overarching super-hegemony include centralized (super-hegemonic) capital accumulation? Was accumulation fed through the inward flow and absorption of economic surplus generated in and/or transferred through other (sub)-hegemonic centers? The answers to both questions are in general affirmative, for which we can find ample historical evidence if we only look for it. For instance, William McNeill (in conversation with Frank) suggests that China itself accumulated capital by absorbing surplus and capital from the West in the several centuries before 1500 AD. Was China therefore super-hegemonic? Prior to China, India was possibly super-hegemonic in the world system. In the period of the eighth and ninth centuries AD, the Abbassid caliphate, with its great metropole at Baghdad, may have been super-hegemonic. The development of European domination over the Mughal, Qing, and Ottoman empires should however also be understood in terms of the conjuncture of European expansion and these regions' entropic phases of accumulation and hegemony. In the nineteenth century, Great Britain is a candidate for super-hegemonic status, followed by the United States in the mid-twentieth century, and possibly Japan in the very late twentieth and early twenty-first centuries.

Thus, super-hegemony need not be limited only to the capitalist world economy, but may have existed at other times in the history of world system development. Super-hegemony is more flexible than empire, or imperialism. Super-hegemony operates not only through political and interstate levels of diplomacy, alliance, and war, but also and maybe more importantly, through super-accumulation.

If super-hegemony existed before recent times, how, when, and why did the super-hegemonic center of the world system, the most favored locus of accumulation, shift around the world system? What effects did such shifts in super-hegemonic centers have upon, and what "functional" role, if any, did they play in, the world system's development? For instance, the super-hegemony of the Abbassids in the eighth century was reflected in their ability to defeat Tang China at Talas in 751, their treaty of alliance with the Tang in 798 AD, and their continued ability to control Central Asia. Perhaps the super-hegemony of Britain contributed to its ability to arbitrate the balance of power on the continent of Europe and to defeat bids to impose a unitary hegemony, such as that by Napoleon? The super-hegemony of the United States after 1945 allowed it to restructure the international order and greatly expand its economic and military influence in the world system. It remains to be seen whether or how Japan might translate super-hegemonic status in world-accumulation processes into further political and economic power in the world system in the twenty-first century.

Cumulation of accumulation

How long, then, has there been an overarching and interpenetrating world system process of capital accumulation, which affected the structure of the structures of which it is composed? In other words, how long has there been a cumulative process of capital accumulation on a world system scale? The (occasional and temporary) existence of super-hegemony also implies super-accumulation at those times, as noted above. Even in the absence of super-hegemony, however, the process of accumulation in one zone of the world system would not have been the same without the linkages to the process of accumulation in another zone or zones of the world system. Therefore, even competing hegemonies and linked structures and processes of accumulation could have contributed to the world system wide cumulation of accumulation. Indeed, such an overarching structure of accumulation and the resulting process of cumulation of accumulation implies that there may be a unitary "logic" of systemic development.

The cumulation of accumulation in the world system thus implies not only a continuous, but also a cumulative, historical process of ecological, economic, technological, social, political, and cultural change. Cumulation of accumulation involves or requires no uniformity among these processes throughout the system or its parts, no unison among its parts, no unidirectionality of change in either the parts or the whole, and certainly no uniformity of speed of change.

On the contrary, both the historical evidence and our analysis suggest unity in diversity (to use the phrase Mikhail Gorbachev used at the United Nations). The unity of the world system and its cumulative process of accumulation are based on the diversity of center–periphery–hinterland, mode-of-accumulation, and hegemonic differences we have emphasized. Of course they also rest on the variety of social, gender, racial, ethnic, cultural, religious, ideological, and other differences, which characterize humankind. Historical change in both the whole (system) and its parts takes place in many "progressive" and "retrogressive" directions, and not unidirectionally or even in unison between here and there.

For this reason among others, historical change also takes place and even cumulates, not uniformly, but at changing rates, sometimes fast, sometimes slowly, sometimes (degenerating) in reverse. Indeed, as in physical transformations and in biological evolution, historical change suddenly accelerates and/or bifurcates at critical junctures. More than likely, contemporaries are rarely aware that they are living and acting in such "special" periods – and many at other times who think they are, are not. Hindsight seems to throw more light on history than foresight or even contemporary sidesight or introspection. Yet even historical hindsight has a long way to go, especially in grasping the dynamics and variability of historical change. We briefly return to these problems below under the subtitle "dynamics."

A HISTORICAL-MATERIALIST POLITICAL ECONOMY AND RESEARCH AGENDA

Historical-materialist political-economic summary conclusions

In this chapter we have made three key arguments. The first is that the world system predates the development of modern capitalism, perhaps by several thousand years. The second is that accumulation processes are the most important and fundamental processes of the world system throughout its development. The third argument is that, though the mode of accumulation underwent many historical transformations, there has been a continuous and cumulative process of accumulation in the world system. Therefore, we argue that a new research agenda is needed to focus more analysis on these cumulative processes of accumulation over the entire historical development of the world system – of some 5,000 years. The secular trends, cycles, and rhythms of the modern capitalist world system thus become contextually more understandable within the much longer cycles, trends, and rhythms of the historical world system, and particularly within its process and cycles of accumulation.

We base our argument upon a new set of criteria for defining what constitutes a "systemic" interaction. The transfer or exchange of economic surplus is the fundamental criterion of a world systemic relationship. Diplomacy, alliances, and conflict are additional, and perhaps derivative, criteria of systemic interaction. Thus, we introduce the criterion of "interpenetrating accumulation" into the definition of the world system. By applying these criteria we saw the origins of the world system recede by several millennia. The world system had its ultimate origins in the development of an archaic Afro-Eurasian economic and political nexus, which first developed in the area now known as west Asia, the Middle East, and the eastern Mediterranean about 2500 BC. Once in existence, this world system continued to develop and expand and deepen. It eventually assimilated and/or merged with all other center–periphery–hinterland zones to form our modern world system. Its relatively unbounded economic nexus is perpetually in contradiction with a more bounded political organization of the economic nexus. Cycles of accumulation and cycles of hegemony, like center–periphery–hinterland relations, have characterized the world system and its subsystems from its inception.

World system history forms a genuine continuum within which cycles of accumulation and cycles of hegemony are the two most fundamental phenomena. These two cyclical phenomena are causally systemically interrelated to one another. They are the basis of our assertion that there are cumulative accumulation processes in the world system over such an extended time frame.

Significant aspects of our argument were anticipated by Kasja Ekholm and Jonathan Friedman over a decade ago (Ekholm and Friedman, chapter 2 in this book). We agree that the "forerunner of the present kind of world system" emerged in ancient Mesopotamia. However, in our view this original formation of the world system was more the result of interregional relations between Mesopotamia and other regions in the "Middle East" and the Indus Valley, rather than their "incorporation" by the Mesopotamian Early Dynastic system. We agree that the world system then expanded and took on certain "general properties", which still define it today. We concur that such general properties "are common to ancient and modern worlds irrespective of specific local forms of accumulation."

Ekholm and Friedman and we agree on the centrality of capital accumulation in this long historical process and system(s) and that "capital" exists not only under "capitalism" and "is not tied to a specific form of exploitation." However, our concept of capital and its accumulation is broader than theirs. They define capital as abstract wealth represented in the concrete form of metal or money that can be accumulated in itself and converted into other forms of wealth. We stress the existence and combination of both state and private capital, as does Chase-Dunn (1989), and we include nonmonetary forms of the production, extraction, transfer, and accumulation of surplus. We also pay more attention than they do to the interregional dimensions of accumulation and supra-regional superaccumulation. Moreover, we stress the cumulative, albeit cyclical, process of capital accumulation – which also contributes to continuity in the world system.

Ekholm and Friedman argue, as we do, that the system is also characterized by center–periphery structures that are unstable over time and that centers expand, contract, and sometimes collapse as regular manifestations of shifts in the locus of accumulation. We have extended this to include the hinterland, which in our view also contributes to accumulation in the center and to transformation in the system as a whole. Moreover, again, we stress the systemic relations among various center–periphery–hinterland complexes, which make up the world system as a whole.

We agree with Ekholm and Friedman that systemic economic relations tend to be more extensive than political ones, and that this is a fundamental "weakness" or contradiction of the world system(s). This contradiction gives rise to instability in and transformation of the system. Yet as Ekholm and Friedman point out: "The development of total systems is not equivalent to the development of individual societies." We discuss these relations and transformations as cycles of hegemony. We also relate hegemony to the center–periphery complex and to accumulation within it. However, we also urge the study of possible overarching system-wide super-accumulation and super-hegemony.

Our debate with Ekholm and Friedman is primarily over the issue of continuity within the world system. They stress "the fundamental continuity between ancient and modern world-systems" and admit the possibility of the same world system. We completely concur with their view that the forms of accumulation have not changed so significantly and that the forms of exploitation and oppression have all existed from very ancient times, though in different proportions and in varying combinations. However, we wish to stress a fundamental similarity and continuity not so much of ancient with modern world systems. We are definitely talking about common characteristics and continuity within the *same* world system.

Ekholm and Friedman continue to argue that "the similarities between empirically delimited systems are great enough to warrant a continuity hypothesis." For them this continuity is of global processes and not of a "physically delimited portion of the globe," and "system" refers to "systemic properties of globally open processes rather than to an operationally definable empirical entity." The distance between their position and ours may not be as great as it might appear and is certainly bridgeable. We recognize and endorse their attention to the nature of local structures and the attempt to establish to what degree they are products of the same larger system, rather than simply connected to it. Because Ekholm and Friedman view global systems as multistructural, that is, containing many articulations among local and global processes, they argue that there is "no obviously established 5,000 year old system." Nevertheless, the gap between our positions is narrowed by their final conclusion that world history is marked by "repetition compulsions and a scenario of imprisonment in larger systems." Their global systemic anthropology is a necessary complement to our world system hypothesis and clarifies issues of the articulation of the local and global processes within a context of global systemic continuities.

Therefore, there is good reason, justification, and merit in constructing a historical-materialist political economy of world system history. Almost all historical and (other) social-scientific analysis of the world and its parts before 1500 AD (and most analyses of the time since then also) have neglected these systemic aspects of world-historical political-economic processes and relations. Some scholars (e.g. Tilly 1984) have considered undertaking such a world system history and have rejected the task as inadvisable or impossible. Others, like Farmer (*et al.* 1977, 1985), Chase-Dunn (1986, 1989), Ekholm (1980), and Ekholm and Friedman, in chapter 2, have started down this road, but have apparently taken fright and stopped or even turned back. A few scholars, especially Childe (1942), McNeill (1964, 1990), Stavrianos (1970), and most recently Wilkinson (1987, 1989) have made pioneering advances toward writing a world system history. Frank (1990) examines their and many other theoretical and historical considerations and rejects their reservations as unfounded. He then proposes why and how these and other pioneering works should be extended and combined for a history of the world and its world systemic historical-materialist political economy along the present lines.

Political, economic, and cultural three-legged stools

A historical-materialist political economy of cumulation of accumulation in world system history does not exclude or even downgrade social, political, cultural, ideological, and other factors. On the contrary, it relates and integrates them with each other. Nor need such a study be "economic-determinist." On the contrary, this study would recognize the interaction and support of at least three legs of the social stool, without which it could not stand, let alone develop. These three legs are: organization of political power; identity and legitimation through culture and ideology; and management of economic surplus and capital accumulation through a complex division of labor. Each of these is related to the other and all of them to the system as a whole and its transformation.

A historical-materialist political-economic analysis of the historical development of this world system should incorporate ecological, biological, cultural, ideological, and of course political factors and relations. Thus, there is justification and merit in also seeking to explain many political institutions and events and their ideological manifestations through the ecological and economic incentives and limitations that accompany if not determine them. In particular, we should pay much more attention to how the generation and capture of economic surplus help shape social and political institutions, military campaigns, and ideological legitimation. Economic institutions, such as Polanyi's (1957) famous reciprocity, redistribution, and market, appear mixed up with each other and always with some political organization. Many political institutions and processes also have economic aspects or "functions."

The three component aspects, the three legs of the stool, are embedded in the mode of accumulation. No mode of accumulation can function without a concomitant *ideology of accumulation*; an *economic nexus* founded on a complex division of labor in which class relations facilitate extraction of surplus; and finally a *political apparatus*, which enforces the rules and relations of accumulation through the ultimate sanction of "legitimate" coercion. The ideology and political apparatus are integral aspects of the mode of accumulation. They are not super-structurally "autonomous" from each other or from the characteristics of the economic nexus. However, ideology and political competition and emulation sometimes appear to take on at least a semi-autonomous character. Even if we grant this, it does not invalidate the alternative assertion that overall they are not autonomous from the economic nexus.

We reject any vulgar unidirectional schema of causality whereby the economic nexus must necessarily determine the ideology and political apparatus of a mode of accumulation because they are not in fact separate. We suggest an alternative concept of the mutual intercausality among the three aspects of a mode of accumulation which is historically specific to each case. Indeed, particularly in periods of transition between one mode of accumulation and another, ideological and political forces can play an extremely significant role in determining the structure of the economic nexus that emerges from the transition. It is in these periods especially that broad-based social movements intercede in world (and local) history. These social movements are often neglected altogether, or they are considered but not sufficiently analyzed in their structural and temporal world systemic context. We can well depart from vulgar economism, but not necessarily from a form of "economic" determinism, if by economic we mean giving the political economic processes of accumulation their due.

Analytic and research agendas on the structure and dynamics of world system history

Most important perhaps are the dynamics of the world system, that is how the world system itself operates, behaves/functions, and transforms (itself?). Are there trends, cycles, internal mechanisms of transformation in the pre-(and post-)1500 world system? When and why does historical change accelerate and decelerate? What are the historical junctures at which quantitative turns into qualitative change? What are the bifurcations at which historical change takes one direction rather than another? And why? Perhaps general-systems theory offers some answers or at least better questions also for this (world) system. For instance, Prigogine and Sanglier (1988) analyze how order is formed out of chaos and how at critical times and places small changes can spark large alterations and transformations in physical, biological, ecological, and social systems.

Recent studies by, for instance, Ekholm and Friedman (chapter 2 in this book) and Chase-Dunn (1989) are looking into both structural and dynamic properties of partial "world" systems before 1500. However, it may be possible to trace long (and within them shorter) cycles of accumulation, infrastructural investment, technological change, and hegemony much farther back in world system history. Not only may they have existed, but they may often have had considerable relative autonomy from policy and politics *per se*. Indeed as in more recent times also, much of this policy was and is instead more the effect of and response to largely uncontrolled cyclical changes. Moreover, policy tends to reinforce more than to counteract these cycles and trends. This cyclical process and policy response may be seen in the decline of various empires, including the present American one.

In particular, to what extent has the process of capital accumulation and associated other developments been cyclical? That is, were there identifiable subsystemic and system-wide acceleration/deceleration, up/down, swings in structure and process? And were any such swings cyclical, that is endogenous to the system, in the sense that up generated down and down occasioned up again? This kind of question has been posed and some answers have been offered for the world system (or its different economic and political interpretations) since 1500. For instance, Wallerstein (1974) and Frank (1978a, b) find long cycles in economic growth and technology. Modelski (1987) and Goldstein (1988) find long cycles in political hegemony and war. Wallerstein also posits a life cycle of expansion and foreseen decay of the system. Toynbee (1973), Quigley (1961), Eisenstadt (1963), and others have made comparative studies of the life cycles of individual civilizations before 1500. So have archaeologists like Robert M. Adams (1966). But to what extent were there also world system wide fluctuations and cycles, and what role have they played in the transformation and development of the world system?

Infrastructural investment apparently occurs in cyclical or phased patterns, and in direct correspondence with the cycle/phase of accumulation and of hegemony. Newly formed hegemonic orders are usually associated with a subsequent intense phase of infrastructural investment, followed by general economic expansion and a concomitant increase in accumulation. Therefore, it could also be fruitful to search for a long-lasting continuous up-and-down cycle of super-hegemony.

Thus, infrastructural investment cycles would be related to cycles of accumulation and cycles of hegemony in the world system. Are there also cumulative aspects of infrastructural investment that affect subsequent world system development? An affirmative answer does not imply we take the position of a single "capital-imperialist" mode of production based on the use of imperial political power as a political apparatus of accumulation throughout world history as posited by Ekholm and Friedman (1982). How did private and state infrastructural investment interact in world system development? For instance, what is the role of private infrastructural investment in creating and sustaining the complex logistical interlinkages of the world system? To what extent does state infrastructural investment create and sustain the logistical interlinkages of the world system? How does the conjuncture and synchronization of phases among contemporary hegemonies affect the respective cycles of infrastructural investment?

If we view the entire five-six millennia development of the world system as a unified cumulative continuum and seek to explain its most significant trends, cycles, and rhythms, based on a historical-materialist political economy, then a "world system history" should follow. Such a world system history should not merely be a comparative history of the world or even a comparative history of world systems. A historical-materialist world system history would regard class formation, capital accumulation, state formation, and hegemonic construction throughout the world system as being integral aspects of the one, cumulative, process of world-historical world system accumulation and development. This history would not be Eurocentric, and should avoid any other form of centricity. A comprehensive world system history would be humanocentric.

NOTE

This chapter first appeared in 1990/1 as "The cumulation of accumulation: theses and research agenda for 5000 years of world system history," in *Dialectical Anthropology* (New York/Amsterdam), 15 (1) (July 1990): 19–42. An expanded version was published as "5000 years of world system history: the cumulation of accumulation," in *Precapitalist Core Periphery Relations* edited by C. Chase-Dunn and T. Hall, Boulder, CO: Westview Press, 1991: 67–111.

REFERENCES

Adams, Brooks (1943) *The Law of Civilization and Decay: An Essay on History*, New York: Alfred A. Knopf.

Adams, Robert M. (1966) *The Evolution of Urban Society: Early Mesopotamia and Prehistoric Mexico*, Chicago: Aldine.

Amin, Samir (1989) "Le Système mondial contemporain et les systèmes anterieurs" (manuscript).

Arrighi, Giovanni and Drangel, Jessica (1986) "The stratification of the world-economy: an exploration of the semiperipheral zone," *Review* 10 (1) (summer): 9–74.

Chase-Dunn, Christopher (1986) "Rise and demise: world-systems and modes of production" (manuscript) (Boulder: Westview Press, forthcoming).

—— (1989) "Core/periphery hierarchies in the development of intersocietal networks" (manuscript).

Chase-Dunn, Christopher and Hall, Thomas D. (eds) (1991) *Precapitalist Core/Periphery Relations*, Boulder: Westview Press.

Childe, Gordon (1942) *What Happened in History*, Harmondsworth, Pelican.

—— (1951) *Man Makes Himself*, New York: Mentor.

de Ste Croix, G.E.M. (1981) *The Class Struggle in the Ancient Greek World*, London: Duckworth.

Curtin, Philip (1984) *Cross-Cultural Trade in World History*, Cambridge: Cambridge University Press.

Eberhard, Wolfram (1977) *A History of China*, 4th rev. edn, London: Routledge & Kegan Paul.

Eisenstadt, S.N. (1963) *The Political Systems of Empires*, Glencoe, IL: The Free Press.

Ekholm, Kajsa (1980) "On the limitations of civilization: the structure and dynamics of global systems," *Dialectical Anthropology* 5 (2): 155–66.

Farmer, Edward L. (1985) "Civilization as a unit of world history: Eurasia and Eurasia's place in it," *The History Teacher* 18 (3) (May): 347–63.

Farmer, Edward L. *et al.* (1977) *Comparative History of Civilization in Asia*, Reading, MA.: Addison-Wesley.

Frank, Andre Gunder (1978a) *World Accumulation 1492–1789*, New York: Monthly Review Press; London: Macmillan.

—— (1978b) *Dependent Accumulation and Underdevelopment*, New York: Monthly Review Press; London: Macmillan.

—— (1981) *Crisis: In the Third World*, New York: Holmes & Meier; London: Heinemann.

—— (1990) "A theoretical introduction to five thousand years of world system history," *Review* 13 (2) (spring): 155–248.

Gernet, Jacques (1985) *A History of Chinese Civilization*, Cambridge: Cambridge University Press.

Gills, Barry K. (1989) "Synchronization, conjuncture and center-shift in east Asian international history," paper presented at the joint International Studies Association, British International Studies Association Conference, London, 1 April.

Gilpin, Robert (1981) *War and Change in World Politics*, Cambridge: Cambridge University Press.

Goldstein, Joshua (1988) *Long Cycles: Prosperity and War in the Modern Age*, New Haven: Yale University Press.

Hall, Thomas D. (1986) "Incorporation in the world system: toward a critique," *American Sociological Review* 52 (3): 390–402.

Johnstone, Paul (1989) *The Seacraft of Prehistory*, London: Routledge.

Kennedy, Paul (1987) *The Rise and Fall of the Great Powers*, New York: Random House.

Lattimore, Owen (1940) *Inner Asian Frontiers of China*, Boston: Beacon Press.

—— (1962) *Studies in Frontier History: Collected Papers 1928–1958*, Oxford: Oxford University Press.

Mann, Michael (1986) *The Sources of Social Power*, vol. 1: *A History of Power from the beginning to* AD *1760*. Cambridge: Cambridge University Press.

McNeill, William H. (1964) *The Rise of the West. A History of the Human Community*, Chicago: University of Chicago Press.

—— (1982) *The Pursuit of Power: Technology, Armed Force and Society since* AD *1000*, Chicago: University of Chicago Press.

—— (1990) "*The Rise of the West* after twenty-five years," *Journal of World History* 1 (1).

Modelski, George (1987) *Long Cycles in World Politics*, London: Macmillan.

Polanyi, Karl (1957) *The Great Transformation: The Political and Economic Origins of Our Time*, Boston: Beacon Press.

Prigogine, Ilya and Sanglier, Michele (eds) (1988) *Laws of Nature and Human Conduct. Specificities and Unifying Themes*, Bruxelles.

Quigley, Carroll (1961) *The Evolution of Civilizations. An Introduction to Historical Analysis*, New York: Macmillan.

Rowlands, Michael, Larsen, Mogens, and Kristiansen, Kristian (eds) (1987) *Center and Periphery in the Ancient World*, Cambridge: Cambridge University Press.

Schneider, Jane (1977) "Was there a pre-capitalist world system?", *Peasant Studies* 6 (1): 30–9.

Stavrianos, L.S. (1970) *The World to 1500. A Global History*, Englewood Cliffs: Prentice-Hall.

Teggart, Frederick J. (1939) *Rome and China: A Study of Correlations in Historical Events*, Berkeley: University of California Press.

Thompson, William (1989) *On Global War: Historical-Structural Approaches to World Politics*, Columbia: University of South Carolina Press.

Tilly, Charles (1984) *Big Structures, Large Processes, Huge Comparisons*, New York: Russell Sage Foundation.

Toynbee, Arnold (1973) *A Study of History*, Oxford: Oxford University Press.

Wallerstein, Immanuel (1974) *The Modern World-System*, vol. 1, New York: Academic Books.

—— (1988) *The Modern World-System*, vol. 3, New York: Academic Books.

—— (1989) "The West, capitalism, and the modern world-system," prepared as a chapter of Joseph Needham, *Science and Civilization in China*, vol. 7: *The Social Background*, part 2, sect. 48: "Social and economic considerations" (forthcoming).

Wight, Martin (1978) *Power Politics*, New York: Holmes Meier.

Wilkinson, David (1987) "Central civilization," *Comparative Civilizations Review* 17 (Fall): 31–59.

—— (1989) "The future of the world state: from civilization theory to world politics," paper presented at the annual meeting of the International Studies Association, London, 28 March–1 April.

Wolf, Eric (1982) *Europe and the People Without History*, Berkeley: University of California Press.

4

HEGEMONIC TRANSITIONS IN THE WORLD SYSTEM

Barry K. Gills

INTRODUCTION

The purpose of this chapter is to present an argument in favor of a new general organizing concept for the study of world history and the central role within it of the world accumulation process and hegemonic power. Rather than viewing transitions between discrete modes of production as the general organizing concept, world history can be analyzed as a series of hegemonic reorganizations or "hegemonic transitions" entailing shifts in the locus of accumulation in the world economy. These hegemonic transitions are very far-reaching in their overall economic, social, and political consequences, composing what might be called a transition in the "mode of hegemony" and thus affecting the character of world order as well as the composition of all the "societies" in that order. The hegemonic transitions reflect the underlying rhythm of competition in the world system and especially the cycles of accumulation in the world economy. However, I argue that the conventional single-hegemon model is seriously misleading and would better be replaced by a new concept of "interlinking hegemonic powers" which more often characterizes the world system.

In addition, I will argue that the conventional sharp dichotomy imposed between premodern and modern states and economies is unwarranted and misleading. In my view, the world system has always, for thousands of years, been characterized by a mixture of modes of capital accumulation involving both private capital and the state. Most importantly, it should be accepted that trade and commerce have *always* played a crucial determining role in the world accumulation process. This is true even in historical periods supposedly dominated by so-called "bureaucratic empires" or "world empires."

Finally, I argue that beyond the many changes in mixed modes of production, there is perhaps a more fundamental patterning in the world system. This patterning is both economic and political, touching both accumulation and hegemonic power at the same time. It is the cyclical concentration and subsequent deconcentration of control over surplus and capital, by classes within states, classes between states, and between states themselves. This pattern is paralleled in the rise and decline of hegemonic powers and in the occurrence of periodic world crises. This brings us to a tentative conclusion implying a general theory of the causes of periodic economic and hegemonic crises which combines class struggle with cyclical change and conjunctural moments of historical transformation.

HEGEMONY AS A PATTERN OF WORLD HISTORY

The notion of hegemony has probably been the most debated term in international-relations literature in recent years (Higgott 1991: 97). The word derives from the Greek "hegemon," which simply means "leader." Two ideas seem to dominate current thinking on hegemony in the international system. First, hegemony is usually regarded as being more about political and military power than economic power, and secondly it is usually held that hegemony passes from one power to another in a succession from "like to like" insofar as the attributes of each hegemonic power are held to be very similar. Conceiving hegemonic succession as long historical patterns of the "rise and fall" of empires or great powers has been a very common way in which scholars have acknowledged it to be a fundamental pattern of change in the international system (Toynbee 1946; Eisenstadt 1963; Wight 1977, 1978; Gilpin 1981; Doyle 1986; Mann 1986; Chase-Dunn 1989; Modelski 1987; Kennedy 1987).

While it is true that the conventional understanding of hegemony focuses on a hierarchy of power, most scholars who study hegemony and long historical patterns of ascendance and decline recognize that hegemonic power is not simply or solely a matter of military and political power. Recently, Paul Kennedy examined the relationship between economic power and military-political power in the rise and fall of the great powers over the past five centuries (Kennedy 1987). Kennedy's thesis emphasizes the very close interrelationship between these dimensions of power: in the long run military-imperial power is unsustainable without a sufficient economic base. Michael Mann (1986) defines social power as being broader than military power alone, yet remains traditional in his orientation, i.e. he dubs his magnum opus "a history of power," thereby declaring his interest is primarily in political institutions. George Modelski and W.R. Thompson (1988) are even more traditional, since they focus explicitly on military, and specifically naval, indices of power in their study of successive "world leaders" in the past five centuries. Nevertheless, they also recognize a very complex and critical relationship between technological change and the pursuit of power.

Alternatively, some scholars suggest that we should have a definition of hegemony that focuses explicitly on economic processes, while not separating these completely from the realm of politics and military power. Wallerstein (1974, 1980, 1988) defines hegemony in a way that depends primarily on very specific economic criteria, whereby a core achieves supremacy sequentially in the spheres of production, commerce, and finance. Keohane (1980, 1984) defines hegemony using both economic and power-political criteria. His formula relates economic capabilities, expressed as a high concentration of economic power, to attainment of hegemonic political power. Keohane's work sparked off much debate on "hegemonic stability," which implicitly recognizes the importance of economic processes to hegemony and vice versa. Frank (1978) views the world capital-accumulation process, with its characteristic cycle of expansion and contraction, as the underlying context of hegemonic competition in the world system from 1492 to 1789, and indeed to the present. Braudel (1982) focused not on the familiar succession of political-military hegemonic states, but rather on a succession of key cities identified by their primary role in capital accumulation in a world economic, or at least regional European, framework. His departures from a state-centric analysis to one based on shifts in the locus of accumulation in the world economy is indicative of a fundamental change of the unit of analysis.

Gills (1987, 1989a, b) and Gills and Frank (chapter 3 above) explicitly define hegemony as a hierarchical structure of accumulation between classes and states, mediated by force. In this definition of hegemony, economic and political dimensions are inseparable. The essential feature of hegemony therefore is not formal political domination *per se*, but rather a hierarchy of centers of accumulation, as well as polities. This hierarchy apportions a privileged share of surplus, and the political-economic power to this end, to the hegemonic center/state and its ruling/propertied classes (Gills and Frank, chapter 3). Force is always an element in the exercise of hegemonic power, though other "economic" means of attaining surplus are also at work. This formulation does not require that either military power explains the attainment of economic power or vice versa. Rather it assumes that both are always employed in the pursuit of hegemonic power.

Hegemony is more than just a hierarchy of power among states. It is a complex pyramid of actors operating at many levels of social organization. At the apex of the hegemonic pyramid are the elite classes in the hegemonic coalition, classes located both in the center and in the periphery, i.e. dispersed throughout the pyramid at key points. These classes are themselves composed of elite families and individuals. Inter-elite relations within a hegemonic pyramid combine elements of competition, cooperation, and subordination, whatever the modes of production through which accumulation is occurring. This way of understanding hegemony is intended to synthesize two dimensions of analysis: military-political competition in systems of states, and economic processes of surplus transfer and its centralization (i.e. accumulation).

By contrast, realist models of international relations that assume that all states are intrinsically equal or similar because they are states either ignore or at least do not adequately account for the hierarchy of accumulation. Nor do they recognize the effects on each actor of its structural position within the hierarchy of accumulation. They admit a hierarchy of power, based on unequal distribution of capabilities between states, but the paradigm treats these states as if each is a completely separate discrete actor in the economic sphere. In short, the sociological-economic dimension of realism is too crude. In reality, no state is as impermeable or discrete an entity as they represent it.

This definition of hegemony is also quite distinct from that employed by Immanuel Wallerstein. In particular, a distinction must be drawn between the Gills and Frank conception of how hegemonies operate in the world economy and Wallerstein's concepts of the world-empire and the world-economy. Wallerstein holds these two to be not only distinct, but really opposite types of political economy. A world-economy is distinguished by a multiplicity of states, whereas a world-empire is an economy presided over by one overarching imperial state. The capitalist mode of production requires and at the same time sustains a multiplicity of states and therefore remains a world-economy. According to this concept, if a world-empire were to emerge, the capitalist world-economy would cease to exist – having become something quite different.

Wallerstein's terms perpetuate a sharp dichotomy between the idea of a politically determined mode of accumulation (the world-empire) and the economically determined form of the (capitalist) world-economy. Wallerstein has devised them in such a way as to emphasize the supposed sharp historical break in forms around 1500 AD. In our terms a world-empire has probably never actually existed on the scale of the world system as a whole. The only "world-economy" we recognize is the sole world economy of the entire world system. Therefore we prefer to drop the use of Wallerstein's terminology and we speak of hegemonies, defined above, rather than world-empires. The world economy we recognize has virtually always been characterized by a multiplicity, not only of states, but of interlinked hegemonic powers. Thus there was no sharp historical break in hegemony in the world economy around 1500 AD in the sense that Wallerstein would have it. There *was* an important hegemonic reorganization in the world economy at that time however, entailing a historical shift in the locus of accumulation from "East" to "West."

A definition of hegemony that emphasizes the integral nature of the hierarchy of power and the hierarchy of centers of accumulation shares much in common with the emerging Gramscian approach to international relations (Cox 1981, 1983, 1987; Gill 1990, 1991; Gills 1993). What they share is a move away from the single-power model of hegemonic succession and toward a more complex multilayered international political economy of hegemonic transition.

The key significance of the emerging Gramscian perspective on international hegemony is that it encourages us to examine not only the military and productive capabilities of states as the motor of hegemonic transition, but also, and perhaps most importantly, to examine how class coalitions are constructed and how ideology and culture are employed both to construct and to legitimate a hegemonic order. It is very rare in history that any elite dares to rule by force alone. It must seek consent, if not consensus, for its leadership or even domination. In my view this very "political" perspective actually enriches a materialist analysis of hegemonic power. It also reinforces the shift toward a more fluid and flexible concept of hegemonic power, one in which power is much more diffuse than any model of single-state hegemonic succession implies.

HEGEMONIC TRANSITION AS THE CENTRAL CONCEPT OF CHANGE

Previously, the term "transition" was usually reserved for change on a very broad sociohistorical scale. For historical materialists in particular, the most important transitions that shaped the course of world history were those between modes of production. I will argue that "hegemonic transition" is as useful a concept, if not more so, as transition between modes of production, or as "hegemonic succession" for understanding the patterns of change of accumulation, power, and world order throughout world history.

Taking this general point somewhat further, I would argue that it is possible to view all of international or world history as a series of hegemonic transitions entailing recurrent shifts in the locus of accumulation in the world economy. It follows from this hypothesis that these hegemonic transitions, or alternatively "center shifts," are a central form of historical change, i.e. as much a fundamental change as transitions between "modes of production," "historical social systems," or "civilizations" were previously presumed to be. Perhaps hegemonic transition and center shift are more real than transitions between the above, which exist primarily as analytical constructs, and therefore their boundaries are more easily identified.

If hegemonic transition is the central concept this implies a fundamental rethinking of the agencies of change in world history. It poses anew the problem of the relationship between "internal" and "external" factors as explanations of historical change. This debate was already begun between "productionists" and "circulationists" some time ago. However, if the nature of the "international" or "external" arena is reconceptualized as a hierarchy of centers of accumulation in which the hierarchy of power is embedded, the debate could enter a new phase. It also re-poses the problem of the relationship between change "from above" and change "from below" in the social hierarchy.

My intention is to build upon the insights of Janet Abu-Lughod (1989), who argues that a world system is not always dominated by a single hegemon, but may be characterized by a number of coexisting core powers (or in my terms interlinked hegemonic powers) that via both conflictual and cooperative relations become increasingly integrated. To Abu-Lughod, therefore, "hegemonic transition" would not be best understood as a process of absolute rise and fall by states. Rather, she emphasizes relative position in a complex multilayered hierarchy. Over the course of world history some nations, or groups of nations, gain relative power vis-à-vis others. Thus they occasionally succeed in "setting the terms of their interactions with subordinates." This is a "rise." Conversely, the loss of such a (temporary) advantageous position is referred to by Abu-Lughod as a "decline" (Abu-Lughod 1989).

Within Abu-Lughod's formulation there is an implicit conception of movement up and down a complex, multilayered hierarchy of economic and political power in the world system. The hierarchy of political power is embedded or "nested" in a hierarchy of economic power embedded in the world economy. If we accept that there has been a world economy at Eurasian scale for far longer than the past five hundred years (Chase-Dunn 1989; Gills and Frank, chapters 3 and 5) then several other points follow. First it becomes possible to view hegemonic rivalries as a continuous process accompanying the development of the world economy. Secondly, it becomes necessary to distinguish between purely regional hegemony (the "empires") and world hegemony. I would argue that hegemony on the scale of the world economy, unlike the regional form of hegemonic power (and perhaps not even that), has never been held *exclusively* by a single power or its ruling/propertied classes. Rather, especially global or world hegemony is always *shared* hegemony, exercised through a complex network composed of class coalitions, and also alliances and other forms of association between states, including competitive ones.

The world system as a whole is certainly never simply dominated by one great hegemonic power, but rather is characterized by *interlinking hegemonic powers* – which are typified in their mutual relations by both competitive and cooperative interactions, i.e. "independence," "interdependence," and "dependence". Changes in the configuration of relations between these hegemonic actors can have a truly profound impact on the course of history and social development. This impact may be equal to or even greater than the impact of class struggle between the exploiter and the exploited classes (i.e. the accumulating and the producing classes). In fact, the outcome of class struggle may often depend ultimately on the outcome of these hegemonic struggles, at least as much, if not more, than the other way around.

This idea flows from a conception of the world system as an interlinked hierarchy of centers of accumulation, as opposed to a simple hierarchy of states and their power. For example, the Pax Americana is probably better understood as a complex coalition of classes and states in a shared global hegemony than as the overwhelming power of a single state (Gill 1990; Van der Pijl 1984). The consolidation of US hegemony after 1945 is accompanied by west European and Japanese economic power, of course, but also by European and Japanese political influence, operating largely in subordinated harmony with US power. This coalition operated in a context of global rivalry with the Soviet Union and other communist powers for hegemonic position. Likewise, British global hegemony in the nineteenth century cannot be properly assessed in isolation from the coexisting (global) imperia of other contemporary great powers and the specific relations established among the great powers within Europe after the Congress of Vienna. To venture much farther back in world history for a moment, our western view of the sole dominance of the Roman empire in the ancient world is fundamentally flawed by the prevailing Eurocentrism. In reality, the regional Roman imperium coexisted with other very powerful and wealthy hegemonic actors, such as the Parthians in Mesopotamia, followed by the Sassanid Persian empires, all of which were embedded in the same Eurasian-wide economic relations, which included Indian, Central Asian, and Chinese states and empires as well.

As an alternative conception to the single-hegemon-succession model, it can be argued that the world system as a whole goes through a cycle composed of periods when several hegemonic powers rise and coexist together, and periods when several hegemonic powers decline together or when hegemonic power is in disarray and competition and conflict increase, i.e. a period of general world political and economic crisis. These hegemonic power cycles seem to be correlated with long cycles of economic expansion and contraction (or at least slower growth or some form of dislocation). Gills and Frank (in chapter 5) trace the occurrence of these cycles back at least two thousand years. These are not simply parallel developments, but are *synchronized*. That is to say, there is a common causal link between them. My preferred hypothesis is that this link comes from their mutual participation in the world economy and in its single hierarchy of accumulation. However, though some hegemonic powers decline there are always ascending powers, even in periods of general crisis. Even the worst economic crisis, though it certainly brings about much political, social, and economic restructuring and a change of the geopolitical landscape, does not mean the disappearance of hegemonic power altogether. The world economy as a whole never "falls," rather the ways in which it is constituted and the linkages through which it operates are changed. This process favours some at a particular time while discriminating against others, and so on through time.

The world historical process to which I refer above is not merely a rearrangement of players through time and space, but entails the restructuring of all the players as well as of the world system itself. It could be more broadly understood, as I have argued elsewhere, as

> a perpetual politico-economic process of mutual societal penetrations and transformations . . . [in which] coexisting classes and states interlock in competitive/cooperative relationships of accumulation and rivalry. These relationships not only determine shifts in the "balance of power" or configuration of international hierarchy over time, but equally, if not more importantly, they constantly force restructuring on all of the classes, states, and societies inter-locked into these competitive/cooperative relationships. This constant process of societal restructuring should be recognized as the real subject matter of the discipline of international relations.
>
> (Gills 1993; see also Gills and Palan 1993)

From this (new) perspective, hegemonic transitions in the world system may be viewed as an unbroken series entailing cumulative development: but composed of both *secular* and *cyclical change*. Over the *longue durée*, the long passage of sociohistorical time in which fundamental social structures are embedded, the world system expands spatially, for instance (a secular trend), while simultaneously undergoing internal restructuring (often of a cyclical character) or "deepening." The hegemonic transition is therefore not simply a repetitive cycle. At the beginning of each new historical period certain conditions will have changed that make it different from the preceding period. In particular, as the pace of technological change increases the difference between one hegemonic period and another may be considerable, despite other continuities.

For example, underpinning all hegemonic transitions is a secular developmental and underdevelopmental process which restructures the hierarchy of center–periphery relations, and center–center relations. This constant process of restructuring occurs locally, regionally, and now globally. There is an underlying process of capital accumulation on a world scale, which itself demands that certain types of restructuring occur in order for world accumulation to continue and expand. Therefore, secular developments in technology and the organization of the production system intertwine with cyclical rhythms of capital formation, and both with social and political developments. Mandel (1980) has examined in a very sophisticated manner the developmental logic of such interacting secular and cyclical patterns for the period of modern history since the 1780s. The long-term relationship of consumption to production, the rates of profit, investment, and exploitation, the technological cycles of innovation, the Kondratieff waves, and the form of social regulation, all appear in Mandel's examination of the development of modern capitalism. However, Mandel did not fully integrate the notion of hegemonic-power transitions into his otherwise impressive analysis. The locus of accumulation, and with it the locus of hegemonic power, shifts in response to all of these world historical forces above, operating in conjunction with one another.

I argue that the accumulation process is the ultimate driving force of hegemonic transition and thus of world order. This materialist analysis of the primacy of economic processes in the evolution of world order is not a "return" to past positions, but is even more relevant today than in the past. It stands in contrast to the explanations of a reinvigorated and redeployed idealist analysis of world order which explains macrohistorical change as the working out of some great historical idea, such as "freedom," or more topically "democracy." If world history has any real "end" it is most likely the (capital) accumulation process itself, in whatever specific historical form. Hegemonic power is a *means* to that end. *As the forms of accumulation change so do the forms of hegemonic power and thus the form of world order.* I believe that the historical evidence shows that the sequence is ultimately in that order and not the other way around.

HEGEMONIC TRANSITION AND THE ROLE OF SURPLUS

The second set of insights I wish to expand upon are those of Gilpin (1981) concerning the cycle of hegemonic rise and decline and the role of economic surplus. I hope the reader will pardon the exceptionally long quotation which follows, but it is necessary to do justice to the full range of Gilpin's formulation in order that I may later relate these points to the arguments above and those which follow. According to Gilpin (1981):

> The territorial, political and economic expansion of a state increases the availablility of economic surplus required to exercise dominion over the system (Rader, 1971, p. 46.). The rise and decline of dominant states and empires are largely functions of the general and then the eventual dissipation of this economic surplus [p. 106]. . . .
>
> The type of social formation is extremely important because it determines how the economic surplus is generated, its magnitude, and the mechanism of its transfer from one group of society to another (Amin, 1976, p. 18); it influences the distribution of wealth and power within societies as well as the mechanism for the distribution of wealth and power among societies [p. 108]. . . .
>
> The distinguishing features of premodern and modern international relations are in large measure due to significant differences in characteristic social formations. The displacement of empires and imperial-command economies by nation-states and a world market as the principal forms of political and economic organization can be under-

> stood only as a development associated with the change from an agricultural formation to industrial formation [p. 110].
>
> . . . the predominant form of political organization before the modern era was the empire . . . the history of interstate relations was largely that of successive great empires. The pattern of international political change during the millennia of the premodern era has been described as an imperial cycle (Rader, 1971, pp. 38–68; Rostow, 1971, pp. 28–9). World politics was characterized by the rise and decline of powerful empires, each of which in turn unified and ordered its respective international system. The recurrent pattern in every civilization of which we have knowledge was for one state to unify the system under its imperial domination. This propensity toward universal empire was the principal feature of premodern politics. . . . The principal determinant of this cycle of empires was the underlying agriculture-based social formation . . . the size of the economic surplus from agriculture and imperial tribute was principally a function of the extent of territorial control. Therefore, other things being equal, the greater the territorial extent of an empire and of its political control, the greater the taxable surplus and the greater the power of the empire. . . .
>
> Although the generation of an economic surplus during the imperial era was dependent on agriculture, its distribution was frequently influenced by commerce and international trade . . . the control of trade routes has been an objective of states and a source of great wealth and power. The great and enduring empires frequently have arisen at the crossroads of trade, and struggles over control of the principal arteries of commerce have been constant sources of interstate conflict. Changes in the control of these trade routes and changes in the locations of the routes themselves have played decisive roles in the rise and decline of empires and civilizations. . . .
>
> The cycle of empires was broken in the modern world by three significant interrelated developments: the triumph of the nation-state as the principal actor in international relations; the advent of sustained economic growth based on modern science and technology; the emergence of a world market economy. These developments reinforced one another and in turn led to displacement of the cycle of empires by the European balance-of-power system and, later, a succession of hegemonies in the nineteenth and twentieth centuries [pp. 110–16].

Since it is my firm contention, following Ekholm and Friedman chapter 2 above and Silver (1985) that "capital" existed in the ancient economy in much the same form as later in world history, and that capital accumulation is the driving force of world-historical development (Gills and Frank, chapter 3 above), it follows that the history of capital accumulation and the history of hegemonic-power transitions are inextricably linked not only for the modern world but throughout most of world history. Chase-Dunn (1989) already argued that "both political-military power and the appropriation of surplus value through production and sale on the world market play an integrated role" in hegemonic-power cycles. But how far back in world history could this be said to hold true? Perhaps much farther back than we are normally led to think is the case. Chase-Dunn explains that the "low overhead strategy" of Venice, which was later emulated by Holland, Britain, and the USA, relies for its success on a decentralized political apparatus of domination which reduces the cost of administration of empire, while surplus extraction is accomplished by trade. By contrast, "high-overhead" imperia which rely on a direct and centralized political apparatus of control and extraction of surplus via coercion/tribute are less successful when in competitive relations with the low-overhead types.

We have been taught that ancient economy and empire were basically about coercion, bureaucratic centralization, and tribute. I believe there is much evidence to the contrary. Gilpin's statement suggests that the regional power dynamic of empire cannot readily be separated from the trade dynamic transcending regional territorial boundaries. Many important and long-lasting hegemonic or imperial powers in world history depended not only on the agricultural surplus or on direct extraction of the same, but crucially upon exchange of products via market relations conducted over long distances. That is, they were embedded in a world economy and their power position was interrelated with their economic position within it. States, even ancient ones, pursue wealth through the pursuit of sources of surplus, of which trade has always been a key, if not decisive, element.

Even the earliest cities of Sumer prospered via long-distance trade, though they engaged in imperial rivalry and expansionism in order to protect or expand their vital trade. The example of the Minoan thalossocracy comes to mind as another ancient example of a centre of accumulation prospering not primarily through military imperium or territorial expansion but through long-distance trade. Even more so, the early trade cities of the Levant and later the Phoenician cities provide an example of ancient capital accumulation on the "Venetian" model that was very successful for many centuries. Many of the principal classical Greek cities also rose to economic prominence in a similar manner, and eventually in competition with the Phoenicians, both of the Levant and of Carthage. The Byzantine empire's strength probably persisted for so long due to the important role the metropole of Constantinople played in the world economy, because of the strength of its gold currency and its pivotal geopolitical location. The list could easily be expanded.

Perhaps it would be more correct to hypothesize that tribute has never been the sole, or the most effective or competitive, means of accumulation, but rather that it has always been trade and commerce which constitute the most significant means of accumulation. This significance lies in the key role that transfer of surplus via trade has in determining change in the hierarchy of accumulation and power, and also in stimulating social change (Denemark and Thomas 1988; Denemark 1990). Therefore, our both crude and incorrect inherited notions of ancient "command-economy" (Gilpin 1981: 112) and of "tributary" modes of production (Amin 1976, 1989), determined by coercion or political means of extraction (Anderson 1974), require significant reformulation.

Gilpin is perfectly right to argue that the rise and decline of empires, great states, hegemons, etc., is a function of the generation and dissipation of economic surplus. He is also right to imply that this is a principle which applies to all world history and not only to the modern world. The quotation above from Gilpin illustrates, if only implicitly, that both the "domestic" character of surplus extraction and the "international" arena of competition over control of the flows of trade are probably of equal historical and analytical importance when attempting to understand the patterns of hegemonic transition. Likewise, he is right to say that changes in the form the surplus takes and the method of its accumulation significantly influence the form of political power that dominates a historical period. Indeed, I would elevate this to a cardinal principle in the study of world history and world order.

If capital accumulation existed via trade even in the ancient world economy and this was a key element in continuous hegemonic rivalry processes, then Gilpin's sharp break between the premodern and modern forms of hegemonic power may not be quite so sharp after all. "Trading empires" are not rare in history, as we have seen, even in the premodern era. "Command economies" are not rare in modern history, indeed the twentieth century seems to have been a period of remarkable (temporary) revival of such economic systems – in direct competition with the trading nation-states which Gilpin identifies as the dominant modern form of hegemonic power. As in the past, the trading state of the twentieth century proved itself to be a superior form in competition with the command economy. Therefore, the putative historical break between the "cycle of empires" and the "succession of hegemonies" may not be quite as clear as Gilpin suggests.

The reason for the success of both premodern and modern trading states seems straightforward. Participation in world trade is participation in world accumulation. This participation greatly increases access to surplus being exchanged and thus offers the opportunity to capture more surplus than would be possible based on a purely self-reliant national economy. This has always been true. Likewise, participation in world trade is an avenue to acquiring technology and production techniques also not necessarily available to a closed, self-reliant economic system. It is likewise a stimulus to achieve superiorities in the production system which allow a state's exports to be competitive in other markets, including other core markets.

Even the so-called imperial command economies of the premodern era, and particularly their elite classes, on closer scrutiny, were most often simultaneously engaged in pursuit of wealth through trade. This was certainly true of the most ancient Mesopotamian empires beginning with the Akkadian, and of Assyria, Persia, Rome, Byzantium, the Arab caliphate and subsequent Islamic empires, Parthia, Sassanid Persia, Bactria, the Kushan empire, Tang and Song China, the Ottoman empire . . . the list could go on. Therefore, the "propensity toward universal empire" should not be explained solely on the basis of the desire to expand territorially in pursuit of more tribute and tax revenue from the agricultural base. It can also be explained in many cases by a desire to control key trade routes, the source of key materials, and key cities which generate "liquid" revenue in monetary form.

So if there is an important premodern-to-modern historical break it may not be so much due to the existence or nonexistence of trade as a key element of the pursuit of power, but rather to a change in the character of that trade. Chase-Dunn argues that "the thing which distinguishes a capitalist world-economy from earlier world systems is the exent to which states in the core rely on comparative advantage in production for the world market instead of political-military power" (Chase-Dunn 1989: 111) Nevertheless, this statement would be difficult to defend even for the relatively "modern" mercantilist states of the seventeenth and eighteenth centuries, which systematically deployed naval military power on a global scale to secure their share of surplus from world trade.

Change in the character of trade seems to reside first and foremost in the production system. The modern industrial change in the production system – made possible by advances in science and technology – led to a change in the form of surplus, or at least to a drastic change in the proportions being produced via agriculture and industry, which in turn led to a change in the forms of accumulation, increasingly via commodity exchange in price-setting markets and the wage-labor form at the point of production, and then in the form of state power, and thus to a change in the form of hegemonic power and world order. We have become very accustomed to referring to this modern historical period as "capitalism," or the "capitalist world-system," i.e. characterizing the historical period by a term for its dominant mode of production.

Though Gilpin and Chase-Dunn are right to highlight the importance of a switch from agricultural surplus and territorial expansion to modern industry, the spread of market relations, commodification, and wage labor, and the appearance of the modern nation-state, it is important to note that these modern forms never entirely displaced other coexisting forms of accumulation. Following Chase-Dunn (1989), it should be accepted that nonmarket variables are important to modern "capitalist" accumulation processes. "Capital" can be defined as a social relationship in which labor transfers a surplus to appropriating classes. These appropriating (accumulating) classes are composed both of owners of means of production and of political elites. Therefore, the "capitalist class" can be either a private or a state elite which organizes production in order to appropriate surplus from labor. "States are part of the relations of production in capitalism" and "there are many degrees and forms of the commodification of labour" so that "the subjection of labour to the logic of profit-making . . . is accomplished by a variety of institutional means." "Real capitalism," and the accumulation of capital in it, includes both private and state "capitalists'" accumulating via the world market, and a mix of "competitive production of commodities and political-military power." The larger arena of "capitalism" allows various forms of commodified labor, not only the wage-labor form, and includes "geopolitics," i.e. the competitive quest for accumulation and military-political hegemonic power among states. Interestingly, "peripheral capitalism does bear a greater similarity to pre-capitalist societies based on the tributary mode of production than does core capitalsm" (Chase-Dunn 1989: 1–43, 121).

In my reading of world history, despite many apparent changes in modes of production, or modes of accumulation, the fundamental patterning of hegemonic transitions, i.e. consolidation and deconsolidation of hegemonic power, and the concomitant concentration and deconcentration of accumulation, seems to persist and indeed to transcend change in the mixture of modes. Let us briefly consider how modes of accumulation interface with hegemonic transition. Just as hegemonic power is better understood as a multilayered hierarchy rather than a unipolar dominance, so also modes of production or accumulation are better understood as a multilayered hierarchy, i.e. always being a complex articulation of modes.

I follow Geoffrey de Ste Croix (1981) and Ekholm and Friedman (chapter 2 above) in recognizing that all the primary forms of extraction of surplus known to the modern world were already in existence even in the ancient world. As discussed in chapter 3 above, in order to retain the notion of discrete modes of production, such as the slave mode of production, de Ste Croix developed an interesting formulation. He decided to characterize a mode as that through which the ruling elite derives the main part of its surplus. This obviates the need for one mode to be overwhelmingly common in the social formation. It is only important that it be the form through which the elite derives the main source of its wealth from other classes. That is, it characterizes the key form of the transfer of surplus; the main form of the accumulation process in that socioeconomic formation at that period of history. It can and does coexist with many other modes.

Taking this pespective even further, perhaps to its logical conclusion, I would argue that the notion of transition between discrete modes of production breaks down altogether. If the reality is always a mixture of many modes in a complex articulation then what actually takes place is a change in the composition of this mixture and the hierarchy within it, not a clean transition from one mode to another. The crucial change is at the top layer of accumulation. This form changes in correspondence with a host of social, political, military, technological, demographic, and other factors. But perhaps it is not only a matter of the historical form the surplus takes, but crucially, change in the distribution of surplus between fractions of the accumulating classes whch constitutes the ultimate key to understanding what drives hegemonic transitions.

If change in the configuration of modes is only one element, change in the configuration of power among the accumulating classes is another very important and too neglected dimension of historical transitions. Despite many changes in modes the fundamental patterning of hegemonic transitions seems to persist and remain a profound influence on the course of social history. The current confusion over whether the world is witnessing a transition from "socialism" to "capitalism" or may yet experience a transition from "capitalism" to "socialism" illustrates my point that perhaps what is happening in the world today would be better understood primarily as a hegemonic transition rather than primarily or solely a transition between modes of production. The same lesson applies to the earlier "transition" between "feudalism" and "capitalism." Chase-Dunn (1989) and Gills and Frank (chapter 5) criticize Wallerstein for regarding India and the Ottoman empire as separate world systems in the sixteenth century because they were allegedly not "capitalist" while the Eurocentered world economy was "capitalist." Wallerstein has substituted mode-of-production criteria for his material-exchange criteria, but by doing so has to reinterpret the very important and extensive trade relations among Europe, India, the Ottomans, and also China. Far better to recognize that "Europe was never (or only briefly) a separate world-system according to the definition of material exchange networks. Rather, there has existed for at least two millennia a multi-centric Eurasian world-system" (Chase-Dunn 1989: 45).

As the present world situation clearly illustrates, a hegemonic transition is largely set in motion by shifts in the relative position of classes and states in the hierarchy of accumulation, but has profound effects on social development and is therefore by no means merely a rearrangement of players on a chessboard. Therefore, by focusing on hegemonic transition as the key concept of change in world history, we need not abandon the problems that modes-of-production analysis sought to address – namely how struggles over accumulation affect the course of larger sociopolitical and economic development in world history. The two are inseparable. "Modes" certainly exist, but they need to be relocated in our scheme of social change, within a framework governed by patterns of interelite rivalry and the accompanying hegemonic transition.

CLASS STRUGGLE AND THE SPATIAL/TEMPORAL INTERFACE OF HEGEMONIC CYCLES

Two of the fundamental axes of change in the world historical process of restructuring are the spatial and the temporal. Both time and space are very real dimensions of historical change, as important as material exchange and institution building. In the discussion to follow I explore the interface of these two axes in hegemonic transition; synchronization, conjuncture, and center shift are concepts I will employ in this exploration of the effects of space and time on hegemonic transition (Gills 1989a). Though from the perspective of the world there is only one unified sociohistorical time, from the point of view of any locality in the world developmental process there are separate or distinctive streams of sociohistorical time. The interaction of these distinctive sociohistorical times is one of the key elements of historical change.

The interaction of different local sociohistorical times (synchronization) produces specific combinations in a moment of world time (conjuncture), which in turn may also result in the spatial rearrangement of the world system (center shift) which will be an expression of the hierarchy of centers of accumulation. This process constitutes a hegemonic transition.

Of course it is not time and space themselves which interact, but rather real social formations and states. These social formations and states each have their own respective cycles of accumulation and cycles of hegemony. These local/regional cycles are in turn themselves constitutive of the one world system cycle (Gills and Frank, chapter 5). Following Gilpin, the consolidation and deconsolidation, or rather rise and decline, of hegemonies can be understood as being part and parcel of a parallel pattern of the concentration and deconcentration of accumulation, both within and between states. What I seek to do is to build up a framework of how all the cycles interact. That is, how each of the local/regional patterns of change affect each other and how each of these local/regional cycles is affected by and in turn affects the patterns of the world system as a whole.

According to my own reading of world history, every regional empire seems to have experienced a cyclical pattern of concentration and deconcentration of accumulation. They all seem to have alternating periods of more centralized accumulation and periods of more decentralized accumulation. Every region in world history also seems to have experienced some form of cyclical pattern of political power, alternating between periods of more centralized power and periods of more decentralized power.

If we accept that cycles of accumulation and cycles of hegemony are very common, possibly universal phenomena, then the key question is what historical forces propel and perpetuate these cycles?

The answer is *class struggles*. Historically, class struggles or class conflict, both between the elite and the exploited, and between elites, are essentially a struggle over political means to determine the shares of surplus apportioned to the classes. The ruling/propertied classes tend to want to increase the level of surplus extraction, since this surplus is the tangible wealth they enjoy. The exploited classes tend to want to decrease the level of surplus extraction, since this is their primary means of safeguarding their standard of living (to use the modern term). In the modern capital–labor relationship capital tends to seek a higher rate of surplus transfer from labor to capital. This is done by pressure to keep wages low and to lengthen the working day. Labor, particularly in its organized trade-union form, tends to want to decrease the transfer of surplus value to capital, by increasing wages and shortening the working day. Capital can and does circumvent the "natural" limits of surplus extraction inherent in labor's reproduction costs by substituting technology for labor and thus increasing productivity. While this is not the time or place to venture further down this well-worn path, the main point is that we should not assume that the essence of the modern capital–labor relation is quite so unique as some would have it, though the logic of development it sets in train has certain important new historical features. Capital has always sought to increase the transfer of surplus from labor to capital, whatever the method of extraction.

In short, class struggles are as old as "civilization" itself, and are essentially about the same thing. It is impossible to argue that class struggles have ever come to an end. That would indeed be the "end of history." The utopianism of early Marxist analysis lies precisely in its view that class struggles would someday end. However much this ideal may appeal to us, it is a risky notion to carry over into analysis of world history as it has so far actually happened or can be realistically expected to happen in the future. This idea of the end of class struggle was an expression of nineteenth-century notions of progress and is implicit in the model of transition between modes of production. By contrast, a model of hegemonic transitions does not assume any necessary end of class struggles, and of their concomitant economic and political cycles, nor does it assume progress in a linear or historically necessary direction.

Goldstone (1991) has recently argued that cycles of social rebellion (which one could argue are very intimately related to cycles of accumulation and cycles of hegemony) are essentially demographically driven, at least for the past few centuries. Demographic change may play an important role in cycles, but in my view it would be a mistake to explain these cycles on the grounds of demographic factors. Goldstone, of course, does not explicitly focus on cycles of accumulation and hegemony.

But there does seem to be a general historical correlation between concentration of accumulation and social rebellion. When extraction of surplus is excessive, and when it is heavily concentrated in a few hands, these conditions seem to lead time and time again, in many different cultures, states, and empires, to a reactive rebellion, and also to possible disintegration, war, invasion, or collapse. Indeed, Geoffrey de Ste Croix (1981) explains the "fall" of the Roman empire in the western provinces on the basis of the social effects of overconcentration of accumulation in the hands of a small oligarchic elite and the resultant overextraction of surplus by both private propertied classes and the state. Similar patterns can be found in many other historical cases.

In preindustrial socioeconomic formations this cyclical development was focused on a struggle between private vs. state elites for control over the mainly but not exclusively agrarian-derived surplus. That is, it is primarily interelite conflict or competition which governs the pattern. The struggle over control of the surplus was not primarily between the elites and the exploited masses of the population. It has to be recognized that most of the time in most places the "masses" are so subordinated to the elite-constructed institutions of social life that they are more objects than subjects of history. Even when the masses are set in motion, i.e. temporarily become self-determining subjects of history, usually via rebellion, they very seldom gain real "progress" in the end. This does not mean they should not struggle. They should and do. It means simply that the outcome of class struggle "from below" is not often what is expected. Class struggle "from above," by contrast, seems to be the real meat of hegemonic rivalry and does seem to have very profound effects on sociohistorical forms, though not very "progressive" effects from the point of view of the exploited.

Returning to Gilpin, it is true that for much of history a particular dynamic characterized the rise and demise of most empires. The centralized state contended with the landed "aristocracy," or landowning classes, for shares of the available agricultural surplus. When the demands of this struggle grew so excessive as to undermine the basis of material life for the exploited masses, they rebelled. It is thus at a particular historical point that the masses enter history as agents of change. This is usually a response to overextraction and underinvestment, often accompanied by "privatization" or "aristocratization" of the state and a resultant overconcentration of power and wealth in the hands of a few.

Private accumulation posed a constant centrifugal, disintegrative force vis-à-vis centralized state accumulation (Gills 1987: 268). Eisenstadt (1963) analyzes the dynamic of bureaucratic agrarian empires according to a model of levels of structural differentiation and the development of "free (flexible) resources," i.e. the availability of social surplus that is not constricted by the "fixed commitments of ascriptive kinship and status groups, but which could be allocated directly." The state establishes direct relations of surplus appropriation with producers and both requires and facilitates the expansion of commodified labor, upon which it becomes dependent. Thus the state's economic activities, even in the ancient world, promoted the extension of the commodity nexus and deepening of the division of labor. One example of this is the minting of coinage to pay armies and to employ artisans on contract.

Eisenstadt recognizes that "it was the combination of external and internal pressures that constituted the major foci of change in the empires." He gives five determinants of structural change in bureaucratic agrarian empires: 1) the continuous needs of the rulers for different types of resources and especially their great dependence on various flexible (free) resources; 2) the rulers' attempts to maintain their own positions of control, in terms of both traditional legitimation and of effective political control over the more flexible forces in the society; 3) the great and continuous sensitivity of the internal structure of these societies to various external pressures and to political and economic developments in the international field; 4) the consequent need of the rulers to intensify the mobilization of various resources in order to deal with problems arising out of changes in military, diplomatic, and economic international situations; and 5) the development of various autonomous orientations and goals among the major strata and their respective demands on the rulers (Eisenstadt 1963).

According to Eisenstadt "strong contradictions" between these different determinant factors developed especially when the state elite "emphasized expensive goals which exhausted the available economic and manpower resources." He identifies a pattern in which overexploitation of the resource base by the state elite depletes the flexible resources necessary to the state's existence. This overexploitation exacerbates a countertendency for resources to revert to subordination to "more conservative, aristocratic-patrimonial (or feudal) elements." This process is associated with the "aristocratization" of the state, usually via the bureaucracy. When this occurs the state elite increasingly indulges in "parasitic exploitation," i.e. the growth of consumption by the elite relative to redistribution and investment of the surplus. This type of parasitic appropriation of surplus is most marked during periods of decline. The process creates "new ascriptive positions and groups" which eventually mount a challenge which undermines "their already overdeveloped bureaucracies." As the state succumbs to aristocratization, in cases where the center is relatively weak and where international exigencies are strong, there is a tendency for such systems to undergo final disintegration and reversion to "simpler, patrimonial, or at most feudal, units" (Eisenstadt 1963). Therefore, "feudalism" is not a mode of production that (all) societies experience at a certain stage of linear historical development, but rather a phase in a hegemonic cycle experienced across much of historical time. The history of virtually every region and every empire or civilization seems to bear this out.

Following Eisenstadt, I suggest there is a pattern in the premodern era of the centralization and decentralization of accumulation. In the centralization phase of empires the state elite is dominant and subordinate private and landed elites to state ends. The power these classes derived from the concentration of wealth in private hands is reduced via state action and reform. The result is an increase in state revenues, since the state is receiving an increased share of the available surplus vis-à-vis these (rival) private elite classes. The strengthened central state is free to develop the bureaucracy, invest in infrastructure, and promote imperial expansion. Through measures to integrate the economy and standardize administration the productive base of the economy is stimulated toward expansion, and more "free" flexible resources are created by the state. Thus there is usually a period of economic and concomitant demographic growth following the success of a centralization phase. Such growth is temporary, however, and is eventually overtaken by inertia as the costs of maintaining the system grow and the private elite erodes the dominance of the state elite and increase its share of surplus appropriation.

In the resulting decentralization phase, the private elite increase its share of surplus at the expense of the state and of producers. Its surplus appropriation is more parasitic and thus the ratio of consumption grows as that of redistribution and investment declines. This process undermines the stability of both the state and the economic base of society. The state enters fiscal crisis and in order to maintain control may increase the level of state surplus appropriation through both taxation and expropriation. But this increase in state appropriation often falls upon a narrowing tax base and thus exposes it to greater exploitation which damages the base, immiserates producers, and stifles economic growth, thus eventually stimulating social rebellion. Many producers flee the jurisdiction of the state and seek a haven under the auspices of local private elites, thus transferring the surplus to them rather than to the state. In this manner the sovereignty of the state begins to be "feudalized" or parcelized. At the most actute stage, the state may collapse altogether, leading to a period of anarchic local rivalries.

Michael Mann has posited the alternation of two historical variants of "power configuration" as evidence of a dialectic of change in world history. These two power variants are 1) "empires of domination," and 2) "multi-power-actor civilizations." The empires of domination are characterized by "combined military concentrated coercion with an attempt at state territorial centralization and geopolitical hegemony." The multi-power-actor civilizations are characterized by "decentralized power actors . . . [which] compete[d] with one another within an overall framework of normative regulation." Mann suggests there is a dialectical relationship between the two variants of power configuration. Empires of domination may be the culminating development of preceding multi-power-actor civilizations. Mann also makes allowance for contiguous and contemporaneous interactions between the two variants of power configuration. That is, region A may be in variant 1 and region B in variant

2 in the same period of world history. For example, Mann cites the coexistence of the multi-power-actor civilization of the classical Greek and Phoenician city states with the "near Eastern Empire," by which I presume Mann means the Persian empire. Martin Wight similarly regarded the interlinkage of Hellas and Persia as two variants of international systems coexisting in the same overarching "secondary states system" (Wight 1977). Likewise, Wight, similarly to Gilpin, suggests that most multi-power-actor civilizations, or "states-systems" have ended in a "universal empire." In fact, Wight held that most states systems experienced a succession of hegemonies, in which one power after another tried to transform the states system, or even to abolish it, by reducing it to unity (Wight 1977).

Mann's formulation of a dialectic between the two variants of power configuration can be usefully enhanced by reference to Eisenstadt's model above. According to Mann, the dialectic rests on each variant's internal capacity for innovation. Mann suggests that one type gave way to the other when further social development was possible only "when its polar opposite type arose to exploit precisely what it could not." One has to be cautious with this type of formulation. I would prefer to suggest that the outcome of transition between types is a consequence of structural forces in historical motion and largely outside the conscious control of actors themselves. For Mann the internal dynamic of multi-power-actor civilizations "seems to have led toward its opposite, greater hegemonic centralization," and vice versa. Mann suggests this dialectic is the "core of world-historical development." The empires of domination, according to Mann, "unintentionally generated more diffuse power relations of two main sorts within their own interstices: (1) decentralized property-owning landlord, merchants and artisans . . . ; and (2) ideological movements." Mann's hypothesis is that "If these diffuse power relations continue to grow interstitially, a decentralized multi-power-actor civilization may result, either from the collapse of the empire or from its gradual metamorphosis" (Mann 1986).

In modern industrialized socioeconomic formations, the cycles are focused on a

> competitive struggle for the realisation of surplus value in the commodity circuit among separate bodies of capital within and between "national economies", mediated on the one hand by elaborate mechanisms of state intervention and regulation and on the other hand by the use of force in the arena of inter-state competition for the apportionment of the surplus value available for capture in the world market.
>
> (Gills 1987: 268)

Wallerstein maintains that in the modern world-system

> a state's strength correlates with the economic role of the owner–producers of that state in the world economy . . . the modern history of the state . . . [is] one long quest to create structures sufficently *strong* to defend the interests of one set of owner–producers in the world-economy against other sets of owner–producers as well as, of course, against workers.
>
> (Wallerstein 1980: 113–14)

So what is really changing is the configuration of relative power, measured in shares of the capture of surplus in the world market, between sets of owner–producers, backed by their respective state elites, which in turn affects the relative power positions of these state elites one to another.

However, unlike the traditional empires, direct competition between state elites and private elites in the modern "capitalist" state is not the main problem. Rather, it is intensification of the competition between private elites, and thus possibly also of their associated states, in the world market that drives hegemonic cycles in the modern era. Wallerstein assumes that capitalist states use both mercantilist and military techniques to assist their owner–producers to compete, but modern states do so most effectively if they can keep the costs of such assistance low enough not to "eat up the profits" (public finance). Each capitalist state's economic activity is more competitive if its political rule reflects "a balance of interests among owner–producers, such that a 'hegemonic bloc' (to use a Gramscian expression) forms the stable underpinnings of such a state" (Wallerstein 1980: 113–14). Much work on the political economy of neomercantilist or "capitalist developmental" states in east Asia emphasizes the importance of a symbiotic relationship between the state elite (including both political parties and the bureaucracy) and the private owner–producers with an aim of achieving competitiveness in the world market (Johnson 1982; Nester 1990).

In the premodern period of world history hegemonic transition on the regional level was primary. Regions alternated between Mann's two power configurations according to their own internal dialectic, though nevertheless affected by external factors as well. Synchronization of cycles between regions was an important feature of international historical change. If the cycles of accumulation and hegemonic power in one region were parallel to those in another, this rhythm obviously had an effect on their mutual interaction. They "rose and fell" together. Therefore their economic expansion and infrastructural investment phases could be mutually reinforcing. If these states came into conflict during their expansion phase the outcome might not be decisive, since both would be in possession of considerable staying power. In their declining phase neither might be capable of taking much advantage of the situation of the other, since both are weakened. The beneficiaries of such a synchronized crisis might be other external actors, from the periphery or hinterland, or another rival empire in a centralization phase. So-called "dark ages" result from a general crisis in which the beneficiary is more backward hinterland peoples and the result of the destruction and disintegration of empires is a degree of economic retrogression.

If, on the other hand, the cycles in one region were not parallel to another contiguous or contemporaneous regional empire, that rhythm would produce potentially very different systemic outcomes. For instance, in the case where region A is in a centralization phase and region B is in a decentralization phase, region A has considerable advantages. This pattern can be identified throughout world history and even as late as the later half of the nineteenth century, when Japan was in a centralization phase and the Qing empire in China was in a decentralization phase. This particular nineteenth-century historical conjuncture brought about a center shift in east Asia toward modern industrializing imperial Japan, which in turn affected the global hegemonic configuration. One of the easiest paths to hegemonic power is a conjuncture in which the major rivals are already weakened by either their own internal dynamic or a general crisis or war. Such a conjuncture was essentially the context for the post-1945 emergence of the Pax Americana.

In the modern era synchronization and conjuncture continue to be important elements of the spatial/temporal interface of historical change. However, the dynamic of alternation between variants of power configuration does not operate in exactly the same way as in the premodern era. The shift in the axis of class conflict is the key to this difference. In the premodern era the main form of class conflict was between state and private elites internally, and between state elites externally. In the modern era, the main form of class conflict internally is between producers and appropriating classes (both state and private) and between private owner–producers of different states, while internally the state and private elites are in a very close alliance. This internal alliance is directed at the producing classes and at rival blocs of private–state elites. However, in some periods of modern history global hegemonic coalitions are built that reduce conflict between rival blocs of private–state elites. This form seems to alternate with periods of more intense direct competition between rival blocs of private–state elites over shares of surplus in the world market.

To conclude, a shift to "hegemonic transition" as the central organizing concept of world history suggests some general hypotheses on the causes of periodic crises. Above all, the primary theme in these crises is always the overall character of the struggle for control of the surplus. The key factors in the onset of crises include the following: an excessive rate of the extraction of surplus (overextraction); an excessive concentration of control over capital (overconcentration); a failure of demand or expansion to stimulate growth (underconsumption); and a failure of investment in productive capacity (underinvestment) which may be reflected in the growth of elite consumption relative to social redistribution and productive investment – but is *always* "parasitic appropriation" as opposed to productive investment of capital. The above are often accompanied by a fiscal crisis of the state and a crisis of political authority. The end result is economic contraction and political fragmentation or dislocation, often accompanied by social rebellion and war.

A *general* world system crisis occurs when the combined cumulative layers of contradictions in the world system cannot any longer be sustained by the existing social, economic, and political arrangements of the world order – thus necessitating drastic transformation. The interaction of all the cycles in the system and the simultaneous occurrence of crises in such conjunctural moments generate a high disequilibrium within the world system, which destabilizes the whole. This disequilibrium is present in both the sphere of world trade and the sphere of political-military power. A shift in both the locus of accumulation and of hegemonic power in the world system is the result. This process is accompanied by economic, social, and political upheavals and usually by wars. A dramatic world hegemonic transition is thus both the result and the resolution of a general world crisis. It is a resolution in the sense that the old world order is eventually destroyed and conditions are laid down for the emergence of a new world order. Out of a crisis of accumulation comes the restored conditions for an expansion of accumulation and a new hegemonic order.

Most importantly, these concepts seem as relevant to today's global economic crisis and on-going world hegemonic reorganization as they are to 5,000 years of world system history. This again renders the supposed sharp historical break around 1500 AD less meaningful than some would have it.

REFERENCES

Abu-Lughod, Janet (1989) *Before European Hegemony: The World System A.D. 1250–1350*, New York: Oxford University Press.

Amin, Samir (1976) *Unequal Development: An Essay on the Social Formations of Peripheral Capitalism*, New York: Monthly Review Press.

—— (1989) *Eurocentrism*, London: Zed Press.

Anderson, Perry (1974) *Lineages of the Absolutist State*, London: New Left Books.

Braudel, Fernand (1982) *Civilization and Capitalism: 15th–18th Century*, New York: Fontana Press.

Chase-Dunn, Christopher (1989) *Global Formation: Structures of the World-Economy*, Oxford: Basil Blackwell.

Cox, Robert W. (1981) "Social forces, states and world orders: beyond international relations theory," *Millennium: Journal of International Studies* 10 (2): 126–55.

—— (1983) "Gramsci, hegemony and international relations: an essay in method," *Millennium: Journal of International Studies* 12 (2): 162–75.

—— (1987) *Production, Power and World Order*, New York: Columbia University Press.

Denemark, Robert A. (1990) "Theories of trade as a political variable," paper presented at the International Studies Association annual meetings, Washington, DC.

Denemark, Robert and Thomas, Kenneth (1988) "The Brenner–Wallerstein debate," *International Studies Quarterly* 32: 47–65.

de Ste Croix, G.E.M. (1981) *The Class Struggle in the Ancient Greek World*, London: Duckworth.

Doyle, Michael (1986) *Empires*, Ithaca, NY: Cornell University Press.

Eisenstadt, S.N. (1963) *The Political Systems of Empires*, Glencoe, IL: The Free Press.

Ekholm, Kasja and Friedman, Jonathan (1982) "Capital" imperialism and exploitation in ancient world-systems," *Review* 4 (1) (summer): 87–109.

Frank, Andre Gunder (1978) *World Accumulation 1492–1789*, New York: Monthly Review Press; London: Macmillan.

Gill, Stephen (1990) *American Hegemony and the Trilateral Commission*, Cambridge: Cambridge University Press.

—— (1991) "Historical materialism, Gramsci, and international political economy," in *The New International Political Economy*, ed. Craig N. Murphy and Roger Tooze, Boulder: Lynne Rienner, 51–75.

Gills, B.K. (1987) "Historical materialism and international relations theory," *Millennium: Journal of International Studies* 16 (2) (summer): 265–72.

—— (1989a) "Synchronisation, conjuncture, and centre-shift in east Asian international history", paper presented at the International Studies Association annual meetings, London (April).

—— (1989b) "International relations theory and the processes of world history: three approaches," in *The Study of International Relations: The State of the Art*, ed. Hugh C. Dyer and Leon Mangasarian, London: Macmillan, 103–54.

—— (1993) "The hegemonic transition in east Asia: a historical perspective," in *Gramsci and International Relations*, ed. Stephen Gill, Cambridge: Cambridge University Press, 186–212.

Gills, Barry and Palan, Ronen, "Introduction" in Palan, Ronen and Gills, Barry (eds) (forthcoming) *Transcending the State/Global Divide: The Neo-Structuralist Agenda in International Relations*, Boulder: Lynne Rienner.

Gilpin, Robet (1981) *War and Change in World Politics*, Cambridge: Cambridge University Press.

Goldstone, Jack A. (1991) *Revolutions and Rebellions in the Early Modern World*, Berkeley: University of California Press.

Higgott, Richard (1991) "Toward a nonhegemonic IPE: an antipodean perspective," in *The New International Political Economy*, ed. Craig N. Murphy and Roger Tooze, Boulder: Lynne Rienner, 97–128.

Johnson, Chalmers (1982) *MITI and the Japanese Miracle: The Growth of Industrial Policy, 1925–1975*, Stanford: Stanford University Press.

Kennedy, Paul (1987) *The Rise and Fall of the Great Powers*, New York: Random House.

Keohane, Robert O. (1980) "The theory of hegemonic stability and changes in international economic regimes, 1967–1977," in *Change in the International System*, ed. Ole Holsti *et al.*, Boulder: Westview Press, 131–62.

—— (1984) *After Hegemony: Cooperation and Discord in the World Political Economy*, Princeton: Princeton University Press.

Mandel, Ernest (1980) *Late Capitalism*, London: Verso.

Mann, Michael (1986) *The Sources of Social Power*, vol. 1: *A History of Power from the Beginning to* AD *1760*, Cambridge: Cambridge University Press.
Modelski, George (1987) *Long Cycles in World Politics*, London: Macmillan.
Modelski, George and Thompson, William R. (1988) *Seapower in Global Politics 1494–1993*, Basingstoke: Macmillan.
Nester, William R. (1990) *Japan's Growing Power over East Asia and the World Economy*, London: Macmillan.
Rader, Trout (1971) *The Economics of Feudalism*, New York: Gordon & Breach.
Rostow, W.W. (1971) *Politics and the Stages of Growth*, Cambridge: Cambridge University Press.
Silver, Morris (1985) *Economic Structures of the Ancient Near East*, London: Croom Helm.
Toynbee, Arnold (1946) *A Study of History* (Somervell abridgement), Oxford: Oxford University Press.
Van der Pijl, Kees (1984) *The Making of an Atlantic Ruling Class*, London: Verso.
Wallerstein, Immanuel (1974) *The Modern World-System*, vol. 1: *Capitalist Agriculture and the Origins of the European World-Economy in the Sixteenth Century*, New York: Academic Press.
—— (1980) *The Modern World-System*, vol. 2: *Mercantilism and the Consolidation of the World-Economy, 1600–1750*, New York: Academic Press.
—— (1988) *The Modern World-System*, vol. 3: *The Second Era of Great Expansion of the Capitalist World Economy, 1730–1840*, New York: Academic Press.
Wight, Martin (1977) *Systems of States*, ed. Hedley Bull, London: Leicester University Press in association with the London School of Economics.
—— (1978) *Power Politics*, New York: Holmes & Meier.

Part III

USING THE THEORY TO REANALYZE HISTORY

5

WORLD SYSTEM CYCLES, CRISES, AND HEGEMONIC SHIFTS, 1700 BC TO 1700 AD

Barry K. Gills and Andre Gunder Frank

> It has not been sufficiently appreciated that a theory of cyclical change also includes a theory of shifts of centres in space. In other words, expansion and contraction processes have rarely been stable. This may involve intra-regional shifts in influence between competing centres within a single core area . . . [and also] oscillations in intra-core hegemony are interspersed by much larger scale shifts in arrangements of centres and their peripheries. . . . It is ultimately the temporal that is seen to dominate over the spatial shifts in the waxing and waning of particular centres. This is generally true of all the long cycle theories.
>
> (Rowlands 1987: 10)

> Thus the cliche "rise and fall," which has been indiscriminately applied to nations, empires, civilizations, and now world systems is too imprecise. In the course of history, some nations, or at least groups of them, have gained relative power vis-a-vis others and have occasionally succeeded in setting the terms of their interactions with subordinates. . . . When this happens, it is called a "rise." Conversely the loss of an advantageous position is referred to as a "decline." . . . [There is a world system] rise when integration increases and . . . decline when connections along older pathways decay. Such restructuring is said to occur when *players who were formerly peripheral* begin to occupy more powerful positions in the system and when *geographic zones formerly marginal to intense interactions* become foci and even control centres of such interchanges.
>
> (Abu-Lughod 1989: 334)

INTRODUCTION TO ECONOMIC CYCLES AND POLITICAL HEGEMONY

In this paper, we explore the relationship between economic cycles and crises of accumulation and their relation to hegemonic shifts in the world system. Our basic theoretical approach is that the fundamental cyclical rhythms and secular trends of the world system should be recognized as having existed for some 5,000 years, rather than the 500 years that has become the conventional timespan in other world system and long-wave approaches (Wallerstein 1974; Modelski 1987). We have already set out this approach both jointly and individually elsewhere (Gills and Frank chapter 3 above; Frank 1990a, b, 1991; Gills 1989). Our focus is upon accumulation of surplus or capital accumulation as the "driving force" of the expansion and dynamic of the world system. We see accumulation to have been continuous but cyclical over several thousand years. We believe that the world process of capital accumulation has gone through identifiable economic crises, which have also been reflected in political crises of hegemony, and vice versa.

This paper seeks to explore this dynamic and these relationships throughout the Afro-Eurasian oikumene as far back as we can trace them. We believe that the pattern of world systemic accumulation, crises, and hegemonic shifts is also relevant to the present crisis and hegemonic decline in the world system.

In this introduction, we confine ourselves to a brief summary of some similarities and differences between our approach and some others. Our perspective and focus are on the world system and its history. For us, the essential defining characteristics of this world "system" are the area or "system" of effective surplus transfer and interpenetrating accumulation. As we discussed in chapter 3 above (p. 93):

> This means that surplus extraction and accumulation are "shared" or "interpenetrating" across otherwise discrete political boundaries. Thus, their elites participate in each others' system of exploitation vis-à-vis the producing classes. This participation may be through economic exchange relations via the market or through political relations (e.g. tribute), or through combinations of both. . . . This interpenetrating accumulation thus creates a causal interdependence between structures of accumulation and between political entities. Therefore the structure of each component entity of the world system is saliently affected by this interpenetration. . . . This transfer [of surplus or political competition for the same] means that no part of the world system would be as it was and is without its relations with other parts and the whole.

Wallerstein and others argue that continuous capital accumulation is the *differentiae specificae* of the modern world-capitalist system. Wallerstein (1988: 108) has also identified other fundamental characteristics of the capitalist world-system, which supposedly distinguish it from all other previous historical social systems. These are: 1) core–periphery structures, 2) A/B phases of economic expansion/contraction (or reduced growth), and 3) hegemony-rivalry. Wallerstein argues that this trinity represents a "pattern maintained over centuries . . . unique to the modern world-system. Its origin was precisely in the late fifteenth century" (1988: 108). Elsewhere, Wallerstein has further elaborated this trinity of characteristics into six points (Wallerstein 1989a: 8–10), and still further into twelve (Wallerstein 1989b: 3–4). However, this elaboration makes little difference. We would only place further stress on another characteristic of the world system, which Wallerstein and others have also observed. That is its "economy/polity contradiction." The economic interlinkages and integration of the world economy are always more intensive and extensive than its political ones, which tend to be more fragmented and territorially bounded. Other scholars, including Chase-Dunn (1986), Abu-Lughod (1989), and Wilkinson (1987, 1989), have also identified these same characteristics earlier than 1500 and outside Europe or a Eurocentric world system.

We agree that these three patterns characterize the modern period of the world system. However, we argue that they are equally appropriate for the world economy/system before 1500, whether fully "capitalist" or not. With specific reference to Wallerstein's "characteristics," this argument is spelled out in chapter 6 below. In general, we identify these same characteristics over several thousand years throughout the world system in all our above-cited work, and also again in the present chapter.

However, in this paper we examine this economy/polity contradiction by concentrating on exploring "only" how apparently world system wide economic expansion/contraction affects hegemonic political developments, and vice versa. Related center/periphery structures, for instance, will also be implicit or visible along the way; but they are not explicitly dealt with here.

Much of world system theory to date has focused on identifying a succession of hegemons since 1500. This succession is usually conceived as a succession from one single power to another, and from "like to like" in terms of the role or function of the hegemon in the world system. Even so, all analysts also recognize periods without a single hegemon and/or with acute rivalry among would-be hegemons. We argue in this chapter that this same pattern can and should be traced much farther back through world system history.

Moreover, the emphasis on a single hegemon and/or the succession from one to another is perhaps misplaced. Like Fernand Braudel and Janet Abu-Lughod, we find many periods without a single all-encompassing hegemon, but rather with a set of interlinking hegemonies, which characterizes the entire world system at any given point in time. However, if we concentrate exclusively on the role and properties of that one predominant hegemon, we may miss the character and importance of the entire set of the interlinking hegemonies. For example, "the world system of the thirteenth century was organized on a very different principle. Rather than a single hegemon, there were a number of coexisting 'core' powers, that both via conflictual and cooperative relations, became increasingly integrated" (Abu-Lughod 1989: 341).

Similarly in the sixteenth century, overemphasis on the role of Portugal in the world system leads to a distortion of the actual overall structure of interlinking hegemonies in that period. Portugal may have been a leading or predominant maritime power, but certainly also coexisted and interlinked with a set of other very significant hegemonies, such as the Hapsburgs, the Ottomans, the Mughals, and the Ming. Therefore, the fixation on a single hegemon, and the succession from it to another, may exaggerate the role and importance of that hegemon to the detriment of an understanding of the role of others. We can best understand the political organization of the world economy by taking into account this wider framework of interlinking hegemonies.

Before going on to discuss hegemonic transitions, it is useful to discuss briefly hegemony itself. In our view, hegemony should be defined with an emphasis on accumulation. In this way, the definition of hegemony is more general, and therefore perhaps more flexible. As discussed in chapter 3 above, hegemony may be defined as a

> hierarchical structure of the accumulation of surplus among political entities, and their constituent classes, mediated by force. A hierarchy of centres of accumulation and polities is established that apportions a privileged share of surplus, and the political economic power to this end, to the hegemonic center/state and its ruling/propertied classes.

From this perspective the primary object and principal economic incentive of a bid for hegemony is to restructure the regional if not overarching system of accumulation in a way that privileges the hegemon for capital/surplus accumulation. Therefore, hegemony is a means to wealth, a means to accumulation, and not merely or perhaps even primarily a means to "power" or to "order." The political and economic processes involved in accumulation and hegemony are so integral as to constitute a single process rather than two separate ones. Therefore we need not be drawn into debate over infrastructural versus superstructural determinants of change, nor need we attempt to separate the state (and states) from the social formation or to derive one from the other.

Only on some historic occasions can we say that, among these interlinked hegemonies, there was one hegemonic power which is in some sense in an overall predominant economic or military position. As noted earlier in chapter 3 we call that a "super-hegemon" which engages in "super-accumulation" in the world system. In that case, we can and must analyze hegemonic transitions on the scale of the world system as a whole. Super-accumulation is defined as "a privileged position . . . [in the world system as a whole], in which one zone of the world system and its constituent ruling-propertied classes is able to accumulate surplus more effectively and concentrate accumulation at the expense of other zones." This position of super-accumulator may be translated into further political (and economic) power via a bid for "super-hegemony" in the world system. That is, a super-hegemon is the hegemon among hegemons. The focus of super-accumulation has shifted over time and space in the development of the world system and it is indeed one of our central research goals to explain why and how these shifts occurred when and where they did, and to explore the effects on the world system as a whole. In the past, the focus of attention on transitions between modes of production deflected attention from the great significance of these hegemonic transitions. The concepts of super-accumulation and super-hegemony allow us to study both the single succession of super-accumulating super hegemons *and* the overall context of the interlinking hegemonies within which this occurs.

If coexisting, interlinked hegemonies, in their ups and downs, appear to be occurring simultaneously (i.e. "synchronized"), this might be evidence that there exists some connection among them and their respective patterns that may be more than the sum of the parts. The identification of correlations in events, like those which Frederick Teggart (1939) established between Rome and China (and which we shall examine below), may be empirical evidence also of their mutual connections and perhaps for the existence of a world system wide process and rhythm. This rhythm affects all parts of the world system simultaneously, though differently (not necessarily all at exactly the same moment), and thus accounts for the synchronization we observe. Therefore, this rhythm should be regarded as specific to the world system and not simply to the parts. Nor should this rhythm be regarded as a mere coincidence in parallel patterns among various regions.

Thus, a framework of analysis built upon understanding the mutual relations of the entire set of coexisting and interlinking hegemonies, generates a different set of questions than one based upon the idea of a succession of single hegemonies. In our suggested framework, the dynamic interaction of the constituent hegemonies is the central focus. In particular, we highlight how the "internal" cycles of each hegemonic structure are affected by and in turn affect the "internal" cycles of other hegemonies, and how these are related to any world system wide economic and political cycles. For instance, do different hegemonies go "up" or "down" together? If so, is there an explanation for this in an independent variable such as a world systemic economic cycle? If the cycles of the different hegemonies are not synchronized, then how does that affect each of them and the overall organization of the world system? For instance, if one hegemon is in a phase of consolidation and is centralizing accumulation and expanding while another is in a phase of disintegration, decentralization of accumulation, and contraction, how do they affect one another? Clearly, the overall set of interlinking hegemonies is always characterized over the long term by the dynamic "rise and fall" among the coexisting and yet rival hegemonies.

We suggest that there may be a very long-term and world system wide general rhythm in the pattern of hegemonic transition. At several points in world history we find a period of simultaneously consolidating hegemonies. That is, several hegemonies are expanding simultaneously over the scope of the world system as a whole. During such a period, there is usually a high level of infrastructural investment. This facilitates higher-intensity economic exchange both within and among these hegemonic entities. This economic exchange occurs through world system logistical interlinkages (Gills and Frank chapter 3 above). Thus, such periods of simultaneously expanding hegemonies seem to be generally characterized by economic expansion in the world economy as a whole. In contrast, hegemonic stability theory (Keohane 1980) argues that one stabilizer, one hegemon, provides a framework within which the rules of the international economy are enforced and that this situation facilitates economic order and expansion. However, Keohane also argues that once an international regime is established, cooperation among the principal powers in the world may continue (Keohane 1984). Thus Keohane, perhaps without realizing it, moves closer to a conception of interlinking hegemonies as the solution to the problems he confronted in the single-hegemon-succession model.

In the down phase, we find a period of simultaneously disintegrating hegemonies. In this period there is usually a general decline in infrastructural investment, and disruption and decline in the intensity of economic exchange. Logistical interlinkages suffer from disruption, decline, or underutilization. The period is characterized by economic and political contraction in many regions, and decline (or reduced economic growth) over the world system as a whole. In this period, there is usually also a series of social and political conflicts and wars related to this contraction and hegemonic disintegration. Hegemonic states become increasingly dysfunctional. Nonetheless, some hegemonic powers do develop in an otherwise generalized down phase. The cases we will identify in our historical review below lead us to suspect two things about these hegemonic powers. First, it might be argued that the ascendance of these hegemon(s) is due not only, or perhaps even not so much, to their own "internal" strength, as it is to the absolute and relative weakness of their neighbors and rivals. For instance, American postwar hegemony was built on the exhaustion of its rivals in the Second World War. This weakness may in turn be due in part to the inauspicious time for capital accumulation in that down phase. Secondly, the hegemonic power does not last very long, possibly also because of the generalized obstacles to capital accumulation during the down phase.

The world-historical rhythm, the world system cycle, is an alternation between these two phases. Moreover, the two phases may be causally linked, in such a way that the "up" phase conditions the eventual onset of the "down" phase, and in turn the "down" phase conditions the emergence of the following "up" phase. If that is the case, the world economy/system never "collapses" or "falls." Rather, it alternates cyclically between periods of relatively high (hegemonic) integration and concomitant economic prosperity, and periods of relatively less integrated hegemonies and concomitant economic retrogression or contraction.

Of course, we should not expect *all* the world (system) to have been going up and down at the same time. Indeed, it is precisely because *some* enterprises, regions, and states get out of phase that the transformation and development of and in the system can take place. In the modern period, and still today, some – indeed, often *the* – most privileged region and/or hegemonic power was/is unable to take full advantage of an expansionary A phase. Concomitantly, a peripheral or, more often, semiperipheral region is able to grow in a B phase of contraction or slow-down, that constrains the (previously) more central ones at whose expense the new one "develops." So it has been historically in the world system in medieval, classical, and ancient times. Therefore, we try below to identify such long A phases of expansion and B phases of contraction and their related hegemonic transitions in an exploratory and tentative way. Accordingly, also, for the time being a number of question marks must remain, especially with regard to the exact timing of the periods.

ANCIENT MARKETS, COMMODIFICATION, AND CAPITAL ACCUMULATION

Our entire analysis of the world system, and of hegemonic transitions within it, is derived from the competitive process of capital accumulation through markets, power, and a combination of both. However, the very existence of large-scale markets and capital accumulation before 1500, or even before 1800, is widely disputed. Nonetheless, other scholars have also claimed to demonstrate the existence of markets and capital accumulation in the ancient economy. The assertions of Karl Polanyi, Moses Finley, I.M. Diakanoff, and others regarding the nonexistence of markets and capital accumulation in the ancient economy are well known. However, Gordon Childe and other scholars in his tradition, as well as an increasing number of archaeologists like Robert Adams, have recently provided ever more empirical evidence and analytic arguments to demonstrate that market production, distribution, and accumulation are age-old.

Philip Kohl (1989) and also Morris Silver (1985) have critically re-examined the theses of Polanyi *et al.*, and found them to be inaccurate. Silver systematically scrutinizes key assertions by leading scholars like Polanyi. The latter contends that

> as late as the seventh century, no sign of market development was forthcoming in Greece. For at least a thousand years before that time, the continental empires of Mesopotamia, Asia Minor, Syria and Egypt and the seafarers of Ugarit and Crete carried on large scale trade without . . . the market as the regulator of supply and demand.
>
> (1981: xli, 146)

Silver argues instead that in the case of Assyrian trading stations in Anatolia, for instance, "the evidence on price formation . . . is fully consistent with the operation of market forces of the usual kind" (1985: 74). Likewise, Silver refutes both Polanyi (1981) and S.C. Humphreys (1978: 56) in regard to their view of the grain trade in the ancient economy (Mesopotamia for Polanyi, Rome for Humphreys) as primarily a function of the collection of taxes, tribute, and state redistribution. Silver assembles evidence from the primary sources that indicates the widespread existence of private warehouses and merchant middlemen in the ancient grain trade, including even in "redistributional" Egypt (1985: 80–4). Likewise, Silver finds evidence, following Piotr Steinkeller, for third-millennium concern loans made by private persons (1985: 84).

Diakanoff argues that "Commodity circulation did exist . . . but commodity production as such did not – i.e. there was no system having as its object the creation of profit by the production of commodities specifically for the market. Hence *no accumulation of capital took place*" (1974: 523). Silver bluntly responds that "The evidence points in the opposite direction" (1985: 107) and cites considerable evidence for the existence of production for export particularly in the archaic metals trade. Most importantly, he marshals evidence for widespread investment in capital goods in the ancient economy, motivated by market opportunities.

> Evidence is abundant of the accumulation of human and material capital, including circulating capital not directly involved in the production process – warehouses, specialized pack animals, navigational channels, and large, purpose-built cargo vessels – and fixed capital – tools of artisans and agriculturalists, machines for lifting water, irrigation channels, metallurgical facilities, industrial installations for wine, oil, cloth, and ceramics, terracing and other forms of land improvement and reclamation, specialized animal stock, and significant investments in tree and vine stock.
>
> (1985: 163)

Silver concludes his critique of Polanyi and others as follows:

> The relatively high costs of communicating, contracting, and transporting did not prevent the emergence in Near Eastern antiquity of recognizable markets for goods and factors of production. . . . The direct evidence for trade, occupational specialization, supply–demand-determined prices, investment in material and human capital, and other "modern" phenomena is uneven with respect to time and place but is, nevertheless, abundant. The availability of a large labour force for seasonal work in agriculture and irrigation canal repair testifies to significant economic differentiation and division of labour. Indirect evidence of the importance of trade is also provided by major transformations in the economies of Sumer, Pharaonic Egypt, and southern Babylonia to take advantage of new commercial opportunities.
>
> (1985: 165)

Similarly, Philip Kohl argues that "Farber's detailed study of prices during the Old Babylonian period shows a consistent pattern for the long-term fluctuations of the relative prices of basic commodities such as barley, oil, land, and slaves, revealing a sharp rise in prices and wages during the reign of Abieshuh (early seventeenth century B.C.)" (1989: 226). Commenting on Kohl, Joan Oates also observes that

> Recent works have increasingly emphasized the inadequacy of such views [as those of Polanyi] for interpreting the growing data for long-distance trade in the early historic periods in the Near East. Indeed, cuneiform studies now confirm the presence of a profit motive already in the mid-3rd-millennium-B.C. (pre-Sargonid) documents, while textual evidence from the immediately succeeding Sargonid period clearly supports the view that by this time there was a true commodity market. Recent analyses also recognize the importance of entrepreneurial activity together with the interdependence of trade and production. Thus the main theses of Kohl's article are not new, but, his intelligent and perceptive contribution [on which we will rely below] is much to be welcomed.
>
> (1978: 408)

HISTORICAL REVIEW OF EVIDENCE ON WORLD SYSTEM CYCLES OF ACCUMULATION AND HEGEMONY

Thus, there is ample ground to enquire into the process of capital accumulation in ancient times. The same goes for the possible cycles of accumulation and of hegemony and their interrelations. The question arises to what period of history our approach is applicable. To answer that question, we rely on what Frank calls John K. Fairbank's second rule, which helps avoid arbitrary and conventionally mistaken beginnings: "The rule seems to be, if you want to study the mid-period . . . , begin at the end of it and let the problems lead you back. *Never* try to begin at the beginning. Historical research progresses backward, not forward" (1990a: 162–4). Only time and diligent effort will tell how far back this historical research can progress. However, history itself did develop forward in time; and so should our exposition of it. If only for the sake of convenience, then, we will begin our historical account in the third millennium BC. However, this historical review can be no more than an exploratory and suggestive preliminary effort by nonspecialists. No doubt, specialists in various periods and regions will be able to find fault with some of our datings, inclusions, and exclusions. We hope they will – and thereby also help reformulate some of our questions or even our putative "certainties."

The Bronze Age period, 3000 to 1000 BC

Elsewhere, we have provisionally traced the origins of the world system back to the interlinking hegemonies in the confluence of Mesopotamia and Egypt in the third millennium BC. These have traditionally been regarded as self-contained systems, whose development was only internally determined. Yet,

> during a short time around 3000 BC, apparently sophisticated, complex systems . . . appeared across an area stretching from the Nile and Aegean in the west to central Asia in the east. It is not impossible that these regional developments may represent a loosely integrated and related series of changes . . . that may in part be attributable to an interplay between local and external forces. In this regard, one possible effect of their outcome may have been a "primitive accumulation of capital" and its role as a force for such change. Such conclusion would include a measure of "market forces" in these periods. . . . Between the late fourth and third millennia, . . . faint, highly buffered "market mechanisms" may have operated for different periods of time and in different regions along these networks.
>
> (Marfoe 1987: 25, 30, 34)

Indeed, we could argue that the later states system of pre-Sargonid Mesopotamia was in fact also a framework of interlinking hegemonies, which included such important locally hegemonic cities as Mari, Ebla, Elam, Lagash, Ur, Nippur, Kish, Uruk, and Akkad. It was out of the context of the hegemony-rivalry process among these interlinking hegemonies that the Akkadian empire emerged. In Sumer, agricultural yields declined over a long period from 2400 to 1700 BC; and (consequently?) population also decreased after 1900 BC. Then, the neighboring Harappan civilization in the Indus Valley declined, to virtual extinction, by 1500 BC, after having maintained trade and other relations during its maturity with Akkadian Mesopotamia. On the other side, Egypt suffered a "time of troubles," low floods, starvation, political fragmentation, and foreign incursions from 2250 to 1950 BC. We do not, and may never, know just how connected these events were. However, Philip Kohl suggests that "if one refuses to despair, the only way to proceed is first to comprehend the whole area that was engaged in some form of regular interregional exchange during the Bronze Age" (1989: 232), which included southern Central Asia, the Harappan civilization in the Indus Valley, the Persian and Anatolian plateaus, Mesopotamia between them, and Egypt. Among these, "profit-motivated trade extended far beyond the political borders of any state and connected . . . [all of these] into a single world system" (1989: 227):

> Foreign trade in the mid-third millennium was an exceedingly complex process, involving the movement of finished luxury commodities, raw materials, and staple products, and was probably conducted both by state agents and by private entrepreneurs. . . . It does show that developments in southwestern Asia were not limited to the alluvial plains and that widely separated communities were linked by complex, well-defined exchange networks.
>
> (Kohl 1978: 466)

A and B phases, 3000–2000 BC?

However, "the period of maximum foreign trade in finished products and raw materials prior to the first attempts at direct political control did not last long" (Kohl 1978: 473). Kohl cites Oppenheim to stress that for Mesopotamian Sumer "the frequency and intensity of contact had reached a peak early in the third millennium B.C." (465–6) After that,

> "International" relations changed over the greater Middle East during the first half of the third millennium with the collapse of the proto-Elamite "hegemony" in southern and Central Iran . . . according to archaeological evidence from Central Asia, Baluchistan, southeastern Iran and the Indus Valley . . . across the Iranian plateau, in the Gulf area (particularly the Oman peninsula), Mesopotamia, the Anatolian plateau and the Caucasus. . . . But it is unclear what happened to foreign relations in the later third and early second millennia with the collapse of Akkadian rule and the subsequent rise of and demise of the highly centralized Ur III dynasty. Dales (1976) explained the collapse of proto-urban settlements throughout the Indo-Iranian borderlands (during the so-called urban phase) as due to the cessation of long-distance overland trade and development of direct maritime trade between Mesopotamia and the Indus Valley. His theory only represents an unproven hypothesis but deserves serious consideration.
>
> (Kohl 1984: 242)

The competition for control over resources was inherent in the organization of trade. Thus conflict is generated around the attempt by each power to subordinate rivals and thereby establish their own hegemony (Childe 1942: 102; Gills and Frank chapter 3 above) from the earliest period in the world system. The organization of trade and the effects of hegemonic conflict to that end can in itself represent a "contradiction" and an obstacle to further economic expansion. Too much conflict can be mutually exhaustive and economically ruinous. Too much domination by one hegemon may bring an increase in trade, but the benefits of the trade may be very disproportionate to the members of the system. That is, the hegemon may reign parasitically while other areas suffer deprivation. Childe recognizes the organization of accumulation as a contradiction.

Thus, in Childe's theory, "If the economy of the Early Bronze Age cities could not expand internally owing to the over-concentration of purchasing power . . . the urban economy must – and did – expand externally" (1942: 139). Childe explains the development of center–periphery relations through the need for the center to induce the periphery to render up a surplus. The task of the center, in trade relations, was to "persuade their possessors to exchange the needed raw materials for manufactures" (1942: 140). According to Childe this trade was from the beginning a political trade between elites in the center and elites in the periphery.

Childe provides a fascinating economic explanation for the creation of the first world system imperium under Sargon of Akkad. First, he points out the underlying economic rationale of all Sargon's key conquests, e.g. "reaching the Cedar Forest (Lebanon)," and the "mountain of Silver" (Taurus), and causing the ships of Meluk, Magan (Oman, source of copper) and Dilmun (Bahrein?) "to anchor at the quay in front of Agade." Sargon's son continued the project of economic imperialism by taking possession of "as far as the Silver mines and from the Mountains of the Lower Sea he carried off their stones" (1942: 142–3). His grandson Naram Sin broke through to the Mediterranean in Syria by destroying the power of Ebla. Childe argues that his seizure of vast booty and employing it to adorn the capital and pay the armies constituted "the forcible distribution of the wealth hoarded in conquered treasuries" which thus "spread purchasing power in Mesopotamia. Production was thereby stimulated. . . . War captives swelled the supply of service producers. . . . Merchants could make profits. . . . The middle class profited from imperialism. . . . Money economy spread" (1942: 143).

Such economic imperialism was possible for the center by virtue of its superior metal weaponry, division of labor, political organization, and the organization of trade. It placed a constant systemic pressure on the hinterlands and the periphery to maintain at least a defense capability in military terms, and at the maximum to emulate the center in economic and political organization, and perhaps even innovate in order to surpass the center.

Thus the territorial space of the world system expanded. As Childe formulates it:

> As a result of one activity or another on the part of the original nuclei, new cities, new centres of civilization arose around the original foci and beyond them barbarians abandoned neolithic self-sufficiency . . . And of course each Bronze Age city or township became itself a new centre of demand irradiating, if only by reflected light, an ever-widening hinterland.
>
> (1942: 144)

The world economy then already encompassed barbarian Europe, as well as West Asia, Central Asia, and even India and perhaps China. Expansion in this period may be attested to by the increase in the number of cities. However, this period of simultaneous consolidation culminated in Hittite–Egyptian rivalry over Syria and the Levant, which was at that time the key node of the logistical interlinkages in the world system.

The recurrent waves of invasion out of Inner Asia into the belt of civilizations around its perimeter may provide us with a clue as to possible cycles in early world system history, which extend back even into the archaic period. Childe argues that soon after 2300 BC, the hegemony of Akkad and the great state structures of Egypt and Indus and the economic systems they dominated "disintegrated." The era of prosperity was followed by "dark ages" during which Gutian invaders ruled in Mesopotamia. Childe says this was a period in which "imperial monopolies" were overthrown and "hoarded wealth collected in treasures was brutally restored to circulation, or simply annihilated, great households were broken up" (1942: 151). In Egypt too, the collapse of central state power of the Old Kingdom gave way to decentralized power and concomitant economic chaos and contraction. But these did not constitute total collapse, and merchant classes and trade recovered, as eventually did the states. The city of Ur established a wide hegemony and the "security for foreign trade" to allow economic recovery and expansion. However, this imperial recovery was eclipsed also in a period marked by a wave of invasion from the hinterland. The Amorites displaced the Sumerian ruling classes. A second "dark age," that is, a period of economic dislocation and contraction, took hold.

The phases in Egypt and Mesopotamia were not synchronized, and so just as Ur collapsed, Middle Kingdom Egypt recentralized and entered a period of economic expansion. Some two centuries later, Egypt again succumbed to disintegration and invasion by the Hyksos. The next recovery in Mesopotamia accompanied the Amorite hegemony of the city of Babylon, which was however in turn overturned by new invasions of Kassites, Hittites, and the Elamites, and a new period of economic contraction followed, accompanied by a multipolar system of interlinking hegemonies.

B phase, 1700–1500/1400 BC

In the period 1700–1500 or 1400 BC, the world system seems to have undergone a simultaneous crisis of the interlinking hegemonies then in existence. While the Hittites and Kassites conquered Anatolia and Mesopotamia, the Hurrians and Hyksos overran the Levant and Egypt, the Aryans inundated the Indus, where Harappan civilization was on its last legs. At the same time, the Shang charioteer aristocracy established itself in north China. This period of simultaneous disintegration of hegemonies was accompanied by inevitable economic disruptions. Silver notes the onset of the "dark age" (1600–1347 BC) and says that "During this era urban life and legal documents relating to private commercial activities decline steeply" (1985: 161). The dark age is also marked by the "disappearance. . . . of all vestiges of social reform – or experiments – of the Hammurabi era" after his death about 1750 BC (Oppenheim and Reiner 1977: 159).

A-phase expansion, 1400–1200 BC

The next period, and especially the fourteenth–thirteenth centuries BC, was another period of economic recovery. The dominant but interlinking hegemonies were the Hittite empire, based in Anatolia and dominant in northern Mesopotamia, and the empire of New Kingdom Egypt. The period was clearly marked by the prominence of interlinking hegemonies, including Babylon, Assyria, and Mitanni, all of which took a full part in the well-developed diplomatic discourse of the period. There was for a time something like a concert of powers among these interlinking hegemonies. The Mycenaean trade supplanted the Minoan in the east Mediterranean. The application of iron to the weapons industry facilitated a new period of hegemonic expansion.

B-phase crisis, 1200–1000 BC

The next world systemic crisis came with the wave of the "sea peoples" and other invaders during the especially important "dark age" in the twelfth and eleventh centuries BC. Both Egypt and the Hittites had employed mercenaries in their earlier wars, thus familiarizing hinterland warriors with both the wealth and the weapons of the center. Childe says, "So the Bronze Age in the Near East ended round about 1200 BC in a dark age. . . . Not in a single State alone but over a large part of the civilized world history itself seems to be interrupted; the written sources dry up, the archaeological documents are poor and hard to date" (1942: 185). As Liverani observes, this scarcity of surviving documentation "is not fortuitous . . . [but] is itself an effect of the crisis (eclipse of scribal schools and the palace administrations)" (1987: 71).

At the same time, the Mycenaeans in Greece and the Levant were overrun by new waves of invasions, which included the Dorians, Aramaeans, and Phoenicians. The Hittite empire disintegrated. The Kassite dynasty in Babylonia collapsed to Chaldeans and Aramaeans. After the reign of Nebuchadnezzar I (1124–1103 BC) began the "dark age of Mesopotamia." A century later, "between 1024 and 978 B.C. Babylon had seven kings divided between three dynasties in a 46 year period" (Roux 1966: 260). In Egypt, Libyan mercenaries and Nubians seized power. Even in distant China, the Shang gave way to the more barbarian Zhou. "Nevertheless the continuity of civilization [in/of the world system?] was not completely or universally interrupted" (Childe 1942: 185).

Even though Mario Liverani says of himself, "I belong to that group of scholars who consider . . . internal factors . . . to be pre-eminent," he nonetheless recognizes that "[in] the collapse of Near Eastern civilization at the end of the Bronze Age . . . it is true that the crisis is rather extended and takes place at roughly the same time over a large area" and that in his particular area of study "at the apex of the crisis . . . a shock of external origin is certain for the Syrian coast" (1987: 69).

Kohl aptly summarizes:

> The original Bronze Age world systems did not simply collapse, but left a complex, web-like legacy of political, economic, and, in the broadest sense, cultural interconnections which, in turn, were acted upon and influenced later historical developments.
>
> (1989: 238)

The Iron Age axial and classical periods, 1000 BC to 500 AD

By about 1000 BC the economic recovery of the region was under way again and there followed a period of considerable economic expansion and hegemonic consolidation. The Iron Age was spreading, and in its first 500 years of expansion, more was achieved than in the previous 1500 years of the Bronze Age, according to Childe (1942: 187). The world economy also achieved a new and higher level of integration. The world system expanded territorially on a new scale to encompass a vast hinterland in Eurasia with deeper penetration of the periphery than before. This was indeed the Eurasian oikumene.

A-phase expansion, 1000–800 BC

During this period of economic expansion beginning about 1000 BC, the Phoenician cities and their oligarchies of merchant–princes, who supplanted their Canaanite predecessors, benefitted considerably. They took control from the moribund Mycenaeans and exercised at least commercial (core) hegemony over the markets of the Aegean, which permitted the Phoenicians to accumulate great wealth in the process. Industrial production, financial and trading power, were concentrated in Tyre, Sidon, and other Phoenician cities of the Syrian–Levantine coast, which were ruled by commercial interests.

During this same period after 1000 BC, politically the main beneficiary from the confusion and weakness of the previous system-wide crisis on the mainland was the emerging Assyrian empire. The Assyrians came to dominate northern Mesopotamia. Nonetheless, Assyrian power was under challenge from two rivals.

> There was a shift in the centre of gravity of exporting countries. Assyria, which was a great consumer, had no iron mines; for a time, especially during the earlier half of the eighth century B.C., it was denied access to the mining centres of the southern coast of the Black Sea and Transcaucasus by the neighbouring kingdom of Urartu. Inevitably it turned its attention to Iran. . . . [which obtained this metal from regions inaccessible to Assyria].
>
> (Ghurshman 1954: 88)

Thus,

> The first half of the first millennium B.C. was a turning point in human history. The centre of "world politics" or of the age shifted . . . [from alluvial valleys in the south] more to the north . . . that the struggle for world power was centred . . . [on] three principal actors in the drama: the Semitic Assyrians with their vast empire; Urartu, a powerful kingdom of Asiatic origin, tenacious opponents of the Assyrians . . . and finally the Aryans, the Iranians who, after a long and arduous struggle, triumphed over their two adversaries and, with the spoils, founded the first World Empire [under the Achaemenid kings from the fifth century onwards].
>
> (Ghurshman 1954: 75)

B phase, 800–550 BC

The cities and states of northern India still developed with the spread of iron technology from the eighth century BC onward. However, elsewhere by the eighth century some economic expansion seems to have slowed down again, and by the mid-seventh Assyria was seriously overextended and in decline. The Assyrian empire collapsed in the late seventh century BC. The Massagetae drove the Scythians westward through Central Asia and these in turn pushed the Cimmerians and the Medes west- and southward at the expense of the Assyrians. This gave way to a period of rivalry among the Babylonians, Medes, and Persians. In China, the pretense of formal Zhou hegemony gave place to independent states which entered into a new phase of rivalry.

The expansion of Greek and Phoenician colonization during this period might be taken as an indicator of the economic pressure these areas were under. For instance, Carthage was founded c. 814 BC, after Tyre came under increasing pressure from Assyrian tribute demands. The economic decline of Tyre and other Phoenician cities of the core is a feature of this period. Likewise, Greek colonization was a feature of increasing competition and market saturation. Hesiod speaks of "potter competing with potter and carpenter with carpenter."

The interrelated integration of distant regions into a single world system was reaching a new stage again. "The idea of humanity as a single society, all of whose members owe one another common moral obligations, is an ideological counterpart of an international economy based on the interchange of commodities between all its parts, such as became effectively manifest in the second phase of the Iron Age," as Childe put it (1942: 212). Perhaps it was also this increased new economic and ideological unity which stimulated the rise and spread of new universalist religions across Eurasia. This was the beginning of what Karl Jaspers called the Axial Age of interconnection and transformation.

A phase, 550–450 BC

Teggart (1939) already observed the temporal "correlation" in the rise and subsequent spread of several major new world religions in the sixth century BC. Among them were Zoroastrianism, Jainism, Pythagorianism, Buddhism, Confucianism, Taoism, Ionian philosophy, the Hebrew prophets Ezekiel and second Isaiah. McNeill (1964: 338) observed that the rise of these religious movements may have been a response to common needs, such as protection from exploitation by the propertied classes and the state elite. Indeed, the emergence of universalist religions may also be an indication of the high level of real economic interlinkage and perhaps the attainment of a new level or stage of economic integration, which had already characterized the previous period.

The sixth to fifth centuries BC were another period of economic and political expansion. The expansionary impulse seems to have appeared first in Greek cities such as Aegina, Corinth, and the Ionian cities, which introduced mass production of cheap but high-quality commodities for export using factory-production techniques. The wealth of Lydia, and its introduction of coinage, is another indication of this expansion. The Greek core was ascending as the Phoenician core was declining. This period witnessed the rise of the Achaemenid Persian empire, which stabilized much of West Asia by reimposing a more unified political order in that part of the world economy and system. The Achaemenids from Darius to Xerxes achieved at least a regional position of "super-accumulation" in the world system, on the basis of the imperial tribute system. The Persian empire exceeded even the Assyrian in the degree to which it succeeded in incorporating the most important economic zones of the world system.

There was at this time a shift in the center of gravity of the world economy of very great historical importance. The key area of logistical interlinkage in the world economy/system shifted from Syria and the Levant to Central Eurasia. Achaemenid control of Central Asian cities, such as the great city of Bactra, and the north-west India trading center of Taxila were very important elements in consolidating Persian super-accumulation. The Persian investment in infrastructure included the 1,677-mile Royal Road, which Darius built from Ephesus to Susa, and the road from Babylon to Ortospana (near Kabul). Persian cities, like their Assyrian predecessors, were cosmopolitan; and its armies were multinational.

> It was in this period that the great caravan cities of Syria – Aleppo, Hama, Homs (Emesa), and Damascus, in particular – truly came into their own, receiving goods from the Silk Road as well as spices and perfumes from Arabia's Incense Road and other luxuries brought by sea from India. Arameans . . . were such active traders on these caravan cities that their speech became the commercial language.
>
> (Franck and Brownstone 1986: 65)

The successful accumulating classes of the sea-faring merchant cities also stimulated the many significant scientific advances and the invention of the alphabet and of coinage in this period. Coinage and the prevalence of manufactures in trade, conducted via cheap maritime transport, among these cities made the manufacture of mass-consumption commodities for the market more prevalent than elsewhere. Increasingly export manufacture occurred in factory workshops under the control of a capitalist utilizing slave labor, the cheapest form of labor vailable. The Persian imperial economy was more centralized and accumulation by the imperial state placed a heavy burden on the economy as a whole.

In Persia wealth was increasingly concentrated in the great estates of the nobility, and mass consumption through purchase in the market was limited. Personal debt increased in these economies and real wages fell until it reached crisis proportions in the fourth century BC. The Persian empire sought to compensate by making use of the wealthy cities and their money economy to the "West," as in the case of Sardis, the Ionian cities, and the Phoenician cities; but the Persians failed to complete the conquest. In particular, the Persians recruited the Phoenician fleets of Tyre and Sidon in their repeated attempts to subdue the western Greeks. It is often overlooked that the battle between Persia and Hellas was also a commercial war between Hellas and Phoenicia. For instance, when the Athenian fleet crushed the Phoenician–Persian fleet at Salamis in 480 BC, Athens immediately seized control of the Hellespont and reopened its vital corn trade in the Black Sea.

Nonetheless, it is clear that Persian hegemony was also interlinked with Athenian. At the same time, the Greek regions in the West had generated a surplus of warriors and the export of mercenaries to the East. In the West also, the prevalence of slave labor acted as a constraint on expansion of domestic demand but stimulated external expansion – toward the East. Geoffrey de Ste Croix explains the "natural foreign policy" of Athens as "driven by her unique situation, as an importer of corn on an altogether exceptional scale, towards a policy of 'naval imperialism', in order to secure her supply routes" from the East (1981: 292–3).

B phase, 450–350 BC

Athens profited most from the fifth-century empire. Nonetheless, it also declined when it failed to raise sufficient revenues to sustain its naval forces. Widespread rebellions broke out in the Athenian empire after 450 BC. Then, as de Ste Croix argues, Greek democracy, as represented by Athens, did not just "die out." It was "deliberately extinguished by the joint efforts of the Greek propertied classes, the Macedonians and the Romans" (1981: 293). Rostovtzeff (1941) argued that the economic decline of the cities from the late fifth century can be explained mainly as a result of a contraction of the foreign market for Greek exports due to the diffusion of industry in the periphery and thus to import substitution. However, de Ste Croix questions this explanation and instead maintains that the answer may lie in the class struggles of the period. That is, "not so much that Greece as a whole was poorer in the fourth century as that the wealthy class was now able to appropriate a greater share of the small available surplus than in the late fifth century" (1981: 294–5). He cites the growing export of Greek mercenaries in the fourth century as evidence of their inability to make a living at home. In this crisis in Greece, "the obvious solution, urged early in the fourth century by Gorgias and Lysias, and most presently by Isocrates . . . was a grand Greek crusade against the Persian Empire, which would wrest from the barbarians enough land in Asia to provide a comfortable livelihood for these men and any other Greeks who were in need" (1981: 295). The Persian–Greek wars were the result. They presaged a hegemonic transition in the eastern Mediterranean.

In a real sense the resolution of the crisis in the Hellenic economy and its class struggles spilled over into a momentum that led to the conquest of Persia, which was further testimony to their intimate interlinkage. The fourth century BC was awash with class conflict in the cities of the West, and with popular demands for the cancellation of debts and redistribution of land. These were symptomatic of an underlying economic contraction or slow-down in expansion which precipitated increased class conflict. Rostovtzeff characterized the fourth century as one marked by increased proletarianization, landlessness, unemployment, and food shortage. It was marked by a contraction in the market for manufacturers and the ruin of "free" petty producers. Wealth was overconcentrated in the hands of the commercial and landed ruling classes. Livy notes a series of famines in Italy in 490, 477, 456, 453, 440, and 392 BC. The Celts invaded Italy and sacked Rome, while setting up the kingdom of Galatia in Asia Minor. The hegemonic disintegration of this period is in evidence from the Peloponnesian wars and the successful revolt of Egypt against Persia c. 400 BC and the breakaway of the Indus from the Persian empire c. 380 BC.

We have been (mis)taught to view this period and its wars only through the eyes of the Greeks, who were subsequently but mistakenly denominated as "western". Bernal (1987) and Amin (1989) have recently and justly criticized this Eurocentric perspective. Historically, of course, Greece was a (semi-?)peripheral extension of West Asia; and during this period the Greeks were oriented eastward to the then hegemonic center in Persia. The "heroic" resistance of Athens and the Delian League to Persian conquest, with funds from the silver mines of Laurion and the treasure of the trading cities, was part of a hegemonic transition and a preface to a subsequent hegemonic shift after the Greek cities were unified under Macedonian hegemony. The crisis made way for the new "orientalizing" of Hellas under the Macedonian monarchy, the defeat of democracy and the subsequent spread of Hellenistic ruling classes to all of the former domains of the Persian empire. Alexander destroyed the Phoenician economic rival Tyre and imposed Greek domination over the area. Thus, the great Persian imperium was overturned by the challenge from the (semi-)periphery in the "West." In this manner, the economic and social crisis of the West found a temporary resolution in the conquest of the East.

A phase, 350–250/200 BC

The next phase of expansion included the reconquest of the Persian empire by Alexander the Great. It was intended to be the prelude to an even larger hegemonic project, which would incorporate the Indian cities of the Indus as well as the Roman and Carthaginian spheres in the west Mediterranean. The logic of this plan was to extend the Persian imperium even further to incorporate the economic zones of the West under one all-encompassing super-regional hegemonic unity in the world system. Alexander's campaign in Central Eurasia, and in Bactria and north-west India in particular, indicates once again the importance of control over this area. Alexander tried to establish transregional super-hegemonic power as the basis for would-be transregional super-accumulation. Alexander's political project died with him in 323 BC, and his empire suffered subsequent political fragmentation into three separate political spheres of interest. Nonetheless, much of the infrastructural interlinkage was maintained and strengthened; and economic expansion appears to have continued. There were renewed hegemonic consolidations. In Hellenistic domains a mixture of the polis and oriental depotism was concocted to resolve class contradictions and facilitate economic expansion. Greek science was applied to increases in productivity as never before.

In China, the process of rivalry, accompanied by economic expansion and the introduction of new administrative and productive techniques, culminated in a hegemonic consolidation in the third century BC by the Qin dynasty. Moreover, trade contacts between China and India also increased during this period.

The late fourth and third centuries BC were a period of hegemonic consolidation also in northern India. The Mauryans began their rise in the fourth century BC. However, their vast empire consolidated hegemony in northern India and the Ganges basin in the third century BC, after the failure of Alexander. The Mauryans gained control of the Indus from Seleucus Nicator, gained control of the key trade city of Taxila, and extended their influence into Central Asia up to the borders of Bactria. The Mauryans constructed the 2,600-mile Great Trunk Road from the strategic city of Pataliputra on the Ganges to the far north-west, near the city of Taxila. The state maintained the infrastructure of roads, signposts, guardhouses, water wells, causeways, ferries, etc., and shelters were provided for traders and other travelers.

B phase, 250/200–100/50 BC

However, the Mauryan empire had declined by the beginning of the second century. Then, control over western Central Eurasia passed from Mauryan and Seleucid hegemony to the independent Bactrian kingdom. Bactria stood at the hub of the economic exchange that included Taxila, Antioch, and Alexandria. In eastern Central Asia and China and beginning around 200 BC, the struggles for territory and influence among the Chinese, Xiongnu, and Yuezhi would soon exert effects also into western Central Asia and westward, as we will observe below. However, we should note that China under the Han dynasty experienced a period of hegemonic consolidation and economic expansion in this period and is therefore not synchronized with the economic B phase in areas to its west.

In the Mediterranean region also, the second century BC was again marked by signs of crisis and contraction and slower expansion of the market. In Egypt, the second century was characterized by all the signs of economic decline, such as overtaxation, official corruption, increased debt, and unrest and brigandage. The Rosetta stone characterizes the period by: "pressure of taxes, rapid accumulation of arrears and concomitant confiscations, prisons full of criminals and debtors, public and private, many fugitives scattered all over the country and living by robbery, compulsion applied in every sphere of life" (Childe 1942: 254). In Greece and Italy free peasantry was declining in favor of capitalist landowners. Prices rose relative to wage increases. Class struggle in the Hellenistic hegemonies came into interaction with the power of Rome, an interlinked hegemony. Rome's own internal class struggles were resolved by recourse to imperialism and expansion of the market in barbarian western Europe. Slave revolts occurred widely in Attica, Macedonia, Delos, Sicily, Pergamon, and in Italy. The power of the Roman oligarchy proved great enough to quell unrest in Italy, override the land reform of the Gracchi, and interject itself into the political affairs of the declining Hellenistic states of the East. The logic of Roman political power moved inexorably toward another "orientalizing" solution in the defeat of the lower classes and the centralization of imperial and monarchic power. The widespread use of slave labor accelerated by Rome's imperial expansion placed a further obstacle to increase in productivity through scientific innovation of labor-saving technology.

It was at the end of, and out of, this B-phase crisis that Rome emerged as the predominant, but by no means the sole, hegemon in this part of the world system. Geoffrey de Ste Croix (1981: 328) argues that "sheer rapacity" for surplus extraction was a key motive for Roman expansionism. In his view, the purpose of Roman rule was to increase the rate of exploitation and to concentrate capital accumulation in the hands of the Roman oligarchy. The effect of Roman rule was not a great profit for the Roman state as such, but rather a tremendous profit for private Roman citizens acting on behalf of Rome. In the second and first centuries BC Rome parasitically exploited its new domains. The civil wars, financed with wealth accumulated from the empire, culminated in a true centralized bureaucratic imperial state made possible by Julius Caesar and consolidated by Octavian.

A phase, 100/50 BC–150/200 AD

The late first century BC and the first and second centuries AD again were a period of major economic expansion, international trade and political relations, as well as interhegemonic rivalries. The Roman empire entered a period of internal (hegemonic) peace and economic prosperity and expansion. By the first century AD, the entire world system was politically organized into an unbroken belt of interlinking hegemonies, stretching from Rome in the Mediterranean basin, to Parthia in Mesopotamia and Persia, the Kushan in Central Asia, and the Han in China. Only northern India was not under a single hegemonic state, but Kushan commercial influence extended deep into the Gangetic plain. Indians expanded into "Farther India" in Southeast Asia.

> Among the various explanations that have been proposed to account for the intensification of Indian trading activity in Southeast Asia at about the beginning of the Christian era, perhaps the most credible is that formulated by George Coedes (1964: 44–49), who attributes the reorientation of Indian commercial interests to "changing political conditions in the Mediterranean and Central Asia" which created a shortage of gold in India, which the Indians sought to meet by looking for gold in Southeast Asia.
>
> (Wheatley 1975: 232–3)

For this period and the Afro-Eurasian oikumene as a whole, Hodgson noted that

> mercantile trade was extended and industry fostered; for instance, both the import of silk from China and its working within the empire. Cities increased in wealth and importance; [after 226] the Sassanian monarchs were notable as founders of cities and protectors of trade. The mercantile development represented in part a response to the ever quickening pattern of trade throughout the Afro-Eurasian Oikoumene. Direct trade by sea and land between China and the Indo-Mediterranean regions opened up. . . . Trade elsewhere in the Southern Seas (the seas of the Indian Ocean and eastward) had likewise expanded, as had trade both north of the Mediterranean in Europe and south across the Sahara. The people from the Nile to the Oxus not only took full advantage of their crossroads. They helped develop new fields of trade.
>
> (1974, I: 142)

The Parthians built an empire in the first century BC that stretched from the Euphrates to the borders of Bactria, and briefly controlled Taxila in the early first century AD. They were later faced with the competition of the Tocharians (the Yuezhi), who may have set up the Kushan empire, which took control of Taxila in 60 AD.

It is still in dispute whether it was the above-mentioned Yuezhi themselves or others whom they in turn pushed south-eastward who founded the Kushan empire. It is certain, however, that in the second and first centuries BC, the Central Asian Xiongnu had conflicts with their neighbors both to the east and to the west. It is in dispute "who started" the conflict to the south-east with the Chinese. (Suzuki [1968] traces the ups and downs between 200 BC and 200 AD of Xiongnu relations with the Chinese.) These responded by building the Great Wall, but then taking control of the Tarim basin and the "silk road" through it well beyond that wall, and also by seeking an alliance against the Xiongnu with the latter's neighbors to the west, the Yuezhi. Nonetheless, or perhaps in part therefore, beginning about 177 BC under Meodun, the Xiongnu drove the Yuezhi still further westward as far as present-day Afghanistan. Grousset comments on this

> colossal impact of the first Hunnic thrust on the destinies of Asia. In driving the Yueh-chih from Kansu [in north-western China], the Hsiun-nu had started a sequence of repercussions which were felt as far away as Western Asia and India. Afghanistan was lost to Hellenism: the last vestiges of Alexander's conquest in these regions had been wiped out; Parthian Iran had been temporarily shaken and the tribes thrust back from Kansu had found an unlooked-for empire in Kabul and northwest India. The same process continues throughout our history which is our present study. The slightest impulse at one end of the steppe inevitably sets in motion a chain of quite unexpected consequences in all four corners of this immense zone of migrations. (1970: 32)

Just to the west of the Oxus, Kushan unification of Central Asia and north-west India between the first and third centuries AD also "facilitated commercial cultural and ideological transmission through a vast region, extending from East Asia to the borders of Europe" (Liu 1988: 2–3). "Through all India the merchant community prospered. . . . Not surprisingly, the religions supported by the merchants, Buddhism and Jainism, saw their heyday during these centuries" (Thapar 1966: 109).

The Kushan inherited and continued to utilize profitably the extensive infrastructure established under the prior period of Mauryan hegemony. This included the trunk road from Taxila to Pataliputra. The Kushan elite were particularly keen to administer matters relating to control of trade routes and commercial activity and trade. During the Kushan period, both Central Asia and northern India experienced urban prosperity, i.e. economic expansion. "Eurasian trade – with the Roman world, and from Central Asia to China – was more vital to its treasury than to those of previous Indian dynasties" (Liu 1988: 7). Liu points to a shift in the locus of accumulation in the region as a whole as a result of Kushan orientation to this Eurasian trade. The Kushan political center of the Mauryan hegemony on the middle Ganges "fell into relative oblivion during this period" (1988: 7). Liu claims that trade between the Mediterranean area and India occurred long before the Christian era and was mainly handled by Arabian intermediaries. Regular direct trade began at the end of the first century BC in the reign of Augustus. It was made profitable by learning to use monsoon winds in the Arabian Sea to establish regular maritime commerce between Alexandria and ports on the Indian coast such as Barbarican and Barygaza. Liu, citing evidence in the *Periplus*, maintains that Roman merchants acquired a regular supply of silk and furs from these ports. Furthermore,

> this fact suggests that the main path of the Silk Route during the first two centuries AD coursed through Central Asia to the Indus valley. Going directly to the sea coast along the Indus or detouring through Mathura, it connected with the Roman world by sea. . . . The discovery of the monsoon made the sea route the easiest way to avoid Persian competition.
>
> (1988: 19)

This indicates ongoing competition among routes in the context of a set of rival interlinking hegemonies. Indeed, "During Kushan rule conflicts between Rome and Parthia, especially under the reign of Trajan (98–117 AD), made the route through the Indus and seaports of the west coast essential for Roman trade to Central and East Asia" (Warmington 1928: 94–5). Well known are the Parthian efforts to control and derive monopoly profits from their intermediary position along the silk road(s) between China and Rome. Even though this trade was not in daily necessities, it "nevertheless sustained many caravan cities and seaports from the Mediterranean to East Asia" (Liu 1988: 178). During these same first and second centuries AD, the expansion of international trade, diplomatic missions, and political relations also tied Funan and other parts of Indochina and Southeast Asia more closely to China on the one side and especially to India on the other (Coedes 1968).

Liu also emphasizes how shifts in trade routes affected the locus of accumulation. "The shift of trade routes caused the rise and fall of these cities as effectively as warfare or other political crises" (Liu 1988: 178). From the first century AD, direct Roman trade with India and Africa struck a heavy blow at the urban centers of Arabia, especially those of south Arabia and Yemen, which were dependent on the incense trade (Bowen and Albright 1958).

Thus, this period of interlinking hegemonies was characterized by constant rivalries among the competing hegemons and pretenders in Rome, Armenia, Parthia, Kushan, and farther east.

B-phase crisis, 150/200–500 AD

From the third through the fifth centuries AD, the previous period of expansion and consolidating hegemonies was followed by a major world systemic crisis on a Pan-Eurasian scale. During this world systemic crisis the Han and Roman, as well as the intermediary Kushan and Parthian hegemonic structures simultaneously disintegrated. Frederick Teggart (1939) examined international political economic linkages through Central Asia for the Roman period.

> when war occurred on the routes in the Tarim Basis [in what is now China's western Xinjian region] disturbances broke out in Parthia

> and either in Armenia or on the border of Syria. Evidently then, war in the Tarim occasioned an interruption of traffic on the silk route, and this interruption aroused hostilities at points along the route as far west as the Euphrates.
>
> (1939: 240)

Teggart correlated and compared the timing of wars and barbarian invasions in Rome and China and concluded that

> Thus the effects of wars which arose out of interruptions of the great "silk route" through Persia are plainly visible in the internal history of Rome. . . . Seemingly there could be no better illustration of interdependence of nations than the consideration that a decision of the Chinese government should have been responsible for a financial panic in the capital of the Roman empire.
>
> (1939: x)

However, even Teggart seems to have considered wars and other political disturbances more as the *cause* of interruptions of trade, rather than the other way around. Yet, it may also be argued with equal or greater reason that many uprisings, wars, alliances, and other political developments were themselves stimulated if not caused by changing local, regional, or even system-wide economic conditions and interests.

Thus first the *rise* and then again the *decline* of Han China (and their Central Asian Xiongnu neighbors), Kushan India, Parthian Persia, and western imperial Rome occurred at very much the same time. The political-economic decline of these empires was also manifested in the notable simultaneous decline of Central Asian and maritime trade among them. The fourth and fifth centuries AD seem to have been a period of major Eurasian (system) wide economic and political decline, indeed. This apparently interrelated series of declines is another important instance of what we see as a major world system wide crisis. Therefore, we wish however briefly to examine some of its regional manifestations in greater detail.

The hegemonic disintegration of the Han preceded that of Rome, becoming acute by the late second century AD. The third and fourth centuries in China were a period of economic retrogression, with a significant decline in internal and external trade and demonetization of the economy. Many cities disappeared altogether and the monetary economy practically collapsed. The political center of gravity shifted from the former capital of Chang'an to Louyang, and the economic center of gravity from the Guanzhong region to the Henan region, and thereafter to the Yangtse (Yangzi) Valley. Nevertheless, cities linked to the Eurasian trade continued to exist and prosper, such as the centers in the western Hexi area (the modern Gansu corridor) (Liu 1988: 42–3). Wealthy merchant houses existed in this period of general urban decline and the Northern Wei dynasty seems to have been particularly favorable toward merchant activity up until the early sixth century.

The Kushan empire in north India and Central Asia disintegrated, and India's political center of gravity shifted back to the middle-Ganges plain during the Gupta period (c. 300–500 AD). The Gupta empire in north India rose in the fourth century, and was destroyed by the White Huns in the sixth century. During the Gupta period landed property gained value and land grants by the king increased in significance, while the urban economy in general showed clear signs of decline (Liu 1988: 21). Nonetheless, during the Gupta period some trade between India and China and between India and the West continued. The Ujjain region in the Gupta period prospered from international trade and Barygaza was still an active port (Liu 1988: 32–3). However, this trade was diverted.

> It seems reasonable to conclude that even when north India suffered a general urban decline in the Gupta period, certain cities along the trade route from Kashmir to the north Indian plain prospered . . . political changes in the post-Kushan period disturbed the Eurasian commercial network from the Roman empire to China but did not destroy it. A major shift took place in the north-west, where the route through Kashmir connecting India to Central Asia gained importance. As the seaports in western India continued to flourish the new Kashmir route brought both western India and the Ganges plain closer to China.
>
> (Liu 1988: 35)

Liu maintains that from the third to the fourth centuries a series of political changes in Asia and Europe disturbed the trade network connecting China and the West through the west-north-western Indian routes (Liu 1988: 21, 35, 178). These upheavals appeared across all of Eurasia: China was divided for three centuries after the disintegration of the Han empire (220 AD), except for a brief unification of north China under the Qin (280–316 AD). The Kushan empire (which controlled Kashmir, Bactria, Kabul, and north-west India) collapsed under the weight of White Hun deprivations in the fourth century. As a result, many urban centres in Central Asia declined or became depopulated during the fourth and fifth centuries. Major cities like Bactra and Taxila and many lesser ones experienced significant decline, "became desolate" and ended up "all in ruins" (Liu 1988: 32, 27). Bactria "might have temporarily lost its nodal function because of the pressure of Sassanians, and subsequent damage done by the Hephthalites or White Huns" (Liu 1988: 27). The Roman empire disintegrated and led to the establishment of the eastern Byzantine empire (395 AD).

It is noteworthy that the Gupta empire rose to power and privilege at the expense of regional predecessors during a period of generalized economic crisis, which had weakened its predecessors in the Indian region.

At about the same time, this was true too of the Sassanians, who replaced the Parthians in Persia. For in the third century also the Sassanian empire took control of the former domains of the Parthians and the Kushan in Persia and Central Asia. However, Sassanian power also was in ascendancy, as Roman and Han power declined. The Gupta perhaps less, and the Sassanians perhaps more, successfully managed to retain some power as sort of super-accumulating monopoly rent from their positions along the way while other economic and political powers had already waned or went under in the generalized world system economic and political crisis. However, neither Gupta nor Sassanian power lasted very long. Perhaps that was not only because they suffered from repeated batterings by the White Huns in the fourth–sixth centuries. Perhaps Gutpa and Sassanian power was also a sort of flash in the pan, precisely because they were only able to take advantage of their rivals' economic and political decline in a period of economic downswing; which would also limit and ultimately destroy their own capabilities. (An apparently similar major such instance may have been the rise of the Assyrians at the beginning of the first millennium BC. Another would be the rapid rise and decline of the Mongols in the thirteenth- and fourteenth-century world-economic downturn to which we will turn in due course. Probably, there were other similar instances in between, as well as before and after this period, which merit greater attention.)

Returning to the third and fourth centuries, they were a period of significant economic contraction in the Roman empire. This included contraction in the market and currency devaluation (even demonetization), and reversal of urbanization, especially in the western provinces of the empire. Childe argues that by AD 150 the "frontiers of the civilised world" had been reached and that the external market could expand no more. Thus, "Unable to expand the whole system began to contract . . . by 250 AD all semblance of prosperity vanished" (1942: 273, 275). The hegemonic disintegration forces of the third century were severe, but the empire was formally kept together. Huge quantities of bullion flowed to the east to make up for Rome's chronic structural deficit on its trade in luxury goods with Asia, thus increasing the pressure on the Roman treasury to debase the coinage. The aristocratic ruling class was discouraged by its own ideology from investing in industry, and preferred for reasons of status to invest in land and commerce. The competition of slave labor with free labor depressed wages in the latter and thus depressed the expansion of the market.

Geoffrey de Ste Croix explains the long decline of the Roman economy as the result of the Roman political system and its class structure, which

> facilitated a most intense and ultimately destructive economic exploitation of the great mass of the people, whether slave or free,

> and it made radical reform impossible. The result was that the propertied class, the men of real wealth, who had deliberately created this system for their own benefit, drained the life-blood from their world and thus destroyed Graeco-Roman civilization over a large part of the empire.
>
> (1981: 502)

Economic collapse, particularly in the form of fiscal crisis, came first in Britain, Gaul, Spain, and north Africa in the fifth century, and in much of Italy, the Balkans, Egypt, Syria, and Mesopotamia in the sixth and seventh centuries. However, the eastern or Byzantine part of the Roman empire never suffered such a severe collapse as its western European part.

Western Europe suffered perhaps more than any other region in the world system from the economic retrogression effected by this world systemic crisis. Moreover, many centuries passed before western Europe recovered, and then only partially. A unique amalgamation of late Roman and Germanic institutions took form in the west-European provinces of the Roman empire. The institutions of feudalism were in place by the time of the death of Charlemagne in 814, and western Europe declined into the "Dark Ages." However, we agree with the evidence and arguments of scholars like Dopsch (1923/4) and Lombard (1975) to the effect that even in Europe, trade and markets never declined as much as the more dominant tradition of Max Weber and Henri Pirenne had taught us. Nonetheless, western Europe became an economic backwater in the world system, with concomitantly backward and primitive political institutions. Thus, it would be largely bypassed by the next world economic upturn, which began in the sixth century. When it finally did begin to recover, it was as part of a process of reintegration into the world economy whose center was then located in the East.

The medieval and early modern periods, 500 to 1500 AD

A phase, 500–750/800 AD

A new period of nearly world system wide economic expansion began in the sixth century. The Sassanid empire regained strength and acquired the key Syrian entrepôt of Antioch. Sassanid campaigns of expansion in the early seventh century brought its power into Anatolia, the Levant, and Egypt. Byzantium also expanded during the sixth century, when Belisarius undertook successful reconquests in the West. Both empires seriously overextended and then exhausted each other in a final debilitating war in the seventh century. In India, Sri Harsha rebuilt a north-Indian hegemony from the city of Kanauj in the seventh century. In China, reunification occurred under the Sui dynasty in the later part of the sixth century.

In summary, most of Eurasia, excepting western Europe, but also parts of Africa, were again interlinked and synchronized, in particular through Central Asia. This synchronization thus linked up across all Afro-Eurasia from West to East, and vice versa. Chinese unification brought acceleration of the economic-expansion phase and Chinese extension of hegemonic power into Central Asia under the Tang dynasty, which succeeded the Sui. Simultaneously, Tang China also increased its relations with Indochinese Champa. The new Arab/Muslim state of Arabia and Palestine exploited the exhaustion of the Persian Sassanid empire in the seventh century and quickly conquered the former Persian domains. Egypt and Alexandria were also taken by the Arabs in 643. Central Asia was added to the hegemony in mid-century. The unification of Mesopotamia, Egypt, and Central Asia under one hegemonic structure gave the Ummayyad and its successor the Abbassid dynasty the position of super-accumulator in the world system. The Abbassid and Tang empires clashed head on in Central Asia in the mid-eighth century. The battle of Talas in 751 confirmed Abbassid super-hegemony and accelerated Tang decline.

Thus, the second half of the sixth and the seventh centuries witnessed commercial and political expansion in various regions. From the second half of the sixth century AD, much of Central Asia was conquered and reorganized by the Turks. They expanded westward to dominate the entire area from Manchuria to the Aral Sea. The role of the Turks in trans-Central-Asian trade and its importance to them has been noted by several authors, among them Christopher Beckwith (1987) and Luc Kwanten (1979), who write:

> When the Turks annexed most of the Central Asian city-states – great centers for the east–west and north–south caravan trade – in the second half of the sixth century, they also removed the political obstacles to relatively high-volume transcontinental trade. . . . The Turks' great interest in commerce did not mean that they dominated it; they were its patrons. Most of the international trade during the Early Middle Ages was in the hands of others. . . . Trade was almost totally monopolized by two or three great trading peoples: the Jews, the Norsemen, and the Sogdians. The profits from this trade in silk, spices, perfumes, war material, horses, and other products stimulated not only imperialism, but also local industry and local trade.
>
> (Beckwith 1987: 178–80)

> Trade played an important role in the Turkic empire. Through their victory over the Yuanyuan, the Turks had gained control over Central Asian trade routes, and hence over the lucrative silk trade between China and Byzantium. The Turks had no intention of either abandoning the trade or sharing it with other intermediaries. Inevitably, this

> led to war between the Turks and the Sassanian empire [in Persia who had been the intermediaries].
>
> (Kwanten 1979: 39)

However, the Turkish empire(s) did not last long. In the seventh and eighth centuries they gave way to the Tang dynasty expanding westward from China, the Tibetan empire expanding northward, the Muslims overrunning Iraq and Persia and expanding eastward, the Byzantines still holding their own, and the Frankish empire rising in western Europe. The Islamic caliphate and the "world" economy around it, so masterfully analyzed by among others Hodgson (1974) and Lombard (1975), probably became the driving force, with its driver's seat in Baghdad. It was founded in 762 and by the year 800 already had a population of 2 million.

Marshall Hodgson (1974) has examined the Abbassid high caliphate from 692 to 945 and especially its period of "flowering" and commercial expansion until 813. To introduce his examination of the Muslim caliphate, however, Hodgson observed:

> This period was one of great prosperity. It is not clear how far this was the case throughout the Afro-Eurasian Oikoumene, but at least in China at that time what may be called a "commercial revolution" was taking place. Under the strong government of the T'ang dynasty . . . commerce became much more extensive and more highly organized. . . . The Chinese economic activity was directly reflected in the trade in the Southern Seas (the Indian Ocean and seas eastward), where Chinese ports became an important terminus for Muslim vessels. . . . It can be surmised that the commercial life of the lands of Muslim rule was given a positive impetus by the great activity in China, especially considering the important connections with China both via the Southern Seas and overland through central Eurasia. In any case, commerce also enjoyed the great benefit of an extended peace which the caliphate was able to ensure within its domains.
>
> (1974, I: 234–5)

However, it may be possible to "clarify" further Hodgson's doubts about the extent of prosperity throughout the Afro-Eurasian oikumene during this period. From the mid-seventh century came the rise and expansion of Taika and Nara Japan, Silla Korea, and Tang China in the East. China expanded southward and increased trade relations with Champa in Indochina. The Silendras established themselves at key trading entrepôts at the tips of Malaya, Sumatra, and Java, astride the direct and indirect trade routes between China, the Arabian Sea, and the Persian Gulf via India. At the same time, the Chinese and the Turks also expanded westward, the Tibetans northward, the Muslims eastward, the Scandinavians southward, and the Byzantines consolidated and held their own as best they could. Meanwhile, Indian, Persian, and Axum power in east Africa declined and/ or was replaced by these expansions and rivalries. Trade through north Africa began to flourish, both along its East–West axis and southward across the Sahara to the sources of gold in west Africa. West Europeans languished for another century until Charlemagne was crowned in 800. Yet even then its trade with the eastern Mediterranean languished. Egypt prospered under the Tulunins in the second half of the ninth century. Is it unlikely that these far-flung developments occurred simultaneously only by historical accident? It seems much more likely that they were "a sequence of repercussions in a chain of quite unexpected consequences in all four corners of this immense zone" going through Central Asia, to recall the terminology of Grousset (1970: 32).

B phase, 750/800–1000/1050 AD?

This chain of repercussions also includes what appears to have been a set of "regional" but very widespread political crises in the mid-eighth century. Beckwith notes:

> The eighth century saw the development of serious crises, and major economic, political and cultural changes, in every important Eurasian state. Typologically speaking, these changes followed more or less the same pattern, due no doubt to their common origin in international, specifically economic change, of a fundamental nature. . . . It is a curious fact that, unlike the preceding and following centuries, the middle of the eighth century – specifically the period 742 to 755 – saw fundamental changes, usually signalled by successful political revolts, in every Eurasian empire. Most famous among them are the Carolingian, Abbasid, Uighur Turkic, and anti-Tang rebellions, each of which is rightly considered to have been a major watershed in the respective national histories. Significantly, all seem to have been intimately connected with Central Eurasia.
>
> (Beckwith 1987: 192)

A major event in the interhegemonic history of this period and a turning point in the history of Central Asia and of the world was the reversal of Tang Chinese expansion in Asia at the battle at the Talas river in 751. The Arab Muslims and the Turks combined forces and defeated the Tang General Gao Xianji (lent to the Chinese by the then flowering Silla kingdom in Korea). He had previously led the Chinese expansion into Central Asia during two victorious campaigns across the Pamirs and into Kushan. The same year, the new Khitai confederacy defeated the Chinese in their north-east; and a Chinese expedition to the south-west into Yunnan failed. Four years later, in 755, began the major eight-year-long internal rebellion against Tang rule led by Anlushan. The rebellion was put down with Uighur help from Central Asia. Nonetheless, Tang power and the regime of the Tang dynasty never really recovered from this external defeat at Talas river in 751 and the internal Anlushan rebellion from 755 to 763. The weakened Tang dynasty hung on until 907, after another major rebellion from 874 to 883. China lost all its western territories again; and the Turks and much of Central Asia – eventually right up to the Great Wall of China – became Muslim.

A century later, in the course of the four years betwen 838 and 842, as Beckwith (1987) notes, in the West the trade route between the Volga and the Baltic was closed in 838 (not to reopen for another generation), and in 840 the Frankish empire broke up. In the East, the Uighur empire fell to the Kirghiz in 840, the Tibetan empire was split up in 842, and in the same year began the open persecution of Buddhism and then of other foreign religions in China. At the same time (after the Arab–Byzantine war of 837–42 and Turkish expansion), the last caliph in Baghdad began the persecution of heretics under Islamic rule. Again, it seems unlikely that these political and cultural events were entirely responses to "internal" pressures unrelated to each other. More likely, they were related to each other and to economic problems or even another widespread economic crisis, common to them all and/or transmitted through Central Asia. Of course, we will never find out, unless we look for such interrelations.

Beckwith observes that

> the great crises of the eighth century were followed by absolutely astonishing economic and cultural growth across Eurasia, from Japan to England. The enormous expansion in trade brought about an explosion in the growth of cities and market towns everywhere. Besides the huge metropolises of Baghdad, Constantinople, and Ch'ang-an, the old [Central Asian] centers of Samarkand and Khwarazam, etc., there were fastgrowing cities where once there were none: Rasa, Karabalgasum, Rostov, Quentovic, and many others. The internationalism of the age burst into full bloom, as commerce and culture, hand-in-hand, flourished as never before.
>
> (1987: 92–4)

However, the ninth and tenth centuries may still have been a period of economic slowdown. They also witnessed important setbacks to some regional powers and (therefore?) greater opportunities for others to establish themselves. Tang China languished and then declined, especially in its relations with Central Asia. The Tang decline opened spaces for the temporary growth of some regional powers, such as the Uighurs and then the Kirghiz. At the other end of Central Eurasia in the tenth century, Egypt experienced economic difficulties and declining real wages (Ashtor 1976: 153–4). Elsewhere, "the boom in the Near Eastern economies came suddenly to an end and the unity of the Moslem empire was shattered" (115). Ashtor lays part of the blame on a 14-year revolt by slaves, many of them Blacks, in southern Mesopotamia, beginning in 869. The growth and power of Baghdad failed to continue and its caliphate began its "disintegration," as Ashtor entitles his chapter on the same. Trade with India and China was diminished (147). Lombard dates the "onset of the decline of Baghdad from the end of the tenth century; it continued in the eleventh century under the Seljuk Turks and was completed when the town was captured by [the Mongol] Hulagu in 1258" (1975: 126). "It is evident that the decline of Baghdad [as well as Basra] and of the centrality of the Gulf route [to the Orient] is explainable only in part by purely local and exclusively economic factors. It can be fully understood only within the context of changes in the geopolitical system of the larger region, and indeed, of the world system" (Abu-Lughod 1989: 192). We now turn to these in the next period of expansion.

A phase 1000/1050–1250/1300 AD

The eleventh and twelfth centuries and perhaps more precisely the years 1050 to 1250 were another period of widespread economic growth.

For instance, Wallerstein notes:

> The feudal system in western Europe seems quite clearly to have operated by a pattern of cycles of expansion and contraction of two lengths: circa 50 years and circa 200–300 years. . . . The patterns of the expansions and contractions are clearly laid out and widely accepted among those writing about the late Middle Ages and early modern times in Europe. . . . It is the long swing that was crucial. Thus 1050–1250+ was a time of the expansion of Europe (the Crusades, the colonizations). . . . The "crisis" or great contractions of 1250–1450+ included the Black Plague.
>
> (1989b: 33, 34)

Of course, Wallerstein and others limit their reference to "feudal" Europe. The legitimacy of this limitation has been debated by Wallerstein (chapter 10 below) and Frank (chapter 6 below). There is ample evidence to support the present authors' belief that both the cycle and the period of expansion within it were world system wide. Indeed, that was a major reason for the commercial ventures of the Crusades Wallerstein mentions, as well as for the prosperity, but also the rivalry, of Venice, Genoa, and the other south-European city states, which, increasingly, turned eastward to connect with the growing and profitable trans-Asian trade. However, especially in the hands of the Genovese and the Catalans, trade also prospered in the western Mediterranean and increasingly extended out into the Atlantic in the eleventh, twelfth, and thirteenth centuries. After Gibraltar, it turned both northward toward north-west Europe and southward to the newly discovered Canary Islands and further to west Africa. Simultaneously, Christians pushed their *reconquista* of the Muslim domains in Spain ever southward. Both would eventually culminate in 1492 with the simultaneous expulsion of the "Moors" and Jews from Spain and the "discovery" of America by a Genovese navigator and merchant-shipper, who had been trained in Atlantic voyages to the Canaries. He raised private finance capital in Barcelona and elsewhere but worked in the service of the Spanish queen, for whom he sought a better and cheaper way to the riches of the Orient. Several other regions around the world also prospered during this period; their simultaneous and interrelated growth and decline have been analyzed by Janet Abu-Lughod (1989).

Foremost among the regions of expansion was China. During this period the Song consolidated their empire in China, amid spectacular population growth and economic expansion. The Chinese population grew to 150 million, the city of Hangzhou to 6 million, and Kaifeng to 4 million (while by comparison Venice, Europe's biggest and most trade-dependent city, reached 160,000). Technological revolution, increased agricultural productivity, large-scale industrial production, construction of vast networks of overland transportation and navigable inland waterways, widespread commercialization, high finance, sumptuary consumption, and expansive domestic and foreign trade all characterized the Song period. Nonetheless, the Sung never regained the hegemonic political position in Central Asia which the Tang had lost. On the contrary, throughout the Song period and until the Mongol conquest, China was "among equals" (to use the revealing title by Morris Rossabi) vis-à-vis its neighbors. Indeed, China was on the defensive against repeated threats and incursions by its also economically and politically expanding neighbors in Central Asia, the Kara Khitai empire in particular, and in Manchuria.

Moreover,

> this external threat was not without effect on the social and economic history of the Sung age. It determined the whole Chinese policy from the end of the tenth century to the end of the thirteenth century. Cut off from access to Central Asia, blocked in its expansion toward the north and north-west by the great empires which had arisen on its frontiers, the Chinese world turned resolutely to the sea. Its center of gravity shifted towards the trading and maritime regions of the south-east, which were extended inland by the enormous network of the Yangtse and its tributaries. The sea routes starting from the Abbasid empire and connecting the Persian Gulf with India, South-East Asia, and the Chinese coast no doubt played a part in this call of the sea. . . . China was the greatest maritime power in the world.
> (Gernet 1985: 300, 328, 326)

An important question for us is whether and to what extent Song China can or should be considered to have been in a position of super-accumulation without super-hegemony. Remarks by the eminent world-historian (and author of among other works *The Pursuit of Power*, 1983) William McNeill to Gunder Frank led us to believe that such a situation may have been the case. On the other hand, there is evidence that Song China suffered from a negative balance of both trade and payments, which would be inconsistent with, indeed contrary to, super-accumulation within the world economy. (Other countries, like hegemonic Britain, also had a negative balance of trade over the long term, at least from 1815 to 1914. However, during that time, Britain also enjoyed a positive balance of payments on current account.) Song China, however, seems to have been a net exporter of bullion. Indeed, this apparently long-term structural adversity or handicap of China may have been another one of the reasons why the Ming dynasty finally sought to "de-link" China from the world economy.

Before that, however, the Indian coasts and especially Southeast Asia and China had also experienced a centuries-long economic boom since the eleventh century, which was manifested in fast-growing intra- and interregional trade. Indians, Malays, "Indonesians," and Chinese were especially active in interregional trade to the east of India. On the other side, Indians, Persians, and of course Arabs were active on the west side of the Indian subcontinent. As Janet Abu-Lughod (1989) stressed, in the west Asian/east Mediterranean region, Baghdad, Basra, and the Persian Gulf route declined. One of the reasons was that it was in the interest of the now rising Genovese to favor the more northerly route through the Black Sea and/or for the Venetians to favor the more southerly one through the Red Sea. The development of the latter also benefitted rival Cairo, which consequently rose to prominence and a population of 500,000 under the Mamluks in the thirteenth and early fourteenth centuries, and would even repel the Mongols. "Egypt was a vanguard for the world system" (Abu-Lughod 1989: 227).

> Both before and after the domination of the Mamluks, Egypt had a direct link to India and the East Indies and pushed its communication system as far as Mohammedan Spain and the western [sic] Maghreb. Thus, Egypt was the forerunner of Portugal. . . . At this time in Cairo . . . a group of wealthy people had a horizon which included nearly a third of the whole world.
>
> (Chaunu 1979: 58; quoted in Abu-Lughod 1989: 227)

Venice and Cairo established a "marriage of convenience" in the attempt to monopolize the Asian-Mediterranean trade between them in competition with their rivals. These included Genoa and its attempt to monopolize the Black Sea route. First competition from Venice and only finally the Ottoman conquest of Constantinople in 1453 propelled the Genovese to expand westward through the Mediterranean and out into the Atlantic instead.

In Central Asia in the eleventh century, the Yamini dynasty of Ghazni (near Kabul) also consolidated a new hegemony, ruling from Hamadan and Isfahan in Persia to the headwater of the Ganges in north-west India. Turkish peoples from Central Asia expanded westward and reached Anatolia. They were then Islamicized and later created the Muslim Ottoman empire and modern Turkey. Turks also began a systematic conquest of India in the twelfth century. This process culminated in the consolidation of the vast hegemonic state of the sultanate of Delhi, which by 1235 ruled from Sind to Bengal. Such was the strength of this consolidation in India, with a centralized administration and standing army, that the sultanate successfully repelled the Mongol invasion led by Genghis Khan.

B phase, 1250/1300–1450 AD

The expansion and consolidation of the Mongol empire began at the end of this long period of expansion and at the onset of a new period of contraction. The Mongols used their military superiority to exploit the situation on a larger and more successful scale than any of their Inner Asian predecessors. They struck first at the Qin in north China. Genghis undertook the conquest of Central Asia against the Muslim empire of Khwarizm. The seizure of Central Asia gave the Mongol imperium the opportunity to assume a position of super-accumulator in the world system. However, the ease of the Mongol conquest in Persia and Mesopotamia was facilitated by the weakness of the Muslim states in west Asia. The economically still stronger state in Egypt was able to resist and repel the Mongol advance. However, elsewhere the economic decline had already begun before the Mongols arrived. Then, the economic downturn that began from the middle of the thirteenth century was made even more severe by the widespread destruction that accompanied Mongol conquests, both in the East and in the West. For instance, the progress of the earlier expansion period in urbanization and trade in Russia was virtually eliminated in the Mongol conquest. Most of the cities (Novgorod excepted) were destroyed, and economic retrogression deepened thereafter. Therefore, despite Mongol consolidation of a vast Eurasian hegemony, an economic downturn of severe proportions affected most of the continent during Mongol tenure. In this respect the hegemony of the Mongols differs from the more usual case of hegemonic expansion during a period of economic upswing. Thus, it is reminiscent of the Gupta hegemony in the economically depressed fourth and fifth centuries and requires special attention.

The collapse of the Mongol imperium in the mid-fourteenth century might be taken as evidence of a world system crisis. If it was indeed the culmination of a "down" phase, we would have to question Abu-Lughod's characterization of 1250–1350 as a generalized "up" phase. Yet Abu-Lughod (1989) herself cites ample evidence that transport and other infrastructural investment and expansion in Venice, Genoa, and in the eastern Mediterranean had declined and halted at least two decades before the arrival of the plague in 1348. Below (chapter 9), she says that prosperity peaked in the opening decades of the fourteenth century, after which signs of decline were already evident.

If the construction and collapse of the Mongol imperium did coincide with the down, as in Wallerstein's periodization, a new explanation is possible for the failure of the Mongol imperium. Traditional explanation of the failure of the Mongols as a ruling class to consolidate their imperium revolves around the theme of their nomadic social organization and its presumed inherent limitations for such a task ("you can conquer, but you cannot rule from horseback"). It is true that the unity of the empire was destroyed early on, in 1260, due to dynastic succession struggles. But if the world economy was already on the downturn by 1250, this itself could help explain why the Mongols could so easily set up their conquest states (except in India) on the back of their already depressed rivals. However, the same world economic depression could then also help account for the Mongols' inability to maintain their power, and why they and everybody else went (temporarily) "to hell in a hand basket."

While the downturn lasted the Mongols continued their predatory depredations. Tamerlane, once again using Central Asian cities (Samarkand) as a base, set out to reconquer and reunify the empire from 1370 to 1405. The sultanate of Delhi had entered into a phase of decline and disintegration and therefore could not resist Tamerlane's onslaught as it had that of Genghis over a century before. But Tamerlane's campaigns were again more destructive than constructive. They did have the historical effect, however, of largely clearing the decks of the Mongol conquest states themselves, such as the Goldon Horde in Russia and the Il-Khans in Persia.

The modern world system period

Our purpose here is not (yet) to analyze or reinterpret this period. We provisionally accept the main outlines of others' rendition of the developments, which are relevant to our present study: economic expansion during the "long sixteenth century" from 1450 to 1600+, the "seventeenth-century crisis," renewed economic expansion during the eighteenth-century "commercial revolution," and the conventional dating of the economic ups and downs of the +/−50 year "long" Kondratieff cycles since the end of the eighteenth century. (Frank [1978, written in 1970–3] and more recently Goldstein [1988] also sought to trace these backwards into the sixteenth century.) We also continue provisionally to accept the "associated" political cycles of hegemonic transition and shifts in the now European-centered world system from Iberia in the sixteenth, to the Netherlands in the seventeenth, Britain (twice) in the eighteenth and nineteenth, and the United States in the twentieth centuries.

Therefore, of course, we also value and use the work on long economic cycles of accumulation and political cycles of hegemony in or centered on the West since 1500 by Wallerstein, Modelski and Thompson, Goldstein and many others. (Moreover, Frank's own work [1978] on these cycles was used as a main source for his dating of their turning points by Goldstein [1988].) We recognize the historic significance of the incorporation of the "New World" in the Americas into the world system. Not for nothing did Frank (1978) choose the title *World Accumulation 1492–1789* (the latter date being the political cut-off obliged by the military coup in Chile in 1973). Therefore, we need not here repeat the alteration of A and B phases of the cycle through the period of the "modern world system."

We prefer to turn instead to a couple of other interrelated problems. The major one is the similarities and differences between ours and others' point of view on the fundamental world systemic continuity or discontinuity between this "modern" period and the "medieval" and "ancient" ones reviewed above. This modern period has been much more widely researched, recounted, and debated by generations of other scholars. The arguments of many of these are well known, and we have already indicated our main areas of agreement and disagreement with some of them, and in particular with Immanuel Wallerstein, in our introduction above, as well as in previous writings (Gills and Frank chapter 3 above; Frank 1990a, b, 1991; Gills chapter 4 above). However much these other writers may differ among themselves, most do agree that the period around 1500 (or for some around 1800) represents a fundamental break with the past. For them it is the beginning of the fundamentally different modern-world-capitalist-system. For us, and still too few others, still more important is the fundamental continuity with the past within the same world system and its continuing cycles of capital accumulation and hegemony/rivalry.

In her pathbreaking book Abu-Lughod (1989) argues that there was a "thirteenth-century world system," but that it was a *different* one than that which "began" in the sixteenth century. For her, between the fourteenth-century decline of the world system based in the East and the fifteenth–sixteenth-century rise of the world system centered on the West, there occurred a "declining efficacy" and "*dis*organization" of "the ways in which they were formerly connected." We view these changes rather as a "*re*organization" and consequently as a shift of the hegemonial center of gravity in the system from East to West – but not as a complete failure of the system as a whole, as she suggests. On the contrary, this temporary disorganization and renewed reorganization can, and we believe should, be read as the continuation and evolution of the system as a whole (Abu-Lughod 1989: 342–5).

Therefore, we even more decidedly agree that "of crucial importance is the fact that the fall of the east precedes the rise of the west," as Janet Abu-Lughod (1989: 338) insists. That is, the world systemic economic and hegemonic crisis of the mid-fourteenth century gave Europe "the chance" to ascend in the hierarchy of the old system, in the context of a new economic expansion and hegemonic reorganization during and following the crisis.

> The context . . . undeniably altered. . . . The world-system . . . arena did move outward to the Atlantic and the Atlantic rim nations of Portugal and Spain, before shifting to northwestern Europe. The fact is that the axis of Central Asia-Anatolia-northern India-and the Levant-Egypt – an axis of central importance in earlier times which was scarcely destroyed by the seventeenth century – never again occupied the center stage of the world system.
>
> (Abu-Lughod 1989: 12)

A similar argument had already been made by Marshall Hodgson in the 1950s and by Jacques Gernet in the 1980s:

> The economic weakness of the pivotal Middle East by the end of the Middle Ages, for instance, seems to have been a decisive factor in the economic and political disposition of the world into which Europe was about to expand.
>
> (Hodgson 1954: 718)
>
> What we have acquired the habit of regarding – according to the history of the world that is in fact no more than the history of the West – as the beginning of modern times was only the repercussion of the upsurge of the urban, mercantile civilizations whose realm extended, before the Mongol invasion, from the Mediterranean to the Sea of China. The West gathered up part of this legacy and received from it the leaven which was to make possible its own development. The transmission was favored by the crusades of the twelfth and thirteenth centuries and the expansion of the Mongol empire in the thirteenth and fourteenth centuries. . . . There is nothing surprising about this Western backwardness: the Italian cities . . . were at the terminus of the great commercial routes of Asia. The upsurge of the West, which was only to emerge from its relative isolation thanks to its maritime expansion, occurred at a time when the two great civilizations of Asia [China and Islam] were threatened.
>
> (Gernet 1985: 347)

In general, the Mongol conquests *and* the economic crisis also laid the basis for wide-ranging economic reorientation and political reorganization in the following period of economic expansion during the "long sixteenth century" from 1450 to 1600+. In direct or indirect response to the changes wrought by the previous economic crisis and the Mongol invasions, the Ming dynasty rose in China, Akbar's empire rose in India, the Safavid empire rose in Persia, and Europeans began a worldwide imperial and now also trans-Atlantic venture in the West. It is the latter to which the then Eurocentric historiography has devoted most absolute and relative attention. Perhaps too much. For, as we observed in our introduction, until at least the nineteenth century the preponderance even of hegemonic transformation still did not lie exclusively in the West.

The collapse of the Mongol imperium disrupted the land routes through Central Asia and the uninterest of Ming China adversely affected overland trade, particularly in silk. However, the most marked decline did not occur until the seventeenth-century depression. The route via the steppe to the Baltic was also disrupted. However, in the eighteenth century trade revived along the more northerly route through Siberia. Trade also declined via the Gulf port of Hormuz to the Black Sea. The trade corridor via the Red Sea and Alexandria remained open. However, European trade with Egypt and the Levant was conducted primarily through payment in bullion. This stimulated an even greater need for sources of bullion in the West and in Africa and the desire to bypass the Alexandrian and Venetian middlemen, if possible, by finding a direct sea route to India and the spice islands. When Portugal and Spain discovered such routes, backed by Italian finance capital, the result was a drastic shift in the logistical nexus of the world system and a concomitant shift in the locus of accumulation. Central Asia ceased to be the key node in the world logistical nexus or to be the key area in terms of attaining super-accumulator status.

Thus another problem separating us somewhat from other students of the world system is that we see *other* parts of the world as having been the most important players in the *same* world system earlier on. Therefore, we also see some of them as players *still* in the same world system after 1500 as well. Thus, we will find it necessary to rephrase (or re-pose?) the question of "incorporation" into the system as perceived by Wallerstein and others, e.g. in the 1987 issue of *Review* dedicated to "Incorporation into the world-economy: how the world-system expands." Moreover, the hegemony first of Iberia in the sixteenth century and then of the Netherlands in the seventeenth, as well as the relative monopolies of trade on which they were based, came at the expense of still operative trading powers among the Ottomans and Indians, among others. As we noted earlier, even the director of the English East India Company Sir Josiah Child still observed in 1680 that "we obstruct their [Mogul Indian] trade with all the Eastern nations which is ten times as much as ours and all European nations put together" (cited in Palat and Wallerstein 1990: 26).

Moreover, the Ottoman empire still lay, and indeed expanded, across the East–West trade routes. However, perhaps its ultimate historical fate was influenced if not sealed by the developments in world system history as a whole. The initial Ottoman political expansion occurred during a period of world economic decline in the fourteenth century. Competition with the rising West stopped Ottoman expansion in that direction, overland under Suleiman against the Hapsburgs outside Vienna in 1521, and by sea under Selim II against the Italians at Lepanto in 1571. The more successful Ottoman expansion in the sixteenth century was in the south-easterly direction and westward along the northern coast of Africa, which were politically weakened and rendered economically less profitable by "the decline of the East." Moreover, the same decline of the Central Asian nexus limited Ottoman opportunities in that direction. Finally, the Mughal advance through the relatively still more attractive India under Babur and his grandson Akbar perhaps pre-empted the Ottomans as well.

Another limitation on Ottoman power and expansion, of course, was the neighboring Safavid empire in Iran/Persia. The Safavids built an empire in the sixteenth century on the ruins left by the Mongol invasion and retreat. Under the Safavids, domestic and international commerce was perhaps more favored than anywhere else in the world at the time. The Safavids sought to maintain and further their political economic interests against their Ottoman and Portuguese competitors. Especially under Abbas I, who ruled from 1587 to 1629, they therefore sought and maintained shifting alliances with the French, Hapsburgs, and British. It was in alliance with the latter that the Persians ousted the Portuguese from Hormuz in 1622. The Portuguese had used their fortress on this strategically located island in the Straits of the same name to exact tribute of protection money from traffic across the Arabian Sea to and from India and Asia.

However, Braudel and others have demonstrated that the shift to the Atlantic still required at least one to two centuries after Columbus. "The general decadence comes over the Mediterranean in the XVII century. In the XVII century, we say, not in the XVI, as is usually claimed" (Braudel 1953: 368). Textile manufacture reached its maximum in Venice in 1592. In Livorna, and probably elsewhere in Italy, the bales of silk "unloaded *over the maritime route* continued to the end of the [sixteenth] century: there is not the slightest sign of decline" (Braudel 1953: 368–71). At the same time, there was "prosperity in the Red Sea" and "it is true that the old spice route again recovers and prospers after the middle of the [sixteenth] century." "Thus, the Levant trade was not interrupted, neither in the direction of Syria nor in the direction of Egypt" (Braudel 1953: 457, 459, 469). That is, the maritime trade routes through the eastern Mediterranean retained their prosperity at least through the end of the sixteenth century.

However, so did both the circum-Asian maritime *and* the trans-Asian overland routes through Central Asia. Nor did European intervention, bolstered as it was by its new financial strength derived from the Atlantic trade, change much in the circum-Asian maritime trade. The European sixteenth-century pioneers in this Asian maritime trade were the Portuguese. However,

> The Portuguese colonial regime, built upon war, coercion, and violence, did not at any point signify a stage of "higher development" economically for Asian trade. The traditional commercial structure continued to exist, however much damaged by religious wars breaking out between Moslems and Christians. Trade did not undergo any increase in quantity worthy of mention in the period. The commercial and economic forms of the Portuguese colonial regime were the same as those of Asian trade and Asian authority. . . . The Portuguese colonial regime, then, did not introduce a single new element into the commerce of southern Asia.
>
> (van Leur 1955: 117–18)

Finally, the circum-Asian maritime trade also still did not displace the trans-Asian caravan trade or the place of Central Asia therein in the sixteenth century.

> The destructive effects of the discovery of the sea route to Asia upon the traditional intercontinental trade routes was not felt until after the elapse of an entire century. After a set-back at the beginning of the sixteenth century the trade routes through the Middle East regained their former importance, and at the end of the sixteenth century the transcontinental caravan trade reached dimensions which must presumably be regarded as its historical culmination.
>
> (Steensgaard 1972: 9)

Indeed, around 1600 all the silk still moved overland by caravan. Moreover, the tonnage of spices brought westward and to Europe by caravan through Central Asia was still twice that brought by ship (Steensgaard 1972: 56–7). Thus, to the end of the sixteenth century, Central Asia continued to maintain its place in overland trade against both the South Asian maritime trade and the West Asian, Mediterranean, and Atlantic trades.

Then, in the seventeenth century there was economic decline. But, it was a cyclical decline, which was common to all of these regions and routes, including the Americas, during the seventeenth-century world economic crisis. As already noted, in the eighteenth century, trade revived again across Central Asia, albeit along a more northerly route. However, the eighteenth century also finally brought on the "commercial revolution" and the growth of the "triangular trade" across the Atlantic (Frank 1978). That finally served also to shift the center of gravity of trade from the East, including Central Asia, to the West.

Thus, the world and its economic and political relations were still multipolar well into the seventeenth century. Beyond the intra-European rivalry for hegemony, there were still competing powers in Europe and western and southern Asia among the Hapsburgs, Ottomans, Safavids, and Mughals. The last three were all Muslim, but they were nonetheless as much rivals among each other as they were with the Christian Europeans who were also rivals both among each other and with these Asian powers.

Beyond the retreat into greater isolation of China under the Ming at one end of Eurasia, another major reason that this historical development eventually became a more unipolar rather than a multipolar transition is explained by Blaut (1977) with reference to the other end: the west-European maritime powers conquered the Americas and injected their bullion into their own processes of capital accumulation. The western powers then used the same to gain increasing control over the trade nexus of the still attractive and profitable Indian Ocean and Asia as a whole. Then they used their power to thwart industrial and commercial competition, particularly in India. The subsequent destruction of the Indian textile industry must stand out as a particularly important aspect of Blaut's argument.

For, according to Palat and Wallerstein, by the end of the fourteenth century

> the Indian subcontinent emerged from this crisis as a core production area of cotton textiles in the world economy and became the beneficiary of a huge inflow of bullion as a result of trade surplus. India's trade with West Asia increased exponentially over the next several centuries and tied the economic fates of cities on both sides of the Arabian sea closely together. . . . At the same time, the maritime trade of India to the east, connecting to the China–Malay trade, experienced a new resurgence, following Sung China's decision to lift its earlier ban on merchant trade. In the wake of this, Srivijaya declined as an intermediary in Southeast Asia to the benefit of ports on the Malay coast. Trade across the Bay of Bengal witnessed a chronological simultaneity of the rise and decline of the most prominent ports at both ends of the eastern Indian Ocean: Pulicat and Melaka, and . . . Aceh and Masulipatnam.
>
> (Palat and Wallerstein 1990: 26)

Clearly, though, economic recovery in this nexus was in evidence from the mid-fifteenth century. Palat and Wallerstein are willing to speak only of an evolving Indian Ocean world economy. By 1500, this economy combined a set of intersecting trade and production linkages converging on such nodes as Aden and Mocha on the Red Sea; Basra, Gombroon, and Hormuz on the Persian Gulf; Surat and Calicut on the western seaboard of the subcontinent; Pulicat and Hughli on the Coromande and Bengal coasts; Melaka on the Malay archipelago; and the imperial capitals such as Delhi and Teheran, connected by caravan trails.

Palat and Wallerstein acknowledge that these centers centralized and dominated transregional trade and that they "lived at the same pace as the outside world, keeping up with the trades and rhythms of the globe" (1990: 30–1; also Braudel 1982: 18). Indeed, so powerful was the production superiority of the Coromandel and Gujarat textile industry that it led to the "deindustrialization" of other areas, and only the navigation laws of the mercantilist European nations, including Britain, kept Indian textiles out of the west-African and Caribbean markets (Palat and Wallerstein 1990: 33, 49).

Nevertheless, Palat and Wallerstein insist that three autonomous historical systems existed: the Indian Ocean world economy, which centered on China, and the Mediterranean/European zones, which merely converged at intersections. Yet they note the "swift collapse of these cities once their fulcral positions were undermined." But they would have it that "their riches accumulated from their intermediary role in the trade *between different world-systems*" rather than acknowledge the existence of a single world economy. Furthermore, Palat and Wallerstein conclude that

> despite the temporal contemporaneity of post-1400 expansion of networks of exchange and intensification of relational dependencies in Europe and in the world of the Indian Ocean, the processes of large-scale socio-historical transformation in the two historical systems were fundamentally dissimilar. In one zone, it led to the emergence of the capitalist world-economy. In the other, to an expanded petty commodity production that did not lead to a real subsumption of labour.
>
> (1990: 40)

Of course, we believe that this is an excessively nearsighted view. Alternatively, by relying only on Wallerstein's modern-capitalist-world-system glasses (or is it blinkers?) these and other authors cannot see or adequately interpret their own evidence from the larger and older world system, which is staring them in the face. This essay has been another of our (im?)modest efforts to help them and others reinterpret this evidence from a wider and longer historical perspective. We may try again to summarize some provisional conclusions that seem to emerge from our historical review above.

SOME PROVISIONAL CONCLUSIONS

We do seem to have identified alternating periods of expansion and contraction, which may be part of a world system wide cycle. These may be summarized by Table 5.1.

Table 5.1 A/B economic phases in the world system pre-1500 AD

1	B phase: 1700–1500/1400 BC
	A phase: 1400–1200 BC
2	B phase: 1200–1000 BC
	A phase: 1000–800 BC
3	B phase: 800–550 BC
	A phase: 550–450 BC
4	B phase: 450–350 BC
	A phase: 350–250/200 BC
5	B phase: 250/200–100/50 BC
	A phase: 100/50 BC–150/200 AD
6	B phase: 150/200–500 AD
	A phase: 500–750/800 AD
7	B phase: 750/800–1000/1050 AD
	A phase: 1000/1050–1250/1300 AD
8	B phase: 1250/1300–1450 AD
	A phase: 1450–1600 AD

Our summary table permits the following observations among others:

1 It is possible to identify many economic and political structures and processes over the millennia, which we now (or still) associate with the modern world-capitalist system.

In particular, the trinity of core/periphery, hegemony/rivalry, and A/B-phase cycle seem to be constant or at least recurring structures and processes of the world system. However, so are multiple political hegemonies (or cores) in regional configurations, which are in political economic competition with each other in a wider world economy and system.

2 Over some 5,000 years there seem to have been alternating periods of faster/greater and slower/lower or even negative accumulation. Moreover, these periods apparently were not merely localized or regional and attributable solely to "internal" factors. The periods of alternating expansion and contraction were also interregional and apparently world system wide. For over two thousand years between 500 BC and 1500 AD, these cycles appear to have been four or five centuries long, with up and down phases of approximately two centuries each. This does not exclude possible shorter cycles as well within these longer cycles.

3 Periods of apparently more rapid economic growth are associated with the rise of several regional hegemons, and among them sometimes an apparent transregional or even world system wide super-accumulating super-hegemon. Some important instances appear to have been Achaemenid Persia in the fifth–fourth centuries BC, Tang China in the seventh century AD, and perhaps Song China in the eleventh–twelfth centuries. These all developed during "up" phases of economic expansion. We

note that all these aspired to some control over parts of Central Asia. However, only the Achaemenids and the Tang achieved some control over Central Asia, and it was not very widespread or long-lasting. The Song achieved none at all.

4 The third-century Sassanid, fourth-century Gupta, the eighth–ninth-century Abbasid, and the thirteenth–fourteenth-century Mongol hegemons did extend their hegemony into Central Asia.

5 However, the Sassanids and Guptas and then the Mongols achieved their hegemony during major down phases in the third–fourth and thirteenth centuries, respectively. During these periods their rivals had already been weakened. Therefore, these developments of hegemonic power and perhaps others (the USA) developed their hegemony over rivals who had been weakened by economic crisis and war. To a significant extent, the latter was also true of the spread of Abbasid power after Byzantium and Persia were weakened by their own conflicts. However, Abbasid political expansion began in a period of generalized economic expansion. To what extent the leveling of Abbasid power in the ninth century coincided with or was followed by a period of economic stagnation in the ninth and tenth centuries is not so clear. Perhaps Assyrian expansion at the beginning of the first millennium BC should be interpreted similarly.

6 The period of economic downturn and crisis during the time in which these powers achieved their hegemony may also help to account for the relative brevity and instability of their hegemonic power. Thus it appears that maybe both the ascendance to power and its almost immediate subsequent loss by at least the Sassanids and Guptas and of the Mongols may be traced to the underlying economic downturn. The underlying economic downturn first helped eliminate their rivals and then undercut the economic possibilities of the maintenance of prosperity and power of these short-lived hegemons themselves. Each was a flash in the pan.

7 Thus, even control over the Central Asian economic and trade nexuses proved to be insufficient for the maintenance of hegemony in the periods in which there apparently was a down period in the world economic system as a whole.

We do not wish to suggest that there are only cycles and no trends, even if we have paid little attention to the latter in this paper. On the contrary, we believe that these cycles (and probably other technological and socio-political ones) are a constitutive and necessary element of (evolutionary) trends of "development." Similarly, we reiterate that not only synchronic simultaneity but also dis-synchronic "fits" are essential parts in this historical process.

Of course, many – indeed most – of the problems related to our endeavor remain. Much more empirical and analytical work is necessary to identify, establish, and analyze:

1 The extent and expansion of the world system in history.
2 The economic cycle, the range of whose effects would also help establish the extent of the system, or vice versa.
3 The regions and/or polities which at various times fit into the cycle synchronically, dis-synchronically, or not at all.
4 The relationships between political hegemony and economic coreness.
5 The trade relations and economic competition, political alliances, and war of rival hegemons with each other and their respective peripheries.
6 The degree to which there may have been super-hegemony and/or super-accumulation at one time or another.
7 The transformatory roles of B phase crises, and why some are more so than others; and of course
8 The temporal precedence and causative predominance of economic cycles of growth or political cycles of hegemony.
9 What generates the cycle(s) and makes the system tick?

We will be able to derive some partial and very tentative answers from our historical review of political-economic cycles of accumulation and hegemony above. Of course, much more historical work remains to be done. Some work by social scientists that complements our own is being carried forward by Melko (1990), Wilkinson (chapter 7 below and 1987, 1989), Abu-Lughod (1989), Chase-Dunn and Hall (1991), Vasquez (forthcoming), among others. Additional clues for the 5,000-year period might also be derived from the more extensive and careful analysis of the relations of cycles of growth, hegemony, and war for the past 500 years. This analysis has been much developed by Wallerstein (1974), Frank (1978), Keohane (1980), Gilpin (1981), Vayrynen (1983), Thompson (1989), Modelski (1987), Rosecrance (1987), Goldstein (1988), and Chase-Dunn (1989a, b), among others. However, we leave the pursuit of these questions for another time.

We wish to end this chapter by calling for greater attention to at least two more factors in this history. One is the ecological factors, which possibly underlie in part both economic and political cycles and their combination all through the ages. Ecological factors are not limited to "exogenous" climatic changes, possibly also cyclical. Today, many people are increasingly conscious of the fact that "endogenous" economic, political, and social (mis)organization also have deleterious effects on the environment, including the climate. However, both planetary and regional climatic cycles and the consequences of human settlement/land use through irrigation, grazing, and forestry; migration; war and the consequent neglect or destruction of both natural and wo/man-made productive facilities – and other endogenous effects on the environment are nothing new. Neither is human consciousness about them. For centuries, "indigenous" peoples have been very concerned about preserving the environment they depend on. Many peoples have "gone under" because they neglected or abused their ecological environment, both in the recent and in the distant past. One of the shortcomings of our general work on the world system so far and specifically of this article is our failure to devote due attention to these ecological factors.

Another largely missing factor in our account is the many bottom–up social movements, which not only responded to cyclically changing economic and political conditions, but probably also influenced them. Those social movements and rebellions occurring during the B phases are of particular theoretical interest. These may have had direct effects on the hegemonic transitions occurring in B phases.

Historically, such bottom–up social movements were almost never successful in achieving their demands. Even so, many were probably "successful" in limiting or at least affecting their rulers' options – including their options in their conflicts with their neighboring rulers. Moreover, these effects probably were mostly in unexpected directions, which were not necessarily to the liking of any of those who were affected. In the long history of the world system, *people* do make their own history, but not necessarily as they choose.

EPILOGUE

Within a year of this chapter's first public presentation at the thirty-first Annual Convention of the International Studies Association [ISA], March 20–3, 1991 in Vancouver, the following partial preliminary corroboration of our thesis and dating of long cycles took place:

1 David Wilkinson of the Political Science Department at UCLA presented a paper at the thirty-second Annual ISA Convention specifically to "offer an independent empirical check for the Gills and Frank proposal." Wilkinson tested the datings of our A and especially B phases by calculating increases and declines in city populations (above certain thresholds) previously tabulated by Tertius Chandler (1987). Wilkinson sifted through an enormous number of Chandler's "snapshots" of city sizes taken for convenience or other reasons at times that often did not coincide with our suggested inflection/turning points of A and B phases, and concludes:

> The decline data were consistent with treating phases B1, B2, B6, B7 and B8 (numbered consecutively beginning with the first 1700–1500/1400 B phase in our list) as Old Oikumene decline phases, were ambiguous with respect to B4 and B5, and did not reflect B3. On the other hand there were misfitting decline data

> for A2, A7 and A8, and potential misfits in ambiguous data affecting A6 and A5; A4 could not be tested and A3 was not challenged. These results are favorable to the proposition that the Old Oikumene showed A-B phases at least as early as the mid-second millennium BC; but considerable refinement of phase time-boundaries, and data collection for crucial but unmeasured years, is called for.
>
> (Wilkinson 1992: 30)

Of course, Chandler's city-size data and Wilkinson's use of them are not beyond challenge or dispute, which could further support, modify, or detract from our dating of phases and the geographical regions or civilizational units to which they apply. Moreover, the fits are better for west Asia, from which we took most of our cues, than for east Asia, which was less or later integrated into the "system" – but for which the data may also be less reliable. Significantly however, there was no fit at all between changes in city sizes also tabulated by Chandler for the western hemisphere and the phases we identified in the eastern hemisphere. This trans-Atlantic misfit offers a significant corroboration of our Eurasian-wide system and cycles. It suggests that, as far as it goes in Eurasia, the fit is not spurious; since it disappears entirely if we try to extend it beyond the "system" across the Atlantic before 1492.

2 At the same ISA meeting, George Modelski of the Political Science Department at the University of Washington in Seattle informed us that one of his graduate students, Andrew Bosworth, again independently from Wilkinson, tested and largely confirmed our long-cycle phases. His subsequent paper "World cities and world systems: a test of A.G. Frank and B. Gills' 'A' and 'B' cycles" was presented at the Canadian Association of Geographers Conference, Vancouver, 21 May 1992. Bosworth concludes that

> 1) there is significant support in Chandler's data for the existence of long-waves of economic expansion and contraction, each averaging about 250 years in length. Such regularity further reinforces Frank and Gills' contention that these phases condition one another, generating a cyclic alter[n]ation. 2) Chandler's data lend strong support to Frank and Gills' timing of the following phases: B1; A2; B2; A3; B4; A5; A6; B8. 3) Chandler's data are inconclusive or lend mild support to . . . A and B phases 3000–2000 BC; B4; B5. 4) Chandler's data are inconsistent with the location or timing of B3; A4; B6; A7; B7; A8 [for which Bosworth suggests some minor and some greater adjustments].

3 The archaeologists Andrew and Susan Sherratt of the Ashmolean Museum at Oxford University kindly sent us their paper "From luxuries

to commodities: the nature of Mediterranean Age trading systems," presented in a conference at Oxford in December 1989 and published in its proceedings (1991). Under the subtitle "A historical picture" (367–75) the Sherratts, of course entirely independently from us and without our prior knowledge, distinguish the following Bronze Age periods: 2500–2000 BC, 2000–1700 BC, 1700–1400 BC, 1400–1200 BC, and 1200–1000 BC, which coincide almost exactly with our phase dating. Moreover, their textual description of these periods sounds very similar to our A and B phases, at least for the second millennium BC in that part of the world.

4 Klavs Randsborg (1991) reports and summarizes archaeological evidence on datings of climatic cycles and ups and downs in rural settlements, towns, and other centers, production and exchange, and society, culture, and mentality. Many of his datings and periods for the western end and sometimes more of the geographical area of our "world system" also bear on and often confirm – or offer evidence to permit refinements of – our A and B phases. Moreover, Randsborg notes that "today we realize that at any rate the Western Empire (of Rome) showed signs of weakening long before the rise of Islam and that the Carolingian realm was hardly totally isolated" (1991: 167). After noting that there have been some 500 theories devoted to the collapse of the Roman empire, he writes that the "well known 'third-century crisis' . . . was accompanied and probably caused by a dramatic shift in the economic centre of gravity . . . [to] the Levant [which] did not suffer overall decline" or had been the real economic center all along (1991: 169–70). He notes that, by contrast to the 500 theories about its collapse, "considerably fewer" have been devoted to the expansion of the Roman empire; and he concludes that "to fully understand the emergence of the Roman Empire would require study of the centre–periphery relations in Europe and the Mediterranean area that emerged with the Mediterranean civilizations" (1991: 185).

Our study, of which this article on long cycles and hegemonic shifts is but a part, offers a world systemic approach to the study of this as well as other historical and contemporary problems. We are gratified to learn of the two parallel studies by the Sherratts and Randsborg and the two elaborate attempts by Wilkinson and Bosworth to put our "theory" to empirical tests with independently gathered data within a year of its public presentation, which we therefore hope may promote more of "all of the above."

5 A week after the thirty-second ISA Conference, at the joint meetings of the Prehistoric Societies of Britain and France in Bristol, Kristian Kristiansen gave Frank his "The emergence of the European world system in the Bronze Age. Divergence, convergence and social evolution during the first and second millennium BC in Europe," to appear in *Europe in*

the First Millennium BC edited by Jorgen Jensen and Kristian Kristiansen (Department of Archaeology, University of Sheffield). He also told Frank about his forthcoming book *Europe Before History. The European World System in the Second and First Millennium* BC.

In both works, Kristiansen discusses commercial and other links between Mycenaeans in Crete and in central and eastern Europe peoples through the Black Sea as well as between the western Mediterranean and the Tumulus culture in Europe between 1700 BC and especially after 1400 BC, that is during our A phase, and up to the Bronze Age crisis after 1200 which we identified as a B phase. Kristiansen refers to Phoenician expansion through the Atlantic to France and Britain in the ninth and eighth centuries BC, in our A phase. Most significantly, Kristiansen focuses on important events between about 600 and 450 BC and then between 450 and 350 BC. In the first period, Europe was re- or more fully integrated into the Mediterranean and it in turn into the west-Asian world (system?). In central Europe, the Hallstatt cultures first "climaxed" and then "declined" as trade routes shifted and/or they overexploited their peripheries. Between 450 and 350 BC, that is during what we termed a B phase, smaller, regional-scale, more "democratic" regimes spread throughout Europe as commercial connections were again broken.

Most significantly, it was during this same period during the mid-first millennium BC that we identify the incorporation of east Asia into the west-Asian-centered world system, which were connected by Scythian migrations and trade among others. This is also the middle of the same period of what Karl Jaspers termed the "Axial Age," during which major monotheistic religions emerged and spread in various parts of Eurasia, as we noted above. It seems unlikely to have been accidental that all these events, the spread of the world system and its incorporation of distant Asia to the East and Europe to the West, as well as the rise of these religions, all occurred at the same time. Thus, archaeological and historical evidence and its analysis by others more qualified than ourselves does seem to lend ever more support to at least the central part of our thesis about the emergence, spread, and cyclical development of the world system in the first and probably also the second and perhaps even the third millennia BC. Much more work remains to be done, and we are encouraged that so many others are doing it.

6 Philip Kohl has kindly made available to Frank the still unpublished translation of E.N. Chernykn's *Ancient Metallurgy in the USSR: The Early Metal Age* (Cambridge University Press, 1992), in which the Russian scholar says that "peoples of the EMA [Early Metal Age] cultural zone seem to have shared the same developmental cycle: the formation and decline of cultures at various levels generally coincided. . . . Such explosions follow some regular rhythm in accordance with [which]

various provinces at the same time collapse or emerge." Moreover, Chernykn supplies datings for some of these cycles, which also lend further support to our own suggestions above.

7 Frank has now drawn on the above-cited and other recently available sources to refine the identification, and where necessary/possible revise the dating, of these cycles in the pre-Christian Iron and Bronze Ages and to pursue them further back through the third millennium BC (Frank 1993).

NOTE

This chapter first appeared in 1992 as "World system cycles, crises, and hegemonial shifts 1700 BC to 1700 AD," in *Review* 15(4) (fall): 621–87.

REFERENCES

Abu-Lughod, Janet (1989) *Before European Hegemony. The World System AD 1250–1350*, New York: Oxford University Press.

Adams, Robert M. (1974) "Anthropolgical perspectives on ancient trade," *Current Anthropology* 15 (3) (September).

Amin, Samir (1989) *Eurocentrism*, London: Zed.

Ashtor, Eliyahn (1976) *A Social and Economic History of the Near East in the Middle Ages*, London: Collins.

Beckwith, Christopher (1987) *The Tibetan Empire in Central Asia*, Princeton: Princeton University Press.

Bernal, Martin (1987) *Black Athena: The Afroasiatic Roots of Classical Civilization*, New Brunswick: Rutgers University Press.

Blaut, J. (1977) "Where was capitalism born?" in *Radical Geography: Alternative Viewpoints on Contemporary Social Issues*, ed. Richard Peet, Chicago: Maasoufa Press, 95–110.

Bowen Richard L. and Albright, Frank P. (1958) *Archaeological Discoveries in South Arabia*, Baltimore: Johns Hopkins University Press.

Braudel, Fernand (1953) *El Mediterraneo y el mundo Mediterraneo en la época de Felipe II*, vol. 1, Mexico: Fondo de Cultura Ecónomica.

—— (1982) *Civilization and Capitalism, Fifteenth–Eighteenth Century, 2: The Wheels of Commerce*, New York: Harper & Row.

Chandler, Tertius (1987) *Four Thousand Years of Urban Growth: An Historical Census*, Lewiston/Queenston: St David's University Press.

Chase-Dunn, Christopher (1986) "Rise and demise: world-systems and modes of production" (manuscript; Boulder: Westview Press, forthcoming).

—— (1989a) *Global Formation, Structures of the World-Economy*, Oxford: Blackwell.

—— (1989b) "Core/periphery hierarchies in the development of intersocietal networks" (manuscript).

Chase-Dunn, Christopher and Hall, Thomas D. (eds) (1991) *Core/Periphery Relations in Precapitalist Worlds*, Boulder: Westview Press.

Childe, V. Gordon (1942) *What Happened in History*, London: Pelican Books.

Coedes, George (1968) *The Indianized States of Southeast Asia*, ed. Walter F. Vella, Honolulu: University of Hawaii Press.

Dales, G.F. (1976) "Shifting plateau and the Indus Valley in the third millennium BC," *Colloques internationaux*, dur CRNS no. 567.

de Ste Croix, G.E.M. (1981) *The Class Struggle in the Ancient Greek World*, London: Duckworth.

Diakanoff, Igor M. (1969) *Ancient Mesopotamia: Social and Economic History*, Moscow: Central Dept of Oriental Literature.

—— (1974) "The commune in the ancient Near East as treated in the works of Soviet researchers," in *Introduction to Soviet Ethnography*, ed. Stephen and Ethel Dunn, vol. 2, Berkeley, CA: Highgate Road Social Science Station, 519–48.

—— (1990) "Language contacts in the Caucasus and the Near East," in *When Worlds Collide: Indo-Europeans and the Pre-Indo-Europeans*, ed. T.L. Markey and John A.C. Greppin, Karoma Publishers.

Dopsch, Alfons (1923/4) [1st edn 1918] *Wirtschaftliche und soziale Grundlagen der europäischen Kulturentwicklung, aus der Zeit von Caesar bis auf Karl den Grossen*, Vienna: L.W. Seidel & Sohn.

Finley, M.I. (1985) *The Ancient Economy*, 2nd edn, London: Hogarth Press.

Franck, Irene M. and Brownstone, David M. (1986) *The Silk Road. A History*, New York and Oxford: Facts on File.

Frank, Andre Gunder (1978) *World Accumulation 1492–1789*, New York: Monthly Review Press; London: Macmillan.

—— (1990a) "A theoretical introduction to 5,000 years of world system history," *Review* 13 (2) (spring): 155–248.

—— (1990b) "The thirteenth century world system: a review essay," *Journal of World History* 1 (2) (autumn): 249–56.

—— (1991) "A plea for world system history," *Journal of World History* 2 (1) (spring): 1–28.

—— (1993) "Bronze Age world system cycles," *Current Anthropology* 34 (4) (August to October).

Gernet, Jacques (1985) *A History of China*, Cambridge: Cambridge University Press.

Ghurshman, R. (1954) *Iran*, Harmondsworth: Pelican Books.

Gills, B. K. (1989) "Synchronisation, conjuncture, and centre-shift in east Asian international history," paper prepared for the annual meetings of the International Studies Association and the British International Studies Association, London, 1 April.

Gilpin, Robert (1981) *War and Change in World Politics*, Cambridge: Cambridge University Press.

Goldstein, Joshua S. (1988) *Long Cycles. Prosperity and War in the Modern Age*, New Haven: Yale University Press.

Grousset, Rene (1970) *The Empire of the Steppes. A History of Central Asia*, New Brunswick: Rutgers University Press.

Hodgson, M.G.S. (1954) "Hemispheric interregional history as an approach to world history," *UNESCO Journal of World History/Cahiers d'Histoire Mondiale* 1 (3): 715–723.

—— (1974) *The Venture of Islam*, 3 vols, Chicago: University of Chicago Press.

Humphreys, Sarah C. (1978) *History, Economics and Anthropology: The Work of Karl Polanyi*, London: Routledge & Kegan Paul.

Keohane, Robert O. (1980) "The theory of hegemonic stability and changes in international economic regimes, 1967–1977," in *Change in the International System*, ed. Ole Holsti *et al.*, Boulder: Westview Press, 131–62.

—— (1984) *After Hegemony: Cooperation and Discord in the World Political Economy*, Princeton: Princeton University Press.

Kohl, Philip L. (1978) "The balance of trade in southwestern Asia in the mid-third millennium," *Current Anthropology* 13 (3) (September): 463–92.

—— (1984) "Central Asia: paleolithic beginnings to the Iron Age," *Synthèse* no. 14, Paris: Editions Recherche sur les Civilisations.

—— (1987) "The ancient economy, transferable technologies and the Bronze Age world-system: a view from the northeastern frontier of the ancient Near East," in *Centre and Periphery in the Ancient World*, ed. Michael Rowlands, Mogens Larsen, and Kristian Kristiansen, Cambridge: Cambridge University Press, 13–24.

—— (1989) "The use and abuse of world systems theory: the case of the 'pristine' west Asian state," in *Archaeological Thought in America*, ed. C.C. Lamberg-Karlovsky, Cambridge: Cambridge University Press, 218–40.

Kwanten, Luc (1979) *Imperial Nomads*, Leicester: Leicester University Press.

Liu, Xinru (1988) *Ancient India and Ancient China: Trade and Religious Exchanges AD 1–600*, Delhi: Oxford University Press.

Liverani, Mario (1987) "The collapse of the Near Eastern regional system at the end of the Bronze Age: the case of Syria," in *Centre and Periphery in the Ancient World*, ed. Michael Rowlands, Mogens Larsen, and Kristian Kristiansen, Cambridge: Cambridge University Press, 66–73.

Lombard, Maurice (1975) *The Golden Age of Islam*, Amsterdam: North Holland.

Marfoe, Leon (1987) "Cedar forest to silver mountain: social change and the development of long-distance trade in early Near Eastern societies," in *Centre and Periphery in the Ancient World*, ed. Michael Rowlands, Mogens Larsen, and Kristian Kristiansen, Cambridge: Cambridge University Press, 25–35.

McNeill, William (1964) *The Rise of the West. A History of the Human Community*, Chicago: University of Chicago Press.

—— (1983) *The Pursuit of Power: Technology, Armed Force and Society since AD 1000*, Oxford: Blackwell.

Melko, Matthew (1990) "State systems in harmonious conflict," paper presented at the annual meeting of the Japan Society for the Comparative Study of Civilizations, Kokugaluin University, Tokyo, December.

Modelski, George (1987) *Long Cycles in World Politics*, London: Macmillan.

Oates, Joan (1978) "The balance of trade in southwestern Asia in the mid-third millennium," *Current Anthropology* 13 (3) (September): 480–1.

Oppenheim, A. Leo and Reiner, Erica (1977) *Ancient Mesopotamia*, Chicago: University of Chicago Press.

Palat, Ravi Arvind and Wallerstein, Immanuel (1990) "Of what world system was pre-1500 'India' a part," paper presented at the International Colloquium on "Merchants, Companies and Trade," Maison des Sciences de l'Homme, Paris, 30 May–2 June 1990. To be published in *Merchants, Companies, and Trade*, ed. S. Chaudhuri and M. Morineau (forthcoming).

Polanyi, Karl (1981) *The Livelihood of Man*, ed. Harry W. Pearson, New York: Academic Press.

Randsborg, Klaus (1991) *The First Millennium AD in Europe and the Mediterranean: An Archaeological Essay*, Cambridge: Cambridge University Press.

Rosecrance, Richard (1987) "Long cycle theory and international relations," *International Organization* 41 (2) (spring).

Rossabi, Morris (1982) *China Among Equals: The Middle Kingdom and its Neighbors 10–14 Centuries*, Berkeley: University of California Press.

Rostovtzeff, M. (1941) *The Economic and Social History of the Hellenistic World*, vol. 2, London: Oxford University Press.

Roux, Georges (1966) *Ancient Iraq*, Harmondsworth: Pelican.

Rowlands, Michael, Larsen, Mogens and Kristiansen, Kristian (eds) (1987) *Centre and Periphery in the Ancient World*, Cambridge: Cambridge University Press.

Sheratt, Andrew and Susan (1991) "From luxuries to commodities: the nature of Mediterranean Age trading systems," in *Bronze Age Trade in the Mediterranean*, ed. N.H. Gale, Jonsered: Paul Astrows Forlag, 351–84.

Silver, Morris (1985) *Economic Structures of the Ancient Near East*, London: Croom Helm.

Steensgaard, Niels (1972) *Caracks, Caravans and Companies: The Structural Crisis in the European-Asian Trade in the Early Seventeenth Century*, Copenhagen: Student Litterature.

Suzuki, Chusei (1968) "China's relations with Inner Asia: the Hsiung-nu, Tibet," *The Chinese World Order. Traditional China's Foreign Relations*, ed. John K. Fairbank, Cambridge, MA: Harvard University Press, 180–97.

Teggart, Frederick (1939) *Rome and China. A Study of Correlations in Historical Events*, Berkeley: University of California Press.

Thapar, Romila (1966) *A History of India*, vol. 1, Harmondsworth: Penguin Books.

Thompson, William (1989) *On Global War: Historical-Structural Approaches to World Politics*, Columbia: University of South Carolina Press.

van Leur, J.C. (1955) *Indonesian Trade and Society: Essays in Asian Social and Economic History*, The Hague and Bandung: W. van Hoeve.

Vasquez, John A. (forthcoming) *The War Puzzle*, Cambridge: Cambridge University Press.

Vayrynen, Raimo (1983) "Economic cycles, power transitions, political management and wars between major powers," *International Studies Quarterly* 27 (December): 389–418.

Wallerstein, Immanuel (1974) *The Modern World-System*, vol. 1, New York: Academic Books.

—— (1984) *The Politics of the World-Economy*, Cambridge: Cambridge University Press.

—— (1988) "The 'discoveries' and human progress," *Estudos e Ensaios*.

—— (1989a) "World-system analysis: the second phase," paper presented at the annual meeting of the PEWS Section of the American Sociological Association in San Francisco, 13 August.

—— (1989b) "The West, capitalism, and the modern world-system," prepared as a chapter in J. Needham, *Science and Civilization in China*, vol. 7: *The Social Background*, part 2, section 48: "Social and economic considerations" (forthcoming) and *Review* xv (4) (fall 1992).

Warmington, Eric Herbert (1928) *The Commerce between the Roman Empire and India*, Cambridge (2nd edn, Curzon Press, 1974).

Wheatley, Paul (1975) "Satyanrta in Suvarnadvipa: from reciprocity to redistribution in ancient southeast Asia," in *Ancient Civilization and Trade*, ed. Jeremy A. Sabloff and C.C. Lamberg-Karlovsky, Albuquerque: University of New Mexico Press, 227–84.

Wight, Martin (1978) *Power Politics*, New York: Holmes & Meier.

Wilkinson, David (1987) "Central civilization," *Comparative Civilizations Review* 17 (Fall): 31–59.

—— (1989) "The future of the world state: from civilization theory to world politics," paper presented at the annual meeting of the International Studies Association, London, 28 March–1 April.

—— (1992) "Decline phases in civilizations, regions, and oikumenes," paper presented at the thirty-second Annual ISA Convention, 1–4 April.

6

TRANSITIONAL IDEOLOGICAL MODES

Feudalism, capitalism, socialism

Andre Gunder Frank

INTRODUCTION TO TRANSITIONS AND MODES IN THE WORLD SYSTEM

The present "transition from socialism to capitalism" and the possible future "shift of hegemony from the United States to Japan" are occasions to re-examine several scientific tenets of our politics and political tenets of our social science. Among these are 1) the "transition from feudalism to capitalism," 2) the "transition from capitalism to socialism," 3) the process of "transition" itself, 4) the notion of feudal, capitalist, and socialist "modes of production," and 5) the hegemonic rise and decline of Europe and the West in the modern world-capitalist system. The question arises whether any or all of the above are based on scientific analytical categories, or whether they are derived only from fondly held ideological beliefs. Perhaps both contemporary political reality and available historical evidence should now lead us to abandon some or even all these positions.

My tentative conclusion will be that ideological blinkers – or worse, mindset – have too long prevented us from seeing that the world political-economic system long predated the rise of capitalism in Europe and its hegemony in the world. The rise of Europe represented a hegemonic shift from East to West within a pre-existing system. If there was any transition then, it was this hegemonic shift within the system rather than the formation of a new system. Now, we are again in one of the alternating periods of hegemony and rivalry in the world system, which portends a renewed westward shift of hegemony across the Pacific. To identify the system with its dominant mode of production is a mistake. There was no transition from feudalism to capitalism as such. Nor was there (to be) an analogous transition from capitalism to socialism. If these analytical categories of "modes of production" prevent us from seeing the real world political-economic system, it would be better to abandon them altogether. These categories of "transition" and "modes" are not essential or even useful tools, but rather obstacles to the scientific study of the underlying continuity and essential properties of the world system in the past. They also shackle our political struggle and our ability to confront and manage the development of this same system in the present and future.

A number of recent academic publications offer a good opportunity for such a re-examination of the (un?)holy canons in our historical science and contemporary politics. These publications include *The Brenner Debate* (Aston and Philpin 1985), on the transition from feudalism to capitalism in Europe, *Before European Hegemony*, on the westward shift of hegemony in the thirteenth century, by Janet Abu-Lughod (1989), *The Rise and Fall of the Great Powers* in Europe and America, by Paul Kennedy (1987), *Long Cycles in World Politics* during the past five hundred years, by George Modelski (1987), *On Global War* during the same period, by William Thompson (1988), and *Global Formation: Structures of the World-Economy* then and now, by Christopher Chase-Dunn (1989), as well as other works on hegemonic changes.

Several recent articles by Wallerstein also offer a particularly revealing opportunity to re-examine all the issues posed in my opening paragraphs. Wallerstein (1989a) looked back on the past, and forward to the next, fifteen years of "World-system analysis: the second phase" at the 1989 annual meetings of the American Sociological Association. Under the title "The West, capitalism, and the modern world system," Wallerstein (1989b) considers "why in Europe rather than China" in a contribution to a volume edited by Joseph Needham. In two further articles cited below, Wallerstein (1988, 1989c) hones the definition of his modern capitalist world system and its *differentia specifica* from all others. These articles also offer a good occasion for us to re-examine these issues of transitions and modes, as well as those of origins of and hegemony in the modern world-capitalist system. I will do so in this essay from a historical perspective on a world system history in which Europe was only a Johnny-come-lately and temporary hegemon.

Wallerstein (1989b) asks what is distinctive about the modern "world-system," the capitalist "world-system," and capitalism, which are the same for him. Others might quarrel with him about these identities, but I will accept them for now. Examination of Wallerstein's argument about this distinctiveness will show that it is internally self-contradictory and externally contradicted by the historical evidence. My argument will be that Wallerstein's interpretation is too limited, indeed, self-limiting; because he fails to take sufficient account of the *world* system.

I made a similar argument about feudalism and capitalism already in a previous debate. Under the title "With what mode of production does the hen convert maize into golden eggs?" I already argued with Rodolfo Puiggros in 1965 that "if we are to understand the Latin American *problématique* we must begin with the *world-system* that creates it and go outside the self-imposed optical and mental illusion of the Ibero-American or national frame" (Frank 1965, translated in Frank 1969: 231). I now argue that the same imperative also applies to the *problématique* of transition between feudal and capitalist modes of production in Europe.

In the last generation, all sides of the Dobb-Sweezy (recently reprinted in Hilton 1976) and Brenner (Aston and Philpin 1985) debates, like generations of "national frame" and other Eurocentric scholars before them, have sought the answer through a change in the mode of production *within* Europe. Yet if we are to understand this apparently European *problématique* we must also "begin with the world system that creates it" and abandon the "self-imposed optical and mental illusion of the [European] or national frame." If we (re-)examine Wallerstein's argument and the historical evidence from a *world system* perspective, it appears that the world system was not born in 1500; it did not arise in Europe; and it is not distinctively capitalist.

WORLD SYSTEM COMPARISONS AND SIMILARITIES

Wallerstein identifies the most essential characteristics of the modern world-capitalist system variously in 1, 3, 6, and 12 points.

The single most important and defining *differentia specifica* is:

> this ceaseless accumulation of capital that may be said to be its most central activity and to constitute its *differentia specifica*. No previous historical system seems to have had any comparable *mot d'ordre* of social limitlessness. . . . At the level of this central defining activity of ceaseless growth, the ceaseless accumulation of capital . . . no other historical system could have been said to have pursued such a mode of social life for more than at most brief moments. . . . The one thing that seems unquestionable, and unquestioned, is the hyperbolic growth curves – in production, population, and the accumulation of capital – that have been a continuing reality from the sixteenth century. . . . There was the genesis of a radically new system.
>
> (Wallerstein 1989b: 9, 10, 26)

However, accumulation has played a, if not the, central role in the world system far beyond Europe and long before 1500, as Gills and Frank (chapter 3 above) emphasize under the title "The cumulation of accumulation." Numerous historical and theoretical objections to this thesis, including Wallerstein's, are examined in detail and rejected as unfounded in Frank (1990). A small sample of the vast evidence in support of earlier world system accumulation is presented below.

Perhaps the differences become greater if we compare Wallerstein's modern capitalist world-system with alternatives on more counts than just one. Elsewhere, Wallerstein distinguishes three different characteristics that supposedly set his system apart: "this descriptive trinity (core-periphery,

A/B [cycle phases], hegemony-rivalry) as a pattern maintained over centuries is unique to the modern world-system. Its origin was precisely in the late fifteenth century" (Wallerstein 1988: 108). As it happens, and well before reading Wallerstein's above-cited 1988 article, Gills and Frank (chapter 3 above) emphasized the very *same* trinity of center/periphery, A/B-phased cycles, and hegemony-rivalry as the other central defining characteristics of our world system. Certainly Chase-Dunn (1986), Abu-Lughod (1989), Wilkinson (chapter 7 below and 1987, 1989), among others, have also found these same features earlier and elsewhere. Wallerstein (1989a) himself recognizes this and said so in his above-cited review at the American Sociological Association meetings.

So perhaps we should go into more detail still. Elsewhere, Wallerstein (1989c: 8–10) summarizes six "realities of the evolution of this historical system." Wallerstein (1989a) also does us the service of cutting up these realities into even more detail and extending the list to twelve "characteristics presumed to be the description of the capitalist world-economy":

> (1) the ceaseless accumulation of capital as its diving force;
> (2) an axial division of labor in which there is a core–periphery tension, such that there is some form of unequal exchange (not necessarily as defined originally by Arghiri Emmanuel) that is spatial;
> (3) the structural existence of a semi peripheral zone;
> (4) the large and continuing role of non-wage labor alongside of wage labor;
> (5) the correspondence of the boundaries of the capitalist world-economy to that of an interstate system comprised of sovereign states;
> (6) the location of the origins of this capitalist world-economy earlier than in the nineteenth century, probably in the sixteenth century;
> (7) the view that this capitalist world-economy began in one part of the globe (largely Europe) and later expanded to the entire globe via a process of successive "incorporations;"
> (8) the existence in this world-system of hegemonic states, each of whose periods of full or uncontested hegemony has however been relatively brief;
> (9) the non-primordial character of states, ethnic groups, and households, all of which are constantly created and recreated;
> (10) the fundamental importance of racism and sexism as organizing principles of the system;
> (11) the emergence of anti-systemic movements that simultaneously undermine and reinforce this system;
> (12) a pattern of both cyclical rhythms and secular trends that incarnate the inherent contradictions of the system and which accounts for the systemic crisis in which we are presently living.
>
> (Wallerstein 1989b: 3–4)

I contend here (and defend in Frank 1990 and Gills and Frank chapter 3 above) that 240 of these 242 words by Wallerstein about the 12 characteristics of the world system after 1500 are also equally and totally true of world economy/system(s) before 1500, whether "capitalist" or not. The two exceptions of one word each are under (6) the origins . . . probably in the "sixteenth" century and under (7) that this world system began in "(largely Europe)." Everything else Wallerstein says about the presumed characteristics of the "capitalist world-economy" and the "modern world-system" was equally true also of the medieval and ancient world system.

Thus, if we examine these lists, no matter whether of a single defining *differentia specifica*, or the trinity, or a half-dozen realities, or of the full dozen characteristics, we find that *each* of them is also equally true of other earlier world systems and/or of the *same* world system before 1500. Of course, I do not expect readers to accept this statement only on my say-so. They must undertake these comparisons themselves. Fortunately however, in doing so they will find an excellent guide, no doubt better than me, in Wallerstein himself. For he now has some doubts about his own position and finds "an uncomfortable blurring of the distinctiveness of the patterns of the European medieval and modern world" (1989b: 33). Indeed, Wallerstein himself is among those who chip away at, and *de facto* question, their own "unquestionable" faith in various ways.

> Many of these [previous] historical systems had what we might call proto-capitalist elements. That is, there often was extensive *commodity* production. There existed producers and traders who sought *profit*. There was *investment* of *capital*. There was *wage-labor*. There was *Weltanschauungen* consonant with *capitalism*. But none had quite crossed the threshold of creating a system whose primary driving force was the incessant accumulation of capital.
>
> (Wallerstein 1989b: 35, my emphasis)

> We must now renew the question, why did not capitalism emerge anywhere earlier. It seems unlikely that the answer is an insufficient *technological base*. . . . It is unlikely that the answer is an absence of an *entrepreneurial spirit*. The history of the world for at least two thousand years prior to 1500+ shows an enormous set of groups, throughout multiple historical systems, who showed an aptitude and inclination for *capitalist enterprise* – as producers, as *merchants*, as *financiers*. "Proto-capitalism" was so widespread one might consider it to be a constitutive element of all the redistributive/tributary world-empires the world has known. . . . Something was preventing it [capitalism]. For they did have the *money* and energy at their disposition, and we have seen in the modern world how powerful these weapons can be.
>
> (Wallerstein 1989b: 59–60, my emphasis)

Moreover, Wallerstein also negates the uniqueness of his "modern-world-capitalist-system" in numerous other passages and ways. Since it would be tedious to dissect all these instances, I will limit myself to citing a representative few. "All the empirical work of the past 50 years on these other systems has tended to reveal that they had much more extensive commodification than previously suspected. . . . It is of course a matter of degree" (1989b: 19, 20). So are the relation and relative "political control" and "extra-economic coercion" to the "free" market here and there, then and now (1989b: 14).

After Wallerstein's own recount of (proto)capitalist "elements" and matters of degree far and wide, long before 1500, it would be even more tedious for me to repeat my own as set out in Frank (1990) and even more in Gills and Frank (chapter 3 above). Suffice it to observe here that 1) Wallerstein will readily admit that "hyperbolic growth curves in production, population and accumulation of capital" have been *cyclical* since 1500; and 2) Wallerstein and others must also recognize that in many times and places rapid and massive growth of production, population, and accumulation occurred for much more than "brief" moments long before 1500. Wallerstein himself helps us observe that this was true for instance during the period 1050–1250 in Europe. The same, only much more so, also occurred *at the same time* in Song China. Some centuries earlier, *capital accumulation* accelerated in Tang China, then in the Islamic caliphate, and previously in Gupta India and Sassanian Iran, among many other instances.

However, the economy and polity of the ancient and even the archaic world (system) were also characterized by all Wallerstein's "elements" of (proto)capitalism (capital, money, profit, merchants, wage-labor, entrepreneurship, investment, technology, etc.) emphasized above *and* the ones he synthesized for the "modern" world-capitalist system (capital accumulation, core–periphery, hegemony, interstate system, cycles, racism, sexism, social movements – the lot). Simply recall the examples best known to westerners: Rome, China (great canals and walls), Egypt and Mesopotamia (irrigation systems and monuments). What is more (important for world system analysis), long cyclical ups (and subsequent downs) in accumulation may be said to have been world-systemic if not world system wide. The important reason is that they were systemically and systematically related to each other, e.g. in Han China, Gupta India, Parthian and then Sassanian Persia, imperial and then Byzantine Rome, Axum East Africa, and of course "barbarian" Inner Asia, not to mention other parts of the world.

That is, the historical evidence also meets the more difficult test of the specificity of capitalism posed by Maurice Godelier (1990). Godelier makes a fourfold classification of characteristics similar to those of Wallerstein. Godelier's position is even further from mine than Wallerstein's. Yet even Godelier remarks that the four characteristics of capitalism he identifies did *not begin* with capitalism. However, he argues that the necessary and sufficient conditions of a new (capitalist) economic structure are their "combination in a new relation" and their "mutual connection" with each other (1990: 9–10). Yet the historical evidence shows that even the combination and mutual relation of Godelier's 4, or Wallerstein's 3, 6, or 12 characteristics did not begin with capitalism in 1500.

Significantly, however, Wallerstein and the others, excepting Wilkinson, are only talking about some similarities with *other* "world" systems. Following them so far, I am only arguing from the old adage that "if it looks like a duck, walks like a duck, quacks like a duck (and demonstrably exhibits nine other descriptive realities besides, which Wallerstein summarizes for his world-system), it must also be a (world system) duck." But in that case, it or they could just be one or more *other* world system ducks, as Chase-Dunn argues. Even Wallerstein might admit this comparison, though the similarities might make him uncomfortable. So what is this invisible and still unspecified "something" that distinguishes the modern world-capitalist system? Perhaps, then, it is only the *Weltanschauung* of capitalism itself by Smith and Marx, and Wallerstein and Amin now, as well as by most others, which retrospectively sees a qualitative break around 1500 where historically there was none. We will observe below that the essential something in this *Weltanschauung* they all share turns out to be the supposed identity of the (capitalist) mode of production *and* system. According to Smith and Marx who led me astray in writing my own book two decades ago, the discovery of America and of the passage to the East Indies by the Cape of Good Hope were the greatest events in the history of humankind and opened up new ground for the bourgeoisie. That is from a European point of view, of course. But from a wider world perspective these two events, as well as others within Europe, were only developments in the unfolding of world history itself. Why were these two new passages to the East and West Indies important, even for Europeans, and why did they want to go there in the first place, if it was not because of what was going on there – and what was to be gotten there – before 1500?

WORLD SYSTEM TRANSITIONS AND CONTINUITY

Jacques Gernet (1985: 347–8) proposes an alternative *world* perspective:

> what we have acquired the habit of regarding – according to the history of the world that is in fact no more than the history of the West – as the beginning of modern times was only the repercussion of the upsurge of the urban, mercantile civilizations whose realm extended, before the Mongol invasion, from the Mediterranean to the Sea of China. The West gathered up part of this legacy and received from it the leaven which was to make possible its own development.

> The transmission was favored by the crusades of the twelfth and thirteenth centuries and the expansion of the Mongol empire in the thirteenth and fourteenth centuries. . . . There is nothing surprising about this Western backwardness: the Italian cities . . . were at the terminus of the great commercial routes of Asia. . . . The upsurge of the West, which was only to emerge from its relative isolation thanks to its maritime expansion, occurred at a time when the two great civilizations of Asia [China and Islam] were threatened.

In other words, the real issue is not just whether there were *other* world system ducks earlier and elsewhere that had the same 1, 3, 6, or 12 characteristics as Wallerstein's world system duck. Nor is the issue one of transition between one and the other such ducks or systems. The real questions are whether there really was a transition to the birth of *this* world system around 1500, or whether the real historical development of *this same* ugly world system duckling reaches further back in time, and whether this system and the motive forces for its "transitions" were based in Europe or elsewhere in the wider world.

I believe that what Jacques Hamel and Mohammed Sfia (1990) call a "continuist" perspective is appropriate in answering these questions. Such a perspective is suggested in their "Presentation" of Wallerstein, Godelier, and others in *Sociologie et Sociétés*. From that perspective, the historical record suggests that this same historical world economic and interstate system is at least five thousand years old. There was more continuity than discontinuity or even transition in this world (capitalist) economy as a historical system across the supposed divide of the world around 1500. More detailed support for this continuity is presented in Frank (1990) and Gills and Frank (chapter 3 above). Moreover, therefore, if there really was a "transition to capitalism" in the sixteenth century (which is also subject to challenge), it took place not in Europe or especially due to changes within Europe but instead in the long pre-existing world system and importantly due to changes in the system outside Europe. In other words, "to understand the *problématique* . . . [of transition 'in' Europe] we must begin with the world system that creates it!"

To anticipate some academic scientific and practical political conclusions, we may well recognize the last of Wallerstein's above-cited six points about the historical system: the system may well have a life cycle, as he says. But this cycle need not, and did not, begin with any transition from feudalism around 1500 as Wallerstein claims . . . and it need not, and may not, end in 2050–2100 with a transition to socialism as Wallerstein suggests. If we can identify any real transitions, each is likely really to be a transition between a transition and a transition.

On these issues of transition and/or continuity in the world system, Wallerstein's own account is again helpful, even though – or perhaps because – its short-sighted Eurocentric perspective and internally contradictory arguments seriously undermine his own central argument and position. Thus, like Gernet, Abu-Lughod, and others, Wallerstein also takes note of the Mongols and the Crusades, but . . .

> The feudal system in western Europe seems quite clearly to have operated by a pattern of cycles of expansion and contraction of two lengths: circa 50 years (which seem to resemble the so-called Kondratieff cycles found in the capitalist world economy) and circa 200–300 years. . . . The patterns of the expansions and contractions are clearly laid out and widely accepted among those writing about the late Middle Ages and early modern times in Europe. . . . It is the long swing that was crucial. Thus 1050–1250+ was a time of the expansion of Europe (the Crusades, the colonizations). . . . The "crisis" or great contractions of 1250–1450+ included the Black Plague. (1989b: 33, 34)

Thus, even according to Wallerstein there was systematic *cyclical continuity* across his 1500 divide. Moreover, since Wallerstein omits doing so (despite his comparison with China), we may note in passing that not incidentally 1050–1250 was also the time of great advances in technology, accumulation, and expansion in Song China; and that the crisis of 1250–1450 was world (system) wide, including China, as Abu-Lughod (1989) has rightly emphasized. Thus the clearly laid-out "pattern of expansions and contractions," including probably that of "demand and prices" (Wallerstein 1989b: 14) was not just (west) European, but perhaps world system wide. At the very least, their manifestations in Europe were also a function of its (cyclically determined?) changing center–periphery relations of trade and hegemony–rivalry with other parts of the world economy. All these not only merit study *per se* or to put the whole historical jigsaw puzzle together, but they require analysis to make any sense out of changes in Europe – or in any other part of Eurasia and Africa. That is, the systemic relations extended far beyond Europe.

Yet even Wallerstein also recognizes several additional pieces of the jigsaw puzzle outside of Europe. Nonetheless, he is still unable to put it together; because he remains wedded to his old *Weltanschauung*.

> The collapse of the Mongols [was a] crucial non-event. . . . The eleventh-century economic upsurge in the West that we have discussed was matched by a new market articulation in China. . . . Both linked up to a Moslem trading ecumene across the Middle East. China's commercialization reinforced this model [why not system?]. . . . The Mongol link completed the picture. What disrupted this vast trading *world-system* was the pandemic Black Death, itself

> quite probably a consequence of that very trading network. It hurt everywhere, but it completely eliminated the Mongol link.
>
> (1989b: 57, 58, my emphasis)

For Wallerstein, the collapse of the Mongols was the last of "four elements in an explanation" of the rise of capitalism in the West out of "the effect of the cumulated collapses." The other three were "the collapse of the signeurs, the collapse of the states, the collapse of the Church" (1989b: 47). There were political-economic factors behind all four collapses. "Most governments became bankrupt . . . incapable of controlling their mercenaries. . . . The Church was a major economic actor itself, and was hurt by the economic downturn in the same way that both signeurs . . . and states . . . were hurt" (1989b: 47–55). Yet Wallerstein refuses to draw the logical – and historical – conclusions: to put the whole picture in the jigsaw puzzle together, we must liberate ourselves from the imaginary transition within the imaginary system confined to Europe. The solution to the puzzle of the four simultaneous and cumulative collapses and to the "crisis of feudalism in Europe" itself was (to be) found outside the limited and optically illusory framework of "feudal Europe." We must instead look at the real transitions in the real world system and its history as a whole. The resolution of the "crisis of feudalism" involved changing relations within, and further expanding of, the whole world system itself – of course, at a world *system time*, which propitiously rendered this solution possible if not necessary.

REAL WORLD SYSTEM ISSUES AND PROPOSALS

To understand this and subsequent transitions therefore, we should:

1 **Abandon the schema of a "European" world (system)** and look outside. Wallerstein and so many others look out the window from their European house; but they still cannot see its (still marginal) place in the world landscape. The Mongols are seen as "the link" in a Chinese–Islamic "trading world-system" before 1500 and yet Wallerstein and others still refuse to accept the prior existence of this *system*.
2 **Look at the whole world system**. China, the Mongols, the Islamic world, and Europe, not to mention other parts of the Afro-Eurasian oikumene were linked into a trading and interstate world system in the thirteenth century, *à la* Abu-Lughod. Should we recognize that this was the world system out of whose crisis hegemonic European capitalism emerged? Posing the right question is getting more than half the right answer. Wallerstein provides another part of the right answer himself. Of course, however, since he refuses to pose the question, he also does not see the answer. Was the "crucial cycle" limited to Europe? Most probably not. Wallerstein himself suggests some of its extra-European

elements. Indeed, all four of the political economic elements of his explanation for the rise of capitalism in Europe include extra-European elements: the Mongols most obviously so, but also the financial crises of the governments, landlords, and Church in Europe. All were related to – in part reflections of? – the development of the 1250–1450 crisis outside Europe and in the world system as a whole. Similarly, the 1050–1250 expansion in Europe had also been part of a world (system) wide expansion (or else why would or could the Crusaders have gone eastward to seek fortune?). The crucial cycle was in the world system itself.

3 **Recognize long cycles of development in this world system**. Wallerstein recognizes that "it is the long swing that is crucial: "1050–1250 up-swing and 1250–1450 downswing . . . and 1450–1600 long sixteenth century" (renewed) upswing, before the renewed "seventeenth century crisis." Moreover, Wallerstein recognizes that it was the "crisis" during the 1250–1450 downturn that led to "cumulative collapse" and then to regeneration and a new "genesis." However, Wallerstein and others neglect to ask – and therefore to find any answer – to the crucial question: crisis, collapse, new genesis *in what system*? Of course, as George Modelski (who is also incapable of seeing this system, *vide* Modelski 1987) correctly pointed out to my seminar, "in order for us to look for a cycle, we must first be clear about the system in which this cycle occurs." So there are two possibilities: the same European system predates 1500, or Europe was part of a world system (also the same) that also predates 1500. Either way Wallerstein's and others' temporal and Eurocentric myopia blinds them to seeing the whole picture of systemic historical reality.

4 **Consider the probability of a continuous cyclical process of development** in/of the *same single* world system. Of course, if there was a long cycle and it was crucial, the 1050–1250 upswing and the 1250–1400 downswing must have been the cyclical expression and development of an *already existing system*. However, in that case of course, also, the 1050–1250 upswing may well have been a (re)genesis from a previous crisis/collapse/downswing, which in turn was the culmination of a previous upswing, and so on . . . how far back? Curiously, Wallerstein sees a single cycle, at least in Europe, but a variety of "unstable" systems around the world, each of which "seldom lasted more than 4–500 years" (1989b: 35). On the other hand, Abu-Lughod (1989) sees a single world system, certainly in the thirteenth century, on which she concentrates, but also in earlier periods. However, each of her world systems cyclically rise (out of what?) and decline (into what?). Neither Wallerstein nor Abu-Lughod is (yet?) willing to join their insights in the additional – obvious? – step to see both a single world system and its continuous cyclical development.

5 **Realize that hegemony in the world system did not begin in Europe after 1500**, but that it shifted to Europe in the course of hegemonic crises and decline in the East of the same world system. Even Wallerstein quotes Abu-Lughod (1989) that "Before European hegemony, the Fall of the East preceded the Rise of the West." Abu-Lughod is at pains to show how and why the various parts of the East declined at this time in world-systemic terms. Therefore, the root causes of the rise of the West to hegemony *and* the transition to capitalism in Europe cannot be found within Europe alone, but must be sought in the course of the development of the world system – and also within its other parts – as a whole. "If we are to understand the *problématique* . . . we must begin with the world system that creates it!"

6 **Pursue the origins of the world system** – and of its development in the past half-millennium – as far back in time and out in space as the historical evidence and our ability to analyze it permit. Wallerstein (1989b: 37) writes:

> Obviously, any historical occurrence has immediate roots whose derivation can be traced back, *ad infinitum*. However, if we believe that the critical turning-point was 500–2500 years earlier, we are coming up with a cultural-genetic explanation which in effect says that the development of capitalism/"modernity" in the West, and in the West first, had been rendered "inevitable" by this earlier "civilizational" system.

The first sentence is true, and so is the premise in the first half of the second. However, the conclusions in the remainder are totally unwarranted and triply false. Tracing the roots of the present world system backwards in no wise obliges us to come up with cultural-genetic explanations; still less with civilizational ones; and least of all with the inevitability of the present or future outcome. It is at least equally possible – and as I argue here, much preferable – to come up with a longer and wider historical systemic explanation, within which earlier civilizational factors play only a partial role, and inevitbility none at all. Therefore, Wallerstein's otherwise correct rejection of causation by alternative civilizational factors and their various interpretations by others is largely beside the point.

The "explanation" is not to be sought through the civilizational roots of the rise, nor the decline, of Rome, which Wallerstein (1989b: 37–9) discusses after other authors. The same goes for his discussion (pp. 39–47) of the "hurrah" for later culture in England and Italy schools. Instead, we should seek the explanations in the development of the world system, within which Rome (and its rise and decline) were only regional parts (along with Parthian Iran, Gupta India, Han China, Central Asia, and Africa) and transitional phases. The same goes for Italy and England. This holistic systematic analysis does not, of course, deny the importance of local, national, regional, or other developments. It only places them in systemic contexts, which also influence these developments – and are in turn influenced by them. However, the whole is more than the sum of its parts, and the *problématique* of no part is properly understandable in isolation from the whole of which it is but a part. Wallerstein, of course, understands this truth full well – for the period since 1500. But he (still) subjectively refuses to admit it for the time before, despite the evidence he himself cites, which objectively supports it. I examine much more evidence for tracing this world system back at least 5,000 years and challenge as unfounded the even greater reservations of others against so doing in Frank 1990 and Gills and Frank chapter 3 above.

7 **Do not pursue the idea of "proto-captalism"** into the blind alley it is likely to be. The first supposed resolution of the feudalism–capitalism debate a quarter-century ago was to try to "compromise" on "semi-feudalism" going on to become "semi-" "proto-" capitalism. I thought that this "compromise" was a nonstarter then; and experience has shown that the "mode of production" debate detracted from better understanding of the *problématique* analyzing the world system that creates itself. Wallerstein made his major contribution by taking this high road himself. It is likely only to befuddle our analysis again to argue now that the essential characteristics of the modern world-capitalist system, quoted in 240 of the 242 words of Wallerstein's 12-point synthesis above, also are "proto-capitalist" "elements," which can be found all around the world in different times and "systems." It is better to proceed as Wallerstein (1989b: 16) does with the

> effort . . . to establish a continuous pattern of scientific/technological advance, located in many different world regions (China, India, the Near [to us] East, the Mediterranean zone), into which recent western scientific efforts have fit themselves, primarily since the sixteenth century. By underlining the continuities, this argument reduces the distinctiveness of what occurred in western Europe. Furthermore, it has been argued that, in this arena as in many others, Europe had previously been a "backward" or "marginal" zone, implying therefore that any explanation of significant change could not be accounted for exclusively or even primarily in terms of some west European affinity . . . or tradition.

Of course, this means that recourse to the idea of "proto-capitalism" in "different" and "earlier" systems is not at all helpful. Instead, it is much more useful to recognize that technical change *and capital accumulation*, as well as all other characteristics of Wallerstein's "modern" world system also characterized earlier times and system(s). In that case indeed, "we find an uncomfortable blurring of the distinctiveness of the patterns [of capitalism and proto-capitalism] of the medieval and modern world" (1989b: 33). What is it then that makes Wallerstein and others so "uncomfortable"? The answer is that this systemic holistic procedure threatens to pull the rug out from under the very foundations of their "scientific" edifice and also of their fondest ideological beliefs!

8 **Liberate ourselves from the optical illusion of the false identity of "system" and "mode of production."** Samir Amin contends that the system could not have been the same system before 1500 because it did not have the capitalist mode of production, which only developed later. Before 1500, according to Amin and others, modes of production were tributary. My answer is that the system was the same no matter what the mode of production was. The focus on the mode of production blinds us to seeing the more important systemic continuity. Wallerstein makes the same confusion between "mode" and "system." Indeed *the single* differentiae specificae *of Wallerstein's modern world-capitalist system is its mode of production.* Wallerstein's identification and also confusion of "system" and "mode" is evident throughout his works and widely recognized by others. So it is in the article I am "dissecting" here. For example:

> the difference between capitalism as a mode of production and the multiple varieties of a redistributive or tributary mode of production is surely not, as often asserted . . . [in] "extra-economic coercion." For there is considerable extra-economic coercion in our capitalist/"modern" historical system, and markets of some kind have almost always existed in other historical systems. The most we can argue is a distinction that is more subtle.
>
> (1989b: 14)

Wallerstein's system is his mode. So it is for Amin (1989), Brenner (Aston and Philpin 1985) – and also for their ideological opponents on the Right. (It may be appropriate to note parenthetically that our disagreement has generated long friendly discussions with the last named and still permits collaboration in our second joint book on contemporary problems with the first two in Amin *et al.* [1990]. Moreover, both have written responses to my historical arguments in Amin [chapter 8 below] and Wallerstein [chapter 10 below].) Nonetheless, I maintain that once Wallerstein and Amin rattle at this mode so much as to blur its distinctiveness, they also rattle at the scaffolding of the construction of this system in 1500 – to the point of the total breakdown of Wallerstein's argument about the *differentiae specificae* and the beginning of his modern world-capitalist system. The 1, 3, 6, or 12 essential characteristics of the world system, and its beginning, antedate Wallerstein's period by far.

We should *separate* our notions of system and mode. Then, we could at least recognize the real existence and millennial development of the world system. I believe it is high time to abandon the sacrosanct belief in the ideological formulations about these supposed different modes of production or the supposed transitions between them in the millennial world system. A transition is a transition between a transition and a transition, as I learned in Allende's Chile.

Therefore, I agree with Godelier (1990) when he says (p. 35) that there are various ways to be materialist. However, I do not agree with his opinion (p. 28) that making a theory of the articulation of modes of production or the transitions among them is now a task of greatest urgency. On the contrary, I believe that materialism, experience, and good sense urge us to abandon this quest and to seek another more fruitful one based on the material analysis of material world system development.

9 **Therefore, also dare to abandon (the sacrosanct belief in) capitalism** as a distinct mode of production and separate system. What was the ideological reason for my and Wallerstein's "scientific" construction of a sixteenth-century transition (from feudalism in Europe) to a modern world-capitalist economy and system? It was the belief in a subsequent transition from capitalism to socialism, if not immediately in the world as a whole, at least through "socialism in one country" after another. Traditional Marxists and many others who debated with us, even more so, were intent on preserving faith in the prior but for them more recent transition from one (feudal) mode of production to another (capitalist) one. Their political/ideological reason was that they were intent on the subsequent transition to still another and supposedly different socialist mode of production. That was (and is?) the position of Marxists, traditional and otherwise, like Brenner (Aston and Philpin 1985) and Anderson (1974). That is still the position of Samir Amin (1989), who, like Wallerstein, now wants to take refuge in "proto-capitalism" – and by extension "proto-socialism." (Before he was ousted after the Tiananmen massacre, Chinese Premier Zhao Ziyang came up with the idea that China is now only in the stage of "primary" socialism.) If Maurice Godelier and Samir Amin among others would dare to undertake a "transition" from their "scientific" categories, they could spare themselves and their readers some of the political (dis)illusions regarding recent events in the "Second" and "Third" Worlds.

TRANSITIONAL SCIENTIFIC AND POLITICAL CONCLUSIONS

Is there a scientific/historical/academic justification for meddling with "proto-capitalism" in such a supposed long transition from feudalism to capitalism – or from capitalism to proto-socialism? No, definitely not, as the internal contradictions in Wallerstein's argument amply demonstrate.

So is there still a political/ideological reason to hold on to the fond belief in a supposed "transition from feudalism to capitalism," around 1800, or 1500, or whenever – to support the belief in a "transition to socialism" in 1917, or 1949, or whenever? Is there any such reason still to continue looking for this earlier transition and its hegemonic development only in Europe, while real hegemony is now shifting (no doubt through the contemporary and near-future nonhegemonic interregnum) back toward Asia? No, there is none.

Ironically, Ronnie Reagan, Maggie Thatcher, François Mitterrand, and all the capitalists they represent are equally – or even more – infatuated with the ideology of capitalist distinctiveness, except that they glorify it. Their opponents on the Left disagree with this valuation and still want to overcome capitalism through the transition to socialism. The Right, instead, want to preserve and glorify capitalism while they glory in the self-destruction they see of Marxism, socialism, and the Evil Empire of the others. However, their ideological faith in the supposedly universally beneficial glories of the "magic" of the market, of course, also lack scientific foundation in reality. The world system wide reality is the competitive dog-eat-dog war of all against all (*à la* Hobbes), in which only the few can win and the many must lose. And so it has been for millennia, thanks to the world system's unequal structure and uneven process, which Wallerstein helps us identify.

We would all do better to see the reality of the globe-embracing structure and the long historical development of the whole world system itself, full stop. Better recognize this system's "unity in diversity," as Mikhail Gorbachev said at the United Nations. That would really be a "transition" in thinking. This "transition" would help us much better to choose among the diversities which are really available in that world system – *Vives cettes différences!* Moreover, this transition in thinking could also help us to understand the real transitions that there are and to guide us in the struggle for the good and against the socially bad difference – *A luta continua!*

NOTE

This chapter first appeared in 1991 as "Transitional ideological modes: feudalism, capitalism, socialism," in *Critique of Anthropology* 11 (2) (summer): 171–88.

REFERENCES

Abu-Lughod, Janet (1989) *Before European Hegemony. The World System A.D. 1250–1350*, New York: Oxford University Press.

Amin, Samir (1988) *L'Eurocentrisme. Critique d'une ideologie*, Paris: Anthropos.

—— (1989) "Le Système mondial contemporain el les systèmes anterieurs" (manuscript).

Amin, S., Arrighi, G., Frank, A.G. and Wallerstein, I. (1982) *Dynamics of the World Economy*, New York: Monthly Review Press; London: Macmillan.

—— (1990) *Transforming the Revolution: Social Movements and the World-System*, New York: Monthly Review Press.

Anderson, Perry (1974) *Lineages of the Absolutist State*, London: New Left Books.

Aston, T. and Philpin, C. (1985) *The Brenner Debate*, Cambridge: Cambridge University Press.

Chase-Dunn, Christopher (1986) "Rise and demise: world-systems and modes of production" (manuscript) (Boulder: Westview Press, forthcoming).

—— (1989a) *Global Formation: Structures of the World-Economy*, Oxford: Basil Blackwell.

—— (1989b) "Core/periphery hierarchies in the development of intersocietal networks" (manuscript).

Frank, Andre Gunder (1965) "Con que modo de produccion convierte la gallina maiz en huevos de oro?" *El Gallo Ilustrado*, Suplemento de *El Dia, Mexico*, 31 October and 25 November.

—— (1969) *Latin America: Underdevelopment or Revolution*, New York: Monthly Review Press.

—— (1990) "A theoretical introduction to 5,000 years of world system history," *Review* 13 (2) (spring): 155–250.

Gernet, Jacques (1985) *A History of Chinese Civilization*, Cambridge: Cambridge University Press.

Godelier, Maurice (1990) *Sociologie et Sociétés* 22 (1) (June).

Hamel, Jacques and Sfia, Mohammed (1990) "Presentation," *Sociologie et Sociétés* 22 (1) (June).

Hilton, R.H. (ed.) (1976) *The Transition from Feudalism to Capitalism*, London: New Left Books.

Kennedy, P. (1987) *The Rise and Fall of the Great Powers*, New York: Random House.

Modelski, George (1987) *Long Cycles in World Politics*, London: Macmillan.

Thompson, William R. (1988) *On Global War. Historical-Structural Approaches to World Politics*, Columbia: University of South Carolina Press.

Wallerstein, Immanuel (1974) *The Modern World-System*, vol. 1, New York: Academic Books.

—— (1988) "The 'discoveries' and human progress," *Estudos e Ensaios*.

—— (1989a) "World-system analysis: the second phase," paper presented at the annual meetings of the PEWS Section of the American Sociological Association in San Francisco, 13 August 1989; published in *Review* 13 (2) (spring 1990).

—— (1989b) "The West, capitalism, and the modern world-system," prepared as a chapter in Joseph Needham, *Science and Civilization in China*, vol. 7: *The Social Background*, part 2, section 48: *Social and Economic Considerations* (forthcoming). Published in *Review* 15 (4) (fall 1992): 561–619; and as "L'Occident, le capitalisme, et le systéme-monde moderne," in *Sociologies et Sociétés* (Montreal), 21 (1) (June 1990).

—— (1989c) "Culture as the ideological battleground of the modern world-system," *Hitotsubashi Journal of Social Studies* 21 (1) (August).

Wilkinson, David (1987) "Central civilization," *Comparative Civilizations Review* 17 (Fall): 31–59.

—— (1988) "World-economic theories and problems: Quigley vs. Wallerstein vs.

Central civilization," paper delivered at the annual meeting of the International Society for the Comparative Study of Civilizations, 26–29 May.
—— (1989) "The future of the world state: from civilization theory to world politics," paper delivered at the annual meeting of the International Studies Association, London, 28 March–1 April.

Part IV

THE WORLD SYSTEM: 500 YEARS OR 5,000?

Discussing the theoretical, historical, and political issues

7

CIVILIZATIONS, CORES, WORLD ECONOMIES, AND OIKUMENES

David Wilkinson

Interested in wars and their causes, I found that to study them with any hope of success it was important to study the whole system that generated them. This in turn led me to the study of "civilization" and civilizations, which seemed the best name for such macrosocial systems; but this study in turn compelled the study of their subsystems – e.g. cores; of their nonmilitary aspects – e.g. world economies; and of their social "containers" – e.g. oikumenes. And at that point my work intersected the work of Christopher Chase-Dunn, Barry Gills, Andre Gunder Frank, and others, who had arrived at the same subject from their different provenances. The purpose of this piece, then, is to provide a set of definitions and theses which summarize the way I now organize my work on civilizations, cores, world-economies, and oikumenes, so as to present it at once as a counterpart and a contribution to their undertaking.

"CIVILIZATION"

1 In the time and space-bounded "ocean" of human sociocultural phenomena there exists a kind of vast social entity, a *collection of interacting cities*, a *civilization*, which functions in varying degrees as a real unity or "atomism," and as a field. A "civilization" is not a "culture," a "state," or a "nation." Ordinarily the boundaries of this social entity transcend the geographical boundaries of national, state, economic, linguistic, cultural, or religious groups.[1]

2 Due to the interdependence of the whole civilization as a system/field and its parts, these vast civilizational social networks tangibly condition most of the surface ripplings of the sociocultural ocean, including the historical events and life-processes of smaller sociocultural systems and the actions of individuals and groups living in a given civilization.

3 Without an adequate knowledge of the civilization we can hardly understand the structural and dynamic properties of its important parts –

of all its subsystems, regions, and components – just as without a sufficient knowledge of a primate troop as a whole, of its gross structure and gross functioning, we cannot understand the nature and behavior of its member individuals.

"CIVILIZATIONS"

4 Screening a list of some 70 candidates yielded a list of 14 entities which appeared to be societies at a civilized *level* (criterion: cities; further evidence: record-keeping, economic surplus, nonproducing classes, etc.) which were also connected *world systems* – militarily closed, geotechnologically isolated social-transactional networks with an autonomous political history during which they did not take or need not have taken much account of the possibility of conquest invasion, attack (or alliance and cooperation) from any outsiders, although the members of each such system did recurrently conquer, invade, attack, ally with, command, rule, legislate, cooperate with, and conflict significantly and effectively with, and only with, one another.

Table 7.1 gives the resulting roster of civilizations/world systems. Figure 7.1 is a chronogram showing the lifespans and relative (Mercator) location of the civilizations in the roster.

Table 7.1 A roster of fourteen civilizations
(listed in their approximate order of incorporation into Central civilization)

	Civilization	*Duration*	*Terminus*
1	Mesopotamian	before 3000 BC – *c.* 1500 BC	Coupled with Egyptian to form Central
2	Egyptian	before 3100 BC – *c.* 1500 BC	Coupled with Mesopotamian to form Central
3	Aegean	*c.* 2700 BC – *c.* 560 BC	Engulfed by Central
4	Indic	*c.* 2300 BC – after *c.* 1000 AD	Engulfed by Central
5	Irish	*c.* 450 AD – *c.* 1050 AD	Engulfed by Central
6	Mexican	before 1100 BC – *c.* 1520 AD	Engulfed by Central
7	Peruvian	before *c.* 200 BC – *c.* 1530 AD	Engulfed by Central
8	Chibchan	? – *c.* 1530 AD	Engulfed by Central
9	Indonesian	before 700 AD – *c.* 1550 AD	Engulfed by Central
10	West African	*c.* 350 AD – *c.* 1590 AD	Engulfed by Central
11	Mississippian	*c.* 700 AD – *c.* 1700 AD	Destroyed (pestilence?)
12	Far Eastern	before 1500 BC – after *c.* 1850 AD	Engulfed by Central
13	Japanese	*c.* 650 AD – after *c.* 1850 AD	Engulfed by Central
14	Central	*c.* 1500 BC – present	?

5 This roster, in its origins a recension of the rosters of Toynbee (1961: 548–9) and of Carroll Quigley (1961: 37), was produced, like Toynbee's

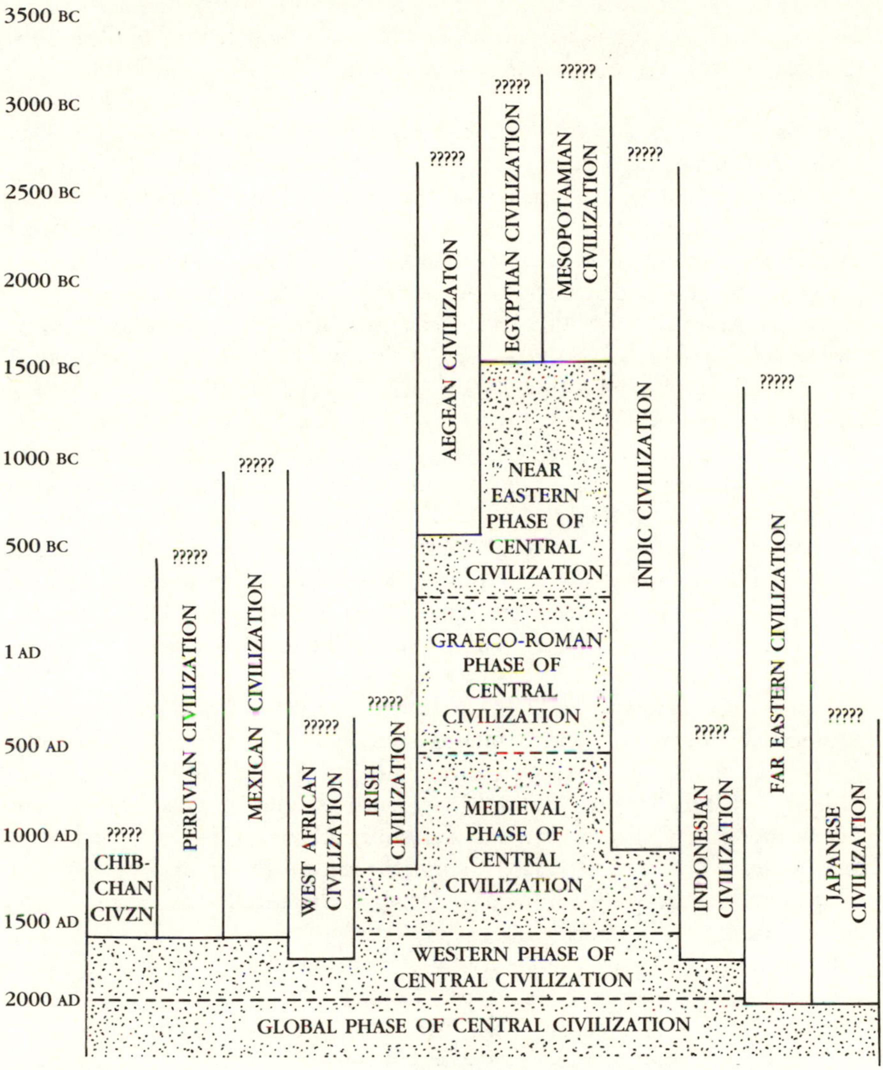

Figure 7.1 The incorporation of twelve civilizations into one "Central civilization"

own 1961 revision of his earlier list, mainly by combining members of the prior rosters. The current civilizations list is different from Toynbee's and Quigley's, but still more different from Spengler's (1926–8) or Danilevsky's (1920).

6 Vis-à-vis Toynbee: of Toynbee's revised 1961 list I recognize Aegean under that name, Egyptic as "Egyptian," Middle American as "Mexican," Andean as "Peruvian," Sumero-Akkadian as "Mesopotamian;" combine Indus and Indic as a single "Indic;" combine Sinic and the Toynbeean "satellites" of Sinic – Korean, Vietnamian, and Tibetan – as "Far Eastern;" promote the Toynbeean satellites Mississippian, North Andean (as "Chibchan"), Japanese, and South-East Asian (as "Indonesian") and a combination of Toynbee's "abortive" Far Western Christian and Scandinavian (as "Irish") to full civilizational status. Of Toynbee's full civilizations, five are not on my list: Syriac, Hellenic, Orthodox Christian, Western, and Islamic are regions or phases of a single continuing civilized society which I call (see Table 7.1 and Figure 7.1) "Central civilization." The same treatment is meted out to some of Toynbee's satellite civilizations – "?Elamite," Hittite, "?Urartian," Iranian, "?Italic," and Russian – and to several of his abortive civilizations – Nestorian, Monophysite, and the Medieval Western City-State Cosmos. Toynbee's abortive First Syriac civilization I have treated as a shared semiperihery of Mesopotamian and Egyptian civilizations.

7 Vis-à-vis Quigley: my list includes Egyptian, Mesopotamian, and Japanese civilizations, and contains reasonable matches to Quigley's Cretan, Mesoamerican, and Andean. I do not accept the separateness of Quigley's "Indic" and "Hindu" civilizations, nor of his "Sinic" and "Chinese." And Quigley's Hittite, Canaanite, Classical, Islamic, Orthodox, and Western civilizations seem to me to constitute cultural regions and epochs within the polyculture of a larger civilization, that which I have called Central civilization.

8 Vis-à-vis Spengler: while my list mentions Egyptian and Mexican civilizations, and contains reasonable matches to Spengler's Babylonian, Indian, and Chinese cases, I do not recognize the separateness of his Classical/Apollinian, Arabian/Magian, Western/Faustian or (suppressed) Russian civilizations; these are, rather, conflicting cultures within a single civilization, namely Central civilization.

9 Vis-à-vis Danilevsky: while my list contains Egyptian, Mexican, and Peruvian entities, and reasonable matches to Danilevsky's Ancient Semitic, Chinese, and Hindu-Indian, I do not recognize the separateness of Iranian, Hebrew, Greek, Roman, Arabian, European, or Slavic civilizations, all of which are (to me) conflicting cultures within the polycultural compost of a single larger society: Central civilization.

10 My differences with the four lists cited reflect my application of a *social* criterion, while Danilevsky and Spengler employed cultural criteria and Toynbee and Quigley used mixed sociocultural criteria. The similarities between lists reflect this coincidence: where e.g. Spengler or Danilevsky found cultural coherence in Egypt, Mesopotamia, China, Mexico, Peru, and India, I found a period of geosocial isolation and historical autonomy.

CIVILIZATIONS AS POLYCULTURES

11 The various civilizations are *not* necessarily based upon any major premise, nor do they necessarily articulate, develop, and realize such, nor are they necessarily logically or aesthetically consistent or complementary. Each civilization is a causal system; it may or may not be a "meaningful" one, or evolve toward or away from "meaningfulness." Since civilizations are not assumed to be "meaningful" unities, they *need* not possess any major premise, prime symbol, ultimate principle, or fundamental value that is articulated by their cultural phenomena. But they might in fact do so.

12 *Do* they in fact do so? I would guess that they do *not*, but, rather, that each will be found to articulate a different evolution of a different dialectic, i.e. a different struggle among a different set of conflicting premises, symbols, etc. Artists, philosophers, charismatics, and prophets within civilizations frequently seek or seem to create or discover meanings, premises, prime symbols, ultimate values, and utopian reorderings in and for their civilizations. Instead they ordinarily create dialectical controversies.

13 Since we need not assume that the cultural field of any civilization is completely unified, nor that it is meaningfully consistent, the question of whether, when, and how cultural unity, consistency, or interaction exist becomes hypothetical, to be explored empirically rather than by definition or axiom.

14 In such exploration, I would begin with the guess that over many generations the culture of any civilization will tend toward greater second-order integration – mutual agreement on what its areas of discord are – with continuing first-order inconsistency (continued discord). Its causal unification will likely be dialectical, organized as a continuing struggle of changing oppositions (though without any final synthesis ever terminating the dialectic).

15 Indeed, the likelihood that we will find all civilizations actually highly and evolvingly contradictory, conflicted, dialectical, is so strong that we might reasonably study civilizations on the assumption that each, far from being an organic cultural unity, is in fact "*a cultural field where a multitude of vast and small cultural systems and congeries – partly mutually harmonious, partly neutral, partly contradictory – coexist*" (Sorokin 1950: 213).

16 On this assumption, one would research a civilization's cultural individuality precisely by identifying, not a prime symbol, major premise, fundamental value or ultimate principle, but the collection of such symbols, premises etc., that coexisted, conflicted, and coevolved within it, their mutual relations of dominance and displacement, challenge and response, fusion and fission.

17 Systematic cross-civilizational cultural research would explore such questions as: is there usually or always a dominant core culture in a civilization? How long does such dominance persist? How is it displaced and by what? When civilizations collide, how is the evolution of cultural dominance affected? Does second-order integration emerge, and at what time scales?

18 I would not want to assume that civilizations necessarily contain a dominant cultural system – the question of dominance is once again properly empirical – but would regard it as an empirical fact that most civilizations, most of the time, indeed contain dominant cultural cores, which have geographic locations and are frequently "dominant" in more ways than one: i.e. militarily, technologically, economically, and demographically, as well as culturally.

CENTRAL CIVILIZATION

19 The most striking effect of the new definition on accustomed lists of civilizations, as has been shown above, is that such familiar entities as classical/Hellenic/Graeco-Roman civilization, Hittite civilization, Arabian/Magian/Syriac/Iranic/Islamic civilization(s), Orthodox Christian civilization, Russian civilization, and even our own familiar Western civilization, must be reclassified either as *episodes* of or as *regions* within a previously unrecognized social-network entity, by my definition both a civilized society and a world system, hence a single civilization. This civilization I have labeled Central civilization.[2]

20 Thus today there exists on the earth only one civilization, a single global civilization. As recently as the nineteenth century several independent civilizations still existed (i.e. those centered on China, Japan, and the West); now there remains but one, Central civilization.

21 The single global civilization is the lineal descendant of, or rather I should say the current manifestation of, a civilization that emerged about 1500 BC in the Near East when Egyptian and Mesopotamian civilizations collided and fused. This new fusional entity has since then expanded over the entire planet and absorbed, on unequal terms, all other previously independent civilizations.

22 Central civilization was created in the Middle East during the second millennium BC by an atypical encounter between two pre-existing civilizations. Civilizations may coexist, collide, break apart or fuse; when they have fused, they have typically done so by an asymmetric, inegalitarian engulfment of one by the other. But the linking of the previously separate Egyptian and Mesopotamian civilizations through Syria was an atypical, relatively symmetric, and egalitarian "coupling" which created a new joint network-entity rather than annexing one network as a part of the other entrained to its process time.

23 The Central city-network, in unbroken existence and process since its inception, has been atypical in another way: it has expanded, slowly by the reckoning of national and state turnover times, but quite rapidly by comparison to other civilizations, and in that expansion has engulfed all the other civilizational networks with which it once coexisted and later collided.

24 "Central" is a historical and positional nomenclature which deliberately avoids any specific geographic or cultural references, thereby indicating that this society is not to be characterized by references to a single river basin, and that its development has not been determined by that of a single culture, nation or people. It would be too parochial to label that civilization by the nomenclatures of any of the nations that have successively populated, of the states that have successively dominated, or of the regions that have successively centered it. At this moment, in this place, and in this culture, it seems not mistaken, and not too parochial, to call it Central civilization.

25 Central civilization is of course positionally "central" only in retrospect, by reason of its omnidirectional expansion: this network, originally Afro-Asiatic in being located where Asia and Africa meet, spread over time in all directions, encompassing the civilized networks of Europe, west Africa, and the Americas by moving west and those of south and east Asia by moving east, and thereby rendering itself historically "Central" as well.

26 The subsumption of a variety of putative civilizations under the single rubric of Central civilization is illustrated by Figure 7.1, which shows two such candidates, "Graeco-Roman" and "Western," as epochs of regional *dominance* within Central civilization; these dominant regions in fact constituted long-lived, but impermanent, *cores* of Central civilization. The Near Eastern, medieval, and global phases of Central civilization also possessed cores; but they were larger and less culturally homogeneous than the Graeco-Roman and Western cores. Another way of comprehending the subsumption is that what has in the past appeared to be the end of one civilization/world system and the beginning of another is easier to comprehend as a core shift within a single continuing civilization – a shift of military, political, economic and cultural domination from one region to another.

27 The taxonomic principles that yield Central civilization as a recognizable entity are three in number. First: any two "civilizations" that were *always* adjacent and vigorously politico-militarily interacting were *ipso facto* parts of a single civilization. In the medieval period of the north-west Old World (i.e. Europe, south-west Asia, north Africa) there were Western cities, Orthodox cities, Muslim cities; there was no Western civilization, no Orthodox, no Islamic civilization. There were civilized peoples and territories in the north-west Old World; they were members of a single civilization.

28 Second: any two historically autonomous civilizations which *become* adjacent and vigorously, continuously politicomilitarily interactive (through expansions or shifts) thereby become a single civilization. Either a new entity emerges (if they unite on relatively equal terms); or one of the old civilizations absorbs the other.

29 Third: any two alleged "civilizations" adjacent in time are but periods in one single civilization unless the earlier civilization's cities are entirely depopulated and abandoned (like those of Mississippian civilization). Unless a civilization's urban centers vanish, it does not fall. It may terminate by fission into two separate and more or less equal autonomous entities which cease to interact dynamically; it may terminate in fusion with some other civilization. Without fission, fusion, or fall there is no end to the civilization's system and process. If there is no end, there can be no succession.

30 Inasmuch as Central civilization combines from 4 to 14 of the civilizations discerned by more pluralist civilizationists using cultural criteria, it is to be expected that, and it is in fact the case that, Central civilization is not a language group, or a religious group, or a state group. Yet it is bonded, bonded oppositionally: for continuing warfare is a social bond, and continuing hostility is a cultural bond. Central civilization is a strongly bonded entity, even though it be a cultural potpourri. Central civilization is a conglomeration of sociocultural phenomena, adjacent in space and time, that is integrated by causal ties – including collision, warfare, and coevolution – and by quasi-meaningful ties of mutual consciousness, awareness of differences, and hostility.

31 Our time is unique in that only one civilization now exists on earth, of global scope, without a periphery into which to expand further. Central civilization seems never yet to have been a "meaningful" but always a "causal" unity; but now that it has reached the limits of its oikumene, after having absorbed the whole human species and all other civilizations, there is a good chance that it will in the future evolve toward a recognizable "meaningful" unity.

32 Central civilization does however have a presently dominant culture within its polycultural mix. Tht dominant culture is what Sorokin labeled "Sensate" – and also theoretic, secular, Promethean, scientific, technological. I would additionally label it cosmopolitan, bourgeois, capitalist, liberal, democratic, and above all "modern." Sensate modernity's culture continues to expand against resistance while simultaneously generating internal schisms and coopting and incorporating external resistances in a manner which maintains both its variety and its dynamism. Being only dominant but not yet all-pervasive, Sensate culture, whose dynamic expansion is called "modernization," has not yet reached its full attainable social limits, and (consequently?) continues to expand savagely against savage resistance, as it has done within Central civilization for the past seven or eight centuries, even while Central civilization itself has been expanding to global dimension.

33 Sensate culture may well be dominant in the now global cultural field, but it is a near thing: there are enormous masses yet being culture-colonized against active or passive resistance. Such masses are to be found, e.g., among Africans and the Indians of the Americas; among non-Protestant Christians, and nonmainstream Protestants; among Muslims, Hindus, Buddhists; among still Marxist-ruled but non-Marxist populations (Chinese especially); among tribal peoples, peasants, and genuine proletarians (Servian, not Marxian – i.e. the urban homeless).

34 That Sensate culture has not expanded to its conceivable demographic and social limit, and that it continues to recruit and expand toward those limits, does not mean that it will get there. There are also signs both of Sensate disintegration and of the beginnings of many countertrends. But the latter are neither integrated nor expansive, and their resistance thus far seems more like diehard reaction than like the genesis of a new counterculture.

CORE–PERIPHERY ISSUES

35 An ideal-type civilization/world system/macrosociety, because its characteristics are unequally distributed over space; and because they are distributed centrically; and because their unequal distributions overlap; and because the inequalities are connected intrinsically to its past history of expansion (for civilizations tend strongly to expand, Central civilization being an extreme rather than an exceptional case), characteristically possesses:

(a) a *core* (central, older, advanced, wealthy, powerful);
(b) a *semiperiphery* strongly connected to the core (younger, fringeward, remote, more recently attached, weaker, poorer, more backward); and
(c) a weakly connected *periphery* (nomads; peasant subsistence producers not yet attached to a city; and other civilizations that trade but do not habitually fight or ally with the subject civilization).[3]

36 Civilizations usually begin in a geographically restricted area composed of cities and the hinterlands their fighters can aspire to control; this is surrounded by an area to which the new cities are politically irrelevant. We may call these zones the (initial) urban *core*, controlled or disputed *semiperiphery*, and uncontrolled *periphery* of the civilization.

37 Civilizations usually expand over time by raiding, invading, and conquering adjacent areas, by sending out colony-cities and military settlements and trading forts, by fascinating and addicting previously indifferent peripheral people to their products (gods, drugs, laws, weapons, music, ornaments, etc.). The territories affected by this civic expansion – whether the expansion be colonialist, imperialist, cultic, developmental – may be considered to have been incorporated by the civilization when their occupants – settlers or settlees – undergo urbanization *and* begin to interact politically on a regular basis – as subjects, allies, tributaries, enemies – with the civilizational core. This area of later expansion and control is the (enlarged) semiperiphery of the civilization.

38 Once a semiperiphery exists, and it comes to exist quickly, it also persists. Thus one of the main continuing patterns that reveals itself in the history of civilizations and world systems is that they tend – not by definition, but empirically – to be markedly geographically tripartite. In the *core*, military force, political power, economic wealth, technological progress, cultural prestige, and theogony are concentrated. The *periphery* is far from the core in all senses, containing peoples and territories known but scarcely noted. The *semiperiphery*, more or less recently penetrated or engulfed, is a zone characterized by military subjection, powerlessness, relative poverty, technological backwardness, low cultural prestige.

39 But while the tripartition of a civilization is very durable, no area has permanent tenure in any role, and tenure of coredom is rather precarious. Cores are not eternal; civilizations can outlast their original cores. A history of cores must therefore be kinematic, describing their rises, shifts, and falls; a theory of cores must ultimately be dynamic, accounting for their motion and change.

40 A civilization's core may have any of several political forms. It may be a single state, as in Mesopotamian civilization, perhaps, during the rise and fall of Assyria, or as in Central civilization during the rise of Media and Persia and Rome, and the era of Justinian. The core may be the metropolitan region of a universal state, as in Central civilization during the Assyrian, Persian-Macedonian, and Roman empires. Or the civilization core may be a functionally divided set of areas in a universal state, as in Far Eastern civilization during the Qin–Former Han and in Japanese civilization during the Kamakura period. The core may contain several states, successively hegemonic: in Mesopotamian civilization, the Sumerian core c. 2500–2360 BC (Ur, Lagash, Umma). It may constitute several states simultaneously balanced, as in Central civilization between its universal empires, and for most of the time since the Roman empire's fracturing. The most frequent core forms are: the single dominant or hegemonic state; several competing states; and the universal-empire metropole.

41 Cores pulsate. Core areas enlarge and contract. Central civilization's core shifts – westward in the Graeco-Roman phase, eastward in the medieval phase, westward again in the Western phase – involved expansion at one edge synchronic with contraction at the other; the global phase saw core expansion east and west. Contractions are naturally enough associated with hegemonic struggles and universal-state periods, expansions with all-core epochs; but not perfectly.

42 Cores shift. Cores may move in a single general direction, or oscillate. The Central core half moved west, then east, then drifted west and north and west again. No signficant patterns are evident.

43 Cores decline and rise. Does past experience as a core preclude or assure return to core status? Apparently neither. Setting aside all the apparent civilizational-startup first-time cores (e.g. Central civilization's Fertile Crescent + Nile valley), there are many cases in which a semiperipheral area, never before a core, rose to core status. In Central civilization, such first-time core entrants included Assyria, Persia, Greece (previously an *Aegean* core), Macedonia, Rome, Byzantium, western Europe, America, Russia. But there are several other cases in which a fallen core area has returned from semiperipheral status, or has regained a solitude it had lost to upstart sharers. In Central civilization: Abbasid Mesopotamia, and the classic case of Renaissance Italy. In the transition from semiperiphery to core, history seems somewhat more favorable to *naissance* than to *renaissance*, but renaissances do happen.

44 Different areas may serve as military-political, economic, and cultural-religious cores, and core shifts may occur in these features at different times. The most notable discrepancies between Central civilization's economic-technical and politicomilitary cores are attested by being corrected: the shift from Rome to Constantinople, the Renaissance-ending invasions of Italy, the revolt of the Netherlands, the involvement of British finance and fleets in Continental wars, and the American entry into the world wars of the twentieth century. There is thus some tendency for geographically separated functions to be pulled together: the politico-military core may conquer the others (the post-Renaissance invasions of Italy), migrate to them (by a movement of the capital, e.g. to Constantinople or Lo-yang), or usurp them (by taxation and subsidy, e.g. Tokugawa Edo); or economic cores may invest in politicomilitary potency (Dutch, British, American).

45 Are semiperipheries necessary? Apparently not, since civilizations are often all-core, i.e. lack a semiperiphery. Central civilization has always had a significant semiperipheral area. Semiperipheries exist more often than not, particularly in universal-empire periods when the metropole is especially favored, but they do not seem necessary features of a civilization: power, wealth, creativity, can all be rather widely dispersed, though dispersal usually alternates with concentration.

46 Tenure in the semiperiphery is more secure than core tenure (cores decline) or peripheral tenure (peripheries are devoured). But there is some upward mobility. A semiperipheral area remains semiperipheral as long as it is politically annexed to, urbanologically subordinate to, militarily dominated by, culturally provincialized by, economically outaccumulated by, technologically outcompeted by, cultically devoted to, the old core. When and where the semiperiphery acquires states as influential, forces as dangerous, cities as populous and wealthy, culture as attractive, technique as progressive, gods as efficacious as those of the core, that part of the semiperiphery *becomes* core; the core area expands to encompass it. And if the old core should peak and decline, be overtaken and passed in its military and political, demographic and economic, cultural and technical and theological development by its semiperiphery (or a part of it), so that the old core becomes a historic backwater, becomes marginal to the affairs of the civilization, while the former semiperiphery becomes the new core, we may properly say that the core of the civilization has shifted. And cores do shift: witness Karnak, witness Babylon.

47 There is some relationship between the transition of a state from semiperiphery to core and its later ability to impose hegemony and universal empire over the states system. Recent arrivals to core status have some advantages in competitions to destroy states systems, but they are not overwhelming, nor entirely self-evident.

48 A theory of peripheries must largely account for their secular decline. Civilization as such – the sum of the territories and peoples of the various civilizations – has expanded continually since its origins, despite some regional setbacks and a single holocivilizational collapse (that of Mississippian civilization), by conquering and colonizing and assimilating its noncivilized peripheral peoples and territories. This contradicts the idea that civilizations rise and fall, rise and fall: they almost never fall. It also contradicts the image of peaceful, sedentary civilized peoples always threatened and occasionally overwhelmed by neighboring barbarians: most of the "overwhelming" has been inflicted by the civilized societies on their peripheral neighbors. When noncivilized peripheral peoples – usually nomads – attack and conquer civilized territory, the result has ordinarily been that they settle down, take over, enjoy ruling the civilization, and continue expanding it; on the whole, peripheral peoples have not developed a sense of peripheral identity and pride sufficient to impel them to destroy the civilizations they have sporadically conquered. Civilizations, on the contrary, strongly tend to destroy their peripheries, through incorporation.

49 "Coreness" and "semipherality" are multidimensional phenomena, but certainly have politicomilitary, economic, technological, demographic, religious, and cultural components. Politicomilitary driving variables seem more obvious and accessible to analysis than others, but are unlikely to function alone. Forces need to be posited to explain both the motions and changes of cores – formations, expansions, pulsations, shuttles, drifts, evaporations – and core persistence and stability.

50 Interesting speculative questions about core and periphery include: can an all-core global society evolve? Would it require a states system?

Does the end of the periphery increase the chances for an all-core society? – or a freezing of current core–semiperiphery boundaries? – or a speedup in core shift? – or a narrowing of the core to a single hegemonic state or imperial metropole?

CENTRAL CIVILIZATION VS. WORLD-ECONOMIC THEORY

51 I have elsewhere (Wilkinson 1987: 48–53) provided some impressions of the economic "facts" about Central civilization which comparative theory needs to accommodate and explain. The civilizationist most noted for attention to economic issues is Carroll Quigley (1961); the analyst of world-systems most so noted is Immanuel Wallerstein (e.g. 1974, 1975, 1979a, b, 1980, 1982, 1983, 1984). To what extent can Quigley's and Wallerstein's ideas be deployed for such an explanatory purpose?

52 Carroll Quigley's economically driven model of the evolution of a civilization is elegant, lucid, consistent, and tight. There are serious problems in its delimitation of the units of macrosocial analysis, and in its dependence upon a relatively homogeneous structure and process to explain fluctuations in relatively heterogeneous social systems. It is not at all clear that such systems have "stages" rather than "phases." Nevertheless Quigley's concept of an instrument of expansion is more generally useful than the alternative "mode of production," which suffers from the same defects while not directly addressing the crucial issue of the general phenomenon of macrosocial expansion. Similarly, Quigley's ideas about core and periphery relationships, and about expansion/stagnation cycles, are of great value in broadening later views of the same topics.

53 The world-systems school of Immanuel Wallerstein and his colleagues has produced a large body of provocative work with great internal complexity. It too delimits the units of macrosocial analysis in ways that seem to call for revision, though in different ways from Quigley's work. It would be useful for world-systems analysts to consider Quigley's work as a potential contributor to their own.

54 For the study of Central civilization, Quigley and Wallerstein are resources despite the fact that Quigley would deny that such an entity ever existed, while Wallerstein would accept it only for the past two centuries or so. Nonetheless this entity displays core–periphery phenomena, and probably buffers "globally" the effects of "local" expansion/stagnation cycles which its world wars probably also "locally" entrain. Even if one does not accept the tight policy–economy linkages implied in the Quigleyan civilizational and Wallersteinian world-systems schemata, one cannot come away from reading Quigley and Wallerstein without accepting that there must be some such linkages: if not quite that posited by either, then perhaps mixtures of their pure types, and perhaps softer, more delayed, sometimes even inverted versions of their harder couplings. No two writers seem better sources for hypotheses concerning the political economy of Central civilization.

55 Extracivilizational as well as intracivilizational trade characterized Central civilization's Egyptian and Mesopotamian predecessors, and Central civilization itself from its inception until its incorporation of the globe.

Wallerstein's propositions about the "rich trades" help to account for the existence, distance, and relatively low impact of such external trade. Still, if it is highly rational to trade what is "worthless" for what is "precious," one must expect traders (and tribute-seekers, and predators) to flock toward preciosity. Such a tendency may help explain the marked inclination of civilizations to couple with or engulf one another, on the assumption that uneven distribution of resources and uneven development of technology tend, while civilizations are separated, to create what will be viewed as "preciosities" as soon as they begin to communicate.

This proposition, and all those hereafter asserted for Central civilization, may well be true of other civilizations, and certainly should be treated as comparative hypotheses or heuristics.

56 There existed an Old World oikumene, an ecumenical macroeconomy, a multicivilizational structure which apparently provided the highest-level largest-scale economic order until the global reach of Central civilization, as the evolving context of the world economies of the various Eurasian civilizations linked by the silk, spice, slave, gold, and ivory trades. This economy was larger than any polity (universal empire or states system) it contained, encompassing Central civilization, Indic, Far Eastern, and others. It may require theoretical treatment as a whole; its theory is likely to be quite special, precisely because of the absence of a polity.

57 Local economies and short-range trade probably account for most economic activity most of the time, with the extraction of food from each city's hinterland and its distribution to the city population of primary importance.

58 World-economic commodities in Central civilization have tended strongly to be elite goods – luxury food, clothing, shelter, and display items – along with the trade tools of elite-supporting soldiers and bureaucrats (weapon-metal; paper for record-keeping). Elites, classes, and the associated inequalities must not be treated as recent phenomena.

59 Early Central trade in precious metals may, and coinage does, imply the development of mobile free persons, merchant classes, and economic (vs. politicomilitary) elites, characterized by private property in portable wealth. These elements of capitalism similarly must not be treated as of recent vintage.

60 The entry into the Central world-economy of fish, wheat, oil, and wine suggests mass consumption driven either by political redistribution (to hire loyalty of armed men, clients, voters, etc.) or by markets, probably varyingly by both. Luxury goods may also have spread more widely through the social structure.

61 The general trend over time is clearly toward a continuing increase in the number and variety of commodities traded in the world economy of Central civilization. Within this trend there are temporary and permanent commodity dropouts, shifts in regional contributions, epochs of faster and slower commodity increase; but the trend remains.

Commodities and commodification too precede modernity, and must be attributed to some early cause, perhaps simply to civilization's division of labor, increased scale, and increased population. Commodities and markets are not intrinsically related: granite appears to be a state commodity for Egyptian monument-builders; granite-hewers worked not (primarily) to build for their own tombs, but to satisfy the monumental egos of the state elite.

The increase in the number and variety of commodities over time is one piece of evidence for a secular trend to expansion in Central civilization over the past 5,000 years.

62 There is as yet discernible no clear increase in the per capita wealth or living standards of the median individual during the premodern periods of Central civilization. It appears that increased production is mostly utilized to increase total population and total urban population. The aggregate wealth of the wealthiest strata (typically politically rather than economically defined) must have increased, but it is not clear that the per capita wealth of these strata also increased.

Modernization seems another story. But if Wallerstein is right regarding "absolute immiseration," it is an even less cheerful story. One wonders, for instance, if the forward days of contemporary world food reserves are more or fewer than in the first food-storing cities. At best, there is room for doubt, and for inquiry.

63 There is no clear evidence of an endogenously economic general crisis or collapse ever having occurred in the Central world economy, although there have been city-level and state-level disasters, and system wide periods of setback and stagnation, usually deriving from politicomilitary events.

This has been argued elsewhere at some length (Wilkinson 1987: 39–48). A very long-term expansive trend appears to underlie various cycles of expansion and stagnation. If Quigley is right, this implies very frequent reforms and circumventions. If an economy is very mixed, with strong regional differentiation, regional failure by institutionalization may lead to the semiperipheralization of the failing region and the destruction of the failed institutions by intruders from another region of the same civilization – a combination of Wallerstein's core-shifting and Quigley's semiperipheral-success ideas.

64 The basic expansive process in Central civilization appears to be circularly causal, dependent upon the presence of an unpopulated or underpopulated geoeconomic periphery and a Malthusian pressure: population expands; more and larger and more dispersed cities with more populous hinterlands extend and intensify settlement; there is greater division of labor and specialization; sufficient demand arises to mobilize new products or longer routes to more distant sources; total production rises; increased production mainly serves to support an enlarged population; etc.

While seas, seabeds, poles, deserts, mountains, forests, tundra, atmosphere, and space remain in many ways peripheries and frontiers of expansion, they are also barriers. Whether the ultimate bounds of human expansion are those of landmasses or of the universe is not clear. Can a civilization avoid taking out all its economic expansion extensively, by a corresponding population growth? Perhaps not.

65 The borders and cities of Central civilization expanded preferentially toward commodity sources, but not always quickly, effectively, or uniformly.

Quigley and Wallerstein employ circumferential rather than radial images of expansion; otherwise their theories meld well with this observation. We may add that a preferred direction of expansion could well be precisely toward "rich trades." Otherwise, areas likely to be brought into the semiperiphery sooner would include likely population outlets and tribute sources.

66 Whatever may be true for state and local economies, it is not correct at any time to describe the world economy of Central civilization as fundamentally feudal, nor slave, nor hydraulic, nor free-peasant, nor communal, nor corporate, nor hierocratic; nor is it fundamentally, in the Wallersteinian sense, either a "world-economy" (capitalist) or a "world-empire" (tributary).

In the fifth century BC, to take an apparently extreme example of variety, but a binding one, what was the Athenian economy? A slave economy (there was a very large slave population)? A peasant economy (most citizens were country-born and bred, and landowners, producing sheep, cattle, grapes, olives, grain)? A merchant capitalist economy (exporting wine and oil, providing coinage and a carrying trade)? An industrial economy (based on the silver, lead, zinc, and iron mines, importing grain)? With an industrial proletariat (slaves included skilled workers; free workers' wages hovered at subsistence)? A world-empire (Athens imposed tribute on other states)? A welfare state (much of the population was on the public payroll via the mass-jury system)? A socialist state (massive expenditures on public works – harbors, fortifications, temples, naval expeditions)? Clearly something of all: a *very* mixed economy. And all this in a tiny fraction of the total area of Central civilization!

67 It is an interesting fact, and one worth reflecting on, not just a given, that Central civilization has never yet been completely penetrated by any particular "instrument of expansion" (in the Quigleyan sense) or "mode of production" (in the Marxian sense).

A possible hypothesis is that there *are* a limited number of possible modes of production (Wallerstein); that all have inbuilt self-destructive propensities (Quigley); and that the only available choices at times of reform or circumvention are the items from the same old menu.

68 A possible reason why the world economy of Central civilization has never been fully statist is that the universal states of Central civilization have been either short-lived, with their extraction capabilities confined to the civilizational core, or tolerant of private property and merchant classes.

Since the same could be said of universal empires in Indic, Far Eastern, Japanese, and Mexican civilizations, we might want to look at the Inca empire, also brief but apparently ultra-statist, to question its extremism, explain its divergence, and thereby explain the norm. Similar questions might be usefully put to statist national economies, e.g. the Soviet and Chinese, within states systems.

69 A possible reason why the world economy of Central civilization has never been fully capitalist (private-propertarian, individualist, marketive) is the unbroken prominence of the political state, based on force, and of political-military-religious elites based on ground rents, taxes, and extraction by force.

Why can these elements apparently not be expunged? How far can they be suppressed, and kept suppressed? These are questions of interest at least to libertarians, and to those socialists who are in touch with the anarchist rather than statist tendencies of that movement. Wallerstein's idea of the marketer's mixed motives and the consequent need of capitalists for states is very much in point here.

70 For whatever reason, the Central economy is at all times a mixed, political economy, embodying trade and war, coercion and bargaining, the one-few-and-many. The balance shifts with time, scale, region, commodity.

And possibly other variables. The determinants of the mix need study. The coexistence, with regional and temporal variations, is so marked as to suggest a theory of the mixed economy as historic norm, and the idea of capitalism and socialism as ideal-typical extremes needs developing.

71 The balance shifts more toward "capitalism" (without ever coming close) as states are small, weak, and numerous, more toward "statism" as they are few, strong and large.

72 One useful indicator of the statist/capitalist balance in the civilization might be the balance between cities of the same size that are state capitals (i.e. power-maintained) and that are commercial centers (i.e. trade-maintained).

73 The core/semiperiphery distinction is not that of a straightforward division of labor between political coercion and economic supply, nor between primary and higher-tech products; but both divisions are notably present.

The element of time-delayed expansion over space, of institutional aging, of destructive core wars, of unequal "materialism" and exogenous technical development will also all doubtless prove factors in determining and shifting cores.

74 It is the politicomilitary predominance of the core, not any purely economic differentiation or "unequal exchange" tradition, that mainly accounts for the tendency for the core to drain the semiperiphery: loot, tribute, taxes, price controls, confiscations, trade route closures, and enforced monopolies are primarily political ventures.

75 A significant fraction of primary products come from within the core, from the hinterlands of core cities.

This becomes less true in the nineteenth century with the development of railroads; the British policy of agricultural free trade may mar the shift. However, it remains true that . . .

76 Citification, and eventually core status, tends to move toward major semiperipheral supply sources.

77 Wherever it is possible to map the distribution of wealth in Central civilization, inequality prominently appears: by city, by region, by political power, by inheritance, in law, by age and family status, by gender. The several inequalities do not appear to be reducible to any one fundamental root inequality.

78 There is abundant scope here for theory and observation, dialectic and eristic, in the contemplation of the world economies of Central and other civilizations. A world system will certainly have a world economy associated with it, and it is worthwhile trying to describe such an economy, and seek theoretical assimilation of the description. Terminology adequate to describe holistically the economic structure of a civilization does not yet exist. It cannot be produced simply by adapting and generalizing "macroeconomic" terminology suited to describe the economy of a state or the economic institutions of a culture, since a civilization is neither a state nor a culture. World economies do not appear to be characterized by sufficiently homogeneous class systems, property systems, production relations, divisions of labor, or instruments of expansion, to make holistic Marxian, Wallersteinian, or Quigleyan characterizations very revealing. There are coexisting and contradictory property types rather than a prevailing property type, coexisting and inconsistent class structures rather than a prevailing class structure, heterogeneous divisions of labor, and several competing instruments of expansion. We have clearly only just begun the theoretically salient description of Central civilization's world economy.

OIKUMENE VS. CIVILIZATION

79 It is the case that there have been economic structures of larger scale than the political structures they contain. I would refer to the theoretical problem of establishing the interconnections between economy and polity when the two are not coextensive as the problem of the oikumene.[4]

80 An "oikumene" is here defined as a trading area, a domain internally knit by a network of trade routes, in which there is enough internal trade so that the whole trading area evolves to a significant degree as a system, while trade outside the area, though perhaps important both to the oikumene and to other oikumenes with which it trades, is not sufficiently dense and significant to cause system-level development to encompass these external systems.

81 Oikumenes may contain no civilization (pre-urban trade networks); may contain and be coextensive with one civilization (the present global economy); may contain but outlie one civilization; may contain and outlie more than one civilization.

82 In an empirical examination (Wilkinson 1992–3), it proved possible on the whole to correlate "civilizations" (politicomilitarily linked urban networks) with "oikumenes" (economically linked urban networks) in which they nested. What similarities and differences exist in the nature and development of oikumenes, as trading areas, and civilizations, as systems of states and empires?

83 A world economy, lacking a coextensive world polity, but containing world polities of smaller area than its own, existed from (at least) the fourth millennium BC (when it linked the world polities of Egyptian and Mesopotamian civilizations) to the nineteenth century AD (when a world polity became global, and coexistensive with the world economy that had theretofore contained it). Other such "oikumenes," trade-linked but not politicomilitarily bonded, probably connected Chibchan with Peruvian civilization, and may have linked Mexican with Mississippian and/or Mexican with Peruvian civilization. But it is particularly noteworthy that Central civilization, from c. 1500 BC to c. 1900 AD, formed a politically coherent social system smaller than, nested within, expanding in pace with and into the space pioneered by, an economically coherent but politically unlinked oikumene. Because that oikumene seems to have been the globe's oldest "world economy," it is designated herein the Old oikumene. The Old oikumene is not only the eldest of the several members of its species (there have been Indic, Far Eastern, and Japanese oikumenes at least, in addition to those of the New World); in its expansion it, like Central civilization, engrossed all others, and today, grown to global scope and (for the first time) coextensive with a polity, is the sole survivor of its species.

84 Oikumenes contain civilizations, but not the reverse. Oikumenes organize larger areas more weakly. Why should this be? Perhaps because politicomilitary ties (rule, attack, threat, alliance) are more costly for actors to maintain than economic ties; or because they impose a net economic loss on the whole system that maintains them, while trade ties produce a net gain. Politics (or political economy) may be a negative-sum game, economics a positive-sum game. Western neoclassical economists would be happy to think so; redistributionists would not.

85 Oikumenes tend to expand. Despite occasional setbacks (reflected by losses of urban population), there have been underlying upward trends in numbers of megacities and in their sizes. Oikumenes tend to expand in area as well as in human and urban numbers: the Old oikumene expanded from the Middle East to global scope, in the process colliding with and absorbing the other oikumenes.

86 There is a parallelism between the tendency of oikumenes to expand, collide, and merge and that of civilizations to do the same. But there is also a major difference: namely, the apparent absence of the distinction between the inegalitarian "engulfment" and egalitarian "coupling" relationships in oikumenical fusion. In particular, during the interval between the fusions of the Old oikumene with Indic and Far Eastern oikumenes, and the later fusion of Central civilization with Indic and Far Eastern civilizations, i.e. between about 326 BC and 1000–1600 AD in the Indic case, and between about 622 AD and 1900 AD in the Far Eastern case, it is hard to argue for any kind of extreme inequality in the transactions between the formerly separate oikumenes. Intense complaints and resistance seem to appear as a result not of economic penetration, but of politicomilitary penetration, not of oikumenical fusion but of civilizational fusion, in which politicomilitary predominance also alters the terms of economic redistribution in the direction of the penetrating powers.

87 Civilizations follow oikumenes, and "the flag follows trade," and not the reverse. There appears to be a powerful economic incentive, once trading areas have expanded beyond the politicomilitary reach of the powers in a civilization's political system, for those powers to extend the reach of their rule, violence, threat, and power-bargaining. No doubt there is a reciprocal incentive for traders and colonists to get outside civilizations' polities, and then to reach back for economic ties. Economy flees polity, which pursues.

88 Oikumenes do not allocate their benefits equally and impartially, except in the Malthusian sense that populations ""granted" a surplus tend to use it to become numerous and poor rather than few and rich (though elites within such populations seem to do the opposite). On the assumption that a notable growth (or shift) in megalopolitan population implies, and results from, a notable growth (or relative shift), of "wealth," the question of which world city was the largest when becomes of theoretical interest.

89 No clear system-level processes exist that give or remove primacy of wealth and population to or from chief cities of the civilizations in polycivilizational oikumenes; urban primacy at the oikumene-level appears to be mostly an epiphenomenon of asynchronous imperial unions and collapses at the civilization level.

90 It would seem consistent to expect that in a monocivilizational oikumene (like the current one), economic inequality is likelier to be the result of politicomilitary than of purely economic processes.

91 There are some apparent, though not in principle unresolvable, discrepancies between this argument and the recent and current findings of other workers, notably Barry K. Gills and Andre Gunder Frank (chapter 3 above; cf. Frank 1990: esp. 228–33). On the one hand, their argument that the world system developed from its origins in Mesopotamia, Egypt, and Indus, into the "Asio-Afro-European ecumene" and incorporated the Western hemisphere after AD 1500 (p. 81–2 above) is virtually identical to the interpretation I would put on Tertius Chandler's (1987) city data, though I prefer the term "Old oikumene" to both the "world system" and "the 'Afro-Eurasian ecumene.'"

92 Furthermore, I fully concur with their defense (p. 85–7 above) of Central Asia's very important and unduly neglected role in the development of "the world system" (for me, of Central civilization and of the Old oikumene).

93 On the other hand, I feel compelled to use a substantially later dating of the incorporation of several key areas into "an over-arching system of inter-penetrating and competitive super-accumulation" (p. 81–2 above) than is implied in their work, which brings the Indus zone into the "world system" by about 2700 BC (p. 81–2 above) and China apparently by 500 BC. To the extent that I am constrained by Chandler's data, I see the Indus as inside the Old oikumene in Chandler's "snapshot" for 1800 BC, but Indic civilization as thereafter outside the Old oikumene in 1200, 1000, 800, 650, and even 430 BC, and not back until 200 BC. To that same extent, I see Far Eastern civilization as outside the Old oikumene up to the 500 AD "snapshot" and inside it only in and after the 622 AD "snapshot."

94 The reasons for our differences are two, and the same in these two cases. One reason is approachable by theory, one by research. The theoretical reason is that I am unwilling to accept that the connection of two oikumenes has produced a single system until the trade routes that connect the two have been studded with entrepôt cities whose population and polity are pretty clearly sustained by brokering (and guarding, warehousing, servicing, repackaging, rerouting, and parasitizing) the trade. Thus the rise of Rayy, Balkh, Broach, and Taxila are to me important and necessary indicators of the reincorporation of Indic civilization's private oikumene into the Old oikumene by 200 BC; the rise of Samarkand and Kashgar serves similarly as indicators of the incorporation of the Far Eastern oikumene into the Old oikumene by 622 AD.

95 The researchable reason might, however, reduce or even resolve our chronological disagreement without requiring changes in theory on either side. Chandler's 1987 data takes the threshold of city size down only to 30,000 in 430 BC, and to 40,000 in 500 AD. Were data to be collected down to the threshold of 10,000 which I prefer, it may be taken as certain that each of Chandler's tables of cities would be greatly expanded, perhaps in the case of some of the later tables expanded by one or two orders of magnitude. Inspection of the Chandler tables suggests very strongly that city sizes form a near-Zipfian distribution – the larger the fewer; the smaller the size the more cities at that size. In the process of such expansion, it is highly probable that many cities which, like Samarkand and Kashgar, crossed a 40,000 threshold by 622 AD, would have crossed a 10,000 threshold by 500 AD, and not impossible that they did so much earlier, or that other cities on the same route crossed the lower threshold long before those crossed the higher. It is therefore quite conceivable that further research will fully resolve our chronological disagreements, with or without a resolution of our theoretical differences.

96 A second difference between the argument developed here and that of Frank and Gills has to do with the system-level phenomenology of my "Old oikumene" and their "world system." I have not located prior to the nineteenth century the phenomenon they characterize as "superhegemony": a "privileged position . . . in which one zone of the world system and its constituent ruling and propertied classes are able to accumulate surplus more effectively and concentrate accumulation at the expense of other zones" (p. 103 above).

97 I prefer (to "superhegemony") the term "parahegemony," based on the multiple connotations of the prefix "para-": related to; almost; closely resembling the true form; abnormal; beyond. "*Parahegemony" is a position in an oikumene in which the parahegemon derives economic benefits similar to those which a true hegemon is able to extract by the use or threat of force*. But the parahegemon does so without the need to spend on force, because it has the economic advantage of being a highly privileged forereacher (a center of invention, and/or saving and investment, and/or entrepreneurship) and/or a rentier (monopolizing a scarce resource, a trade-route intersection or choke point, an enormous market, etc.); and because it has the politicomilitary advantage of being strong enough to defend its centers and monopolies, *or* of being outside the politicomilitary striking range of its rivals and/or victims.

98 The terminological difference is not crucial. "Parahegemony" could not unreasonably be called "superhegemony," even though it involves *less* relative power than "hegemony," because it may be more secure, less assailable, cheaper to maintain than genuine politicomilitary hegemony.

99 There have, I believe, been recognizable parahegemons on the world-systems. Britain, often mistakenly styled "hegemonic" in the nineteenth century, was a parahegemon – able to defend itself from anyone though not to conquer or control any of its great-power rivals; advantaged by being first or fastest in industrial development and then in finance.

100 So, after the Second World War, was the United States parahegemonic rather than hegemonic? The USA was incapable of compelling positive compliance by Russia (Stalin's violation of Yalta), China (failure of the Marshall mission; failure of the 1950 Acheson initiative), France (general intractability of General De Gaulle), India (defection from 1950 Korean war support coalition; foundation of nonaligned movement), even North Korea (1950–3) or North Vietnam (1954 ff.). It was, however, fully capable of defending itself, all its trade routes and major trading partners, and it possessed relative superiority in agricultural and industrial capacity and in innovative capacity and achievement. By contrast, the position of the USA in 1991 was far closer to hegemony than to parahegemony: it was better able to coerce, and less able to compete.

101 But were there pre-nineteenth-century parahegemons? I have not found their trace in the Chandler data. The historical traces of oikumenical parahegemony ought to include cosmopolitan accumulation of wealth; and, if we accept that a wealthy cosmopolis will contain a luxuriating patriciate and a proliferant and/or immigrative plebs, remarkable growth in population ought to be as usable a sign of parahegemony as would be the accumulation of palaces and temples, pleasances and theaters, monuments and brothels, warehouses and ministries, harems and hippodromes.

102 The largest city in an oikumene is, then, *perhaps* also the sign of the oikumenical parahegemony of the state within which it lies. But there are other possible explanations for cosmopolitan size. A city might be largest by reason of direct hegemony (not parahegemony) over the oikumene as a whole. Or it might be largest for reasons accidental to the oikumene but well-grounded for some region within the oikumene, e.g. because its state was locally hegemonic (or parahegemonic) to the most populous or wealthiest region within the oikumene.

103 In reviewing Chandler's list of "Cities that can have been the largest" (Wilkinson 1992–3: Table 30) most such seem to have their status plausibly explained on grounds that relate to their *regional* rather than their *oikumenical* role. Most commonly they rose in population as their state acquired hegemony, empire or universal empire, not within the whole of the Old oikumene but within a civilization that was a politicomilitarily linked region within the economically bound system of the oikumene, and they fell in size in proportion as the scope of the regional domination of their state shrank.

104 On the whole, therefore, the achievement of oikumenical parahegemony seems to be a relatively recent phenomenon. Why? The answer is no doubt partly to be found by closer examination of the rise of nineteenth-century London and twentieth-century New York; but also in the failure to reach parahegemony of earlier plausible candidates. These would be those cities that acquired large populations without acquiring empires large enough to account for those populations, and which accordingly probably prospered mainly through success in trade, but which never rose to demographic primacy: perhaps this list should include Kerma (Nubia), Hazor, Ugarit, Saba (Yemen), Hastinapura, Miletus, Broach, and Canton; surely it would include Tyre, Athens, Carthage, and Venice. If the experience of the latter quartet is characteristic, then the usual pattern of the failure on the road to parahegemony is dual: one becomes a target for the attacks of dominant powers on *their* way to hegemony or universal empire, and is thereby distracted from wealth-seeking to defense, or destroyed, or taken over and drained; and/or one turns from the road to economic parahegemony to the parallel but different road to politicomilitary hegemony, and finds oneself unfitted to be a hegemon by just those social characteristics that made one a fit candidate for parahegemony, e.g. (perhaps) an open, fluid, volatile, mercantile social order.

105 Whether the USA has acquired the attributes needed by a hegemon, and in the process lost those required of a parahegemon, is a question that might be raised in this connection; but not in this paper.

106 Since Gills and Frank do not as yet ascribe "superhegemony" to any particular pre-nineteenth-century state, it cannot be said that we are as yet in substantive disagreement. But I am now pessimistic about the likelihood that empirical research will in future locate such an entity, while I believe they remain rather more hopeful. To the extent that their "superhegemon" and my "parahegemon" mean the same thing theoretically – the overlap is not complete, but substantial – this difference of expectations is also resolvable by research rather than otherwise.

I have tried in this essay to begin where my own independent research began, and to end by coming to grips with the challenging, stimulating, and important theses about the world system and superhegemony lately articulated by Gills and Frank. Certain issues divide us still, and these are always to me the more interesting. I regard the question of hegemony, parahegemony, and superhegemony as the premier issue for the next phase of the debate, which this collection opens.

NOTES

1 This proposition, like most of those in the next three sections, is derived by way of a critical encounter with the work of Pitirim Sorokin. See Wilkinson forthcoming.

2 For an expanded treatment of this issue, see Wilkinson 1987.

3 These issues are treated at greater length in Wilkinson 1991.

4 This problem is investigated further in Wilkinson 1992–3.

REFERENCES

Chandler, Tertius (1987) *Four Thousand Years of Urban Growth: An Historical Census*, Lewiston/Queenston: St David's University Press.
Danilevsky, Nikolai Ia. (1920) *Russland und Europa*, trans. Karl Notzel, Stuttgart: Deutsche Verlags-anstalt.
Frank, Andre Gunder (1990) "A theoretical introduction to 5,000 years of world system history," *Review* (Fernand Braudel Center) 13 (2) (spring): 155–248.
Quigley, Carroll (1961) *The Evolution of Civilizations*, New York: Macmillan.
Sorokin, Pitirim A. (1950) *Social Philosophies in an Age of Crisis*, Boston: Beacon.
—— (1956) *Fads and Foibles in Modern Sociology and Related Sciences*, Chicago: Henry Regnery.
—— (1964) *Sociocultural Causality, Space and Time*, New York: Russell & Russell.
—— (1966) *Sociological Theories of Today*, New York: Harper & Row.
Spengler, Oswald (1926–8) *The Decline of the West*, trans. Charles Francis Atkinson, New York: Knopf.
Toynbee, Arnold J. (1961) *Reconsiderations. A Study of History*, vol. 12, Oxford: Oxford University Press.
Wallerstein, Immanuel (1974) *The Modern World-System*, vol. 1: *Capitalist Agriculture and the Origins of the European World-Economy in the Sixteenth Century*, New York: Academic Press.
—— (1975) "The present state of the debate on world inequality," in *World Inequality: Origins and Perspectives on the World-System*, Immanuel Wallerstein, Montreal: Black Rose Books, 9–28.
—— (1979a) *The Capitalist World-Economy*, Cambridge: Cambridge University Press.
—— (1979b) "Underdevelopment and phase-B: effect of the seventeenth-century stagnation on core and periphery of the European world-economy," in *The World System of Capitalism: Past and Present*, ed. Walter L. Goldfrank, Beverly Hills: Sage, 73–83.
—— (1980) *The Modern World-System*, vol. 2: *Mercantilism and the Consolidation of the European World-Economy, 1600–1750*, New York: Academic Press.
—— (1982) "World-systems analysis: theoretical and interpretative issues," in *World-Systems Analysis: Theory and Methodology*, ed. Terence K. Hopkins, Immanuel Wallerstein, *et al.*, Beverly Hills: Sage, 91–103.
—— (1983) *Historical Capitalism*, London: Verso.
—— (1984) *The Politics of the World-Economy*, Cambridge: Cambridge University Press.
Wilkinson, David (1985) "General war," *Dialectics and Humanism* 12 (3–4): 45–57.
—— (1986) "Kinematics of world systems," *Dialectics and Humanism* 13 (1): 21–35.
—— (1987) "Central civilization," *Comparative Civilizations Review* (fall): 31–59.
—— (1988) "Universal empires: pathos and engineering," *Comparative Civilizations Review* (spring): 22–44.
—— (1991) "Cores, peripheries and civilizations," in *Core/Periphery Relations in Precapitalist Worlds*, ed. Christopher Chase-Dunn and Thomas D. Hall, Boulder, CO: Westview Press, 113–66.
—— (1992–3) "Cities, civilizations and oikumenes," *Comparative Civilizations Review* (fall 1992): 51–87 and (spring 1993): forthcoming.
—— (forthcoming) "Sorokin vs. Toynbee on congeries and civilizations: a critical

reconstruction," in *Sorokin and Civilization: A Centennial Assessment*, ed. Michel Richard, Palmer Talbutt, and Joseph B. Ford, Rutgers, NJ: Transaction Books.

8

THE ANCIENT WORLD-SYSTEMS VERSUS THE MODERN CAPITALIST WORLD-SYSTEM

Samir Amin

The modern world has produced a general image of universal history founded on the proposition that (European) capitalism is the first social system to unify the world. The least that can be said in that respect is that this statement seriously distorts reality and – I submit – is basically an expression of the dominant Eurocentric ideology. In fact, societies prior to the sixteenth century were in no way isolated from one another but were competitive partners within at least regional systems (and perhaps even a world system). Overlooking their interaction, one can hardly understand the dynamics of their evolution.

Simultaneously I maintain that capitalism is a qualitatively new age in universal history which started around 1500. Therefore I insist upon distinguishing the modern capitalist overall structure from protocapitalist elements which indeed appeared in anterior societies, sometimes since quite ancient times; I also insist upon the specificity of the capitalist center/periphery dichotomy vis-à-vis previous forms of polarization.

THE SPECIFICITY OF CAPITALISM VIS-A-VIS ANTERIOR SOCIAL FORMATIONS

The theoretical contribution of the Marxist concept of the capitalist mode of production is crucial to this discussion. Its eventual dilution (fashionable nowadays of course) does not help clarify the issues. The capitalist mode of production entails private ownership of the means of production which are themselves the product of labor, namely, machinery. This in turn presumes a higher level of development of the forces of production (compared to the artisans and their instruments) and, on this basis, the division of society into two fundamental classes. Correspondingly, socially necessary labor takes the form of free wage labor. The generalized capitalist market thus constitutes the framework in which economic laws ("competition") operate as forces independent of subjective will. Economistic alienation and the dominance of economics are its expression.

No society prior to modern times was based on such principles. All advanced societies from 300 BC to 1500 AD are, from one end of the period to the other, of a profoundly similar nature, which I call tributary in order to show this essential *qualitative* fact; namely, that the surplus is directly tapped from peasant activity through some transparent devices associated with the organization of the power hierarchy (power is the source of wealth, while in capitalism the opposite is the rule). The reproduction of the system therefore requires the dominance of an ideology – a state religion – which renders opaque the power organization and legitimizes it (in contrast to the economistic ideology of capitalism which makes economic exploitation opaque and justifies it through this means, counterbalancing the relative openness of political relations, itself a condition for the emergence of modern democracy).

Having taken a stand on some of the debates of historical materialism, I believe it helpful to recall my essential conclusions. They affect my suggestions on the nature of the one (or more) premodern system(s). I have rejected the supposedly Marxist version of "five stages." More precisely I refuse: 1) to regard slavery as a necessary stage through which all the societies that are more "advanced" have passed; 2) to regard feudalism as the necessary stage succeeding slavery. I have also rejected the supposedly Marxist version of the "two roads." More precisely, I refuse to consider that only the "European" road (slavery-to-feudalism) would pave the way to the invention of capitalism, while the "Asiatic" road (the supposed Asiatic mode of production) would constitute an impasse, incapable of evolving by itself. I have described these two interpretations of historical materialism as products of Eurocentrism. I refer to my alternative suggestions in *Class and Nation*. I suggested the necessary succession of two "families of modes of production": the communal family and the tributary family. This suggestion comes from highlighting two qualitative breaks in the general evolution: 1) later in date: the qualitative break from the dominance of the political and ideological instance (state plus metaphysical ideology) in the tributary phase into the dominance of the economic instance (generalized market and economistic ideology) in the capitalist phase; 2) previously: the qualitative break from the absence of a state and the dominance of the ideology in the communal phase into the crystallization of social power in the statist-ideological-metaphysical form in the tributary phase. This proposition entailed identifying various forms of each of the two phases and, more particularly, defining the "central/peripheral" forms of the tributary phase, with precisely the description of feudalism as a peripheral tributary form.

To some, the forms I call "tributary" would not constitute "a" mode of production in the sense that they believe Marxism attaches to the concept of the mode of production. I shall not indulge in this kind of Marxology. If it is a "nuisance" I am ready to replace the term "tributary mode of production" with the broader expression "tributary society." Of course my suggestions remain within a framework dominated by the search for "general laws." Include in this, on the basis of these conceptualizations I have suggested, their "transition" toward capitalism, marked by the development of the "protocapitalist" elements which appeared earlier in history. There is of course a strong current nowadays rejecting any search for general laws and insisting on the "irreducible" specificity of various evolutionary paths. I take this epistemological orientation to be a product of a Eurocentrism concerned above all with legitimatizing the "superiority" of the West.

THE SPECIFICITY OF THE CAPITALIST WORLD-SYSTEM

The first question the debate on this subject encounters concerns the character of worldwide capitalist expansion. For my part, along with others (including A.G. Frank), I hold that the processes governing the system as a whole determine the framework in which local "adjustments" operate. In other words, this systemic approach makes the distinction between external factors and internal factors relative, since all the factors are internal at the level of the world-system. Is there any need to stress that this methodological approach is distinct from prevailing (bourgeois and even current Marxist) approaches? According to the latter, internal factors are decisive in the sense that the specificities of each ("developed" or "undeveloped") national formation are mainly due to "internal" factors, whether "favorable" or "unfavorable," to capitalist development.

My analysis remains broadly based on a qualitative distinction (decisive in my view) between the societies of capitalism, dominated by economics (the law of value), and previous societies, dominated by the political and ideological. There is, as I see it, a fundamental difference between the contemporary (capitalist) world-system and all the preceding (regional and tributary) systems. This calls for comment on the "law of value" governing capitalism.

On that ground I have expressed my point of view in terms of what I have called "the worldwide expansion of the capitalist law of value." Generally speaking, the law of value supposes an integrated market for the products of social labor (that then become commodities), capital and labor. Within its area of operation it brings a tendency to uniformity in the price of identical commodities and returns on capital and labor (in the form of wages or returns to the petty commodity producer). This is a close approximation to the empirical reality in central capitalist formations. But on the scale of the world capitalist system, the worldwide law of value operates on the basis of a truncated market that integrates trade in goods and the movement of capital but excludes the labor force. The worldwide law of value tends to make the cost of commodities uniform but not the rewards for labor. The discrepancies in world pay rates are considerably broader than in productivities. It follows from this thesis that the polarizing effect of the worldwide law of value has nothing in common in terms of its quality, quantity, and planetary scope with the limited tendencies to polarization within the former (regional) tributary systems.

In this context the qualitative break represented by capitalism remains totally valid; it manifests itself in a fundamental reversal: the dominance of the economic replaces that of the political and ideological. That is why the world capitalist system is qualitatively different from all previous systems. The latter were of necessity regional, no matter how intensive the relations they were able to maintain among each other. Until the reversal has occurred it is impossible to speak of anything but protocapitalist elements, where they exist, subject to the prevailing tributary logic. That is why I am not convinced of the usefulness of a theoretical view that suppresses this qualitative break and sees a supposedly eternal "world system" in a continuum whose origin is lost in the distant past of history.

The significance of the qualitative break of capitalism cannot, therefore, be underestimated. But an acknowledgement of it reveals its limited historical application, as it is stripped of the sacred vestments in which bourgeois ideology has dressed it. The simple and reassuring equations can no longer be written, such as capitalism (nowadays "market") equals freedom and democracy, etc. For my part, along with Karl Polanyi, I give a central place to the Marxist theory of economic alienation. With Polanyi, I draw the conclusion that capitalism is by its nature synonymous not with freedom, but with oppression. The socialist ideal of bringing freedom from alienation is thus reinvested with all the force of which some sought to deprive it.

The critique of Eurocentrism in no way implies refusal to recognize the qualitative break capitalism represents and, to use a word no longer fashionable, the progress (albeit relative and historically limited progress) it ushers in. Nor does it propose an "act of contrition" by which westerners renounce describing this invention as European. The critique is of another kind and centered on the contradictions the capitalist era opens up. The system conquers the world but does not make it homogenous. Quite the reverse, it effects the most phenomenal polarization possible. If the requirement of universalism the system ushers in is renounced, the system cannot be superseded. To sum up in a phrase the critique I suggested in *Eurocentrism*: the truncated universalism of capitalist economism, necessarily Eurocentric, must be replaced by the authentic universalism of a necessary and possible socialism. In other words, the critique of Eurocentrism must not be backward-looking, making "a virtue of the difference," as the saying goes.

THE MERCANTILIST TRANSITION IN EUROPE, 1500–1800

The world-system is not reducible to the relatively recent form of capitalism dating back only to the final third of the nineteenth century, with the onset of "imperialism" (in the sense that Lenin attached to this term) and the accompanying colonial division of the world. On the contrary, we say that this world dimension of capitalism found expression right from the outset and remained a constant of the system through the successive phases of its development. The recognition that the essential elements of capitalism crystallized in Europe during the Renaissance suggests 1492 – the beginning of the conquest of America – as the date of the simultaneous birth of both capitalism and the world capitalist system, the two phenomena being inseparable.

How should we qualify the nature of the "transition" from 1500 to 1800? Various qualifications have been suggested, based on the political norms prevailing at the time (*ancien régime* or "the age of absolute monarchy") or on the character of its economy (mercantilism). Indeed, the old mercantilist societies of Europe and the Atlantic and their extension toward central and eastern Europe are problematic. Let us simply note that these societies witnessed the conjunction of certain key preliminary elements of the crystallization of the capitalist mode of production. These key elements are a marked extension of the field of commodity exchanges affecting a high proportion of agricultural production; an affirmation of modern forms of private ownership and the protection of these forms by the law; a marked extension of free wage labor (in agriculture and craftsmanship). However, the economy of these societies was more mercantile (dominated by "trade" and "exchange") than capitalist by virtue of the fact that the development of the forces of production had not yet imposed the "factory" as the principal form of production.

As this is a fairly obvious case of a "transitional" form, I shall make two further comments on this "conclusion." First, the elements in question – that some have called "protocapitalist" (and why not?) – did not miraculously and suddenly emerge in 1492. They can be found long before in the "region," in the Mediterranean precinct particularly, in the Italian cities, and across the sea in the Arab–Muslim world. They had also existed for a very long time in other regions: in India, China, etc. Why then begin the "transition to capitalism" in 1492 and not in 1350, or in 900, or even earlier? Why speak of "transition to capitalism" only for Europe and not also describe as societies in transition toward capitalism the Arab-Islamic or Chinese societies in which these elements of "protocapitalism" can be found? Indeed, why not abandon the notion of "transition" altogether, in favor of a "constant evolution of a system in existence for a long while, in which the elements of protocapitalism have been present since very ancient times"? My second comment explains in part my hesitation in following the suggestions made above. The colonization of America accelerated to an exceptional extent the expansion of the protocapitalist elements indicated above. For three centuries the social systems that participated in the colonization were dominated by such elements. This had not been the case elsewhere or before. On the contrary, the protocapitalist segments of society had remained cloistered in a world dominated by tributary social relations (feudal in medieval Europe). So let us now clarify what we mean here by the domination of tributary relations.

One question we might ask is whether the dense network of Italian cities did or did not constitute a "protocapitalist system." Undoubtedly protocapitalist forms were present at the level of the social and political organization of these dominant cities. But can the Italian cities (and even others, in south Germany, the Hanseatic cities, etc.) really be separated from the wider body of medieval Christendom? That wider body remained dominated by feudal rural life, with its ramifications at the political and ideological levels: customary law, the fragmentation of powers, cultural monopoly of the Church, and so on. In this spirit it seems to me essential to give due weight to the evolution of the political system of "protocapitalist" Europe from the sixteenth to the eighteenth centuries. The evolution that led from the feudal fragmentation of medieval power to the centralization of the absolute monarchy kept pace precisely with the acceleration of protocapitalist developments. This European "specificity" is remarkable, since elsewhere – in China or in the Arab–Islamic world for example – there is no known equivalent of "feudal fragmentation"; the (centralized) state precedes "protocapitalism." I have attributed this European specificity to the "peripheral" character of the feudal society – the product of a grafting of the Mediterranean tributary formation onto a body still largely at the backward communal stage (the Europe of the barbarians).

The (belated) crystallization of the state, in the form of absolute monarchy, implied, at the outset, relations between the state and the various components of the society that differed abstractly from those that were the case for the central tributary state. The central tributary state merged with the tributary dominant class, which had no existence outside it. The state of the European absolute monarchies was, on the contrary, built on the ruins of the power of the tributary class of the peripheral modality and relied strongly in its state-building on the protocapitalist urban elements (the nascent bourgeoisie) and rural elements (peasantry evolving toward the market). Absolutism resulted from this balance between the new and rising protocapitalist forces and the vestiges of feudal exploitation.

An echo of this "specificity" can be found in the ideology accompanying the formation of the state of the *ancien régime*, from the Renaissance to the Enlightenment of the eighteenth century. I stress the "specificity" – and in my opinion advanced character – of this ideology, which broke with the tributary ideology. In the latter scheme, the predominance of a metaphysical view of the world is based on the dominance of the political instance over the economic base. To avoid any misunderstanding, I stress that metaphysics is not synonymous with "irrationality" (as the radical currents of the Enlightenment have painted it), but seeks to reconcile Reason and Faith (see my discussion of this theme in *Eurocentrism*). The ideological revolution from the Renaissance to the Enlightenment did not suppress metaphysics (metaphysical needs), but freed the sciences from their subjection to it and thereby paved the way to the constitution of a new scientific field, that of the social sciences. At the same time of course (far from accidental) concomitance between the practices of the new state (of the *ancien régime*) and developments in the field of ideology stimulated protocapitalist expansion. The European societies began to move rapidly toward the "bourgeois revolution" (1688 in England, 1776 in New England, 1789 in France). They challenged the absolutist system that had provided a platform for protocapitalist advances. New concepts of power legitimized by democracy (however qualified) were introduced. It is also from there on that the Europeans developed a new "awareness" of their specificity. Before the Renaissance the Europeans (of medieval Christendom) knew they were not "superior" (in power potential) to the advanced societies of the Orient, even if they regarded their religion as "superior," just as the others did! From the Renaissance on, they knew they had acquired at least potential superiority over all the other societies and could henceforth conquer the entire globe, which they proceeded to do.

THE ARAB-ISLAMIC AND THE MEDITERRANEAN PRIOR SYSTEMS

Everybody knows that the Arab-Islamic Mediterranean and Middle East region enjoyed a brilliant civilization even before the Italian cities. But did the Arab-Islamic world constitute a protocapitalist system? The protocapitalist forms are present and, at certain times and places, inspired a glorious civilization. The views I have put forward on this subject (see *The Arab Nation*, *Eurocentrism*) tie in with Mansour Fawzy's book (1990) on the historical roots of the impasse of the Arab world, and, in some regards, with the works of the late Ahmad Sadek Saad. Beyond possible divergences – or shades of meaning – we are of the common opinion that the Arab-Islamic political system was not dominated by protocapitalist (mercantilist) forces but, on the contrary, that the protocapitalist elements remained subject to the logic of the dominant tributary system power. In fact, I consider the Arab-Islamic world as part of a larger regional system which I call the Mediterranean system.

I have suggested (in *Eurocentrism*) that we can date the birth of this "Mediterranean system" from the conquests of Alexander the Great (third century BC) and conceptualize a single long historic period running from this date to the Renaissance, encompassing at first the "Ancient Orient" (around the eastern basin of the Mediterranean), then the Mediterranean as a whole and its Arab-Islamic and European extensions.

I have in this regard put forward the thesis that we are dealing with a single tributary system from 300 BC (unification of the Orient by Alexander the Great) to 1492. I refer to a single "cultural area" whose unity is manifested in a common metaphysical formulation (the tributary ideology of the region), beyond the successive expressions of this metaphysics (Hellenistic, eastern Christian, Islamic, western Christian). In this tributary area I find it useful to distinguish between its central regions (the Mediterranean Orient) and its peripheral regions (the European West). Within this entity exchanges of every kind have (nearly always) been highly intensive and the associated protocapitalist forms highly advanced, particularly evident in the central regions (in the period of the first flowering of Islam from the eighth to the twelfth centuries and in Italy for the succeeding centuries). These exchanges have been the means of a significant redistribution of surplus. However, the eventual "centralization" of surplus was essentially tied to the centralization of political power. From that point of view the cultural area as a whole never constituted a single "unified imperial state" (except for the two brief periods of the Alexandrine empire and the Roman empire occupying all the central regions of the system). Generally speaking, the peripheral region of the European West remained extremely fragmented under the feudal form (and this is the very expression of its peripheral character). The central region was divided between the Christian Byzantine Orient and the Arab-Islamic empires (the Umayyad, then the Abbasid dynasties). It was first subject to internal centrifugal forces, then belatedly unified in the Ottoman empire, whose establishment coincided with the end of the period and the overall peripheralization of the eastern region – to the benefit of a shift of the center toward the previously peripheral region of Europe and the Atlantic.

Could this "system" be described as protocapitalist? In support of the thesis is the presence of undeniable protocapitalist elements (private ownership, commodity enterprise, wage labor) throughout the period, expanding in certain places and times (especially in the Islamic area and in Italy), declining in others (especially in barbarian Europe of the first millennium). But in my view the presence of these elements does not suffice to characterize the system. On the contrary, I would argue that, at the crucial level of ideology, what began in the Hellenistic phase of this period (from 300 BC to the first centuries AD), and then flourished in the (eastern then western) Christian and Islamic forms, is purely and simply the tributary ideology, with its major fundamental characteristic: the predominance of metaphysical concerns.

What we are talking about is indeed a "system," but not a "protocapitalist system," that is, a stage in the rapid transition from tributary society to capitalist society. On the other hand, we are dealing with a "tributary system," not a mere juxtaposition of autonomous tributary societies (in the plural), which just happened to share some common elements, such as religion, for example, or integration – albeit of limited duration – in an imperial state, such as that of Rome, Byzantium, or the Umayyad or Abbasid dynasty.

The distinction implies in my view a certain degree of centralization of surplus, which took the form of tribute and not, as in capitalism, that of profit from capital. The normal method of centralization of this tributary surplus was political centralization, operating to the advantage of imperial capitals (Rome, Byzantium, Damascus, Baghdad). Of course this centralization remained weak, as did the authority of the centers concerned. Byzantium, Damascus, and Baghdad could not prevent their staging-posts (Alexandria, Cairo, Fez, Kairouan, Genoa, Venice, Pisa, and so on) from frequently achieving their own autonomy. The entirety of barbarian Christendom (the first millennium in the West) escaped such centralization. In parallel, the logic of the centralization of authority stimulated protocapitalist relations to the point that mercantile handling of part of the surplus never disappeared from the region, and took on great significance in some areas and epochs, notably during the glorious centuries of Islam, and the emergence of the Italian cities following the Crusades. On this basis I have described the social formations of the Arab world as tributary-mercantile formations. All this leads me to conclude that capitalism "might have been" born in the Arab world. This takes me back to other discussions on this issue with which I have been associated. I have argued that once capitalism had appeared in Europe and the Atlantic, the process of evolution toward capitalism was brutally halted in its development elsewhere. The reason why the evolution toward capitalism accelerated in the Atlantic West (shifting the center of gravity of the system from the banks of the Mediterranean to the shores of the Atlantic Ocean), it seems to me, is mainly due to the colonization (of America, then of the entire globe) and contingently to the peripheral character of western feudalism.

DID A SINGLE WORLD TRIBUTARY SYSTEM EXIST?

My methodological hypothesis leads me to regard the other "cultural areas" as further autonomous tributary systems. In particular, it seems to me that the Confucian-Chinese tributary system constituted a world on its own and of its own. It had its own center (China), characterized by a strong political centralization (even if the latter under the pressure of internal centrifugal forces exploded from time to time. But it was always reconstituted), and its peripheries (Japan especially) had a relationship with China very similar to that of medieval Europe with the civilized Orient.

I leave a dotted line after the question whether the Hindu cultural area constituted a (single) tributary system.

This having been said, the question is: was the Mediterranean system "isolated" or in close relation with the other Asiatic and African systems? Can the existence of a "permanent" world-system, in constant evolution, be argued beyond the Mediterranean area and prior to its constitution? A positive response to this question has been suggested to some (notably Frank) by the intensity of exchange relations between the protocapitalist Mediterranean, the Chinese and Indian Orient, and sub-Saharan Africa, and perhaps even the significance of the exchanges in earlier times between these various regions of the ancient world. For my part, I do not believe that it is possible to answer the question, given the current state of knowledge. It is, however, useful to raise it in order to provoke a systematic exchange of views on what can be deduced from our knowledge, the hypotheses it may inspire, and the directions of research indicated for verification of these hypotheses.

I do not intend to substitute my own "intuitive views" for the eventual results of these debates. I advance them here only provisionally, to open the discussion. I should therefore suggest the following (provisional) theses.

First, humankind is one since its origins. The itinerary of the earth's population begins from the nucleus of hominids appearing in East Africa, going down the Nile and populating Africa, crossing the Mediterranean and the Isthmus of Suez to conquer Europe and Asia, passing the Bering Straits and perhaps crossing the Pacific to install themselves (in the most recent epoch) in the Americas. These successive conquests of the planet's territory are beginning to be dated. The following may be the pertinent question: has the dispersal brought a "diversification" of the lines of evolution of the various human groups, installed in geographical environments of extreme diversity and hence exposed to challenges of differing kinds? Or does the existence of parallel lines of evolution suggest the conclusion that humankind as a whole has remained governed by "laws" of evolution of universal application? And as a complement to this question it might be asked what effect have relations between the scattered human populations had on the fate, intensity, and rapidity of the transfer of knowledge, experience, and ideas?

Intuitively it might be imagined that some human groups have found themselves fairly isolated in particularly difficult circumstances and have responded to the challenge by particular adaptations unlikely to evolve of themselves. These groups would then be located in "impasses," constrained to reproduce their own organization without the latter showing signs of its own supersession. Perhaps included here would be the (still highly fragmented) societies of hunters/fishers/gatherers of the Arctic, the equatorial forest, small islands, and some coasts.

But other groups have found themselves in less arduous circumstances that have enabled them to progress simultaneously in mastery of nature (passage to settled agriculture, invention of more efficient tools, and so on) and in tighter social organization. In regard to the latter the question arises of "possible laws of social evolution of universal application" and the role of external relations in this evolution.

Secondly, in regard to societies that have clearly "advanced," can one detect similar phasing followed by all, albeit at faster or slower rates? Our entire social science is based on this seemingly necessary "hypothesis." For the satisfaction of the spirit? As legitimation of a universalist value system? Various formulations of this "necessary evolution" succeeded one another up to and during the nineteenth century. They were based either on the succession of modes of exploitation of the soil and instruments utilized (Old Stone Age, New Stone Age, Iron Age), or on the succession of social forms of organization (the ages of Savagery, Barbarism, Civilization). Various evolutions in these "particular" domains were regrafted on to what we regarded as fundamental general tendencies. For example, the "matriarchal–patriarchal" succession, the succession of the ages of philosophical thought (primitive, animist, metaphysical, Auguste Comte-style positivist), and so on. I shall not spend time here discussing these "theories," which are almost always more or less overridden by subsequent research. I merely point to their existence as evidence of the persistence of the need to "generalize," beyond the evident diversity that is the property of the scientific approach.

It seems to me that the most sophisticated formulation of all the theories of general evolution was that proposed by Marxism and based on the synthetic notions of "modes of production." The latter comes from a conceptualization of the basic elements of the construction (forces of production, relations of production, infrastructure and superstructure, etc.). They are then "enriched" by the grafting on of particular theories articulated to those of "modes of production" (such as theory of the family, of the state, etc.). Here again I shall not discuss whether these Marxist constructs are indeed those of Marx himself, or the product of later interpretations that may or may not be consonant with the spirit of the Marxism of Marx. Nor shall I discuss the validity of these theories in the light of our present-day greater knowledge of the societies of the past. Once again I merely point to the formulations as the expression of this same need to "understand," which implies the possibility of "generalizing."

Thirdly, on the basis of the conceptualization proposed, it is not difficult to identify several tributary societies at more or less the same level of maturity of general development: production techniques, instruments, range of goods, forms of organization of power, systems of knowledge and ideas, and so on. Noteworthy too is a fairly dense web of exchanges of all kinds between these societies: exchange of goods, knowledge, techniques, and ideas. Does this density of exchange justify speaking of a single world-system (albeit described as tributary) – in the singular? Frank and Gills provide an explicit criterion: an integrated system arises when reciprocal influences are "decisive" (A would not be what it is without the relation it has with B). So be it. But the overall question remains: were these relations "decisive" or not?

However, the universality of the laws of social evolution in no way implies the concept of a single system. Two distinct concepts are involved. The first refers to the fact that distinct societies – separated in geographical distance or time – have been able to evolve in a parallel manner for the same underlying reasons. The second implies that these societies are not distinct from one another but ingredients of the same world society. In the evolution of the latter – necessarily global – the laws in question are inseparable from the effects of the interaction between the various components of the world society.

I would in this context make two prefatory comments. 1) Economic exchanges are not necessarily a "decorative" element, making no lasting impression on the "mode of production" and hence on the level of development. Exchanges may be a significant means of distribution of surplus, decisive for some segments of the interrelated societies. The question is not one of principle but of fact. Were they? Where and when? I discount any hasty generalization that they were always (or generally) so or that they were never (or with rare exceptions) so. In the case of the Arab-Islamic region, for example, I have said that the exchanges were significant. They were enough to mark the formation of a "tributary-mercantile" character essential to an understanding of its involuted history of succession from a "glorious" phase to one of "degeneration," and of shifts of the centers of gravity of wealth and power in the region. I have also said that the "protocapitalist" formation of mercantilist Europe (seventeenth–eighteenth centuries) rapidly climbed the step toward capitalism thanks to these exchanges it dominated. But whether the exchanges had a matching role in China, India, the Roman empire, etc., I personally am in no position to say. 2) The exchanges in question must not be limited only to the economic field. Far from it. The writing of the history of the precapitalist epochs puts greater emphasis on cultural exchanges (especially the spread of religions) and military and political exchanges (rise and fall of empires, "barbarian" invasions, etc.), whereas the accent is on the economic aspect of relations within the modern world-system. Was this distinction wrong?

I do not think so. I believe, on the contrary, that the historians – albeit intuitively – have grasped the reversal of dominance, from the political and ideological to the economic, which is the central core of my own thesis. At this level is it possible to speak of a single tributary political and ideological world-system? I do not believe so. I have therefore preferred to speak of distinct tributary "cultural areas" founded precisely on broad systems of particular reference – most often the religious: Confucianism, Hinduism,

Islam, Christianity. Of course there is a certain relationship between these various metaphysics since they express the fundamental requirement of the same type of (tributary) society. The relationship in turn facilitates mutual borrowings.

To approach an answer to the question (of one or more systems), it is necessary to combine three elements: the density of economic exchanges and transfers of surplus distributed through this channel; the degree of centralization of political power; the relative diversity/specificity and hence autonomy of the ideological systems.

Autonomy of the various tributary systems does not preclude economic relations and other exchanges among them, nor even that such exchanges could be significant. It would be impossible to understand many historical facts and evolutions without reference to these exchanges: the transfer of technology of all kinds (the compass, gunpowder, paper, silk that gave its name to the roads in question, printing, Chinese noodles becoming Italian pasta, etc.); the spread of religious beliefs (Buddhism crossing from India to China and Japan, Islam traveling as far as Indonesia and China, Christianity as far as Ethiopia, south India, and Central Asia), etc.

There is certainly no centralization of surplus at the level of a world-system comparable to that characterizing the modern world in the exchanges that led here and there to lively protocapitalist links (from China and India to the Islamic world, the African Sahel, and medieval Europe) and transfers of surplus – perhaps even decisive at key points of the network of exchanges. The explanation is that centralization of surplus at the time operated mainly in association with centralization of power, and there was no kind of "world-empire" or even a "world power" comparable to what British hegemony would constitute in the nineteenth century or US hegemony in the twentieth.

The ancient (tributary) epochs had nothing comparable to the "polarization" on a global scale of the modern capitalist world. The earlier systems, despite significant levels of exchange, were not polarizing on a world scale, even if they were on a regional scale to the benefit of the centers of the regional systems (for example, Rome, Constantinople, Baghdad, the Italian cities, China, India). By contrast, the capitalist system is truly polarizing on a global scale and is therefore the only one deservedly described as a world-system.

This methodology for the analysis of the interactions between the tributary systems may call for a reassessment of the "traditional" findings in the history of the notorious "barbarians" who occupied the interstices of the great tributary cultural areas. Was the role of these "barbarians" really as it has been made out, a purely negative and "destructive" role? Or did their active role in intertributary exchanges give them a certain vocation to take decisive initiatives? The latter would explain their success (not only military) in "unifying" immense territories (Genghis Khan's empire), their capacity to situate themselves at the heart of ideological initiatives (Islam born in Arabia, the "barbarian" crossroads of Mediterranean-Indian-African exchanges), their capacity to hoist themselves rapidly to central positions in a tributary system (the glorious example of the Khwarizm area in the first centuries of Islam), etc.

A final reservation concerning the systematization of the hypothesis of the existence of a single world-system throughout history: is it possible to speak of tributary systems and significant exchange networks among them before the fifth to third centuries BC? I do not think so for the following three reasons at least: 1) because the social systems of the greater part of humankind were still backward at the stage I have described as communal; 2) because the islets of civilization at the stage where the state was the recognized form of the expression of power had not yet found complete tributary ideological expression (see the argument on the ideology of the ancient world in *Eurocentrism*); 3) because the density of the exchange relations between these islets remained weak (this did not prelude some exchange relations; for example, technological borrowings that were able to travel unexpected distances).

A CRITIQUE OF EVOLUTIONISM

The theory according to which all human societies have been forever integrated in a single world-system, in continuous evolution (capitalism not representing therefore any kind of qualitative break in this respect), arises from a philosophy of history which is in the end based on the notion of competition. Certainly it is based on a realistic observation of facts, namely, that all societies on earth, in all eras, are to some extent in "competition" with one another. It would not matter whether the relations they did or did not entertain showed their awareness of it. We know that the strongest must carry the day. At this level of abstraction there is indeed a single world, because there is a single humankind. It might perhaps be added that most "open" societies with intensive relations with the others have a greater chance of measuring up to this competition and facing up to it more effectively. It is otherwise for those who shy away from competition and seek to perpetuate their way of life; they risk being overtaken by the progress made elsewhere and later being marginalized.

This discourse is not wrong, but merely at such a high level of abstraction that it begs the real issue, namely, how this competition is manifested. Two bourgeois historians – themselves philosophers of history – deliberately placed themselves at this most general level of abstraction (in order to refute Marx). Arnold Toynbee in this regard suggests an operative model reduced to two terms: the "challenge" and the "response to the challenge." I suggest that, as a model valid for all times and all places, it teaches us nothing that is not already obvious. Toynbee suggests no law to explain why the challenge is taken up or not. He is satisfied with a case-by-case treatment. There is an almost natural parallel with the contradiction between the axioms of neoclassical bourgeois economics defined in terms claiming to be valid for all times ("scarcity," "utility," etc.) and the historical concept of qualitatively differing successive modes of production, determining specific institutional frameworks in which the "eternal rationality of human beings" is expressed. Jacques Pirenne, far superior to Toynbee in my opinion, suggests a refinement of constant contradiction between (sea-going) "open" societies and (land-based) "closed" societies and does not hesitate to describe the former as "capitalist" (Sumer, Phoenicia, Greece, Islam in the first centuries, the Italian cities, the modern West) and the latter as "feudal" (from ancient Persia to the European Middle Ages). He never hesitated to attribute to what I call "protocapitalist elements" the decisive place in the progress of the "open" societies making them the driving force of development of the forces of production. He likewise never concealed that his thesis was intended to discount the "closed" experiences of the Soviet Union and salute the dynamism of the Atlantic world. Hence Pirenne managed – certainly with skill – to replace class struggle with a constant struggle between the capitalist tendency and the feudal tendency within human societies.

I still believe that Marx's method is superior, precisely because it situates the abstraction at the appropriate level. The concept of modes of production gives back to history its explicit real dimension. At that level the significance and character of the capitalist break can be detected. The break is such that I do not think that competition between societies of earlier times and within the modern world-system can be treated in the same way. First because the competition of earlier times rarely crossed the threshold of consciousness and each society saw, or believed, itself "superior" in its own way, "protected by its deities," even when a looming danger imposed a greater consciousness (as between Muslims and Crusaders). Moreover, the discrepancy between the great tributary precapitalist societies is not such that the superiority of one over another is obvious; it is always conjunctural and relative. There is nothing comparable to the subsequent overwhelming superiority of capitalist societies over the rest. That is why I see the seizing of consciousness of this superiority as crucially important and therefore date the beginnings of capitalism to 1492. From then on the Europeans knew that they could conquer the world and went on to do so (see my arguments on this point in *Eurocentrism*). We know *a posteriori* – but the actors of the time were unaware – that the "strongest" is the one who has advanced to a qualitatively superior mode of production – capitalism. I would add that in the competition of earlier times geographical distance had a blunting effect. However intensive exchanges between Rome and China, I find it difficult to believe that the "external" factor could have a similar impact to that of the discrepancies in productivity of our own times. I believe that this distancing gave strictly internal factors a considerably more decisive relative weight. It also explains why those concerned had difficulty in assessing the real balance of forces. Quite different, it seems to me, is competition within the modern world-system, where consciousness is so acute that it is a plaintive chorus in the daily discourse of the authorities.

A DIAGRAM OF THE TRIBUTARY REGIONAL AND WORLD-SYSTEMS

The diagram opposite (Figure 8.1) illustrates my concept of the "ancient world-system" (reduced to societies of the so-called eastern hemisphere: Eurasia–Africa) for the periods covering the eighteen centuries between the establishment of the Hellenistic system in the Middle East (300 BC), the establishment of the Han state in China (200 BC), the Kushāna and Maurya states in Central Asia and India (200 BC), and the European Renaissance, that is, from 300 BC to 1500 AD. I wish to summarize its characteristics as follows.

First, as I have already said, all societies of the system in question are, from one end of the period to the other, of a tributary nature. Nevertheless, it is possible to distinguish among all these societies those which I would call "central tributaries" from those which are "peripheral tributaries." The former are characerized by a surplus centralization at the relatively high state level, with its redistribution placed under its control; while in peripheral formations, the embryonic character of the state (and even its virtual nonexistence) leads to a complete disintegration of surplus distribution monopolized by local feudal systems. The centers/peripheries antithesis is not, in this case, analogous to that which characterizes the (modern) capitalist world. In the latter, the relationship in question is an economic domination relationship in which the centers override the peripheries (and this is associated with economic dominance). This is not so in the ancient relationship. Dominated by the ideological authority, the tributary structures are either central or peripheral depending on the degree of the completion of the power-centralization process and its expression through a state religion. In the central formations, the latter takes the form of a state religion or a religious-oriented state philosophy with a universal vocation which breaks with the specific local religions of the former periods which I called "communal formations" (see *Class and Nation*). There is a striking relationship between the establishment of big tributary societies in their completed form and the emergence of great religious and philosophical trends which were to dominate civilizations over the ensuing two thousand years: Hellenism (300 BC), Oriental Christianity, Islam (600 AD), Zoroaster, Buddha, and Confucius (all three 500 BC). This relationship – which in no way excluded the reciprocal concessions provided by the

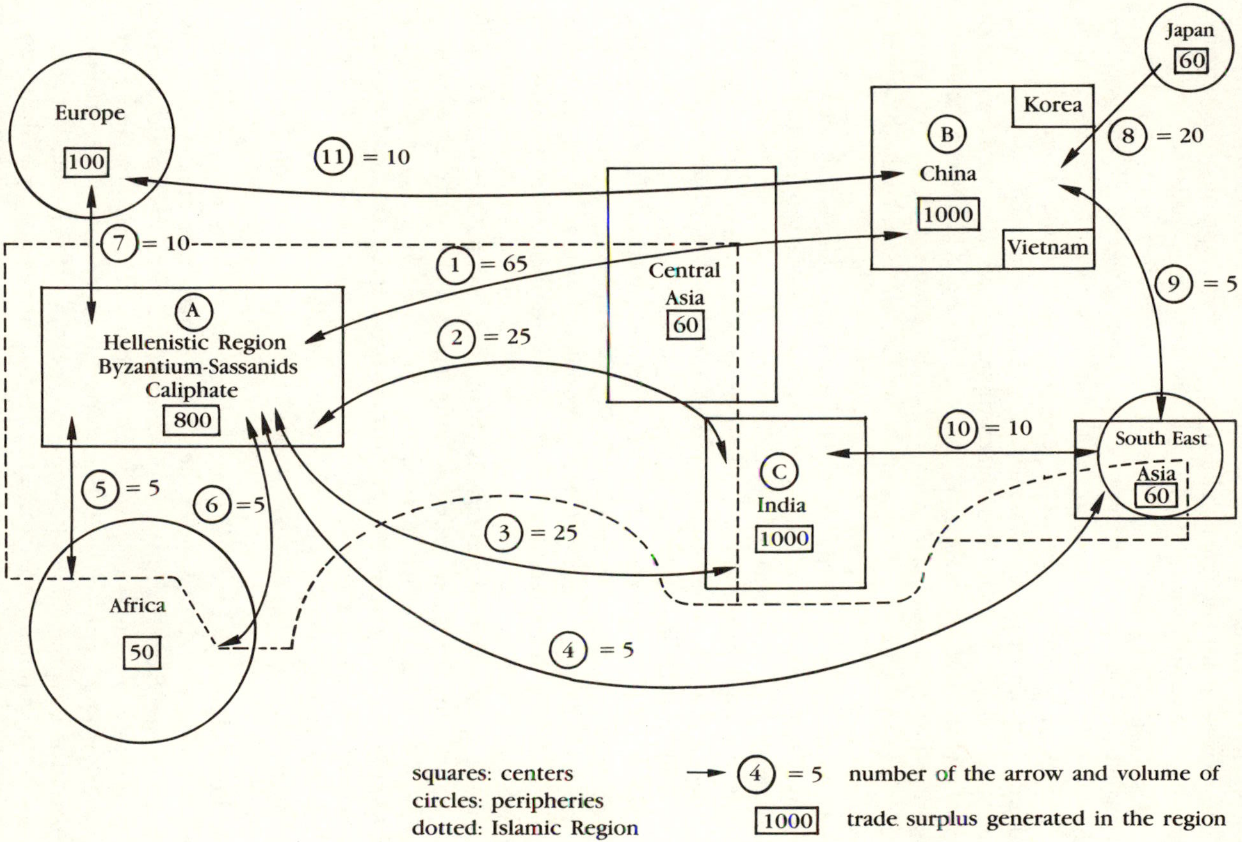

Figure 8.1 The tributary world-system 300 BC–1500 AD

relations that all tributary civilizations maintained among themselves – is not, in my view, an accident, but rather one of the consistent bases of my thesis on the dominant "tributary mode."

The establishment of great philosophical and religious movements associated with the formation of tributary systems represents the first wave of revolutions related to universal history, which is expressed by a universalist-oriented vocation transcending the horizons of the local – almost parochial – line of thinking in the ancient periods. This revolution sets up the tributary system as a general system at the entire level of mankind – or almost does so – for 2,000 to 2,500 years. The second wave of universal-oriented revolutions, which opens up capitalist modernity and its possible socialist overtaking, is marked by the Renaissance (and the revolution in Christianity with which it is associated) and, subsequently, by the three great modern revolutions, the French, Russian, and Chinese revolutions (see *Eurocentrism*).

The "model" *par excellence* of this tributary mode is, in my view, provided by China, which, without, it seems, a long incubation period (there is only one millennium between the Shang and the Zhou and the establishment of the Han dynasty), crystallizes in a form which undergoes no fundamental change, either with regard to the organization of productive forces and production relationships or ideology (the Confucianism–Taoism tandem replaced for only a brief moment by Buddhism), or with regard to power concepts during the 2,000 years between the Han dynasty and the 1911 revolution. Here, surplus centralization is at its height, at the level of an enormous society, not only during the brilliant periods where political unity was entirely or almost entirely achieved in this continent-country by great successive dynasties (Han, Tang, Song, Yuan, Ming, and Qing), but even during the periods of interdynastic disturbances when the country was divided into several kingdoms whose size was nonetheless considerable for the period. At the borders of China, Korea and Vietnam also turned, during the course of the first millennium of our era, into similar tributary systems which, in spite of their political independence with regard to China, borrowed its model of organization and Confucian ideology.

In the Middle East, the tributary system derived its completed form from the conquest of Alexander the Great. I have recommended in this connection (see *Eurocentrism*) this reading of the successive philosophical and religious orientations of Hellenism, Oriental Christianity, and Islam. However, in this region, the incubation period lasted for as long as thirty centuries for Egypt and Mesopotamia, ten centuries for Persia, Phoenicia, etc., and five centuries for Greece. Hellenism, Christianity, and Islam were, moreover, to produce a synopsis which borrowed some elements crucial to each of these ancient components and even from Persia and India as well. Here, too, surplus centralization for the ensuing 2,000 years is remarkable.

Doubtless, the region was split after the precarious political unification in the Alexander era; but it was split into large kingdoms for the period. Hence, divided between even bigger empires – those of Byzantium (300 to 1400 AD) and the Sassanids (200 to 600 AD) – and subsequently reunified gradually through the expansion of the Muslim caliphate, formed in the seventh century AD, which conquered Constantinople at the end of our period (in 1453), the spaces of surplus centralization were still either vast (during the first three centuries of the caliphate), or at the very least, considerable, after the break-up of the caliphate from the year 1000 to the advantage of Arabo-Berber dynasties in north Africa and Turco-Persians in the Mashreq and western part of Central Asia. The western Roman empire finds its place in this reading of history as an expression of an expansion of the tributary model to the banks of the western Mediterranean. Of secondary importance in universal history, the Roman empire owes its place to the fact that it has transmitted tributary ideology – in the form of western Christianity – to the "European" periphery.

A Eurocentric reading of history (see my critical appraisal in *Eurocentrism*) has, in this regard, distorted the achievements which, beyond the Italian peninsula, failed to resist barbaric feudalization (that is, the disintegration of the tributary system).

A third completed tributary center was established on the Indian continent in 200 BC from the Maurya period, followed by the Kushāna state (which overlaps the western part of Central Asia) and Gupta after the long incubation period which began with the Indus civilizations (Mohenjodaro and Harappa – 2500 BC). The Muslim conquest from the eleventh century on which followed after a "pulverization" period (of the seventh and ninth centuries) re-established together with the Ghazhavids, the sultanates of Delhi (1200–1500 AD), and subsequently the Mughal empire (1500–1800 AD), a tributary centralization on a large scale, while the Hindu states of Dekkan, also tributaries, equally represented considerable kingdoms for the period.

Three zones appear in Figure 8.1 whose peripheral character is striking during the entire or almost entire period under consideration (from 300 BC to 1500 AD). Europe (beyond the Byzantine region and Italy, that is, "barbaric" Europe) was the product of a tributary graft (transmitted by the ideal of the Roman empire and Christian universalism) on a social body still organized, to a large extent, on deteriorated community bases. Here, I wish to refer to the analysis I made (see *Class and Nation*) which simultaneously gives an account of the disintegration in the control of surpluses, and which defines feudalism as an uncompleted peripheral form of the tributary system, although the collapse of the state system was partially offset by the Church. Europe was slowly moving toward the tributary form, as testified by the establishment of absolute monarchies (in Spain and Portugal after the *reconquista*, and in England and France after the Hundred Years War). This belatedness constitutes, in my view, the crucial advantage which facilitated the early qualitative strides made by the Renaissance and capitalism (see *Class and Nation*).

Japan constituted, at the other end of the Euro-Asian continent, a peripheral tributary mode whose resemblance to Europe had struck me even before Mishio Morishima came to confirm my thesis. The degraded form of Japanese Confucianism, the feudal disintegration which preceded the belated formation of a monarchical centralization from the Tokugawa state (1600 AD), bear testimony to this peripheral character (see *Eurocentrism*), which, here, too, explains the remarkable ease with which Japan switched over to capitalism in the ninteenth century.

Sub-Saharan Africa constituted the third periphery. It was still lingering at the communal stage developing toward tributary forms. At this stage the tributary surplus centralizations still operated only on societies with limited size. Disintegration therefore remained the rule.

The status of Southeast Asia was ambivalent. It seems to me that here it is possible to recognize some central type of tributary formations – even if they only cover smaller spaces than those of other great Asian systems – and peripheral zones (defined by surplus disintegration). To the first type belongs the Khmer empire, followed by its Thai, Burmese, and Cambodian successors from the fifth century and, perhaps, in Indonesia, the Majapahit kingdom from the thirteenth century. On the other hand, the organized societies of Malaysia and Indonesia which crystallized into states under the influence of Hinduism (from the fifth century) and subsequently Islam, seem, in my view, to belong to the peripheral family, crumbled by the scattering of the surplus, collected in very small and relatively numerous and fragile states.

The status of the Central Asian region was special. The region itself is less defined in its borders than the others. Some large states were established in this region at an early period – such as the Kushāna empire – which directly linked up the Hellenistic Middle East and the Sassanids and then the Islamic Middle East to India and China. The region itself became the center of gravity of an immense empire at the time of Genghis Khan (1300 AD). Before and after this final crystallization, it had entered the Islamic orbit. Its modes of organization were tributary-oriented, at one time advanced (where the expression of centralized power on a large scale makes it possible), at another time relapsing into "feudal" disintegration. But the major feature of the region was that, by virtue of its very geographical position, it was the indispensable transit zone for East–West trade (China, India, the Middle East, and beyond to as far as the peripheries of the system). Having been in competition with the sea route from time immemorial, the continental route lost its importance only belatedly in the sixteenth century.

As for the second characteristic of the ancient world-system: during the entire eighteenth-century period under consideration, all the societies represented in Figure 8.1 not only existed together, but still maintained trade links of all types (trade and war, technological and cultural transfers) which were much more intense than was generally thought. In this very general sense, one can talk of the "general system" without, of course, mistaking its nature for that of the modern (capitalist) world-system. In Figure 8.1, I represent these links by eleven arrows. Of course, the intensity of flows that each of these arrows represents varied considerably with time and space. But above all – and I wish to emphasize this point – their connection with the internal dynamics peculiar to the different tributary systems they link up is not only fundamentally different from that which characterizes the "international links" within the modern world-system, but has also operated differently from one tributary formation to another.

To clarify things, I want to distinguish four sets of links:

1 The links mutually maintained between the three major centers (A – Rome and Byzantium, the Sassanid empire, the caliphate; B – China; C – India) are marked by arrows 1 (Middle East–China through Central and northern Asia), 2 (Middle East–India across western Central Asia), and 3 (Middle East–India by sea route). These links were undoubtedly the most intense of all, merely in view of the wealth and relative power of the centers in question, at least in the glorious years of their history.
2 The links maintained by the Arabo-Persian Islamic center with the three peripheries (Europe, Africa, Southeast Asia) are shown by arrows 4 (Middle East–Malaysia, Indonesia sea route), 5 (north Africa–African Sahel trans-Saharan route), 6 (Middle East–Swahili eastern coast sea route), and 7 (caliphate and Byzantium–Europe). The trade in question was less intense than that of the previous group (due to the relative poverty of the peripheries), and especially important is the fact that it was asymmetrical (a concept that I clearly distinguish from the specific inequality of the centers/peripheries relationships of the modern world) in the sense that they were perhaps neutral in their effects on the center, but crucial for the development of the peripheries. These relationships considerably accelerated the establishment of states in the African Sahel and East Africa (see *Class and Nation*) as well as in Malaysia and Indonesia and thus opened the way for the Islamization of these regions (Islam then replacing the ancient local religions in line with the needs of the tributary world). They also contributed immensely to the emergence of Italian trading cities, and, through these cities, of infiltration throughout the whole of feudal Europe.
3 The links maintained by the Chinese center with the Japanese periphery (arrow 8) and the Southeast Asian periphery (arrow 9) are of the same nature as those in the second group. Here, I wish to refer to arrow 11,

which indicates a direct communication establishment between China and Europe, using of course the routes of Central Asia but without passing through the canal in the heart of the Islamic caliphate. This direct relation existed only for a relatively short period, within the framework of the Mongol Pax (the Genghis Khan empire in the thirteenth century). But it was crucial for subsequent events of history because it made it possible for Europe to resort to China's vast technological accomplishments (gunpowder, printing, the compass, etc.); Europe was mature enough to do this and take the qualitative leap from a peripheral tributary (feudal) system to capitalism. Furthermore, shortly thereafter, Europe substituted the sea route it dominated for all ancient forms of long-haul transport, thus establishing direct links between itself and each of the other regions of the world (Africa, India, Southeast Asia), "discovering" and then "conquering" America at the same time.

4 The links maintained by the Indian center (Buddhist and Hindu) with its Southeast Asian peripheries (arrow 10) are similar to the China–Japan links.

It obviously appears that the relative intensity of "external" flows, as compared with the different masses constituted by the regional formations under consideration, varies considerably from one region to another. The three key central regions, A, B, and C (Middle East, China, India), represented, in terms of economic weight, a multiple of what constituted each of the other regions. If, therefore, the volume of the surplus identified in each of these key central regions is measured by index 1,000, it could hardly have exceeded index 100 for each of the other regions (Europe, Africa, Japan, Central Asia, and Southeast Asia). Moreover, only a part and probably a relatively minor part (10–20 per cent perhaps) of this surplus could involve long-distance trade.

The four arrows which concern China (major 1, minors 8 and 9, and transitory 11) could, for instance, represent an index "value" of about 100 (10 per cent of the surplus produced in China). The three arrows which concern India (majors 2 and 3 and minor 10) probably hardly exceeded index 50 or 70. All historians have observed that the "external" trade of these two continental masses were marginal as compared with their volume of production.

On the other hand, the weight of external trade seems more pronounced for region A, which is the only region in direct relationship with all the others. To major arrows 1, 2, and 3 representing A's trade with B and C (total index value: 115 in our assumption) is added the region's trade with the peripheries of Europe (arrow 7), Africa (arrows 5 and 6), and Southeast Asia (arrow 4), making a total index value of about 25. In sum then, external trade, in this case, would have represented an index value of 140 (almost 20 per cent of the surplus?).

For each of the peripheries too the contribution of external trade would appear relatively considerable: index 20 for Europe, 10 for Africa, 20 for Southeast Asia, and 20 for Japan, that is, 20–30 per cent of the surplus generated in these regions. Similarly, transit flows through Central Asia (arrows 1, 2, and 11) on the order of index 100, might have accounted for a volume even greater than that of the locally produced surplus.

The index values assigned to both the surplus volumes produced in each region and the trade volumes indicated by each of the arrows are, of course, mere fabrications on my part created with a view to suggesting some relative orders of magnitude. It is for historians to improve upon them. Failing this (and we have not found any figures in this regard) the figures I have used constitute some orders of magnitude which seem plausible to me and which can be summarized in Table 8.1 below:

Table 8.1 Locally generated external flows

	Surplus (1)	(2)	% (2/1)
Middle East	800	140	18
China	1,000	100	10
India	1,000	60	6
Europe	100	20	20
Africa	50	10	20
Japan	60	20	33
Southeast Asia	60	20	33
Central Asia	60	100	166

Geography has assigned to key central region A an exceptional role without any possible competitor until modern times, when Europe, through its control over the seas, overcame the constraints. Indeed, this region is directly linked to all the others (China, India, Europe, Africa) and is the only one as such. For two millennia, it was an indispensable transit route to Europe, China, India, or Africa. Besides, the region does not reflect a relative homogeneity similar to that of China or India, either at the geographical level (stretching from the Moroccan shores of the Atlantic to the Aral Sea, Pamir and to the Oman Sea, it does not have the features of a continental block as in the case of China and India), or at the level of its peoples, who themselves are products of the early proliferation of the most ancient civilizations (Egypt, Sumer, Assyria, Mesopotamia, Iran, Hittites, Phoenicians, and Greeks) and speak languages from various families (Semitic, Hamitic, Indo-European). The conquest of Alexander the Great and the triumph of the Hellenistic synthesis triggered a collective awareness which was subsequently strengthened by Oriental Christianity (limited by the Sassanid border) and subsequently and, above all, by Islam.

One of the keys to the success of Islam relates, in my view, to this reality. The region was finally firmly established within the short period covering the first three centuries of the Hegira. It was thus composed of the three superimposed strata of Islamized peoples, namely, the Arabs from the Atlantic to the Gulf, the Persians beyond Zagros to Pakistan, the Turks in Anatolia and in the entire Turkestan from the Caspian Sea to China proper. Thus, Islam did not only unify the peoples of the so-called classical "East" but annexed, at the same time, Central Asia, the indispensable transit route to China and northern India. I think that this success should be attributed to the fact that, in spite of all the conflicts witnessed by history internal to this region, it created a certain solidarity and strengthened the sense of a particular identity with regard to the "others"; that is, specifically, the Chinese, Indians, Europeans, and Africans that the Muslim Umma borders on along each of its frontiers. In Central Asia, the success of Islam created regional unity, which, until then, was absent. For the civilization in this region, in which trade flows represent larger volumes than the surplus produced locally, depended on the capacity to capture, in passing, a part of these transit flows.

The magnitude of the links with the others for the entire key central region A and its Central Asia annex bestows on its social system a special character which I venture, for this reason, to call "mercantile-tributary," thus indicating even the magnitude of protocapitalist forms (commercial links, wage labor, private property, or estate) in the tributary societies of Islam. Moreover, beyond the original boundaries of Islam, the gradual conquest of African and Southeast Asian peripheries is also worth putting into close relationship with its mercantile dynamism of region A (see *The Arab Nation* and *Class and Nation*).

Thirdly, the world-system described above for the eighteen-century period preceding the Renaissance is not analogous to the modern system that follows it (in time). To talk about the ancient system in its spatial and time universality or even in its Arab-Islamic component as the "ancestor" of the modern system would be misleading. For this is only a platitude – succession in time and nothing more; or it implies that there was no qualitative break but only quantitative development and a "shift" of the system's center of gravity from the southern shore of the Mediterranean to its northern shore (Italian cities) and then to the Atlantic shores, and this boils down to eliminating the essential, that is, the qualitative change in the nature of the system: the law of value which governs the dynamics of the modern system but not those of the tributary system. This universalization of the law of value is exclusively responsible for the establishment of one single antinomy which operates worldwide (a center composed of historically established national centers as such and peripheries all economically dependent on this center), thus creating an *ever increasing* differentiation from one period to another between the center and the peripheries,

Table 8.2 The early roots (up to 200 BC)

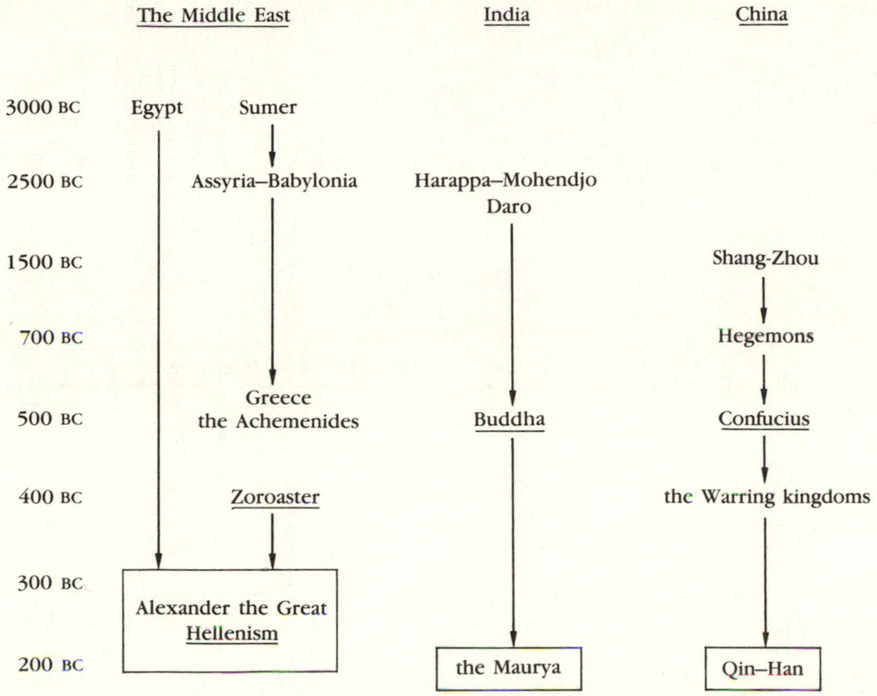

over the entire five-century history of capitalism and for the entirely visible or imaginable horizon within the framework of its immanent laws. In this connection, there is nothing comparable to the lasting relative balance (for 2,000 years!) between the key central regions of the tributary period. This qualitative difference forbids talking about "interdependence" – unequal, as it were – of the different components of the ancient system in terms similar to those that govern the modern world. Key regions A, B, and C are certainly in "relation" with one another (and with the other regions); it remains to be demonstrated that this "interdependence" would have been essential. The parallelism in their trend is no evidence of the crucial nature of their "relations"; it only reflects the general character of the laws governing the social development of all humankind (thus defining the status of the "specificities"). The possible concomitance of the "rise" and the "fall" of states of the past is far from obvious.

A cursory glance at Table 8.3, which describes the parallel history of the three key centers and the other regions, shows that this concomitance is merely a matter of pure chance.

Pirenne had already observed – a view taken up by Andre Gunder Frank and Barry K. Gills – the concomitance of the fall of the Roman empire

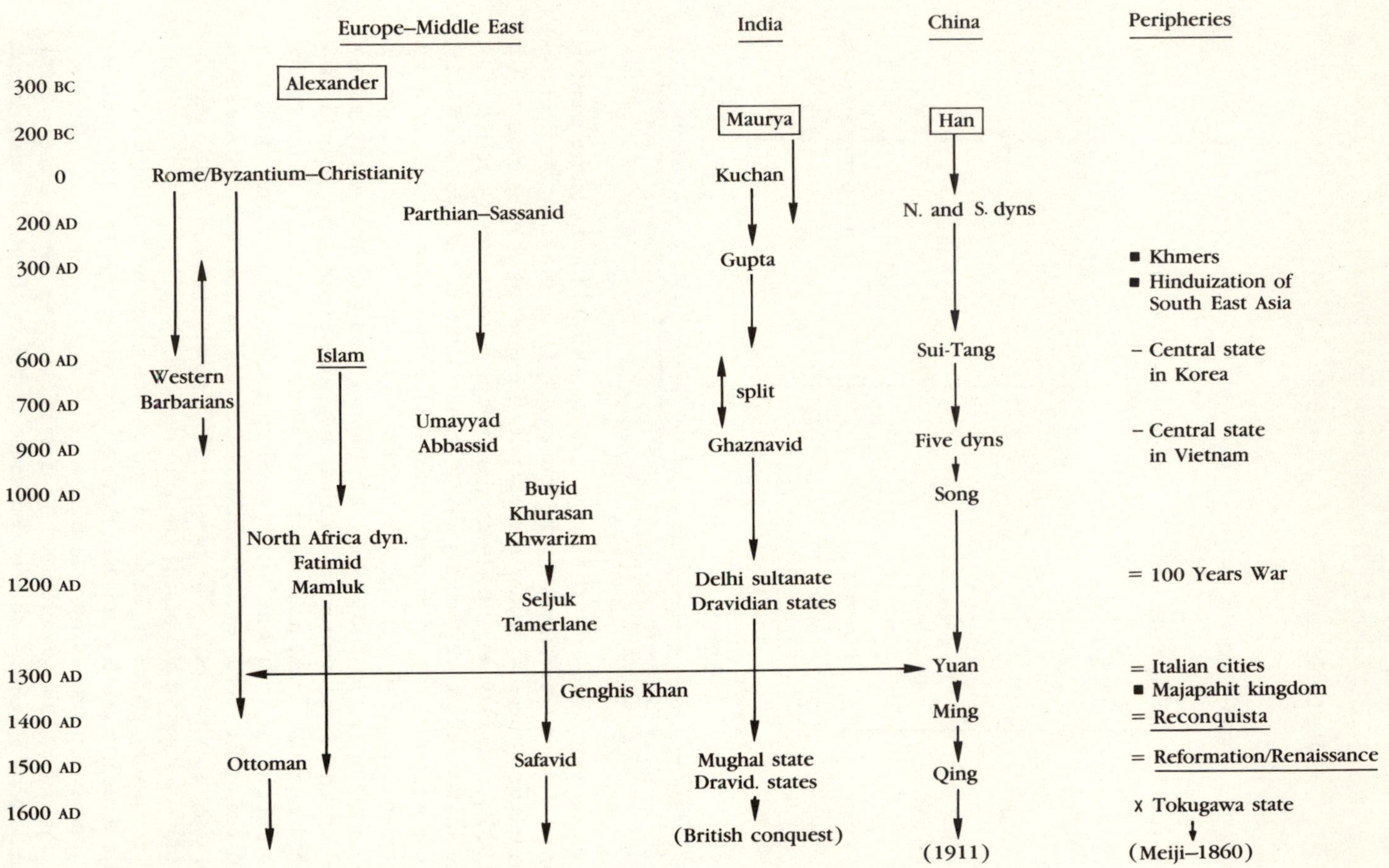

Table 8.3 The tributary systems (300 BC–1500 AD)

and that of the Han dynasty. But the Roman fall was followed by the rise of Byzantium, the Sassanid, and the Kushāna state, while the decline of the Hans was followed, right from the year 600 (the height of barbarianism in the West) by the rise of the Tang, and, three centuries earlier, by that of the Guptas, whose fall coincided (also by chance) with the rise of Islam. There are no clues to the identification of the "general" cycles of the rise and fall. The very term "fall" is, even in this context, misleading; it is the fall of a form of state organization in a given region, but, in most cases, as regards the development of productive forces, there is no parallel fall. I am struck rather by the opposite phenomenon, that is, the continuity of these long parallel historical events: from Rome–Byzantium–Sassanids–Islam to the Ottomans and the Safavids, from the Maurya dynasty to that of the Mughal state, from the Han dynasty to those of Ming and Qing, there were only a few qualitative changes but a great quantitative progress on the same organizational (tributary) bases. This does not exclude the fact that, in examining local developments, it is possible to explain any particular political rise (or fall) – which may still be relative – by a special link in which "external relations" have occasionally played a role. Once again, there is nothing similar to the "cycles" of the capitalist economy, whose scope is really global as a result of the universalization of the law of value, the basis of the modern capitalist economy.

The crystallization of a new modernity in Europe which was achieved within a short time (from the rise of Italian cities to the Renaissance; three to four centuries) is not the "repetition" of a "general" phenomenon under which would be subsumed all together the "birth" of civilizations (Egypt, Sumer, Harappa, Shang) and the "establishment of empires" (Achemenid, Alexander, Rome, Byzantium, Sassanid, Umayyad, Abbasid, Ottoman, Safavid, Maurya, Gupta, the Mughal state, Han, Tang, Song, Ming, Qing, and the Genghis Khan empire).

I proposed an explanation of this fact (see *Class and Nation*) that the qualitative break is first made within a tributary periphery (Europe) and not in one of its centers (A, B, or C) and is then repeated in another periphery (Japan). I based my explanation on the contrast between the flexibility of the peripheries and the rigidity of the centers, that is, while keeping to the logical context of the *general* nature of the laws of the evolution of societies (the "uneven development" which is the general form of an identical overall evolution). I consider this explanation more satisfactory than those proposed by the different characteristically Eurocentric conceptions (see *Eurocentrism*). I also think it is more satisfactory than Pirenne's theory, which I have referred to as being based on the permanent contrast between "capitalism" (the synonym of "openness," especially in "maritime" terms) and "feudalism" (the synonym of "closure," especially in "landlocked" terms). Like Andre Gunder Frank's and Barry K. Gills's (which is close to the extreme), Pirenne's theory is a transformation of the Eurocentric deformation: it "attributes" the European miracle to the maritime openness of the region, since each of the theories is based on the negation of the specific nature of the capitalist modernity.

Of course the crystallization of capitalism in Europe has a history (it is not done by magic, in 1493 for instance) and entails specific consequences for the subsequent evolution of the other regions. The rapid development of Italian cities, which of course accounted for such crystallization, is in turn a result of the tributary mercantile expansion of the Arabo-Islamic region. However, it is because it operated within an outlying zone (feudal Europe) that this Italian expansion set fire to the grassland and accelerated the rate of evolution to the extent of creating in Europe a system that was qualitatively superior to that of the formerly more advanced societies. I have given (in *Class and Nation*) a detailed explanation of this conjuncture which establishes a link between the state's weakness and the establishment of an area of autonomy for a veritable new class – the middle class – to appear, then the state's alliance with the latter in order to go beyond the breaking up of the feudal system by creating a new absolutist and mercantilist state, and so on. The general consequence of the new crystallization of Europe (capitalist and no longer feudal) is obvious: it blocked the evolution of the other societies of the world, which were gradually marginalized in the new global system. Moreover, the capitalist crystallization of Europe brought about a specific hostility toward the Arabo-Islamic region. We recall at this juncture the observation I made earlier about the specific position of the Islamic world in the old system. In order to establish direct links with the rest of the world to its advantage, Europe had to break the indispensable monopolistic and intermediary position enjoyed by the Islamic world. Ever since the early attempt of the Crusades, which was followed immediately by the establishment of the link between Europe and China that was opened by the Mongolian peace during the era of Genghis Khan, this hostility has been pursued to date and has found expression in a particularly neurotic attitude toward Muslims and generated in turn a similar response from the opposite direction. It is finally to break up this inevitable intermediate zone that Europeans set off on the seas. Contrary to Pirenne's thesis, such a choice was not the result of some geographical determinism.

Fourthly, the remarks made concerning these 2,000 years are not valid for the previous periods: on the one hand, the civilized societies known during previous periods – *a fortiori* the barbarians – were sometimes organized in a manner that was different from those of the subsequent tributary period; on the other hand, the network of relations that they engaged in among themselves was also different from the one illustrated with Figure 8.1 and Table 8.3.

Certainly, our scientific knowledge of the past becomes even less as we recede further in time. Nevertheless, it seems to me that two lines of thought relating to the "pretributary" eras can be distinguished (two philosophies of history). Pirenne's theory – which on this basic point is similar to the points of view defended by Andre Gunder Frank and Barry K. Gills – does not recognize any qualitative break around 300 BC, either around the Christian era or from the end of the Roman empire (the end of Antiquity, according to contemporary textbooks), just as it does not recognize any qualitative break separating "modern times" from "ancient times." Indeed, as I already mentioned, according to Pirenne, all periods of human history are marked by the same contrast between open, maritime, and "capitalistic" societies and closed, landlocked, and "feudal" societies. Moreover, like Frank and Gills, Pirenne emphasizes the exchange relations that existed among the societies at all times, irrespective of the distance separating them (for example, on the exchanges among Sumer, the Indus civilization, Egypt, Crete, Phoenicia, and Greece). Like Frank and Gills, Pirenne's theory is based on a philosophy of linear history: the progress is quantitative and continuous, without any qualitative change; in the words of Gills and Frank, it is the "cumulation of accumulation." On the other hand, the commonly accepted theory of Marxism distinguishes three stages of civilization that are different in terms of quality: slavery, feudalism, and capitalism. I do not enter into this field of Marxology, to resolve the question of knowing whether this theory is really that of Marx (and of Engels) – and to what extent – or whether it is only that of the subsequent Marxian common understanding. In any case, this theory states that all the societies listed in Table 8.3 are "feudal" societies: for Europe, from the end of the Roman empire; for the Byzantine and Islamic Middle East, right from their constitutions; for India, since the installation of the Maurya dynasty; and for China, since the Han era. Previously, on the other hand, according to this theory, they must have passed through a phase of "slavery" whose obvious and indisputable existence would be exemplified by Greece and Rome. In my opinion people put forward by analogy a state of slavery in China (from the Shang to the Han), in India (the Indus and Aryan civilizations), in the Middle East (in Mesopotamia). The existence of slavery located elsewhere and later on in certain regions of Africa, produced by the disintegration of earlier forms of communal formations, proves – according to this theory – that the passage through slavery constitutes a general requirement.

I do not share this point of view (see *Class and Nation*) and have offered instead a theory according to which: 1) the general form of class society that succeeded the previous communal formations is that of the tributary society; 2) the feudal form is not the general rule but only the peripheral form of the tributary type; 3) various conditions determine the specific form of each tributary society (castes, estates of the feudal era in the European sense – *Stände*; peasant communities subjected to a state bureaucracy, etc.); 4) slavery is not a general requirement – it is absent from most of the landmarks of history (Egypt, India, China); it hardly undergoes any important development unless it is linked to a commercial economy and is therefore found within ages that are very different from the point of view of the development of productive forces (Graeco-Roman slavery and slavery in America up to the nineteenth century). Are the periods before the "break of tributary societies" which is marked in Table 8.3 not then to be distinguished from the rest of the precapitalist history? For instance, Egypt in particular offers the example of a tributary society having practically nothing to do with slavery whose history begins 3,000 years before the crystallization of the Hellenistic era. Assyria, Babylon, Iran of the Achemenids and probably pre-Mauryan India and pre-Han China sometimes practiced slavery but this practice did not constitute the main form of exploitation of productive labor. Finally, according to my theory, a tributary society is not crystallized into its complete form until it produced a universal ideology – a religion based on universal values that go beyond the ideologies of kinship and country religions peculiar to the previous community stage. In this perspective, Zoroaster, Buddha, and Confucius announce the crystallization of the tributary society. Until then, I prefer to talk about "incubation" or even the "long transition from communal forms to the tributary form." This transition, which is perhaps relatively simple and rapid in China, is made more complicated in India as a result of the Aryan invasion that destroyed the Indus civilization. In the Middle East the diversity of the peoples and trajectories, as well as the mutual influence of one people by the other, compels us to consider the region as a "system." I place within this context the early maturing of Egypt into a tributary society, the distinctive mercantile nature of slavery in Greece, and therefore I give particular importance to the Hellenistic synthesis, the prelude to the Christian and Islamic revolutions which were to take over the unification of the region.

Does the intensity of the exchange relations among the societies of these distant eras make it possible to talk about a "system"? I doubt it, considering that the civilized societies, that is, those advanced in the transition to the tributary form, still remain islets in the ocean of worlds of communities. Even when they are parallel, the trajectories do not prove that the societies in question do constitute a system but establish only the validity of the general laws of evolution.

NOTE

This chapter first appeared in 1991 as "The ancient world-systems versus the modern capitalist world-system," in *Review* 14 (3) (summer): 349–85.

REFERENCES

Ahmad, Sadek Saad (1985) *Tarikh Misr al Ijtimai*, Cairo.
Amin, Samir (1978) *The Arab Nation*, London: Zed.
—— (1980) *Class and Nation, Historically and in the Current Crisis*, New York: Monthly Review Press.
—— (1989) *Eurocentrism*, New York: Monthly Review Press.
Fawzy, Mansour (1990) *L'Impasse du monde arabe, les racines historiques*, Paris: L'Harmattan.
Frank, Andre Gunder (1990) "A theoretical introduction to 5,000 years of world system history," *Review* 13 (2) (spring): 155–248.
Pirenne, Jacques (1948) *Les Grand Courants de l'histoire universelle*, 4 vols, Louvain.
Polanyi, Karl (1987) *La libertà in una società complesse*, Milan: Boringheri.
Toynbee, Arnold (1962) *A Study of History*, 12 vols, Oxford: Oxford University Press.

9

DISCONTINUITIES AND PERSISTENCE

One world system or a succession of systems?

Janet Abu-Lughod

I've recently published a book on the world system in the thirteenth century, entitled *Before European Hegemony*.[1] It was intended in part as a corrective to Immanuel Wallerstein's work on the sixteenth-century *et seq*. world-system.[2] My criticism was that Wallerstein, while creatively extending the work of other historians and correcting for some of their biases, had still accepted the main line of western historical scholarship: namely, that the "story" becomes interesting *only* with the "Rise of the West" after 1450.[3]

This, I contend, is much too late. Because his account begins essentially with the sixteenth century, Wallerstein tends to overemphasize the *discontinuity* between the new Eurocentered capitalist world economy that began to come into being then and the system of world-empires and world-economies that had preceded it. And what is less defensible, he refuses to "dignify" any pre-sixteenth-century patterns of global trade by applying the term "world-system" to them. Indeed, he defends reserving *that* term only for the *modern* world-system, with its capitalist structure.

In contradistinction, my position is that a very advanced world-system already existed by the second half of the thirteenth century, one that included almost all regions (only the "New World" was missing) that would be reintegrated in the sixteenth century. Indeed, nascent capitalism was present in various parts of that system, without actually succeeding in dominating all parts.[4] However, it was a world-system that Europe had only recently joined and in which it played only a peripheral role. Furthermore, this earlier world-system was organized in a very different way from the one over which Europe would ultimately exercise hegemony. The major metatheoretical dilemma in my work was (a) to see elements of continuity and discontinuity between what I conceptualized as successive but linked world-system stages; and (b) to account for *how and why* the transition occurred *when* it did.[5]

Andre Gunder Frank and I are now having a friendly debate – conducted by long-distance mails in which, I confess, he has been writing more regularly and voluminously than I have been answering. Like the earlier one I had by mail with Wallerstein when I was writing my book, this disagreement also has no resolution.[6]

Both debates have been over some "simple" (but ultimately unanswerable) questions:

1 Has there been *only one* world-system, the one that began with the *sixteenth century*?
2 Have there been *several successive world-systems*, each with a changing structure and its own set of hegemons?
3 Or has there been only *a single world-system* that has continued to evolve *over the past 5,000 years*?

Wallerstein espouses the first position, I have taken the second, and Frank and Gills contend the third. The present volume is part of this debate.

Is this a real controversy or is it merely a frivolous debate of the kind in which academicians sometimes engage for the sake of selling more books? I hope not the latter. What I would like to explore here is not whether one answer is right and the others wrong; clearly, there is no right answer. Rather, what I want to do is challenge us to think about what can be gained, intellectually and in terms of a research agenda, from a strategy that emphasizes continuities, versus one that emphasizes discontinuities.

It might be useful, however, to distinguish two levels of the argument: one on the regional level, the other on the international. On a regional (or what I have called a subsystem) level, one can argue not only for *continuity* but even development and expansion of economic and cutural linkages, without having to assume that the international system itself exhibited such continuities. To put it another way, one might find that local patterns persist and even prosper, while, at the same time, acknowledging that the role of the local region in a wider system has undergone a real transformation. Such an approach might help to explain long-term consequences in a more fruitful way.

First, then, I would like to support the argument about persistence. This might best be illustrated by reference to the series of maps (based on McEvedy) that were prepared for and appear in *Before European Hegemony* (pp. 138–40, reproduced here as Figures 9.1, 9.2, and 9.3). If one examines only the right halves of the maps, one is struck by the remarkable continuity in trade routes and volume in the region under discussion. But one can make an equally good case for *systemic* transformation. The left halves of the maps illustrate that the context within which this continuity existed was undergoing a radical expansion and restructuring, which made its meaning in the larger system more problematic.

The editors of this volume have asked me to set the historic stage by

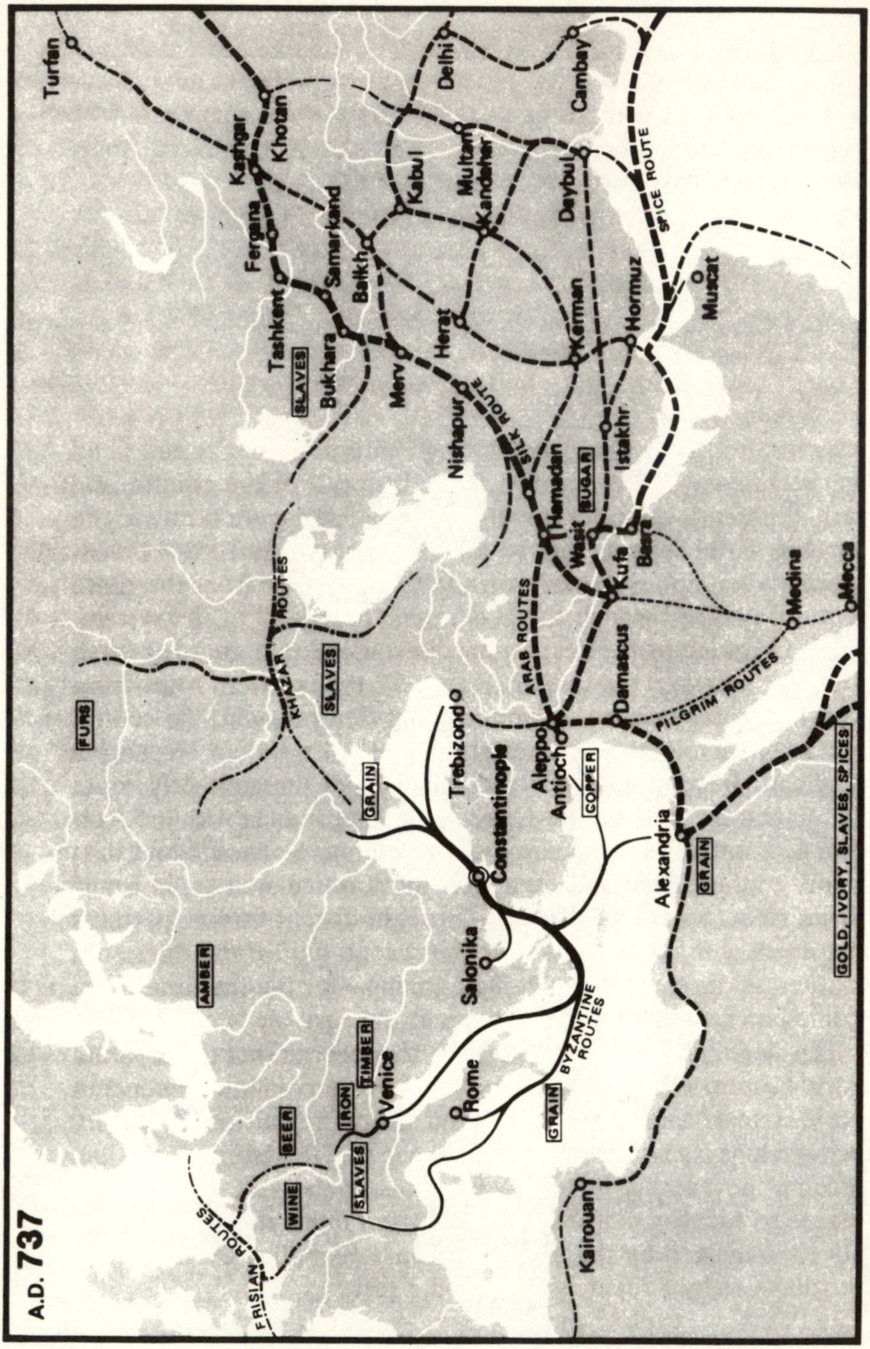

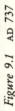

Figure 9.1 AD 737

Figures 9.1 to 9.3 The gradual reticulation of trade routes from the Mediterranean across Central Asia and toward the Indian Ocean AD 737–AD 1478 (based on Colin McEvedy's *The Penguin Atlas of Medieval History*, 1961)

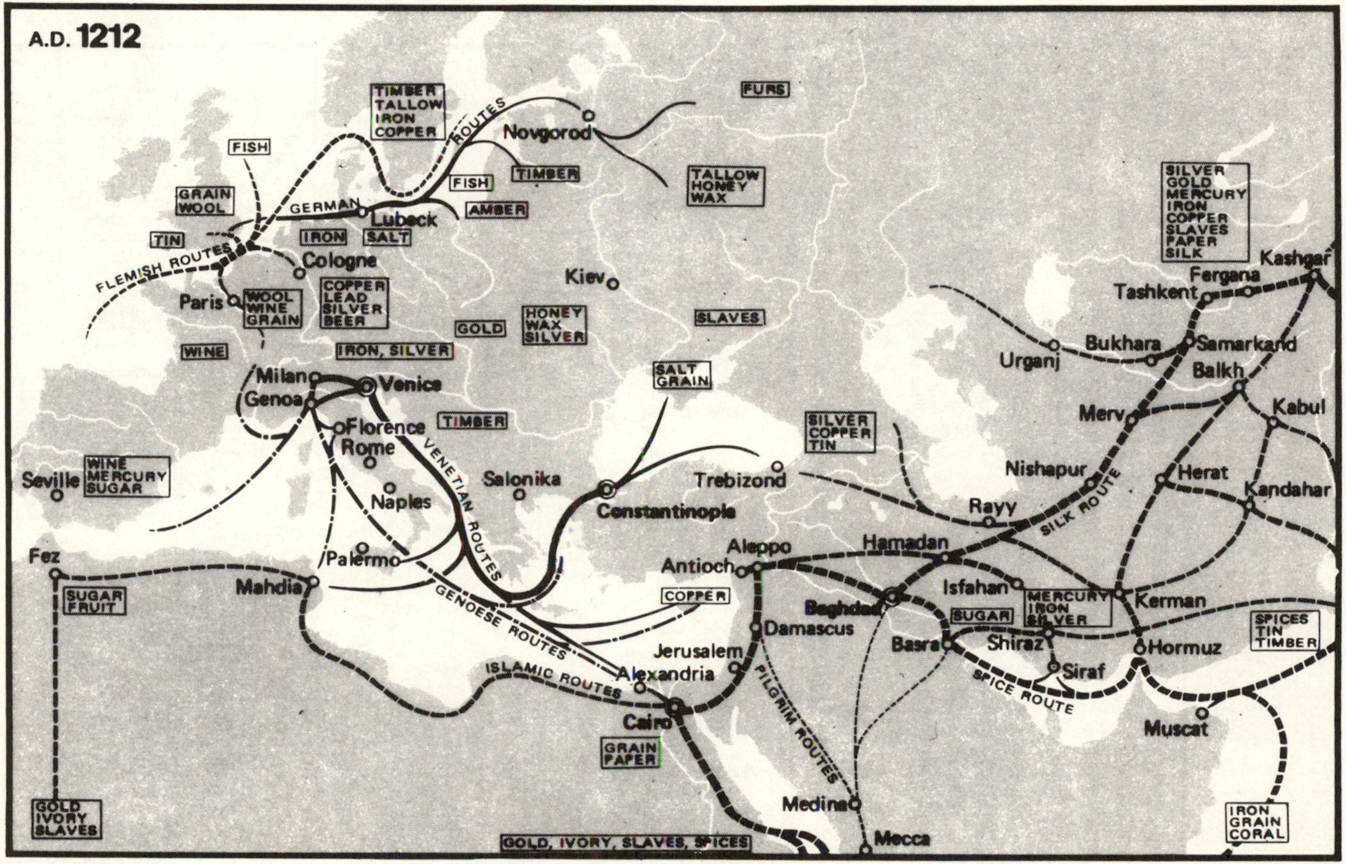

Figure 9.2 AD 1212

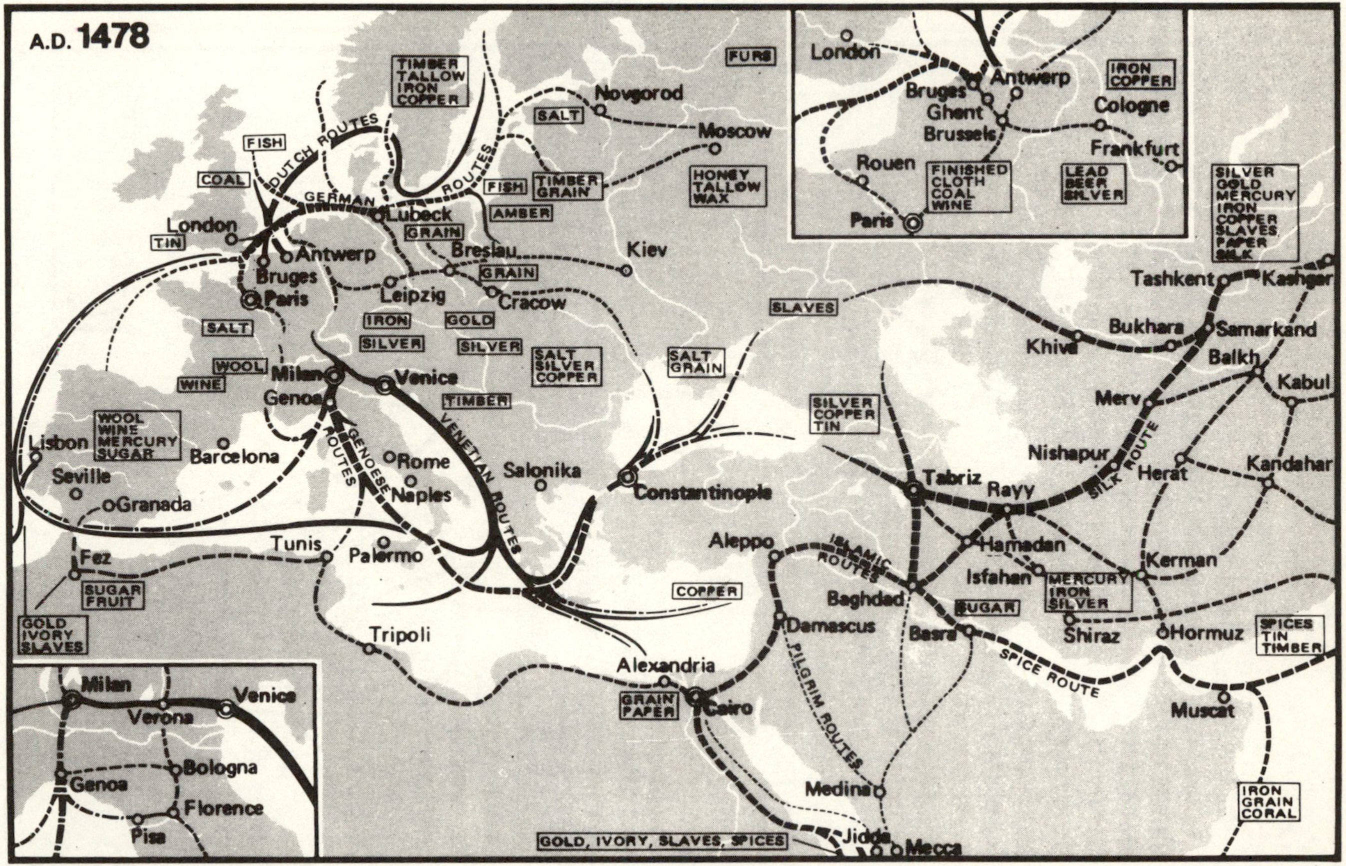

Figure 9.3 AD 1478

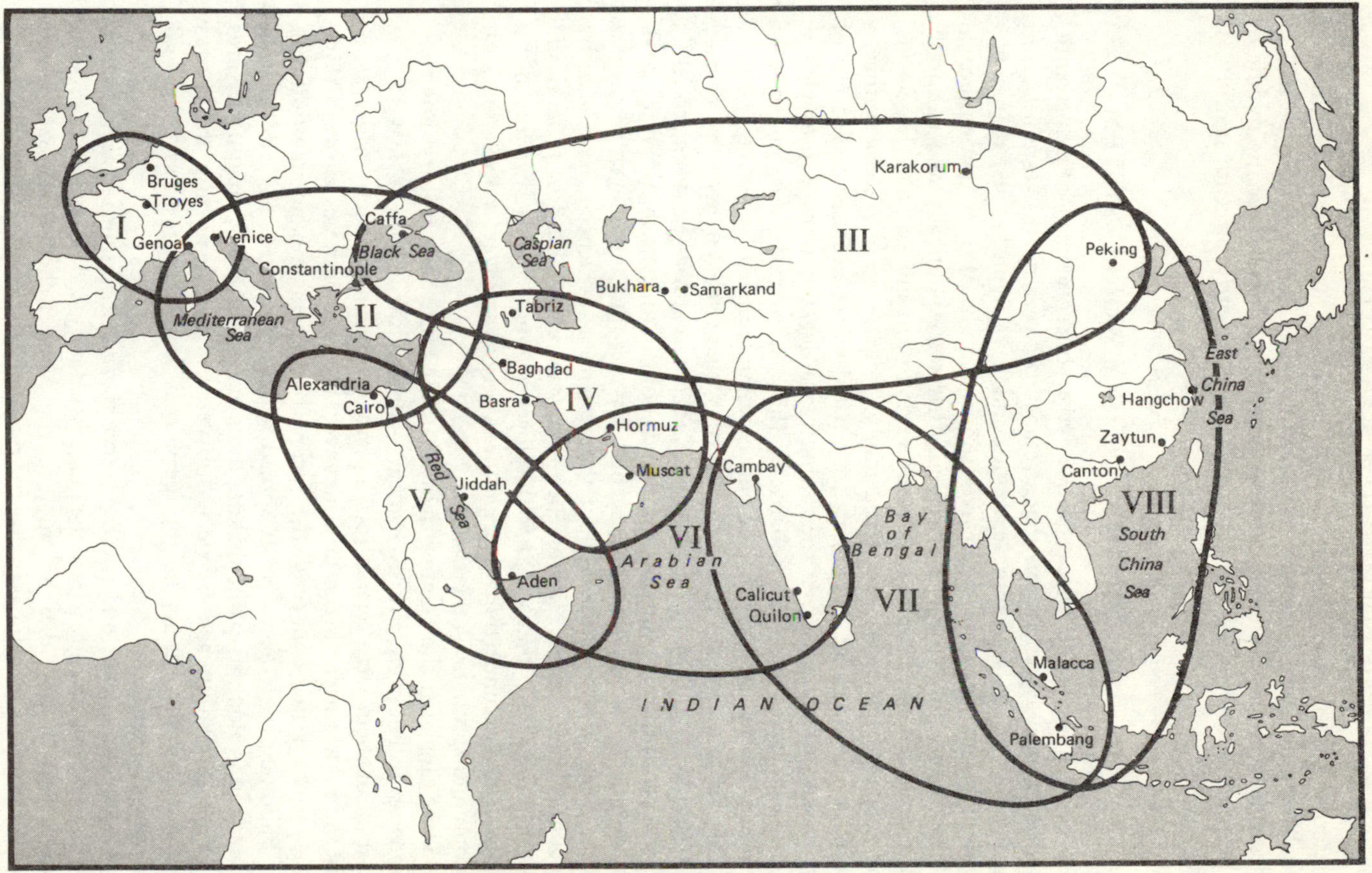

Figure 9.4 The eight circuits of the thirteenth-century world system

describing what was going on in the world in the thirteenth century. I shall do this, but I cannot resist moving beyond that time period to describe how the containing system drastically altered after the middle of the fourteenth century and especially after the early fifteenth century. It would be totally transformed by the sixteenth.

THE THIRTEENTH-CENTURY WORLD-SYSTEM

As can be seen from Figure 9.4, I have conceptualized the thirteenth-century world-system as one that stretched between north-western Europe and China at its geographic extremes and have hypothesized that it was internally organized into eight overlapping circuits of trade that connected three (or possibly four)[7] core regions that were politically and culturally distinctive. While each of these core regions had one or more hegemons, no single subsystem exercised hegemony over the entire system. Rather, a rough and somewhat stable balance existed – not necessarily because of *détente*, but because, given the technological level of transport, as well as significant cultural-religious barriers, there were real limits to span of control that fell far short of the entire system's scale.[8]

My book traces the processes whereby these subsystems were formed and gradually linked to adjacent ones in the centuries between, roughly, the eleventh through the opening decades of the fourteenth, when the peak of commercial integration was reached. By that time, high levels of surplus were being produced throughout the system, as evidenced, *inter alia*, by a cultural and artistic efflorescence that was remarkable for its level and extensiveness. My thesis is that this level was not only a *symptom* but a *product* of the connections that had been forged and were stimulating local economies throughout the system.

Some time after the opening decades of the fourteenth century, however, signs of decline were already evident – although it is hard to make a case that all of them were related to what was happening in the world-system. By the mid-fourteenth century, however, the case becomes clearer. Along the pathways that connected the various subregions a pandemic outbreak of bubonic plague occurred. It spread widely (see Figure 9.5), decimating populations along its path, shaking dynastic power bases, creating fissures and breaks within and between subsystems, and disturbing the *modus vivendi* that had, at its height, permitted almost frictionless trade and exchange.

One century later, one could observe these discontinuities very clearly. At the eastern extreme, where the plague evidently had originated, a process was set in motion that led first to the Ming Rebellion (1368), which overthrew the Yüan dynasty that for two centuries had unified China with Central Asia and facilitated trans-Eurasian land trade, and eventually (after 1430) to the withdrawal of the Chinese fleet (and its subsequent port rot)

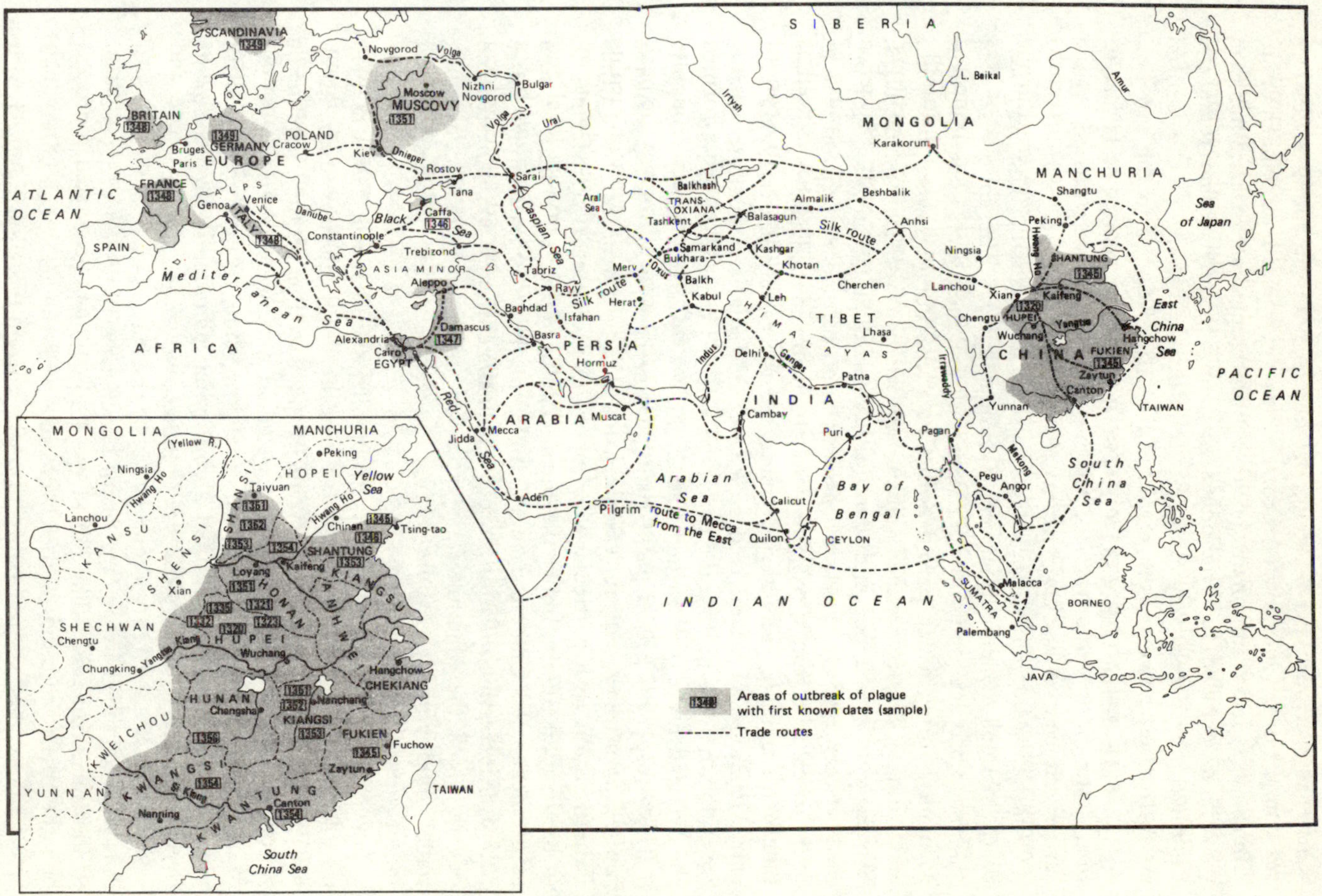

Figure 9.5 The congruence between trade routes and the spread of the Black Death *circa* 1350

which had previously played so important a role in maintaining the eastern sea connections. Once again, Central Asia was poised in opposition to China – as it had traditionally been[9] – and presented a barrier rather than (what I have called) a "frictionless medium" through which trade and exchange moved relatively freely. Even after the closing of the Central Asian frontier, however, the sea trade from the Red Sea to the east persisted, as we shall see. It was only *after* a later Ming policy shift that its final destinations – the ports of south-east China – were closed, which further reduced volume and viability.

Within the Middle East, the effects were no less dramatic. The Egyptian-based Mamluk system underwent a similar cycle.[10] The apogee of that subsystem was achieved under the Ayyubids and their successors, the Bahri Mamluks, during which period both Crusader incursions were thrust out and Mongol threats repelled, albeit not without the loss of Baghdad. Especially under the long, if discontinuous, rule of Sultan an-Nasr Mohammed between 1293 and 1341, prosperity was great, thanks to the operations of the so-called Karimi merchants who sustained and mediated the Mediterranean sea trade of the Italians, conducted the eastern sea trade via port entrepôts along the Islamicized west coast of India, and finally reached a working arrangement with the newly Islamicized Ghazanids in Iraq, along the overland route of reopened trade.

This prosperous period peaked roughly in the first few decades of the fourteenth century, but it was short-lived. The plague hit the Middle Eastern region with particular virulence, and the eventual transformation of the Mamluk system under the Burji Mamluks (after 1381) may be seen as parallel to the Chinese changes. In Egypt the fifteenth century was a period of increasing inflation during which the currency was debased, and one in which the Mamluk state expanded its active role in controlling trade, monopolizing export crops, squeezing local producers, and intimidating external traders.

Finally, the conquest of Constantinople by the Ottoman Turks in 1453 must be viewed in the context of a shift in the European subsystem, which had also been set in motion by events of the preceding century. The major European actors in the sea trade that linked northwestern Europe to the Middle East were the Genoese and Venetians, whose rivalry for sea control in the Mediterranean constituted a continuing plot-line in how the post-twelfth-century world-system was organized.

Between 1204 and 1261, Venice had been the major power in Constantinople and thus the guardian (and major beneficiary) of the northern gateway to Central Asian trade. The fall of the Latin kingdom in the latter year, or rather the restoration of Byzantine rule with the assistance of Venice's arch rival, Genoa, led to a redirection of Venetian trade via Egypt. It was a partnership that would benefit both for decades to come.

But Genoa's relative exclusion from the system was not without its eventual effect. By the last decade of the thirteenth century it had already turned its attention to the Atlantic, effecting a sea link with Flanders that bypassed central France and making forays down the western coast of Africa along a path that would eventually be opened by Portugal, Genoa's new rival in the Atlantic.

In the mid-fourteenth century, however, both Venice and Genoa were hard hit by plague mortalities. Thanks to their sea connections with the Black Sea, from which the plague spread from Mongols to Europeans, the two port city states suffered proportionately greater mortalities than any other parts of Europe that were more peripherally situated. This led to a mid-century depression in both cities, from which Venice eventually recovered, but Genoa did not.[11] Indeed, the period 1378–84 marks the substantial defeat of Genoa in the Mediterranean rivalry between the two powers, although the final *coup de grâce* was not administered until the end of the fourteenth century.

The relevance for Middle Eastern developments, and particularly for the subsequent rise of Ottoman power, should now be clear. In the course of the thirteenth and early fourteenth centuries, a division of labor, or a *modus vivendi*, had been worked out. Genoa gained priority over the northern land route via its preferred status in Constantinople and its dominance over the Black Sea and the trading ports on it. (Genoese traders also benefitted from their role as providers of new recruits to the Mamluk dynasty centered on Egypt.) The middle route, which went overland from Palestine to the Persian Gulf, underwent a severe decline as an attractive alternative, after the last Crusader kingdom was eliminated towards the end of the thirteenth century (the so-called "fall" of Acre in 1291). This left, as the major rival to the Black Sea–overland route to China, the southern route, in which, thanks to the increasingly close symbiosis between the Mamluks and the Venetian traders, the Venetians were becoming more important in the sea trade with the farther east. The Egyptians still dominated that trade via their monopoly over the Red Sea route.

With the reduction in trade over the northern land route, occasioned by the plague and then the break-up of the Mongol empire that had unified Central Asia with China, the Genoese were no longer in a strong position vis-à-vis their rival, Venice. Indeed, there are no records of any Genoese traders in China after 1340. Thus, Genoa was weakened economically and, consequently, militarily. The expansion of the Ottoman Turks into (newly named) Istanbul was in part the fruit of Genoa's final defeat in the Mediterranean.

This left the southern, mostly sea, route as the only one to which Europeans (largely through Venetian traders) had access. While throughout the fifteenth century this route continued to prosper, the peculiar alliance between the Mamluks, who controled access to eastern markets and suppliers, and the Venetians, who transshipped most of the eastern goods to

European markets, was controling a larger share of a declining amount of world trade. This monopoly was finally broken by the Portuguese, beginning in the early sixteenth century.

THE FALL OF THE EAST PRECEDES THE RISE OF THE WEST[12]

This is the final argument in my book. In it, I contend that the entire Indian Ocean arena lay open to foreign "conquest" for two reasons. First, patterns of nonhegemonic trade had prevailed for many centuries in that arena.[13] Multiple naval powers not only shared the trade, but even carried each others' goods and merchants. This meant that the powers involved in the Indian Ocean trading system had absolutely no preparation to resist the Portuguese incursion into their waters in the early decades of the sixteenth century. The second reason, of course, was the prior Chinese withdrawal from the sea and the rotting in port of its former navy.[14] Since the Chinese fleet was the only force that (earlier) could have marshaled sufficient strength to offer resistance to the Portuguese, the latter's ability to "skim" the surplus from the continuing sea trade could not be prevented.[15]

The successful conquest of the Mamluk empire by the Ottoman Turks, which was roughly contemporaneous with Portuguese expansion into the Indian Ocean, must in part be attributed to these changes in the larger system. When Egypt came under Ottoman rule in 1516, the ease with which the former was defeated was not unrelated to the setbacks it had earlier experienced in the eastern trade.

The rest is, as they say, history. By the latter part of the sixteenth century, not only had the Ottoman fleet been defeated by the Venetians (in the battle of Lepanto in 1571) but they ceased any pretensions to remaining a sea power. After that, the Mediterranean was not a Muslim "lake." Furthermore, the major arena of the world system had begun to shift to the Atlantic. Braudel documents the eclipse of the Mediterranean in his two-volume work on the Mediterranean in the age of Philip II,[16] while there is voluminous work on the growing importance of the so-called "New World." There is no need to document this.

However, these naval defeats did not mean that Ottoman power declined, nor did they mean a break in the continuity of the land system that connected Anatolia with south-eastern Europe (notably the Balkans) or with northern India and beyond. But they did mean that thereafter the Ottoman strength was to be over land. The importance of Turks and Arabs in the sea trade of both the Mediterranean and the Indian Ocean was at an end.

WHAT CAN BE GAINED BY CONCEPTUALIZING THE TRANSITION AS A STRUCTURAL REORGANIZATION OF THE WORLD-SYSTEM, I.E. PERSISTENCE

None of this global analysis implies that regional subsystems disappeared, or even declined, if measured in absolute terms. In this sense, Gunder Frank is correct to speak of one long march, rather than a set of equal cycles. My own metaphor is one of a very long up-cycle with fluctuations that at times are so extreme that it is analytically useful to speak of "breaks" and restructuring. There is, then, no necessary contradiction between seeing the persistence and even improvement in economic activities over time *within a given region* and seeing that this region was falling increasingly below the average change for the system or the exponentially increasing shift in a region that, due to restructuring, was far outdistancing the subregion in question.

It is not enough to fight the stereotype of decay in the Ottoman–north-India region, because, despite its prominence in historical discussions, it was just not true. At least, my readings of the serious work that has been done by scholars of the seventeenth century on that region is a sufficient refutation of the stereotype.

I would suggest, however, that we need to pay more attention to the changed role of the region in question in terms of the larger system. In the final analysis, although the Venice–Cairo axis continued to operate down through Ottoman times, and the rumors of the demise of the spice trade were exaggerated, the fact is that the context of this trade had undeniably altered. The Venetian fleet did vanquish the Ottomans. The world-system did eventually restructure away from the Mediterranean and the sea powers that controled it. The real arena did move outward to the Atlantic and the Atlantic rim nations of Portugal and Spain, before shifting to north-western Europe. The fact is that the axis of Central Asia, Anatolia, northern India, and the Levant–Egypt – an axis of central importance in earlier times which was scarcely destroyed by the seventeenth century – never again occupied the center stage of the world-system. I urge study of not only the continuities at the subsystem level, but also the discontinuities most evident at the large scale.

NOTES

This chapter first appeared as a manuscript in 1990 as "Discontinuities and persistence: one world system or a succession of systems?" from the New School of Social Research in New York.

1 See *Before European Hegemony: The World System* A.D. *1250–1350*, New York: Oxford University Press, 1989.

2 Particularly Immanuel Wallerstein, *The Modern World-System*, vol. 1, New York: Academic Press, 1974.

3 The term is, of course, drawn from the title of William McNeill's famous book, *The Rise of the West: A History of the Human Community*, Chicago: University of Chicago Press, 1963, even though the lengthy text of his book stresses the earlier and continuing importance of the East.

4 Contention over the meaning of "capitalism," and over when it began (whether in the thirteenth century or the sixteenth), has been going on for a very long time, and I have no wish to enter that debate in this article. It is, however, amply covered in my book.

5 See my "Restructuring the premodern world system," in *Review* 8 (spring 1990): 273–85.

6 See his review essay of *Before European Hegemony* in *Journal of World History* 1 (2) (fall 1990): 249–56, in which he sets forth his own views. He has been sending me materials and book outlines for the past year.

7 At the minimum, the cores were north-western Europe, centered on the triangular axis of Flanders, central France, and northern Italy, the Middle East, radiating from Baghdad and then Cairo, and China, along the axis of the Grand Canal that connected the Yellow River with the Yangtze. The intervening zone – including the Indian subcontinent and the East Indian archipelago – is harder to conceive of as a "core" since its mixed character and shifting limits often fragmented it into parts that were within the orbits of separate cores. I would not argue strongly against viewing this central region as a core, so long as political factors were excluded.

8 In the thirteenth century these limits had expanded considerably over those that prevailed in the two preceding world-system formations: the first which centered on the Mesopotamian-Indus Valley connection several millennia before Christ, the second which connected the western Mediterranean with the west coast of the Indian subcontinent in the centuries just before and after the start of the Christian era. The limits of the second era were somewhat widened during the early centuries of Islam, eventually expanding to encompass those in force in the thirteenth century.

9 Barfield's book is significant for our purposes because it indicates that the thirteenth century Yüan period was the *only* exception to the long history in which nomads from Central Asia were pitted against the settled population of China. See Thomas J. Barfield, *The Perilous Frontier: Nomadic Empire and China*, Cambridge, MA: Basil Blackwell, 1989.

10 These vicissitudes can best be traced through studying the capital city of that empire, Cairo, whose growth and decline sensitively reflected Mamluk fortunes. See my *Cairo: 1001 Years of the City Victorious*, Princeton: Princeton University Press, 1971.

11 See, among others, B.Z. Kedar, *Merchants in Crisis: Genoese and Venetian Men of Affairs and the Fourteenth-Century Depression*, New Haven: Yale University Press, 1976.

12 See my "Did the West rise or did the East fall? Some reflections on the thirteenth century," presented to the annual meetings of the American Sociological Association in Chicaco in summer 1987 and subsequently printed as Working Paper No. 50, New York: New School for Social Research, Center for Studies of Social Change, 1987.

13 In this evaluation I depend heavily on the prior work by K.N. Chaudhuri, *Trade and Civilisation in the Indian Ocean: An Economic History from the Rise of Islam to 1750*, Cambridge: Cambridge University Press, 1985.

14 The Ming withdrawal from the sea is a subject of considerable debate in the field. While scholars disagree on why, they do agree on when. The scuttling of

the Chinese fleet did not occur as soon as the Yüan dynasty was overthrown. In fact, Admiral Cheng-Ho's "treasure ships" continued their voyages up through the early 1430s in a remarkable show of force that carried them to the Persian Gulf, as well as to all important intermediary ports. Nevertheless, the Chinese navy was left to rot in ports after that, which meant that they could offer no resistance to Portuguese men-of-war when they arrived some seventy years later.

15 A small fleet mounted jointly by the Mamluks and the Indian Muslim rulers to protect their control over the Arabian Sea between them was easily defeated near Diu in the first decade of the sixteenth century by far superior Portuguese armed ships.

16 See Fernand Braudel, *The Mediterranean and the Mediterranean World in the Age of Philip II*, 2 vols, New York: Harper & Row, 1972.

10

WORLD SYSTEM VERSUS WORLD-SYSTEMS

A critique

Immanuel Wallerstein

I wrote my article "The West, capitalism and the modern world-system" (Wallerstein 1992) before I read Andre Gunder Frank's and Barry K. Gills's various recent writings in which they insist that there was no historic transition from anything to capitalism (anywhere, and specifically not in sixteenth-century Europe) because whatever happened in Europe in the sixteenth century was simply a (cyclical?) shift *within* the framework of an already existing "world system," which has existed (for Frank and Gills) for several thousand years. Frank and Gills refer primarily to a geographic zone, called by some the oikumene, which goes from eastern Asia to western Europe and southward to include at least south Asia, south-west Asia, and northern Africa.

This is an interesting and important thesis, but its argument is directed at me only to the degree that it is directed at anyone and everyone who does not wish to "abandon [the sacrosanct belief in] capitalism as a distinct mode of production and separate system" – apparently so large a group that it includes (*dixit* various acknowledements) even the "friends" whom they have asked to make "reflective comments" on their papers.

My paper was written not at all *contra* Andre Gunder Frank and Barry K. Gills but rather *contra* all those – from Maurice Dobb to E.L. Jones to W.W. Rostow – who believe two things simultaneously: (a) something distinctive occurred in (western) Europe which was radically new somewhere in early modern times; (b) this "something" was a highly positive or "progressive" happening in world history. My position is that (a) was true but that (b) was distinctly not true.

I shall not repeat the detailed argument of my previous paper. But permit me to spell out the logic of my presentation there. Basically, the paper has two parts. First, I sought to establish that most of the traditional ways of distinguishing capitalism from other previous historical systems used weak distinctions in that they did not hold up under the light of empirical investigations. These traditional *differentiae specificae* included extensive commodity production, profit-seeking enterprises, wage labor, and a high level of technology. I called all these elements "protocapitalism" since, without them as a *part* of the whole, one couldn't have capitalism. But I argue their presence was not enough to call a historical system a capitalist system.

They were not enough because, I argued, each time the agents who used these elements seemed as if they might be able to go further and create a true capitalist system, they were repressed or destroyed in one way or another. And what then distinguishes a self-sustaining long-lived capitalist system, I asked? To which my answer was that the *differentiae specificae* was, and was *only*, that the system was based on a structural priority given and sustained for the *ceaseless* accumulation of capital. Not, I insist, merely for the accumulation of capital, but for the *ceaseless* accumulation of capital.

It is my view that such a system was created, initially in Europe in the sixteenth century, and then expanded to cover the entire world. It is my view also that no historical system that ever existed before can be plausibly seen as operating on the principle of structural priority to the *ceaseless* accumulation of capital.

I made this argument not (I remind readers) in order to counter Frank and Gills but in order to counter all those who regarded such a transformation as a progressive "miracle." That is what brought me to the second half of my article – the attempt to account for the peculiar *weakness(es)* of western Europe that it permitted such a disaster to occur. I found the weakness in the implausible contemporaneity of four collapses – those of the seigniors, the states, the Church, and the Mongols.

Let me speak to the Mongols issue once again, since Frank reopens it in chapter 6 above. The importance of the Mongols is negative. My argument was that the three other "collapses" were not enough since one might have expected that they would have led, by occurring jointly, to the conquest of western Europe by an external power, which would have ended the possibility of the descent into capitalism. However, since the Mongols "collapsed," this led (through several intervening steps) to the momentary collapse of the world trading system of which Frank speaks, the weakening of its component sectors, and hence the impossibility for anyone to conquer western Europe at that particular moment in time. For one moment in historical space-time, the protective anticapitalist gates were opened up and capitalism "snuck in," to the loss of all of us.

Having restated my position on the "contra-miraculous" nature of the origins of capitalism as a historical system, let me briefly address Frank's own views. In his article (1990), he makes a case for the growth over thousands of years of an interrelated trade network that he calls the "world system." I believe in fact his account is a fairly acceptable initial and partial outline of what had been happening in the world between 8000 BC (or so) up to 1500 AD. I agree that there were many major nodes of political-economic activity, which I prefer to call "world-empires," and that these world-empires entered into long-distance trade (often? regularly? this is still to be demonstrated) with each other. I agree too that these world-empires included in the trading network of the oikumene various zones that were not organized as "world-empires." I even agree that, as a consequence, there may have been some common economic rhythms between them.

However, I do not believe that this trading network at any point of time was based on an axial division of labor involving integrated production processes. And therefore, for me, by axiom they did not form a single historical system, since I use that term to mean precisely something based on an axial division of labor involving integrated production processes. Of course, we may all define terms as we wish. This is the definition I have found useful, since it is the only one that accounts for the lives of limited duration of all these various systems, and for the ways in which they have functioned historically during their lives.

I do not believe that trade alone makes a system. I have tried on at least four occasions (Wallerstein 1973, 1976, 1989: ch. 3; Hopkins and Wallerstein 1987) to spell out the distinction between trade in "luxury" goods and trade in "bulk" goods or "necessities," and to indicate the consequences of the distinction. Even if it is difficult on occasion to draw the line empirically between the two kinds of trade, I continue to believe the distinction to be key analytically. It permits us to distinguish trade *within* a historical system (primarily in "necessities") and trade *between* separate systems (primarily in "luxuries"). Because of the technology of transport before modern times and hence because of its high cost, "long-distance" trade had necessarily to be in low-bulk, high-profit goods, and these had to be "luxuries."

Note a detail in word usage that distinguishes Frank and Gills from me. They speak of a "world system." I speak of "world-systems." I use a hyphen; they do not. I use the plural; they do not. They use the singular because, for them, there is and has only been one world system through all of historical time and space. For me there have been very many world-systems. For example, I do not consider that what many historians call China or the Chinese empire has been one system. There have been a number of successive systems in the geographic zone called China. The Han rose and fell. The Tang or the Ming is not the same historical system, even if the geographic location, the outward form (a "world-empire"), and some cultural features were the same. The "modern world-system" (or the "capitalist world-economy") is merely one system among many. Its peculiar feature is that it has shown itself strong enough to destroy all others contemporaneous to it.

This brings us to the hyphen. My "world-system" is not a system "in the world" or "of the world." It is a system "that is a world." Hence the hyphen, since "world" is not an attribute of the system. Rather the two words together constitute a single concept. Frank and Gills's system is a world system in an attributive sense, in that it has been tending over time to cover the whole world. They cannot conceive of multiple "world-systems" coexisting on the planet. Yet until the nineteenth century, or so I contend, this has always been the case.

Far from being Eurocentric, my analysis "exoticizes" Europe. Europe is historically aberrant. In some ways this was a historical accident, not entirely Europe's fault. But, in any case, it is nothing about which Europe should boast. Perhaps Europe and the world will one day be cured of this terrible malady with which Europe (and through Europe the world) has been afflicted.

This brings us to the future. For that we have to return to a schematic view of the past. Thus far, I believe, we have had three historical eras on the planet earth. There was the period before 8–10,000 BC about which we still know very little. The world was probably composed of a large number of scattered minisystems.

Then, there was the period from 8–10,000 BC to circa 1500 AD. There were in this period multiple instances of coexisting historical systems (of the three main varieties: world-empires, world-economies, minisystems). None of them was "capitalist" in that none of them was based on the structural pressure for the ceaseless accumulation of capital. *Gloria Deo!* As I said, I do not disagree that, among many of the major "world-empires," there was a growing network of long-distance trade. And perhaps this "crowding together" accounts in part for the outbreak of the malady that is capitalism. I say perhaps, because I do not like the teleological implications of this. I prefer my explanation of a fortuitous simultaneity of events. The two modes of explanation are not necessarily incompatible one with the other.

The third period began circa 1500 AD. The aberrant system, our capitalist world-economy, proved aggressive, expansive, and efficacious. Within a few centuries it encompassed the globe. This is where we are today. I do not think it can last too much longer (for my arguments, see Wallerstein 1982). When its contradictions make it no longer able to function, there will be a bifurcation, whose outcome it is not possible to predict. This outcome, however, will be radically affected by small input, hence by our input. The world is neither continuing to inch forward to a perfect oikumene, as some might suggest, nor remaining in a relatively stable state of social imperfection. Just because our inadequate analyses based on nineteenth-century social science are now proving to have badly misled us does not mean we have to fall into a variant of eighteenth-century triumph of universal reason. Just because it is useful to probe more intelligently into the patterns of the pre-1500 era does not mean we may ignore the unpleasant and dramatic caesura that the creation of a capitalist world-economy imposed on the world. Only if we keep the caesura in mind will we remember that this historical system, like all historical systems, not only had a beginning (or genesis), but that it will have an end. And only then can we concentrate our attention on which kind of successor system we wish to construct.

NOTE

This chapter first appeared in 1991 as "World system versus world-systems: a critique," in *Critique of Anthropology* 11 (2).

REFERENCES

Frank, A.G. (1990) "A theoretical introduction to 5,000 years of world system history," *Review* 13 (2) (spring): 155–248.

Hopkins, T.K. and Wallerstein, I. (1987) "Capitalism and the incorporation of new zones into the world-economy," *Review* 10 (5/6) (supplement): 763–79.

Wallerstein, I. (1973) "Africa in a capitalist world," *Issue: A Journal of Africanist Opinion* 3 (3) (fall): 1–11.

—— (1976) "The three stages of African involvement in the world-economy," in P.C.W. Gutkind and I. Wallerstein (eds) *Political Economy of Contemporary Africa*, Beverly Hills, CA: Sage, 35–63.

—— (1982) "Crisis as transition," in S. Amin, G. Arrighi, A.G. Frank, I. Wallerstein, *Dynamics of Global Crisis*, New York: Monthly Review Press; London: Macmillan, 11–54.

—— (1989) *The Modern World-System*, vol. 3: *The Second Great Expansion of the Capitalist World-Economy, 1730–1840s*, San Diego, CA: Academic Press.

—— (1992) "The West, capitalism, and the modern world-system," *Review* 15 (4) (fall): 561–619. Prepared as a chapter in J. Needham (ed.) *Science and Civilization in China*, vol. 7: *The Social Background*, part 2, section 48: "Social and economic considerations" (forthcoming).

11

REJOINDER AND CONCLUSIONS

Andre Gunder Frank and Barry K. Gills

In this book about history in the "old" Afro-Eurasian world system oikumene, the central debate is really about *how* to write a world (system) history. We editors/contributors view the world system primarily as a "world economy" or better as a "world political-economic system." It has been the "same" system by virtue of its real historical continuity and the persistence of its structural patterns and processes for at least 5,000 years. However, these patterns themselves promote change, especially through the constant competition among the participants. In our view therefore, we are dealing with the *same* world system over 5,000 years, even though it is not always the same.

The debate among the contributors has been primarily about continuity versus discontinuity in world history. There are two main positions in this debate. One position is that political/ideological determination of the mode of production or social formation in world history before about 1500 AD and of ceaseless capital accumulation and economic determination (through the "law of value") at least in the modern capitalist world-system thereafter makes for a sharp break or discontinuity between the pre-1500 and post-1500 periods. This first position is taken here by Amin and Wallerstein, who at least therein represent the nearly universally accepted received wisdom on this matter. The other position is that the capital accumulation did not begin or become "ceaseless" only after 1500 AD, but has been the motor force of the historical process throughout world system history. Therefore, there was no such sharp break between different "systems" around 1500. This second, still very small-minority, position is taken by us editors/contributors and by Ekholm and Friedman. Though Wilkinson does not emphasize it, his long-term analysis also seems closer to this second position. Abu-Lughod seems closer to the first and still dominant position, despite her reference to a "thirteenth-century world-system." In his contribution here, Wallerstein clarifies this difference between many historical world-systems (with a hyphen) and one world system (without a hyphen), while Abu-Lughod tries to take an intermediary position.

Wallerstein and other world-system theorists stress the material transcivilizational exchanges in the world system via the "division of labor," which in turn determines their approach to the issue of "incorporation" into the world(-)system. We and others (e.g. sociologists Chase-Dunn and Hall, political scientist Wilkinson, and Kohl and other archaeologists) prefer a framework based on center–periphery complexes and a larger hierarchy of such complexes. Whether center–periphery relationships are "developmental" or "underdevelopmental" (Kohl takes a position against underdevelopmental relations in the ancient world) is an important but in our view not a crucial debate.

The real debate/disagreement revolves around the question of what structures constitute a "system" or a "world(-)system" in particular. We contend that a hierarchy of center–periphery (and hinterland) complexes within the world system, in which surplus is being transferred between zones of the hierarchy, necessarily implies the existence of some form of an "international" (though this is not the best term) division of labor. In our view, Amin and Wallerstein continue in the footsteps of Polanyi and Finley and underestimate the importance of capital accumulation via trade and the market in the ancient world system. Therefore, they do not see participation in the system in the same way we do and look for the "incorporation" of peoples and their societies and economies into the world-system at a point when we see them as having long been part and parcel of the historical development of the world system.

The real dispute then is over the *character* of the "international" or world system division of labor – not over its very *existence*. It may be true that as time passes the world system division of labor becomes ever more integrated, and time and space become ever more "shortened" (in the long run at least – allowing for temporary historical "setbacks" in the process – particularly in crisis periods). Wallerstein stresses what in our view is only a *particular* modern phase in the development of this world system division of labor at a higher level of integration than may have generally prevailed earlier. In his contribution in chapter 7 above, Wilkinson is prepared to accept our world system framework, albeit as manifested through more connections than economic trade and political conflict. However, the dating of the formation of such a "Central world system" (as Chase-Dunn and Hall would have us term it to satisfy all of us) is later and its geographical extent is consistently smaller through the ages for Wilkinson (e.g. as displayed in the date maps that accompany some of his writings) than it is for us editors/contributors. The reason is that Wilkinson asks for more stringent, empirically verifiable criteria of system inclusion, in particular demonstrable strings of connecting entrepôt cities between hegemonic centers. Yet Wilkinson also recognizes above, and even more so in his still unpublished "test" of our chapter-5 cycle datings, that his *de facto* operational criteria may be too stringent. For instance, he relies on Chandler's data on city sizes with a lower cutoff at 40,000 people. This restriction probably makes many cities escape the net, which would be there if we had readily available data for cities of say 10,000 population.

We have no objections to and indeed welcome such "tests" and refinements of our definition and identification of the world system. We see no reason why such procedures should contradict our own premises about the existence and importance of a world system division of labor *much earlier* and perhaps (though this remains to be empirically established) at a lower "intensity" of integration. To take a more contemporary example, no one can any longer reasonably deny that China or India are part of the modern world system, though reference to China's "socialist system" might give this (false) impression. Their "internal" division of labor may be less intensely integrated into the world system wide division of labor than that of Singapore or South Korea, but China and India are not "out of it." We disagree with those, among whom Charles Tilly is prominent, who suggest that we set arbitrary (trade and/or other) percentage levels of integration or systemicity in our definition of world system. We still believe this would be neither necessary nor useful and could be very misleading. (Until the 1970s, foreign trade accounted for no more than 5 per cent of American exports or imports; but not for that was the United States "out" of the system!) Such arbitrary limits/requirements on the level of system integration could constitute a barrier to posing questions about world system developments/interactions/correlations/exchanges, which we regard as so important. We do not accept criteria that may amount to a projection of the prevailing conditions of the present onto the past. We reject this as a form of "now centrism." The evidence suggests to us that there has been a world system wide division of labor even in the distant past some 5,000 years ago. Its form does not necessarily have to be identical with the modern form. Why should it? The labor of the ancient lapis-lazuli miners of Afghanistan and the textile workers in urban Sumeria was surely interlinked in a "world" economic/system division of labor even in the fourth or third millennium BC. They were both in the same world economy and the productive labor of one was connected, though perhaps indirectly, to the labor of the other in one overall exchange nexus.

In her contribution in chapter 9 on the other hand, Abu-Lughod recognizes long continuities on a *regional* level, such as Anatolia to India, which she calls "subsystem levels." However, she declines to "assume that the international system itself exhibited such continuities." So what she so magisterially analyzed in her book *Before European Hegemony: The World System A.D. 1250–1350* and the earlier Islamic "system" to which she refers in passing were each only one-shot deals for her. We editors/contributors stand by our argument with her that the system-wide "disorganization" and "failure" to which she refers should be recognized as being rather recurrent phases of a continuing "international" world system, whose continuity is far longer than any of her "regional subsystems." Indeed, is there not a contradiction in her own reference to a long-lasting "subsystem level" in the absence of a continuous world system?

We also find a contradiction in Abu-Lughod's qualification of her thirteenth-century world system first as one of booming economic expansion and then as economic crisis and decline. Both could be admissible if the boom appelation were only to the first part of her 100-year period; but it was not confined to that. Or the decline and fall could have started only after 1300. However, by our reckoning, and also by Wallerstein's and others' at least for Europe, the declining B phase of a long cycle began around 1250, that is her starting date, and lasted until 1450. By that reckoning, Abu-Lughod's entire world-system and period were part of a long B phase of decline between two periods of A-phase expansion in the eleventh–twelfth centuries and again in the "long sixteenth century" from 1450 to 1600, both of which are also recognized by Wallerstein and others. In that case however, as we have already argued, especially in our chapters 5 and 6 above, how is it possible to deny world systemic and long-cyclical continuity over this period, if not a still longer one? This area is certainly open to future investigation and debate. Hopefully such further explorations of this issue will help clarify our respective positions and perhaps break new ground.

Another area for future refining of positions over similarities and differences in the world system is the form of hegemony. We editors retain the concept used by economic (Wallersteinian) and political (Modelskian) world-systems and international relations theorists (Keohane), historians (Kennedy), and others. However, we insist again that hegemonic dominance over the world system, not to say the entire globe, has only rarely been achieved, if ever. More common, in the modern world system as well as in the world system before 1500, have been a series of simultaneous regional but unstable, temporary hegemonic powers. We see these regional hegemons both as forming a "system" of hegemony and of being constituent parts of the "world system," whose own structure and dynamic is also expressed by these hegemonic powers as well as their rise, fall, and mutual rivalries and alliances. Their hegemony, however, is not only "political." It is also "economic" in the sense that they centralize and use to promote their own "development" the economic "surplus," which they derive from their at least in that sense "dependent" peripheries and even hinterlands. *That*, and not only "power for its own sake," is why they seek to expand, maintain, and defend their hegemony as far and as long as they can. In chapter 3 especially, we editors/contributors broached the idea of a "super-hegemon" who "super-accumulates" on a world system wide scale. However, Wilkinson says he can find no example of such super-accumulating super-hegemony in the world (system) before 1500; and he is doubtful even about the only two recognized instances of hegemony since then, the British in the nineteenth century and the American in the twentieth century. The Mongols in the thirteenth century, whom we put forward as a possibility in chapters 3 and 5, may well be a doubtful case. However, we contend *per contra* Wallerstein and Modelski, that the case for super-accumulating super-hegemony on a world system scale was greater for the thirteenth-century Mongols than for Portugal in the sixteenth century and Holland in the seventeenth century.

These issues in our debates about system continuity also intercede in some older, indeed "classical," debates. In the classical Marxist view, capitalism was progressive. Capitalism developed the means of production and opened up new areas of the world to the concomitant process of capital accumulation in the "world capitalist system." Bill Warren (1980) among others also defended this position against writers who had begun to question it explicitly or implicitly. Baran, Sweezy, Frank, Amin, and others had begun to argue that capitalism as a world-historical process also generated the "development of underdevelopment" in the periphery and therefore was not progressive, at least for most of its people. Amin and Wallerstein have argued that most people in the modern world(-system) are now worse off than their forefathers and mothers were in premodern times. Wallerstein and other world-system theorists also argued that the semiperiphery represented an avenue of mobility within the world system hierarchy that also provided for the rise and decline of hegemonic powers.

On these issues, the present contributors largely do agree. None of us can support Marx's (or rather Stalin's) unilinear view of capitalist agency in world history. However, we can retain and seek to refine the basic perspective of *historical materialism*, which of course was neither original nor exclusive to Marx. However, the contributors differ in the role they assign to the *capitalist mode of production* or the supposed transitions between them in world history. On this issue, Amin and Wallerstein remain in the classical Marxist tradition; and we editors, Ekholm and Friedman, and Wilkinson do not. Why? Because we find too many big patterns in world history that seem to transcend or persist despite all apparent changes among modes of production and supposed transitions between them. The evidence available to us (notwithstanding our ignorance in comparison to specialists) suggests to us that there has been a profound misunderstanding of the character of modes of production. In particular there has been widespread underappreciation or underestimation of the role of capital accumulation, markets, the profit motive, "entrepreneurial elements," and of long-distance trade for *most* of world history.

Therefore, also, as contributors to this debate, we editors seek to extend the insights of dependency and world system theory much further back. We argue that the world system is rather like a giant and never-ending game of musical chairs. This "game" is not child's play but is based on incessant "rat-race" and "devil-take-the-hindmost" competition among the "players." The driving force behind this game is competitive capital accumulation, whether by state or by private elites, and usually by both. In the course of this competitive "game," particular "players" and areas change position within the world system from one time to another. This change is particularly accelerated, if not generated, during periods of system-wide economic crisis and the accompanying hegemonial shifts when "the music stops" or at least slows down. Peripheral (regional and political-economic) positions within the world system act as a mechanism of exploitation via transfer of surplus to the distant center(s) and the subordination of the periphery's "development" to the requirements of the center's "development." Some "development" may take place even in the periphery; but this is not the real point, at least over the long pull. The important issue is the position in the world system, and how, when, why, and where that position does or does not change and permit or deny – and literally in any case unevenly distribute – the benefits (and costs) of development in and of the world system as a whole.

The outcome of "development" in any particular part of the system is part and parcel of the prevailing conditions of "development" (especially capital accumulation) of the whole world system. This seems to be a general law of all world system history. This game of musical chairs is literally as old as the hills and as old as the world system in any event, and it continues right up to the present. The recent collapse of the Soviet Union and the regimes in eastern Europe and their subordination to the International Monetary Fund and the Group of 7 (*de facto* G3) is a case in point. The attempt to understand these events as a transition between modes of production, let alone as a change of "system," can only confound much more than it clarifies. Instead, these dramatic events should be seen as the outcome of these regions' and regimes' inability to compete adequately in the accentuated rivalry during and because of the present period of world-economic crisis within the world system as a whole. Reaganomic "star-wars" bankrupted *both* "super-powers," although the USA has been able to paper over the "twin deficits" in its budget and balance of payments through capital shots in the arm by its allies (but even more its competitors) in Europe and Japan, which have bailed the United States out (so far but for how long?). We are not witnessing a "reincorporation" of the "socialist East" into the world economy run along the canons of the "free market/capitalist" West. On the contrary, the East – no less than the South, of which most of it had been and now again will be a part – had been in a disadvantaged position in this same world system all along; and that is the principal reason why it failed.

We editors/contributors view this change in position in the world system as part and parcel of change in the overall development of the world system itself and as the result of its governing motor-force process of competitive capital accumulation and hegemony–rivalry. Thus our position reaffirms the earlier break by Frank, Wallerstein, and others with the then dominant state-centric framework and unilinear modernization theory. We reaffirm the correctness of the shift to the whole world system as the essential unit of analysis. However, we seek to carry it further in space, time, and analysis than Wallerstein and other "world-system" theorists. This is not to say that the world system simply "determines" *everything* that can or cannot happen or the "chances of mobility" of any regional, social, or individual "player" within the system. However, the whole is more than the sum of its parts, and *no* part can ever be understood apart from the whole system, which helps determine if not its fate, at least its choices or lack of them.

Therefore, we argue that it is not the mode of production which determines the overall developmental patterns and outcomes of this game – but the nature of the game itself, of which the various modes are (only) an element. The search for any supposed "transitions" between such "modes" only obscures the essential continuity of participation in the same one and only world system. Soviet "socialism" was an element in the game after 1917, but it never determined the nature or pattern of the game. Similarly, the whole period of world history since 1500 has been less "defined" by "capitalism" than it was generally defined and characterized by shifts in the routes of trade, centers of accumulation, and the location of hegemonic power from "East" to "West." The now emerging period of world history is again, or rather still, characterized by competition between centers of accumulation, which may possibly even be accompanied by a continuous westward shift of the center of accumulation back to Asia in "the East," if there is not a (temporary) "breakdown" of the world economy into rival political-economic zones.

We are arguing that the nature and rules of the game do not change so much as the players change position. Techniques of competition change, but it is also true that many basic techniques have been around for millennia. However, the world system process of competitive capital accumulation goes on and remains the ultimately determining process in world system development – and in the (temporary) costs and benefits, which particular peoples and regions derive therefrom, mostly on the basis of their (also temporary) under/privileged, competitive, or monopoly/oligopoly position in that same world system. This is what *we* mean by the continuity of and in the world system, by comparison with which the discontinuities are only minor from a longer world-historical (system) perspective.

The point on which we cannot agree with either Amin or Wallerstein concerning discontinuity is the role of capital accumulation in world history. We affirm Ekholm and Friedman's challenge to the Polanyi and Finley orthodoxy on capital in the ancient economies. The evidence suggests to us (overwhelmingly) that there was no sharp break pre- and post-1500 in the predominance or even in the supposed nodes of capital accumulation in the world system. What there *was* was a dramatic and important shift in what McNeill refers to in his foreword as the communications network of the world system. That is, pre- and post-1500 there was a historic shift from trade centering on the three corridors in the east Mediterranean, west and Central Asia to transatlantic linkages, which however did not really replace the former until the eighteenth century (*not* the sixteenth!). Within this shift there was the "windfall" profit to European centers of accumulation of the conquest and incorporation of the Americas as a periphery to the rising European core, thus bolstering its new world system position. The surplus and especially the bullion extracted from the Americas (*à la* Blaut) was injected into global exchange circuits in Europe's favor while also stimulating within Europe what is usually called the "rise of capitalism."

The key in these changes is a shift in locus of accumulation in the world system accompanied by a shift in hegemonic power and the global reorganization of centers and peripheries. These shifts were part of the underlying changes in competitive position in the world accumulation process, but they are much older than "modern" "capitalism" in the world system. Polanyi *et al.* were mistaken about the supposed absence of capital accumulation in the ancient economy. We believe that Amin and Wallerstein are still mistaken about the in/*significance* they accord to capital accumulation in pre-1500 world history, even though both admit the *existence* of capital accumulation before 1500.

This question of continuity/similarity versus discontinuity/differences in the debate is related to other patterns and issues about which the contributions to this book contend as well. Among these issues are the following:

1. Long cycles of expansion and contraction in the world economy.
2. Hegemonic world system cycles of simultaneous rise and decline.
3. Large-scale periodic migrations and invasions during crisis periods.
4. Ideological confusion and fragmentation during crisis periods.
5. The increase of repression, heightened class conflict and greater incidence of war and general destruction during crisis periods.
6. Shifts and the rise of new centers of accumulation during crisis periods.
7. The economic, social, and political *retrogression* of some regions during crisis periods (so-called "dark ages"), which involve less well-developed connections to the centers of world system economy and "reversion" to locally more self-reliant economies.
8. The eventual re-establishment of a renewed exchange and communications network, renewed economic growth, and new hegemonic structures.
9. Shifts in centers of production and accumulation, related to shifts in trade routes and urban and demographic settlement patterns in the world system in periods of renewed expansion.

10 New urban growth and larger demographic growth and the territorial expansion of the world system as a whole in periods of expansion.
11 Periods of economic expansion accompanied by growing trade at long distances over both land and maritime routes, higher frequency of diplomatic contact, cosmopolitan exchange of ideas and technologies, consolidation of political systems and hegemonies, all of which contribute to higher rates of capital accumulation.
12 Eventual overconcentration of capital, which leads to "overaccumulation" and "underconsumption," growing gaps between rich and poor, overextension of the state apparatus, falling rates of investment and profit, slowdown of expansion, and contraction of economic growth.

All of these patterns may be associated with "capitalism" since 1800 or the "modern world-system" since 1500. However, inspection of the evidence shows that they were equally present and significant over at least 5,000 years of world system history.

Albert Bergesen (1992) suggests that neither the "pre-" nor the "post-" 1500 camp in this debate has yet made a breakthrough to a new theory of world system history. Perhaps not. However, we suggest that the extension of post-1500 insights to the long pre-1500 period may indeed constitute the kernel of a new theory of world system history and of its center–periphery structure and governing processes of capital accumulation and hegemony–rivalry. This one world system process develops, underdevelops, brings "progress," peace, prosperity and also war, destruction and depression in its wake. This is the stuff of all world (system) history. The challenge for world system theorists is not only to *rewrite* all world history in this light, but also to help guide at least some of the more destructive processes of world system history into socially more benign if not beneficial channels.

This new departure in world history writing leads us "full circle" back to the issue of ecology. The world system's origins lie in ecology, as does its entire developmental history and of course its future. We agree with McNeill, writing in the foreword of this book, that one of the next steps in the new rewriting of world history must be a new understanding of how world system development both altered and was in turn altered by the natural environment. The natural environment places limits on and establishes parameters for world system development. Ecological crisis and perhaps even ecological cycles have accompanied world system development in the past. The now looming ecological crisis reminds us of the urgency of this emphasis on ecology in world history.

Thus, this is not an arcane debate about ancient history. The disagreement goes to the nub of a larger theoretical argument over how best to study the modern world (system). This debate is at the fulcrum of historical-materialist, including Marxist, analysis of world history. The questions we debate above must be answered satisfactorily in order better to be able to address pressing political questions about "what is to be done." Both "camps" in this debate (perhaps surprisingly to some) share the *same* good political intentions. Namely, how to change the world for the better in the interests of its people and not just its present or future rulers. These political implications may explain why some of the disagreements debated in this book sometimes arouse such strong feelings: they are related to the question "what is to be done?" Three of the present contributors, Amin, Frank, and Wallerstein, along with Giovanni Arrighi and Marta Fuentes, recently addressed this question jointly under the title *Transforming the Revolution: Social Movements and the World-System* (1990).

Thus McNeill may be right (though excessively generous in his foreword) that our debate may be a potential turning point in the writing of world history. McNeill says that whether or not the "5,000-year world system" framework (which he suggests is a "confluence of Marxism with more inchoate liberal ideas about world history") will constitute a "landmark" or not depends partly on the future of Marxism and partly on the future of world-history writing as a professional undertaking. The key to this, and again we agree with McNeill, is how *material processes* are treated in the writing of world history. We are very adamant that capital accumulation, as well as its long cycles of world system wide economic expansion and contraction, merits much greater recognition in world historical analysis and writing.

If this point is recognized, as McNeill says, the debate about the unit of analysis takes on a very different and less central aspect. Traditionally, the unit has been framed as "nation-state" "societies" or "civilizations" and more recently "world-systems." Following McNeill, *material transcivilizational processes* in the entire Afro-Eurasian oikumene (or world system) would become much more central to the concern of world-historians and express the "unity in diversity" of humanity in world history. McNeill proposes that we emphasize the material transcivilizational exchanges in the "communications network," which act as the skeleton of the world system body. In that case, the "awkwardness of terminology" recedes in importance.

The "central question" is whether such material exchanges have *really* been the key determining process in world (system) history. We agree with McNeill about these material processes in the world system and that their recognition does not require or imply the exclusion of civilizational or ideational aspects of human experience. Rather, we suggest that due recognition of these long-term "material" structures and processes can provide a framework through which to analyze these "ideal" aspects in an organized way. We also accept that the world system develops in and through a dynamic communications network across which capital, surplus, commodities, peoples, armies, ideas, technologies, diseases, and more travel. Thus, McNeill's suggestions do not contradict and are entirely compatible with emerging world system history framework, premises, or hypotheses – and vice versa. His suggestions can help refine, develop, and elaborate our framework for the writing of world history as well. We can only look forward to this new joint enterprise and invite our supporters and critics alike to continue the debate over the ideas developed in this book.

The editors' perspective on world system history extends and deepens the rejection of Eurocentrism that was made by earlier world-system theory. However, all the contributors in this book agree on and participate in this important task. We affirm that in the future all world-history writing must be *humanocentric* and as objectively as possible assess the overall *unity* of human history while encompassing the *diversity* of its cultural expressions. No centrism based on the temporary historical "glory" of any nation or region should any longer be allowed to distort our *universal* human understanding of our one world history.

REFERENCES

Amin, S., Arrighi, G., Frank, A. G., and Wallerstein, I. (1990) *Transforming the Revolution: Social Movements and the World-System*, New York: Monthly Review Press.

Bergeson, (1992) Political Economy of the World System (PEWS) Newsletter.

Warren, B. (1980) *Imperialism: Pioneer of Capitalism*, London: New Left Books and Verso.

INDEX

A/B phased cycles 4, 144, 149, 188–95, 203, 300; Bronze Age 153–7; Iron Age 157–71; Medieval and early modern periods 171–80; modern world system period 180–7
Abbas I 184
Abbassid dynasty 172, 173, 189
absolute monarchy 251, 252, 265
absolutism 252, 253, 274
Abu-Lughod, Janet 5, 8–10, 25, 30, 45, 46, 75, 120, 143, 145–6, 176–8, 180, 181–2, 190, 201, 203, 208–11, 297, 299–300
accumulation: concentration of 131–2; cumulation of 105–6, 202; hegemony 100–6; historical-materialism 106–12; infrastructural investment 90–2; interpenetrating 92–4, 106, 144; political-economic modes 97–100; private 68–9, 97, 99, 102, 132–4; process 115–35; public 97, 99, 102; relations 92–7; state 97, 99, 102, 132–4; of surplus 92–7, 144; surplus transfer 92–7; of wealth 78, 107, 125, 127, 128, 243; world system origins 81–5; world system routes/nexuses 85–90
accumulation cycles 70; hegemonic cycle 33, 36, 91, 98, 102–3, 107, 111–12, 130–1, 136, 181; hegemonic shifts and 143–51; historical review 151–87
accumulation modes 93–4, 97–100, 115, 128
Adams, Brooks 83
Adams, Robert 6, 111, 149
Adelson, H.L. 23
Aegean–Black Sea–Central Asia corridor 88, 89
Africa 16, 24; Iron Age 165, 167, 171; Medieval and early modern period 172, 173–4; modern world system period 184; tributary system 263, 266
"Afrocentrism" 11, 21
Afro-Eurasian oikumene 144, 157, 165, 173, 209, 239–43 *passim*, 297, 306
agriculture 65, 66; -based production states 69–70, 98, 124, 127; bureaucratic empires 132, 133; commercial 62–3; surplus 82, 92, 132
Ahmad, Sadek Saad 253
Akbar 184
Akkadian empire 84–5, 152, 153
Albright, Frank P. 167
Alexander the Great 89, 162–3, 253–4, 264–5, 269
Algaze, Guillermo 7, 20
Allen, Jim 69
Allen, Mitchell 6
Allende regime 214
Allerdyce, G. 14
Ambrose, W.R. 69
American Sociological Association 201, 203
Americas 85, 181, 186
Amin, Samir 3, 5–6, 11, 19, 21, 30, 45–8, 95, 123, 126, 162, 206, 213–14, 306
Anlushan 175
an-Nasr Mohammed, Sultan 286
analytic agenda 110–12
ancien régime 251, 252, 253
ancient history, classicism in 21–2
ancient markets 149–51
ancient world-systems (*versus* modern

191–3, 210; political hegemony and 10–11, 143–9, short 4, 11
economism 110
economy/polity contradictions 100, 145
"egocentric illusion" 17
Egypt 65–7, 81–2, 84; Bronze Age 152–3, 155–7; Iron Age 163, 171; Mamluk rule 24, 178, 286, 287, 288; Medieval and early modern period 172, 174–5, 178–9; modern world system period 183, 184
Eisenstadt, S.N. 111, 116, 132–3
Eisler, R. 43–4
Ekholm, H. 6, 7, 18, 45, 61, 74, 76, 94, 107–9, 111–12, 124, 128
elitism 33–4, 92–3, 98–9, 102, 117, 119, 128, 132–4, 154; state elites 136, 137, 159
Emmanuel, Arghiri 203
empires 70–1, 134, 135; *see also* "world empires"
endogenous factors (ecology) 190
Enlightenment 252, 253
entrepôt cities 241, 298
entropic phases 102, 103, 104
environment 40, 92, 190–1, 305
equal exchange 93
"equal time" concept 12
ethnic studies 42–3
ethnicity 42–3, 75
ethnocentrism 74
ethnogenesis 42
Eurasia 12, 14, 21–2, 24–6; Afro-Eurasian oikumene 239–43, 297, 306; Iron Age 157–71; Medieval and early modern periods 171–80; modern world system period 180–7
Eurocentrism 129, 207; capitalist world system 247–50, 253, 265, 273; challenged 3, 11–12, 15–17, 21–2, 112, 121, 307; ecnomic history 26–30; medievalism 22–4; modern world system period 183
Europe 273–4, 295; medieval 22–4; mercantilist tradition 251–3; modern world system period 180–7; *see also* Eurocentrism
"European" world system 209–12
evolution of interlocal structures 63–6
evolutionism 41, 260–2
exchange relations 127, 251, 256, 258–9, 260, 276
exchange systems 101; supralocal 60–1, 63, 74
exogenous factors (ecology) 190
exploitation 62–3, 92–3, 95–6, 98, 120, 130–1, 133–4, 144; capital and 66–9
exports 61, 63, 65–8, 161
expropriation (of surplus) 134

factory system 251
Fairbank, John K. 151
Farmer, Edward 13, 24, 109
Fawzy, Mansour 253
Featherstone, M. 12, 35, 43
feminism 43–4
feudalism 10, 23, 176; capitalist world system 248, 252, 255, 262, 265–6, 273–5; in economic history 27–30, 33; feudal disintegration 262, 265–6; hegemonic transition 129, 133; transitional ideological modes 46, 47, 75, 200–15
Finley, Moses 18, 59, 149, 298, 303
five thousand-year world system 3–4, 306; anthropology 41–2; archaeology 18–21; civilizationism 17–18; classicism 21–2; development studies 38–40; early modern history 32–4; early modern to modern history 24–6; ecology 40; economic history 26–30; ethnic/race relations studies 42–3; Eurocentrism 11–12; gender relations 43–4; implications 44–8; international relations 36–7; macro historical sociology 30–2; medievalism 22–4; political geography 35; world historiography 12–17; world system theory 5–11
food trade/reserves 234, 235
forereacher 242
formalism 41, 59
Franck, Irene M. 160
Frank, A.G. 3–8, 10–12, 15–17, 19–25, 29–30, 32–3, 35–40, 42, 46–8, 71, 74–6, 94–5, 109, 111, 117–18, 120–1, 124, 129–30, 144–8, 151, 154, 176, 178, 180–1, 185, 190–2, 194–5, 202–3, 205, 207, 212, 221, 241–2, 244, 271, 273, 275, 278–9, 292–5, 306
free (flexible) resources 132, 134
free will 44, 45
freedom 123
Friedberg, C. 61

Friedman, J. 6, 7, 18, 43, 45, 61, 74–6, 94, 107–9, 111–12, 124, 128
Fuentes, Marta 48, 306

Galtung, Johan 63
Gao Xianji 174
gender relations 43–4
general systems theory 110–11
Genghis Khan 87, 179, 180, 259, 266, 268, 274
geopolitics 35, 128
Gernet, Jacques 26, 97, 177, 182, 206–7
Ghurshman, R. 158
Gibbon, Edward 23
Gill, Stephen 36, 118, 121
Gills, B.K. 3–6, 8, 10–11, 17, 19–25, 29, 32–3, 35–7, 40, 46, 74, 102, 117–18, 120–2, 124, 129–30, 132, 135, 144, 146–8, 154, 181, 191–2, 202–3, 205, 207, 212, 221, 241–2, 244, 292–5
Gilpin, Robert 36, 96, 116, 123, 125–7, 130, 132, 135, 190
Gimbutas, Marija 43
glacier analogy 84
Glazer, Nathan 42
global: civilization 226; culture 35, 229; hegemony 8, 36, 121; systems 79, 108–9
globalization–localization 12, 35, 43
Godelier, Maurice 205–6, 214
Goldstein, J.S. 10, 11, 36, 101, 111, 180–1, 190
Goldstone, Jack A. 31–3, 131
Gorbachev, Mikhail 43, 47, 105, 215
Gorgias 161
Gouldner, Alvin 33
Gramscian approach 36, 119
Great Trunk Road 163
Great Wall of China 165, 175
Greece 21, 22, 27; Iron Age 159–65, 171
Group of Seven 342
Grousset, Rene 166, 174
guild structure 69
Gupta empire 169–70, 179, 189

Hall, J.A. 27
Hall, S. 43
Hall, T.D. 18, 19, 96, 190, 298
Hallstatt cultures 194
Hamel, Jacques 207
Hammurabi 156
Hapsburg state 28–9
Harsha, Sri 171
Hegel, G.W.F. 43
hegemonic cycles 35, 36, 91, 98, 102–3, 107, 111–12, 136, 181; and class struggle 130–8; historical review of evidence 151–87; *see also* accumulation cycles
hegemonic powers 37, 100–3, 116–19, 123–9, 138, 300, 304; interlinking 36, 115, 120–1, 146–8, 152, 155–6, 167
hegemonic shifts 8–10, 46–7, 193, 200; *see also* world system cycles (crises and hegemonic shifts)
hegemonic transitions (in world system) 115; as central concept of change 119–23; class struggle 130–8; hegemony as pattern of world history 116–19; role of surplus 123–9
hegemony 89, 136, 210–11; parahegemony 242–4; pattern of world history 116–19; regional 4, 120; rivalry and 4, 7–8, 47, 120–2, 126, 132, 152, 181, 185–6, 200, 203; super-hegemony 8, 111, 146–7, 178, 242, 244, 300–1
Hellenistic kingdoms 21, 22
Herodotus 12
Hiebert, F.T. 20
Higgott, Richard 116
'high culture' 61
high overhead strategy 125
Hilton, Rodney 27, 28, 202
Hinduism 259
Hirschman, A.O. 38
historical change: hegemonic transition 119–23; role of surplus 123–9; spatial/temporal interface 130–8
historical materialism 6, 30, 59, 98, 119, 248, 301, 305; political economy 82, 106–12
historical review (world system cycles of accumulation and hegemony) 151; Bronze Age 152–7; Iron Age 157–71; Medieval and early modern periods 171–80; modern world system period 180–7
historical social systems 119
historical sociology (macro) 30–2
historiography, world 12–17
Hodgson, Marshall G.S. 13–16, 24, 165, 173, 182
holism 45, 211–13
Hopkins, T. 25–6, 294

Mycenaeans 194

Naram Sin 154
nation-states 123–4, 127, 306
national/state development 38–9
"national economies" 135
"national frame" 202
natural resources 82–3, 92, 95
naval defeats (Indian Ocean) 288
"naval imperialism" 161
Nebuchadnezzar I 157
"necessities" 294
Needham, Joseph 201
neo-classical economics 27, 30, 261
neo-evolutionism 41
neo-Marxism 30
neo-mercantilism 136
neo-structuralism 29
Neolithic Revolution 82
Nester, William R. 136
New World 76, 85, 181, 186
Nile–Red Sea corridor 88, 89
nomadic societies 16, 41, 42, 43–4, 87, 96–7, 180
nonpatriarchal partnership relations 43
Norman expansion 24
North, Douglass C. 27
Nowak, Leszek 33

Oates, Joan 151
Oceania 77, 85
Octavian 164
oikumene 292, 294; Afro-Eurasian 144, 157, 165, 173, 209, 239–43, 297, 306; Indic and Far Eastern 240, 241; civilization *versus* 221, 228, 234, 239–44; Old 191–2, 239–43 *passim*
oligarchy 69, 132, 164
Oman 20
"open" societies 260, 261
Oppenheim, A.L. 156
Orlin, L. 6
Orwell, George 8
Ottoman empire 24, 178–9, 183–4, 194, 286, 287, 288–9
overaccumulation 305
overconcentration (capital) 98, 137, 154
overextraction/overexploitation 98, 132, 133, 137, 194
overland trade routes 85, 86, 88–90
owner-producers 136

palace sector 67, 69
Palan, R. 29, 122
Palat, R.A. 25, 26, 183, 186–7
parahegemony 242–4
Parthia 164, 165, 167–8, 170
patriarchy 43–4
"patrism" 43
Pax Americana 121, 137
Peet, Richard 35
peripheral tributaries 262
peripheralization process 95, 96
Persian empire 24, 159–62, 164, 168, 170, 172, 174, 178–9, 183–4, 188–9
Persian Gulf corridor 88–9
persistence (and discontinuities) 278–89
petty commodity production 187, 249
phased cycles *see* A/B-phased cycles
Phillip II 288
philosophical implications (5000-year world system) 44–8
Philpin, C. 27, 28, 47
Phoenician cities 157–62 *passim*, 194
Pirenne, Henri 23, 171
Pirenne, Jacques 261, 271, 273–5
plague (Black Death) 10, 24, 25, 176, 208, 284–7
Poland 28
Polanyi, Karl 6, 18, 41, 59, 74, 109, 149–50, 250, 298, 303, 304
polarization, development and 38, 259
political: conclusions (transitional) 214–15; control 82–3, 205; exchanges 258; hegemony 143–9, 300–1; implications (5000-year world system) 44–8; long cycles 36, 37; power 100–5, 109, 116–17, 120, 126, 130
political economy 97–100; historical-materialist 82, 106–12; international 36–7; neomercantilist/capitalist development states 136
political geography 35
political sociology 30–2
polycentrism 21
polycultures 224, 225–6, 228
population 236, 240; *see also* city population/size
Portugal 146, 184, 185
postmodernism 35
power: hegemonic *see* hegemonic powers; political 100–5, 109, 116–17, 120, 126, 130; relations 8–10, 47, 211, 288

thirteenth-century 45, 283–8; world system *versus* 201–2, 292–6
world tributary system 262–76
Wright, Gary 60, 64

Xerxes 160

Yamini dynasty 179

Zenobia, Queen 22
Zhao Ziyang 47, 214
zones 98, 100–1, 103, 105, 147, 187
Zoroastrianism 159